A HUNDRED YEARS OF
ENGLISH GOVERNMENT

AMS PRESS
NEW YORK

A HUNDRED YEARS

OF

ENGLISH GOVERNMENT

by

K. B. SMELLIE

*Professor of Political Science
in the University of London*

GERALD DUCKWORTH & CO. LTD.

3 Henrietta Street, London, W.C.2

Library of Congress Cataloging in Publication Data

Smellie, Kingsley Bryce, 1897-
    A hundred years of English Government.

        Reprint of the 1950 2d ed., rev. published by
Duckworth, London, issued in series: The Hundred
years series.
        Bibliography: p.
        Includes indexes.
        1. Great Britain—Politics and government.
2. Political parties—Great Britain—History.
I. Title. II. Series: The Hundred years series.
[JN216.S55 1977]   320.9'41'08   75-41256
ISBN 0-404-14606-6

From the edition of 1950, London
First AMS edition published in 1977
Manufactured in the United States of America

AMS PRESS INC.
NEW YORK, N.Y.

320.941
S637h

261636

PREFACE

This book was first published in 1937. For the second edition I have rewritten many parts and I have added a chapter bringing the story down to 1949. I have tried to make the going a little easier for the reader by pruning thick and untidy sentences and by dropping some superfluous detail. Foreign affairs (sketchy in the first edition to the verge of absurdity) have disappeared. Local government has been transplanted to another book—there was no room for it to grow here as it should. I have tried to keep the new chapter on the period since 1939 in the key of the original book, but fourteen years on, the self is not the same.

I am most grateful to my research assistant at the London School of Economics, Miss Eileen Barnes, who has carefully checked and where necessary corrected the notes and appendices. She has of course no responsibility for any errors which may remain.

K.B.S.

CONTENTS

CHAPTER I

THE STATE AND SOCIETY, 1832-70

Transformation of the Problem of Government by the Industrial Revolution—Economists and Utilitarians—The Theory of Representative Government—Socialist Critics—Political Points of View—Policies pursued : Free Trade, Combinations and Monopolies—Public Services—The Case of Ireland—Early Capitalism reviewed.

IN the nineteenth century the spirit of science born in the seventeenth century had left its cradle and was abroad in the land ; it had been bodied forth in a machinery of production and transport which was to change the face of the whole world. The spirit of man was incarnate in material things. The external conditions of his life, once almost as everlasting as the hills, would now be mutable as the sea. The problem of government was transformed. Changes in all the conditions of life and labour, of birth and of death, were beginning a new acceleration which could not be controlled and would make towards an end which could not be foreseen. But in the new dangers there lay the possibility of new knowledge and new powers. Hitherto governments and societies had flourished or decayed from causes which could only dimly be guessed. Changes of climate might subtly undermine them, unknown disease ravage them, or barbarian irruptions overwhelm them,

"determined things to destiny held unbewailed their way."

But from the end of the eighteenth century the increase in the rate of change in the conditions of men's lives made it possible for something to be known about the nature of the forces by which society is controlled. As the acceleration of the film can reveal the rhythm of the growing plant so the acceleration of a series of industrial and commercial revolutions was to reveal something of the laws by which societies grow. From Adam Smith to Marx the nature of society was examined in the light of the new knowledge made possible by the quickened pace of the production and distribution of the goods and services by which men live. Just as during the war of 1914-18 and the peace which followed, the spinning dance of currencies enabled the nature of money almost experimentally to be studied, so the industrial revolution of

7

the early nineteenth century laid the foundations of economic science, by revealing the hidden laws which control production and exchange.

From the first Reform Act (1832), which was the first great adjustment made by the old governing order to adapt itself to the new social structure, to 1870, when the rise of modern Germany and a really United States altered our status in the world of States, there are three main currents of opinion about the nature of our government to be considered. There is first the analytical approach developed by the economists and the utilitarians; secondly, there are the criticisms of the first provoked by the limitations of their methods; and thirdly there are the empirical devices of statesmen and administrators who had as best they could masterfully to administer the unforeseen.

(1) When population was so rapidly increasing and when trade and industry were expanding faster than they had ever done before, two problems were always to the fore : to understand the scope and nature of the changes which were taking place, and to adjust the machinery of government to a new social order. Mankind was on the march and the economists were the best scouts it had.

In his *Theory of the Moral Sentiments*, Adam Smith had discovered an harmonious order in nature whereby, under divine guidance, the welfare of man was promoted by the operation of his individual behaviour.[1] In the *Wealth of Nations* the element of divinity was replaced by forces statistical and natural.[2] " Society," he wrote, " may subsist among different men, as among different merchants, from a sense of its utility without any mutual love or affection, if only they refrain from doing injury to each other." Obviously there is much virtue in that " if." For the new science of economics it would provide the grounds for the justifiable activity of the state. In the *Wealth of Nations*, Adam Smith wrote that " government activity is natural enough and therefore good when it promotes the general welfare, and is an interference with nature and therefore bad when it injures the general interests of society." For him the functions of government were natural—by which he meant good—when they were limited to securing that those forces which were known to make for good, should not be interfered with. But what were the forces which were known to make for good ? They were the many forms of the self interest of ordinary men which had made the economic order and which alone were necessary for society, if the State would prevent violence and administer justice. But what is this justice which lurks so slyly in the text ? By justice Adam Smith meant " the duty of protecting as far as possible every member of society from the injustice and oppression of every member of it." This would have assigned to government the reconstruction of the whole economic order.[3] But Adam Smith was not concerned to reconstruct the whole economic order. He took for granted private property, class conflict, and understood by justice the legal and customary code which in his time dealt with property and contract.[4] His real concern was to attack the specific abuses of existing governments which could be shown to hinder the co-operation for which men were in their own interests prepared. He wished to show that, with free trade in land, a free choice of occupations within and between countries would add immeasurably to the wealth of nations. Certain conditions necessary to wealth were not provided by the eighteenth-century State. Adam Smith did not much consider the necessary conditions of peace and justice. He was concerned to analyse a natural economic order; he assumed its social fabric.

After Adam Smith, Ricardo developed a fruitful method of analysis based on a technique of abstraction and applied it to the solution of many urgent practical problems. He formidably assailed that type of sophistry which results from neglecting in an argument the full implications of any changes discussed.[5] He exploded many bad arguments for many privileges by the right method of enforcing the necessity of tracing out the whole series of results.[6] In an age of increasing productivity, but one still of bitter poverty, he showed that the proposition that men could not have their cake and eat it was unaffected by the size of the cake.

In Bentham, the other great formative thinker of the new age, an attempt was made to cover the whole duty of man. But with him, as with Adam Smith, the conception of nature was ambiguous. The principle of utility had for Bentham two meanings : (1) that all men were led by their appetites for pleasure and their dislike for pain to the creation of society ; (2) that the good was pleasure and that it was the duty of all men, but particularly of legislators, so to play on the appetites of all, that they would be led to just those actions which would maximize their pleasures. Mankind was under the domination of two masters, pain and pleasure, but could play them one against the other to the relief of man's estate. The Utilitarians provided the fashionable guides for the alterations in the machinery of government after 1830. " The guides of English legislation during the period of individualism . . . accepted the fundamental ideas of Benthamism . . . their immediate and practical object was the extension of individual liberty as the proper means of ensuring the greatest happiness of the greatest number."[7] Some of them considered that the interests of individuals were harmonious and that only the interference of the State prevented the harmony showing ; others who recognized disharmony considered that clumsy State action would make it worse.[8] Out of their attempt to harmonize their belief that happiness ought to be shared by each according to his capacity, and their experience, that such a consummation, however devoutly wished by some, was prevented by the tenacity by which those who had, held on, they developed a naive democratic theory.

In both the economics of Adam Smith and the sociology of Bentham there is the same difficulty that the place which should be occupied by State action to secure the justice, whose obligation they both assume, is nowhere clearly defined. How came it that the invisible hand seen by Adam Smith had faltered in its cunning? How had the natural order come to be distorted by that " insidious and crafty animal vulgarly called the statesman or politician? " If, as Bentham supposed, mankind was under the domination of two masters, pain and pleasure, how had it come to produce the confusion of the eighteenth-century scene? Now the confusion had been revealed how was it to be cleared? Would the insidious and crafty animal, vulgarly called a politician, find and keep his proper place? Would those sinister interests which as Bentham saw preferred their own pleasure to the pleasures of their neighbours be converted by philosophy to the code of one for all and all for one?

An answer to these questions was attempted by the nineteenth-century English theory of representative government.

The English theory of representative government in the nineteenth century was developed from two assumptions. The first assumption, derived from the rationalist movement of the eighteenth century, was that matters of opinion could be settled by discussion—that truth could get itself accepted when the last king had been duly strangled with the entrails of the last priest. The second assumption was suggested by the astonishing progress of industry and commerce and was that most of the needs of men could be satisfied without the assistance of the State. Matters of opinion could be settled by discussion and the external conditions of life could be satisfied by bargaining in a market. If men were only free to enter into whatever contracts they pleased the interests of each would be harmonized with those of all. Those few matters which experience or tradition placed outside the magic of the market could be dealt with by the democratic formula of " one man, one vote."

Economic progress and democratic theory were closely related. The obvious vitality and seeming harmony of the economic order were a comforting demonstration of the power of reason in society. The swift advance of industry was providing a society which seemed strong enough to stand without the aid of any government. The market which the economists had analysed was providing indirectly the perfect State which philosophers had failed to plan. This strengthening of the social order by the bonds of innumerable private contracts favoured liberty of thought. For long ages liberty of thought and expression had been crushed, because it was feared that a disbelief in existing religious and moral codes might destroy the basis of society. It was believed that the power of government over men's opinions and bodies was too feeble to have stood the shock of general scepticism. The real safeguards of public order were held to be the lethargy of habit and superstitious awe. The new industrial progress, by showing that the essentials of human order were rooted more firmly in men's stomachs than in their minds, prepared the way for freedom of thought. For there could be no objection to the long-run benefits of intellectual freedom when in the short run it no longer threatened the social order. The mind might change but the body remained the same. And the bodies of men seemed able to co-operate for their mutual benefit whatever the colour of their skins or the beliefs in their heads. It was reasonable to believe that the tableau of human progress could be left to the economic loom.

Of course, as Mr. Keynes has pointed out, no economic thinker of repute really believed in a *laissez-faire* which denied the necessity for far-reaching State control. But then no political thinker of repute really believed in the vote as an instrument for the creation of a State. Both the market and the ballot were to be understood in their appropriate context. Freedom of contract assumed a society; freedom of discussion and the ballot a particular form of society. Industrial progress seemed to be producing the particular form of society the successful operation of the ballot required. For it seemed to be producing a form of society in which governments would have less to do. But on the vital question of the necessary functions of government at each stage of the development of the economic order the economists were tantalizingly obscure. The market required the existence of society. Some form of private property, the enforcement of contracts and the suppression of violence were required before the subtle adjustments of human interests, that the mechanism of price provides, could be enjoyed. But to admit the need for the enforcement of contracts was to abandon the philosophy of individualism which much economic thought implied. Enforcement of contracts involves an all pervasive intervention of the organized power of the State, to make men do what they do not wish to do, in the interest of the general good of the community. Why should not the State leave

11

those who do not keep their promises, or those who are poor judges of the promise-keeping nature of others, to the stings of conscience or the natural consequence of vacillation, duplicity or stupidity? In fact the economist was unwilling to consider the fundamental problem of politics or the right use of force. He was inclined to assume that the boundary between force and persuasion had once for all been drawn, though all history shows it to be the most wavering frontier among men. Unless this problem of the right use of force by the community is faced the results are disastrous. For if force is not rightly controlled it will cripple and distort the mechanism of price. Unless price is taught its place justice and violence may pass under its control. Where the State has been enfeebled its powers have reappeared as part of the technique of competitive industry itself. In the United States the weakness of the federal system and the social conditions of a pioneering community allowed the great industries to exercise political powers which they employed in distorting the mechanism of price for their own ends. In the feudal age every landowner was doing the same. Given the proper organization of the market the conflict of a million wits sharpened by self-interest may give a daring and insight to the planning of the economic order that no bureaucracy could achieve. Given peace by enlightened legislators the Cobdens of the world may be left to garner plenty. But who is to secure that there shall be the peace which favours all and not the sword which profits some?

Of the economists it has been said that " their individualistic doctrine of society, combined with their presupposition that respectable men and women are mainly engaged in safeguarding all details of their commercial interests led them to neglect questions of prevalent fact." The presuppositions of political democrats were equally vast. In the English democratic tradition of the nineteenth century it was assumed that there would be such a balance between conflicting greeds and errors that an intelligent and disinterested minority could turn the scale. In his *Representative Government* J. S. Mill argues that justice and the general interest can carry their point only because the separate and selfish interests of mankind are almost always divided.

It was tacitly assumed that reason could always in an industrial society command sufficient votes to prevent its own extinction ; that the change desired by a majority would never be of such a character to lead the minority to challenge the principle of majority rule itself. Mill, and others, recognized that, if racial or religious conflict were to destroy the chance to persuade by discussion, representative government would not work. In Victorian England the rapid growth and the increasing mobility of economic life seemed to promise, for a time, the removal of all differences save those of price.

(2) There were those who, while they might not understand what was true and useful in the economists' method of abstraction, were rightly convinced that there were vital aspects of the social order which the latter ignored. They were concerned with the nature of that society whose existence the economists assumed. What were the conditions of that peace and what was the nature of the justice which Adam Smith took for granted? But with these critics, too, the influence of the eighteenth-century idea of a natural order was powerful and confusing. We find in them two main ideas about the relation of the State to society. The first is, perhaps, most clearly stated by Paine : " the great part of that order which reigns among mankind is not the effect of government . . . society performs for itself almost everything which is ascribed to government . . . government is no further necessary than to supply the few cases to which society and civilization are not conveniently competent . . . all the great laws of society are laws of nature . . . but how often is the natural propensity to society disturbed or destroyed by the operations of government."[9] Paine, like Adam Smith, was so concerned to attack the abuses of existing government that he did not stop to remark that " the few cases to which society and civilization are not conveniently competent " might include the subordination of force to the ends of justice. For the implications of Paine's position were far reaching. Adam Smith had assumed that the existing laws of property and contract were the embodiment of justice. Only simple violence had to be suppressed. But to Paine the whole existing framework of society was the product of violence. In his contrast between society and government he is really contrasting an ideal society with the one in existence. This theme was developed by the early English socialists who sensed that the enemy was no longer feudal privilege but the nascent powers of coercion in the new industrial order. They were concerned precisely with the nature of that society and the technique of its justice and peace which the economists assumed. The economic order might be natural. But were all forms of society natural? " That great man," wrote Hodgkin of Adam Smith, " carefully distinguished the natural distribution of wealth from the distribution which is derived from our artificial right of property." There was the " nature " of reason, of men's interests and their power to co-operate and to persuade, and there was the " nature " of men's passions and their power to coerce. There were other forms of violence than the sword. To the English socialists of the period 1820-30— John Grey : *Lecture on Human Happiness*, 1825 ; William Thompson : *Inquiry into the Principles of Distribution of Wealth*, 1824 ; Thomas

13

Hodgkin : *Labour Defended*, 1825 ; and J. F. Bray : *Labour's Wrongs and Labours' Remedies*—it seemed that the rich were getting richer and the poor were getting poorer. Where Adam Smith had seen a natural harmony they could see only violence and theft. To these socialists the natural harmony possible among men was prevented by the artificial rights of property. Neither they nor the economists, their opponents, seriously considered the nature of that system of property and of laws which would secure the practical working of the market which the economists showed theoretically to be possible. The problem which these early socialists raised of the relation between a possible harmony of equals and the existing conflict of unequals was raised in a different way by the utilitarians. Either men were so made that they each pursued their own interest, and in so doing were led in all things by an invisible hand to pursue the interests of all ; or there were some men who saw that the greatest happiness of all ought to be secured and that it was their duty to arrange the system of rewards and penalties in society to secure it. But if the economist did not know what systems of property or of contract were necessary for the working of his ideal market, the utilitarian did not know what system of legislation was necessary to secure the happiness of all. Political and social theorists after Bentham and Ricardo developed the criticism that the actual conditions of society did not satisfy the conditions which an economist might tacitly assume ; and that even had they done so, there were many services vital to the relief of man's estate which the magic of a market could not command. On the economic side there were two problems which the wide mind of J. S. Mill seized on and developed. (1) The system of landed property in England did not satisfy the conditions that the freedom of the market required. And this criticism of the land laws could be extended to all the monopolistic elements secreted in all communities where custom ruled and violence preyed. (2) There was no necessary connection between a man's value in the market for his labour and the minimum costs of his maintenance as a citizen. This, which is the vital flaw in the attempt to find a natural harmony in the economic order has been now fully admitted by the modern schools of economists who have elaborated the technique of the analysis of marginal utilities. The more subtle and complex the industrial order the less probability is there that the value of any particular worker in the market will be equal to the cost of maintaining that standard of living which the increase in the average productivity of the community makes desirable. On the political side the issues were simple. Even had the utilitarian thesis been true that men ought to seek the greatest happiness of the greatest number, the problem

14

remained to discover the right conduct for utilitarians in a community which had not realized that those principles were true. Always, as Macaulay had tried to show James Mill, there was a living past with which contemporary philosophy must deal.

I suggest, then, that the economists assumed that there was a political order providing the conditions their science assumed while the political theorists looked to the industrial order to give the conditions necessary for theirs. Freedom of thought and freedom of trade were mutually supporting and mutually dependent. But their critics tried to tell them then, and we can see now, that both were dependent upon certain complex conditions of tradition and knowledge which were in rapid change around them.

(3) We must now turn from those who attempted to probe the inner nature of the changing social order to those who had to meet its pressing problems as they arose. Economists, utilitarians and socialists might sense the shape of things to come, but it was the politicians and administrators who had to meet each questioning hour. The analysis of the thinkers had to be applied by the political and administrative talent available. " There is a limit to . . . the amount of work-manlike creative legislation or administration of which any government is capable in a given time."[10] Before 1832 the reforming Benthamites had found their policy thwarted by the opposition or inertness of classes biased by some sinister interest.[11] After 1832 their ideas had to be applied by the politicians which the limited franchise then allowed to power, and in opposition to vested interests still firmly entrenched, and through a legislative machinery unsuited to the action required. Huskisson, whose speeches bring out clearly his relation to the utilitarians,[12] had to exercise the greatest caution because the West Indian interest was so firmly represented in Parliament—an interest that survived until 1874.[13] Free Trade in corn involved the political suicide of Sir Robert Peel, and was only won because the class which wanted cheap bread was politically stronger than the class which wanted dear bread.[14] Peel " in his hesitations, his postulates, his limits, in his honesty of purpose, his receptivity, his mastery of today's business and his often blurred view of its relation with tomorrow's needs " was the embodiment of the British State in the nineteenth century.[15] His pupil, Gladstone, in whom there was no scrap of Bentham's make-up,[16] had to undergo an " exhaustive mental re-habilitation "[17] when he was at the Board of Trade in the 'forties and was transformed from a hope of the stern and unbending Tories into the political partner of Bright. His autobiography has a passage prophetic of the problem of government in a changing world. " The

gradual transfer of political power from groups and limited classes to the community, and the constant seething of the public mind in fermentation upon a vast mass of moral and social as well as merely political interests offer conditions of action that the statesman, in order to preserve the same amount of consistency as his antecessors, must be gifted with a far larger range of foresight."

If the ideas of Bentham were tried out by a Peel, a Gladstone, and a Place, the ideas of the Socialists found their experimenters in an Owen and in the matter-of-fact bargaining of the sporadic trade unionism of the middle nineteenth century, while Coleridge's eloquent presentation of all those aspects of society which the utilitarians ignored found its inarticulate champions in the prejudices of Tory squires and its Machiavellian manipulation in the histrionic genius of Disraeli.

In England the extension of the franchise was so gradual that many traditions and conventions of an aristocratic system were retained. It may be denied that the governing class in England in the nineteenth century deserved the name of aristocracy, but it will be admitted that as an oligarchy with sufficient public spirit to resist tyranny, and sufficient common sense to adapt itself to a changing economic and social order, it was a good teacher for the rising democratic power. For an oligarchy which has won from royal privilege the control of the State becomes, if it survives, a democracy in everything but scale. For however exclusive they may be, the members of the ruling class only retain power by co-operating among themselves. They have learnt how to choose and follow a leader. They are a government of amateurs protected by their very prejudices against the narrowness of experts or the rigidity of bureaucratic routine. Inoculated with corruption they are immune from the worse ravages of that disease. They know something of the subtle relation between discussion and coercion in the management of men. They were able to teach each section of the people admitted to the franchise that there were other problems of government to be solved than the destruction of privilege.

We must now briefly consider the actual policies which were the outcome of the interplay of the various theories and organized interests. They may be considered in four groups. There was (1) the attack on those privileges which were indefensible in theory and lacked also the political power to resist reform. Of these the most famous was the Free Trade movement which swept away the old fiscal system and the privileges of the agricultural community. There were (2) the problems implicit in a *laissez-faire* policy : What was the legal framework appropriate to the free co-operation of men assumed to know their own interests ? Of these we may briefly consider the development

16

of Company law on the one hand and of Trade Union law on the other. In the same group were the special problems presented by economic activities which seemed by their very nature to threaten monopoly. Of these the problem of the railways may be briefly noticed. There was (3) the great group of problems connected with those social and individual needs which the magic of the market failed to provide in practice. Effective demand was lacking for the services of the parson or the schoolmaster. (4) There was the special problem of Ireland where the particular social conditions economists and utilitarians tacitly assume, were not and never had been present.

(1) The problem of Free Trade was comparatively simple. It was to the interest of this country as the first which had specialized in the new machinery of production to remove all political barriers to the development of a market for her goods and the supply of the raw materials which she needed. Acceptance of the new economic order did not require in England as it did in Ireland an actual reduction of the population. There was no conflict between economic interest and the sentiment of nationalism. The interest which was most profoundly affected—the agricultural—had to submit only to a comparative and not to an absolute reduction in importance. Moreover, as previous economic revolutions had destroyed our peasant proprietors, there was no great numerical political force wedded to a traditional way of life to oppose its transformation.

In 1820 the practical needs of the London and Edinburgh merchants impelled them to petition against "every restrictive regulation of trade not essential to revenue." A Commission of 1820 laid it down that "commerce must be a source of reciprocal amity between nations and an interchange of production to promote the industry, the wealth and the happiness of mankind." At that time special interests were in full possession of vested rights to which they laid claim. There was the Corn Law of 1815 ; there were the differential duties in favour of the West Indian proprietors ; the monopoly of the East India Company ; and a rigorous application of the navigation laws against competition. There were heavy duties on raw materials of industry and prohibitive or extravagant duties on foreign manufactures.[18] By 1852, as a result of the work of Huskisson, Peel and Gladstone, customs policy had almost ceased to be discussed.[19] The principles of free trade had been introduced by a skilful interpretation of the mischief of protection.[20] But on the side of the free traders was the balance of political power and a multiplicity of discoveries and events—the first English railway in 1830 ; the telegraph in 1837 ; the first ocean steamer in 1838—which prepared the way for the almost unlimited economic development of 1850-73 which seemed to confirm their policy.[21]

Of (2) the problems implicit in a *laissez-faire* policy, the law relating to companies is one of the most interesting. For here the relation of the State to the very heart of economic individualism was most directly concerned. What were the legal instruments without which the co-operation of every man in his own interest and thereby for the good of all was not possible? In 1844 Gladstone as chairman of a committee on Companies, met lawyers, county magistrates, promoters and artisans, and learnt much about an industrial organization which seemed content to misdirect the wealth of the nation.[22] " The nation was groping blindly for a policy which would regulate the savings of the people by converting all surplus capital into instruments of production . . . and the task of the legislator was to bring home to the investor the full significance of an ordered system of financial regulation."[23] But the State was to show itself slow and uncertain to regulate and control the new economic forms. The essential problem : What were the legal conditions under which those who wished to combine for purposes of trade and industry might do so? involved the whole theory of the relation of the State to the economic order and was a convincing demonstration of the complex legal forms an economic order requires. In the first place the law in 1844 was so absurd and obscure that it was said that a man had either to be a knave or a fool to venture his money in partnership with a stranger. Partnership law was so imperfect that its technicalities amounted to a denial of justice to partners and to their clients. The Registration Act of 1844 gave to trading associations the power of sueing in a corporate capacity. After 1850 there was a demand for the relaxation of all restraints on the free action of individuals in economic activities and in the application of capital.[24] But such freedom required that there should be freedom to combine with limited liability. English law had no objection to limited liability in principle, but the method of notice and agreement which it required was very inconvenient. Only in special cases before 1850 was it possible to secure a charter which confirmed limited liability. Where the object was hazardous and deterrent to small partnerships as in mining, or required capital beyond the resources of a few individuals as in railways, or required extended responsibility as in insurance, or an unusually large membership as in the case of literary societies, such charters were available.[25] But after 1850 it was found that " limited liability was needed for local enterprises of a useful kind, financed by numerous passive investors under the guidance of their richer neighbours."[26] Investments in land or landed securities were much desired by the middle and working classes, but the uncertainty and complexity of titles and the length and expense of conveyance together with the cost of stamps placed them beyond the reach of such investors. The problem of the railways secured the acceptance of the principle of limited liability.[27] By the Joint Stock Companies Act, 1856, any seven or more persons could, by registering a " memorandum of association," become a body corporate with a limited liability. In 1862 a great consolidating Act was passed. In 1867 an official enquiry was held into the operation of limited liability. Though it was thought by some that the government ought to protect people who were ignorant and foolish, the prevailing sentiment was against any additional publicity. Limited liability had been opposed by those who held that it would endanger the reputation of British merchants. It had been secured by those who held to the general principle that perfect freedom should be allowed in the making of contracts between man and man, guarding only against wilful deception. But the legal instruments were difficult to forge. Partnership law was not made adequate until 1890. The Companies' Acts of 1856 and 1862 only mitigated the game of beggar my neighbour for the good of all.

While Company law was concerned with the problem of defining the legal conditions for the co-operation of capital, Trade Union law was concerned with the problem of the co-operation of labour. At the beginning of the century the Combination Acts had been passed because it was feared that unions of workmen under the guise of trade activities might engage in revolutionary propaganda.[28] As the fear of revolutionary activity died down the unions were opposed on the ground that the individual should be free to dispose of his capital or his labour as he chose.[29] But it could be argued that freedom to choose ought to mean freedom to combine, and in the then fluid condition of the market for labour it was rightly argued by Place that to allow combinations of workers for the purpose of bargaining about wages would facilitate the organization of industry and trade. And so in 1824 and 1825 the Combination Acts were repealed. But the real problem was then revealed. The organization of a market for labour requires more than freedom of the workers to combine. It requires that the lowest paid worker shall receive in his wages or by subsidies what a citizen must have—and there is nothing in economic theory to suggest that this condition will be met ; it requires also that there shall be a knowledge of the wages offered and received throughout the economic system ; and it requires that the parties concerned shall be willing merely to persuade and not be tempted to coerce. So the problem of the State was how to regulate the conditions of buying and selling of labour not merely where there might be fraud, but where

19

there might be violence, open or disguised, and where the failure of the parties to agree might threaten the public order. It was dealing with a particular aspect of the central problem of politics—how to control the substance of force within the forms of persuasion.

The issue was complicated by the fact that between 1825 and 1875 the best and wisest of the judges believed " that the attempt of Trade Unions to raise the rate of wages was something like an attempt to oppose a law of nature."[30] While the Act of 1825 had removed the statutory prohibitions of combinations it left them liable to prosecution under the common law if they were in restraint of trade. This doctrine of the " restraint of trade " involved the judges in an attempt to solve a complex problem in economic analysis for which their training was nil, while their social and political prejudices were likely to lead them astray. They developed the doctrine that it was an obstruction of an employer to persuade a worker to leave his service unless paid a certain scale of wages. In 1859, the Molestation of Workmen Act, though it defined more precisely the freedom of combination given by the Act of 1825 and extended it in certain directions, still left it open for the courts to say that the inclusions of any object other than the determination of wages and of hours would make the Unions' action illegal.[31] There was also a controversy as to the distinction between peaceful persuasion and intimidation and threats. The Trade Union Act of 1871, the outcome of exhaustive investigation by a Royal Commission, declared that " the purposes of any Trade Union shall not, by reason merely that they are in restraint of trade be deemed to be unlawful so as to render any member of such Trade Union liable to criminal prosecution for conspiracy or otherwise." The Criminal Law Amendment Act repealed the Acts of 1825 and 1859. But the immunity of strikes and other combinations from criminal prosecutions, either under statute or at common law, for actions which would otherwise have been lawful had they not been in furtherance of a trade dispute, was not fully secured until the passing of the Conspiracy and Protection of Property Act, 1875.[32] But though criminal liability had been removed by statute the judges indefatigably developed the doctrine of civil conspiracy.

It was possible for some economists to argue that a proper currency might be secured by leaving banking business wholly free from legislative interference. But other economists found cogent arguments against this extravagance of *laissez-faire*. McCulloch argued that under competitive conditions the expanding banks would not be controlled by the more conservative, but on the contrary would be compelled to dance to their tune.[33] With ordinary commodities in a competitive system the public secure the best supply at the lowest price while the

20

producers bear the losses due to their own errors and miscalculations ; but " with respect to a paper currency . . . the interest of the public is of a very different kind ; a steady and equitable regulation of its amount by fixed law is the end to be sought and the evil consequence of any error or miscalculation upon this point falls in a much greater proportion upon the public than upon the issuers."[34] How could labourers, women, minors and all the variety of those who do not worship Mammon be expected to distinguish a bad note from a good? The case for regulation was stated by Tooke : " free trade in banking is synonymous with free trade in swindling . . . it was a matter for regulation by the State and came within the province of police."[35]

Whatever the merits of the theoretical discussion, force of circumstances had practically decided that there should be a central bank, with a recognized responsibility for safeguarding the public interest in a pure and stable currency. Since the foundation of the Bank of England in 1694, due to the casual emergency of Charles II's repudiation of his debts, there had developed, out of a series of exchanges of favours between a needy government and an accommodating corporation, a responsibility of the Bank of England which it found impossible to avoid. Though at the time of the Bullion Committee (1819) the Directors of the Bank of England protested to Parliament that they should not have placed upon them the responsibility for " supporting the whole national currency," circumstances were too strong for them. The Bank Act, of 1844, gave to the Bank of England the ultimate monopoly of the note issue. The crises of 1847, 1857 and 1866 were to prove that the government must support the Bank in time of stress, and Bagehot was to reveal in *Lombard Street* that the Bank was the controlling element in the country's credit structure, and that it was under an obligation to pay attention to the public interest in framing its policy and was not at liberty to act merely for the benefit of its shareholders.[36]

The problems of the railways and of shipping may be briefly noticed. In the 'thirties and 'forties of last century the railway presented the threefold problem of safety, of planning, and of possible monopoly. The Acts of 1840 and 1842 introduced a system of Board of Trade inspection which was to develop into a pervasive and meticulous control of the conditions of safety. But thirty years were to elapse before the State secured the power to compel disclosures of the conditions which might have caused an accident. As to planning, the parliamentary procedure for railway bills was concerned more with the adjustment of private grievances of property-holders than with the planning of a railway system.[37] Gladstone seems, from his experience at the Board of Trade, to have thought that there was need for a logical system of railway planning.[38] In 1840 the Railway Department of the Board of Trade was established, but its powers were those of suggestion rather than of positive regulation. From 1844-55 a distinct board for railway matters existed within the Board of Trade. After that railway business was thrown into the ordinary business of the Department. A Railway Commission had a brief life from 1846-51. Gladstone failed in the 'forties to secure any effective control of railway development partly because Parliament was wedded to the system of private bills, but mainly because the threatened monopoly did not develop. Though each committee that reported was concerned at the apparent diminution of competition no monopoly emerged. By 1872 men were convinced that a private system of railways was not necessarily a monopolistic danger.[39]

In the case of shipping the State was to assume the power to watch over a British merchant vessel from the day when her materials assumed the form of a ship to the day when they finally lost that form. The great consolidating Merchant Shipping Act of 1854 carefully regulated apprenticeship, contained a whole wage-paying code, but no wage regulations, and made premature solicitation of seamen by lodging housekeepers illegal.[40] Only in the case of marine insurance did the State fail. It was found impossible to regulate improper contracts without interfering with innocent and proper contracts. This detailed regulation of shipping did not prevent its prosperity or its growth to over 50 per cent. of the known tonnage of the world.[41] Similarly the most regulated industries of cotton and coal became the two leading export industries.[42] But though the Commission of 1867 showed abundant scope for State intervention in agriculture very little was done. " There is," wrote Jevons, " a wonderful contrast to the elaborate regulations of the factory, workshop, shipping, coal mines, metalliferous and other Acts relating to the various branches of manufacturing and commercial industry. It would lead us too far to inquire whether the absence is due to its needlessness or to the unwillingness of land-owning legislators to touch the interests of their own order."[43]

(3) The importance in English politics of organized religion must never be forgotten. For most of our politicians the religion learnt at their mother's knee or acquired in adolescence has been the only philosophy they knew. If they have ever been tempted to forget the English Bible or the Reformation they have been prevented by their Scottish and Irish colleagues. Most of the philosophical reflections to be found in the letters and diaries of many a hard-boiled politician are emotional and muddled references to their adolescent creeds.

Political wisdom has led them to let religious dogs lie, but, at the same time, the code of a gentleman which forbids him to disturb the mind of a friend has made the individualism of the Englishman's religion a formidable political force. As he can only discuss religion with those with whom he is agreed, both toleration and the essential bigotry of minds which are closed have developed side by side.

In the 'thirties of last century Churchmen, Dissenters and Roman Catholics were reported to exist in the ratios of 120, 80 and 4. Such figures are not very precise, for the estimates were made by men who felt immortal longings in them and cannot with indifference have enumerated the saved and the damned. At least 25 per cent. of the population—those who lived by bread alone because they could afford no other food—were without any religious views at all. A fair proportion of the prosperous artisans were a sceptical and thinking race. Many of the middle and upper classes were utilitarians who admitted no religion but humanity. But more than half the population felt that the Church of England—or their particular form of Dissent—was the most important thing they needed here below.

It is, perhaps, of little importance that Disraeli should have defined the organized hierarchical church as " a sacred corporation for the promotion and maintenance in Europe of certain basic principles." But Gladstone is incomprehensible unless it is remembered that he began his political career with the publication of his views on Church and State, views which Macaulay found " after full and calm consideration to be false, to be in the highest degree pernicious, and to be such as, if followed out in practice to their legitimate consequences would inevitably produce the dissolution of society."[44] All save the atheistic poor and the philosophical Radicals felt that some form of organized religion was necessary to the existence of society. Though Bentham had held that the Church of England was ripe for dissolution and James Mill had prepared a scheme by which lay priests should lecture weekly on utilitarian ethics and the elements of natural science, much as Moscow now broadcasts its dialectical materialism, the Evangelical party in the Church of England made possible the humanitarian legislation which the philosophical Radicals could never have carried alone. The experience of the Methodists had far-reaching effects on party and trade union organization. The High Church party was stung by the Liberal attacks on the privileges of the Established Church into the Oxford Movement which, had it not been undermined by post-Darwinian scepticism, might have transformed the political and social life of England.

The Tory felt with Coleridge " that the Christian Church and the

National Church are as little to be confounded as divided ; "[45] that it transplanted to every parish of the United Kingdom a germ of civilization, " that in the remotest villages there is a nucleus round which the capabilities of the place may crystallize and brighten."[46] On the Tory view, writes Leslie Stephen, the relation of State and Church might be compared to that of man and wife in Christian countries where, though the two are one, the husband is bound to fidelity.[47] The Whig regarded the Church as part of a government system providing him with patronage.[48] The Radicals opposed it for the same reason that they opposed the landlords, because it was a monopoly as unjustifiable in the religious sphere as the landed system was in the economic.[49] But when the Church of England was attacked the most notable dissenters flew to the succour of the Church. The cause of the Church became the cause of the country.[50]

After 1832 the English aristocracy clearly recognized that the abuses of the Church of England must be reformed if it was to survive the attack on economic privilege. Its accounts, if not its creed, would have to bear inspection. In 1835 Peel was writing : " I feel it my solemn duty as a minister and as a member of the Church to advise the Crown to administer its Church patronage . . . on a new principle . . . Ecclesiastical sinecures must share the fate to which all sinecures have been doomed . . . I think it impossible to maintain the principle that an office of the Church without corresponding duties shall have large emoluments attached to it, while the cure of souls in some populous districts is wholly unprovided for."[51] The growth and shifting of the population made it necessary to reorganize the financial and administrative system of the Church of England.

At the time the income of Durham was more than twenty times the income of Llandaff, while in St. Margaret's and St. John's, Westminster, with a population of 50,000 there was no decent provision for even a single minister. In 1836 Parliament created a Permanent Ecclesiastical Commission to equalize the incomes of the various bishoprics and to reorganize their territorial extent. The Church Pluralities Act of 1838 virtually abolished pluralism. The Church Establishment in 1850 had been adjusted to meet the financial, if not the philosophical, criticism of the Radicals. The political power of Dissent secured the removal of some of their most serious grievances—the compulsory levying of Church rates, the monopoly by the Church of England of the ancient universities, the legal compulsion to employ an Anglican cleric at their marriage or burial. These would have been remedied sooner but for the opposition of the House of Lords.

The most serious part played by organized religion was neither in

24

the support it gave to humanitarian legislation, nor in the justification it enabled some to find for the privileged station to which God had called them, but in the obstruction it caused to the development of education. " Any attempt at educational reform had to reckon with the most intense of Victorian emotions, sectarian animosity."[52] There were times when the sectarian rivalries of dissent and the Established Church, together with a bigoted anti-Romanism, gave to our internal politics some of the passions of war.

The history of English elementary education cannot here be summarized. When the factory replaced the village neither the parish priest nor the village schoolmaster could prevent barbarism. With the growth and shifting of the population, schools, like roads and drains, required the attention of the State. Nor could the magic of the market be expected to provide for morals any more than it could provide for health. Most statesmen and economists must have agreed with Kaye Shuttleworth that it would be a fallacy to assume " that knowledge . . . is a natural want, certain to assert itself like the want of food or clothing or shelter, and to create a demand." They would have agreed that " all statesmen who have wished to civilize and instruct a nation have had to create the appetite."[53] Nor were the shameful facts in dispute. Graham in 1843 had " no doubt that a frightful case might be clearly established of brutal ignorance and heathenish irreligion," and that it was the paramount duty of the Government to apply a progressive remedy to an evil of such magnitude and danger.[54]

But it was not possible to get the agreement of Parliament to a scheme of national education. " The dissenters would not stand the parson in a State school. The Established Church would not stand anyone else."[55] So the Government's influence was limited to the giving of meagre grants to the two great voluntary organizations—the National Society of the Established Church and the British and Foreign Society of the Dissenters. England, which led the world in drains, was far behind in schools. Not until after the Reform Act of 1867 and the industrial threat of a united North America and a triumphant Germany was it clearly recognized that the voluntary system had failed. The price paid for sectarian passion was that England entered the fierce economic competition after 1870 with artisans the least trained, and a middle class the worst educated in Europe.

It was in Ireland that the limitations of the current English ideas as to the relation between the political and the economic order were most clearly revealed. There was lacking there that underlying unity of character and opinion which enabled the English political system to adjust itself without a civil war to the new society the industrial revolu-

25

tion had made. In Ireland there was an absentee aristocracy, an alien Church, and a starving population. Their poverty was caused by a population of eight millions in 1841 (nearly double what it was to be in 1911) depending upon a primitive system of tillage. The only other occupations were the linen manufactures of Ulster, the distillation of spirits, and the undeveloped fisheries. In 1841 more than 80 per cent. of all the farms were under 16 acres and only 7 per cent. were over 30 acres. Economic causes made for a system of tillage which kept the population dangerously near the level of subsistence. The political system gave to the landlord with a large number of tenants considerable power. English rule was little more than a provisional government in a half-conquered country. The Government had to use military force so that the income of an alien Church might be devoted to one-tenth of the population. In the 'thirties Peel saw that force could give no permanent cure. The remedy, when it came, was to be an agrarian revolution which was to halve the population of Ireland, to create in the United States the political force of the Irish-Americans, one of the most dangerous enemies England has ever had, to create in the British Parliament the Irish Nationalist party, and at last to destroy the English Liberal party for a generation. Free Trade and the great famine of the 'forties compelled a transition from small to large holdings, and from tillage to the pasture. By 1851 26 per cent. of all farms were over 30 acres in size and only 51 per cent. were under 16 acres. The population had sunk to 6.5 millions. Between 1851 and 1911 the number of persons to each 1,000 acres of land would decrease by 30 per cent. while the number of cattle would increase by over 60 per cent., the number of sheep by 88 per cent., and the number of swine by 35 per cent.

It was in this context that the Government had to determine the validity of a system of freedom of contract applied to the ownership of land. In Ireland the law regarded the landowner as the sole owner of the farm, whereas in fact and in equity the tenant was the co-owner. For the tenant in Ireland, unlike the English tenant, provided the stock and the improvements and had moreover, if dispossessed, either to starve or emigrate. The Irish ejectment code was entirely in favour of the landlord. As early as 1816 he could obtain an ejectment order by a simple procedure in the County Court a thing no English landlord could do until 1856. In 1860 Deasy's Act implied that the relation of landlord to tenant should be founded on the express or implied contract of the parties and not upon tenure or service. The Act, as Morley said, imported into Ireland the English ideas of landed property and contract with a definiteness and a formality that would in England have been

26

impracticable. The evictions which followed in the 'sixties were no doubt in the general interest of cultivation. Pasture and the large farm were the only sound basis for Irish economic life. But the methods employed created the political force of the Irish-American in the United States, the Irish proletariat in English cities, and the Irish Nationalists in the British Parliament. In 1870 Gladstone attempted to give a legal recognition to the co-ownership which in fact and in equity existed. His Act gave compensation for disturbances and for improvements, but it failed because of the variety and complexity of its exceptions, the timidity with which it was administered and the fact that the landlords had still power to raise rent at will. When in the 'eighties the fall in agricultural prices began, the land question became amalgamated with the national to the destruction of the English Liberal party, the creation by State action of the most favoured peasant proprietors in Europe and in the fullness of time, the Irish Free State.[56]

What can be said of the part played by the State in the social and economic changes we have briefly sketched? It is clear that no simple formula will cover the interplay between the reason impulses and custom by which material goods are produced and distributed, and the same reason impulses and custom by which the State is run. To certain fundamental questions we shall never know the answer. Had there been a fully representative system, would it have secured a more effective control, and would that control have been to our economic advantage? It is impossible to say how far an emancipated peasantry instead of backward agricultural labourers, or politically enfranchised unskilled labourers, would have affected the main outlines of our economic development. In all these cases the exigencies of our present problems have led to barren speculation on past history. It is, for example, urged that had taxation for home services and development been more thorough, much of the wastage of capital exported abroad would have been avoided—that Birmingham might have had the treasures wasted on Brazil. The difficulty here is that for every hypothetical change there is introduced a maze of possible consequences. The most that can be done is to consider some of the special cases where we have the safeguard of a comparative check. We do not know whether universal suffrage would have produced the sobriety of Switzerland or the intoxication of the Third Empire. We do not know whether a Chartist revolution in 1848 would have produced a Trotsky or a Stalin. But we can say that we produced a political system which satisfied certain essential conditions of order and of liberty and that it was the means of inventing certain essential political tools : a technique of co-operation between local and central authorities ; a method of changing governments ;

27

an ordering of opinions and powers organic enough and large enough to rule by persuasion and not by the bayonet or the bomb. But we can also say that we remained until the end of the century one of the most uneducated nations in Europe ; that our manners and customs were open to the criticism that they were not unfairly pictured in the novels of Dickens. We have the evidence of sensitive contemporaries—of Matthew Arnold, of Ruskin, and of William Morris, that an acquisitive society had a sickness the touch of Midas would not cure. We can guess that many changes were possible without more knowledge than the common people had. We can ask whether the failure to produce those changes was due to a culpable brutality and greed.

Looked at in this way most of the strictures on the early English capitalists will not stand. They were neither Boundabys nor Gradgrinds. Nor can we fairly say that the economic system could have been other than it was. Whether the means of production and distribution should or should not be owned by the State might be a debatable question by the end of the century, but it was not possible at the beginning. The technique of control did not then exist. There were neither the means of communication nor the experience of industry to make that possible. Of little value is the judgment that " it was the British capitalist who, fortified in his faith by the early political economists, first made of the pursuit of pecuniary gain what we may not unfairly call a national religion . . . it was . . . British commercialism that prepared the moral conscience of mankind for the German theory of world power. Bismarck and Treitsche were the spiritual descendants of Ricardo and Nassau Senior."[57] The spokesmen of British commercialism were Cobden and Bright, and it was their faith that if only those elements in the English political system which were based on privileges faintly resembling those of a German caste were removed, universal peace would ensue. It was the privilege and the flunkeyism of British society that they criticized. And it was the privileges and the flunkeyism that were its greatest weaknesses. It was privilege which destroyed Ireland, and flunkeyism which enervated politics. But the theory of pecuniary gain was a rational belief in the only method known for the amelioration of the lot of man. There may have been intellectual error in their rejection of certain proposals : Bright for the fencing of machinery, Senior for the reduction of hours ; but it was caused, not by a religion of pecuniary gain, but by a belief in an analytical argument. It is too often forgotten that, while the early socialists were right in their sensing of the problem of the relation between the economic and the political order, they had at the time no analytical or experimental approach to offer. During the whole of Marx's residence in England no contribution of any importance to technical socialist thought was made by an Englishman.[58] Before 1890 the English socialists were Arnold, Ruskin and Morris, who said that culture and beauty and equality were in peril. But beauty, truth and freedom are always imperilled in pioneering communities. England in the nineteenth century was a frontier civilization. Would she have been better as an armed camp?

CHAPTER II

GOVERNMENT AND PARTIES, 1832-67

The Reform Act of 1832—Development of Parties—Party Creeds—
Changes in the Constitution, 1832-67—Constitutional Crises—Melbourne,
1834—Bedchamber Question, 1839—Repeal of the Corn Laws, 1846—
A second Reform Bill, 1867—Parliamentary procedure—Cabinet
Government.

IN 1859 Sir James Graham, a timid Whig fearful that Bright might
change the House of Commons into a "mere creature of numbers apart
from property and intelligence," wrote to Lord John Russell : " In
1832 we based the representation on property and intelligence and
carefully maintained the balance of power, so blending the influence of
land and numbers in the election of the representative body that collision
with the Crown and an independent House of Lords might be avoided.
It was a question of balance and proportions. Our calculations were
just, our proportions were safe, and our bloodless revolution has yielded
for the last quarter of a century better legislation, greater national
prosperity, more internal peace, less civil discord than any other period
of our parliamentary history can boast."[1] Thus does the perspective of
middle age see wisdom in its own past and the decay of reason all around.
What were the balance and proportion of the bloodless revolution of
1832, and what relations between property and intelligence did it plan
and what did it secure ?

Had the Reform Bill of 1832 not been passed blood would certainly
have been shed. But its balance and proportion are visible only to the
eye of political faith. For it was a complicated compromise framed to
meet a pressing need. " I see no reformer," said Coleridge, " who asks
himself the question what it is that I propose to myself to effect in the
result."[2] The old constitution had lost that minimum of popular support
without which a governing class must try to sit on bayonets. And such
a position an English aristocrat found compatible neither with his
religion, his dignity, nor his purse. If he were to preserve anything of the
constitution whose spirit Montesquieu had praised and Burke had
worshipped, there had to be a drastic redistribution of political power.
Continuity with the past would provoke a revolution. Changes in the

distribution of population, in the value of money, and the economic interests of the governing families had thrown the machinery of government hopelessly out of gear.

There was " Old Sarum with its bare field and two members, contrasted with unrepresented Manchester's rising population of 180,000. Birmingham, Leeds, Sheffield, Wolverhampton, Huddersfield, Gateshead, were also voteless, while eight members sat for the whole of London. The 23 northern counties of England included only 74 of the 203 Parliamentary boroughs in the country, in spite of the fact that the centre of gravity had been rapidly shifting northwards since the industrial revolution. The south coast on the other hand, was dotted with boroughs, while Cornwall alone returned 44 members, one less than the whole of Scotland."[3] In the small boroughs the new-rich were securing a monopoly. Two-thirds of the closed boroughs were held by the Tories.[4] In the Scottish counties the right of voting was attached to the small class which possessed feudal superiority over land, though not necessarily holding the land itself. In Banff 19 voted, and in Ross and Cromarty, 29.[5] Had the electoral system not been reformed a change of government by peaceful methods would soon have been impossible. The franchise was too narrow for a pendulum to swing. Nonconformists, the professional classes, merchants and manufacturers, tradesmen and artisans in towns, and the Whig aristocracy were for the bill. Against it were the Church, the Law, the Universities, the Services, many great bankers, and most farmers and country gentlemen.[6]

To understand the effect of the Reform Act of 1832 it is necessary to consider not only the change in the qualification for the vote, but also the redistribution of seats. The disfranchisement of the rotten boroughs was the main blow to the Tories. Fifty-seven small boroughs which had returned 113 members were disfranchised. From each of 30 boroughs which had returned two members, one member was taken away, and two were taken from each of two other boroughs which had returned four. The allocation of 63 seats to the industrial towns of England was the main hope of the Liberals. Other changes in the distribution of the seats were the giving of 62 additional seats to the counties and the distribution of 18 seats taken from England to Scotland (8), Wales (5) and Ireland (5). Of the changes in the voting qualification the most important were : In the boroughs the enfranchisement of £10 householders, and the abolition of a variety of customary voting rights which had favoured the artisans. In the counties the addition of copyholders, leaseholders for lives and tenants at will paying over £50 per annum to the previous freehold franchise. In the boroughs the artisans were worse off than before 1832 by the loss of the old qualifications. Instead of forming

31

more than half of the total borough electorate the artisans were, after 1832, outnumbered by more than two to one.[7] In the counties the admission of tenants at will actually strengthened the hold of the bigger landowners so long as voting remained public in deference to " legitimate interests."

The total effect was to increase the electorate by 217,000, or 49 per cent., but the distribution of voting-power was fantastically uneven. Although more than two-thirds of the seats withdrawn had come from the south of the Thames and Severn, the advantage of the small boroughs and therefore of the South remained overwhelming. North of the Wash to the Severn line the boroughs returned 86 members, and the counties 39 ; south, the boroughs returned 248, and the counties 123.[8] One in thirty of the population of the United Kingdom had the vote, but the distribution of voting power varied from 1 in 5 in Westmorland to 1 in 37 in Lancashire and 1 in 39 in Middlesex ; in the boroughs from 1 in 4 in the small boroughs to 1 in 45 in the manufacturing towns. Harwich and Lyme Regis returned two members each for an electorate of less than 200. Ireland, with one-third the population of the United Kingdom, would return only 105 out of 658 members.

If the aristocracy accepted reform to save the constitution, the middle and lower classes sought in reform the road to their Utopias. The aristocracy thought a limited reform might save their order and the throne ; the middle class that it might secure in politics the honesty religion taught and business proved was the best policy. It might shrivel up " the monopolies, Church craft, sinecures, armorial hocus pocus, primogeniture and pageantry " which battened on industry and thrift.[9] For the lower class reform might provide a defensive weapon in a competitive age.

The expectations of all three were to be disappointed. The aristocracy thought that they had adjusted the voting power to the new distribution of wealth the industrial revolution had caused. They were giving political recognition to their economic equals. But a franchise based on the rent of houses was to prove a shifting basis for a stable political order. The rise in wages and in rents after the discovery of gold in California in 1848, and in Australia in 1851, enfranchised many which the qualifications of 1832 had been designed to exclude. The Reform Act added 217,000 to an existing electorate of 500,000, but within the next generation the qualifications prescribed added 600,000 more. So great was the rate of economic change that the compromise of 1832 could not acquire the force of custom long unchanged. The slow changes of an agricultural order were replaced by the swift accelerations of an industrial community. The ruling classes were driven to consider

32

the economic basis of the State. The middle class was to discover that there was more in the art of politics than the higgling of a market or the abstractions of fashionable philosophers. The poor were to discover that to compel attention is not to be understood or to know your own mind.

The complexity of the franchise stimulated the development of parties. The Reform Bill of 1832 provided for a registry of those qualified to vote ; but it was left to those who had the right to vote to see that their names were on the register—at the cost in England of 1s., and in Scotland of 2s., and unless they were there they could not vote. " Registration became a gap through which the parties, hitherto confined to Parliament, made their way into the constituencies and gradually covered the whole country with the network of their organizations."[10] In 1835 the Radicals opened a registration office in Cleveland Row with a full-time secretary.[11] In three years they established the Reform Club, the Reform Association, and had attempted to provide the Liberal party with a financial basis. In 1832 the Carlton Club took the initiative in scrutinizing the electoral roll, though the idiosyncrasies of local Toryisms compelled a cautious policy. Between 1832 and 1841 Peel, who saw that the registration of voters was " a perfectly new element of political power . . . more powerful than either the sovereign or the House of Commons," linked up a central party organization with a network of local associations.[12]

An increase in corruption flowed from obvious causes. When the Reform Bill was drafted the King had refused to consider the ballot. The aristocracy clung to the open system of voting as a method of safeguarding the " legitimate interest " of property, and of excluding men from the House of Commons " who would be following impulses not congenial to our institutions . . . men incapable of taking large views and looking only to penny and shilling gains and losses," a course to be disapproved by " all the intelligent and respectable classes."[13]

The " perfectly hideous " system of the hustings remained. It disgraced candidates and depraved electors while the scenes which took place at almost every particular election were, as Bright said, " a frightful price to pay for parliamentary government." With small electorates the possibility of securing a purchasable margin of votes was not to be resisted. The aristocratic system of nomination, which had been practised by the eighteenth-century owner of a rotten borough, was succeeded by the no less aristocratic system of intoxication. The Parliament of 1841 was known as the bribery parliament. Between 1832 and 1854 the 200 electors of St. Albans absorbed in one way and another over £24,000. As late as 1867 it was still common for every voter polling to cost £1 a head.[14] " May I venture," wrote Mrs. Disraeli to Sir Robert Peel, " to name my own humble but enthusiastic exertions in times gone by, for the party or rather for your own splendid self. They will tell you at Maidstone, that more than £40,000 was spent through my influence alone."[15] If those who had the vote were prepared to sell it dear, those who had no vote used what influence they could command. In 1837 " Sir William Graham at Carlisle was hunted through the streets and his son knocked down." Scenes took place which even he found " disgraceful to the free institutions under which we live."[16]

Though the House of Commons condemned bribery, individual members continued to practise it. Disputed elections were tried by parliamentary committees, boldly partisan, but prepared to wink at the obvious collusion of rival candidates in the maintenance of loose practices. Whig committees decided for the Whig candidate ; Tory committees for the Tory. But should the parties desire to split the difference, and in constituencies returning two members divide the spoils, the committee would offer no objection.[17] An Act of 1854 defined bribery but failed clearly to define undue influence. In 1868 the House of Commons imposed upon an unwilling judiciary the trial of disputed elections. The Ballot Act was not passed until 1872, when at the same time the provision that nominations should be made in writing abolished the clamour of the hustings. The indirect power of aristocracy through electoral influence was not firmly controlled until the Act of 1883.

If the confusion and corruption in the constituencies were thick, the confusion in the minds of the party leaders was thicker still. In 1828 the Duke of Wellington had complained " we hear a great deal of Whig principles and Tory principles and Liberal principles . . .but I confess that I have never seen a definition of any of them and cannot make myself a clear idea of what they mean." The Duke's capacity for political analysis was no doubt inhibited by his fear of the " blackguard influence " in politics. But we have a similar complaint of confusion from the " blackguards " themselves. " Politics," wrote the Radical Parkes in 1838, " are about as confused as Bottom's dream, which was past the wit of man to say what dream it was."[18]

The confusion of parties between 1832-67 is profoundly important in the development of the constitution. The insight of Burke had seen that " party divisions, whether on the whole operating for the good or evil, are things inseparable from free government." But the creation of a system of parties which should embody a triple unity of ideas, interests and persons, schooled in co-operation and dedicated to the service of the State, was to be the work of a century. Between 1832 and 1868 we have the transformation of the conflicting cliques within a governing class into the party organization of a democratic State. After 1868 it seemed to popular tradition that Gladstone and Disraeli had given to the airy nothings of speculative thought a concrete embodiment in the interests, the organizations and the traditions of two great parties. But Gladstone and Disraeli learnt their magician's arts in the period we are now considering. It was in this period that the technique of persuasion by discussion, in place of the tyranny of custom and the power of the purse or the terror of the sword, was first systematically developed. The development of parties is inevitably complex. Were all parties expressions of economic interests the complexity would remain. Even in the strategy of a class war there is an opportunity for a variety of tactics. The goal may be determined but the ways to it may be many. A class may advance its own interests in many ways—by the sword, by the purse, or by the tongue. As men do not live by bread or by privilege alone, an economic group may be defending a system of beliefs as well as a group of economic advantages. Even if we can believe that its religion, its morals and its customs have developed as so many defences to its economic privileges, those defences may be manned in many ways. The division between parties was never so trivial that it made politics a game for the prize of office, nor so fundamental that the one desired to destroy the other. The slow extension of the franchise meant that a happy mean between a friendly game and a war of classes was maintained.

In 1832 the Whigs and Tories had been riven and battered by the storm of a changing world. They represented a conflict of interests and a conflict of traditions, and the two struggles were intertwined. " The ideal Tory and the ideal Whig . . . agreed in the necessity and benefit of an exact balance of the three estates ; but the Tory was more jealous of the balance being deranged by the people, the Whig of its being deranged by the Crown " (Coleridge). The Whig party had been disorganized by forty years in opposition, and the problems of the new industrial age were to disintegrate it further. Its principles were vague and general. The Whigs believed in nothing in excess not even constitutional reform or the reduction of corrupt expenditure.[19] They believed that truth would prevail if men were free to argue out their differences, but they held that only in a balanced and complex constitution could such freedom be secured. The prerogatives of the Crown, the privileges of the two Houses of Parliament were a necessary safeguard to the rights and privileges of the people. Universal suffrage would destroy an ordered liberty and create a lawless tyranny. They believed that privilege might be the parent of freedom ; that it was the duty and the privilege of property to extend the empire of reason. Political corruption they convinced themselves was an inoculation against religious prejudice and popular violence. It was an antidote to the religious fanaticism sporadic in a period of rapid social change and disintegrating faiths. An old Whig, like Russell, had " a noble confidence in the power of truth to prevail and a naive confidence in himself as its exponent." But if Russell believed in government by discussion within the forum of privilege, a new Whig like Macaulay could bring his colleagues to accept sweeping constitutional changes, as natural and inevitable consequences of all great changes in the distribution of property and the diffusion of political intelligence. The Whig party compelled the Tories to save property by reconstruction. It saved them from provoking revolution by reaction.[20]

The Conservative party was new born in 1833. " Unlike the Whigs it had no traditions, but it had interests and it was alive . . . Its strength lay in the support of substantial interests alarmed at the prospect of radical change."[21] If the Whigs represented the eighteenth-century blend of rationalism with the constitutional traditions of 1688, the Conservatives represented the economic interests most severely threatened by the new industrial and commercial order. There was the corn interest, the cattle interest, the sugar interest. But there was also the tradition of reconstruction as a method of defending their order. The Whig would have government corrupt and the Church subordinate to the State so that the people should be safeguarded against despotism and bigotry. The Conservative desired a strong government and was prepared to reform for strength, but he looked to the Church as a bulwark against the lower orders. Sir Robert Peel was the architect of the new party. He thought of it as " a beleaguered garrison whose right and whose duty it was to evacuate and demolish untenable positions in order that what remained might hold out the longer."[22] The essence of his doctrine was that traditional institutions could be conserved in a changing society only if they were incessantly adapted.[23] " His mission was not so much to originate as to moderate, control and instruct . . . he was the great minister of the middle classes who, by rallying them round the reformed constitution, was able to save both his own order and theirs from the revolution which seemed to menace both."[24]

In 1832 it seemed to J. S. Mill that there was " nothing definite and determinate in politics except Radicalism." Through its influence slavery was abolished throughout the British Empire in 1833 ; the Poor

36

Law reformed ; the first grants given to education ; the trading privileges of the East India Company abolished. But the Radicals failed to establish themselves as a third party. Had they done so the House of Lords might have been reformed and the English Church in Ireland disestablished. The limited franchise of 1832 did not allow them to develop into a permanent third party in the House. Neither in 1832 nor in 1865 did the House of Commons have a single representative of any class except the possessing and employing classes. Macaulay wrote in 1833 that a man of honour could not make politics a profession unless he had a competence of his own without exposing himself to privations of the severest kind. No man could write enough to procure a decent subsistence and at the same time make politics a profession. The first reformed parliament was composed for the most part of country gentlemen. More than 400 were without any profession and nearly 200 were related to peers. One analysis of their membership gives 508 as landowners, 73 financiers and 100 members of the Army and Navy. In 1865 the same groups were respectively 436, 163 and 125. Though artisans secured no direct representation, commerce and manufacturers did. In 1832 and 1835 there was an important group of East and West Indian proprietors, and in 1847 the railways were represented by 86, and in 1860 by 160 members.[25]

In 1832 the Radical party had many influential and wealthy members ; barristers, merchants, writers, military and naval officers, bankers, doctors, squires and Whig peers' sons all stood in its interests.[26] But the worst feature of the Reform Bill, it seemed to a contemporary " was the few leading minds created by it. In Parliament many of our really honest Radicals are not fit to be even abbots in a monastery. The system is too costly to allow better men to get in."[27] Neither Hume, nor Grote, nor Buller possessed the art of leadership, and Cobden was the first Radical capable of sitting with credit in a Cabinet.[28] In the constituencies Radicals were at a disadvantage because their indifference in religion and freedom in morals could not command the support of pious dissenters.[29] The £10 householders of the working and small shopkeeper class showed a desire for candidates of unimpeachable respectability. Even in 1832 Tower Hamlets, the vastest and dingiest urban constituency sent to the House of Commons Lushington, a Whig ecclesiastical lawyer, and Clay, a wealthy merchant.[30] For a time the Radicals established a complete electoral domination in the Metropolitan area, but the Tories, using the " Church and King cry" with one section of the electorate and " Conservative, not destructive reform " with another, and supplementing these with money for the bribable and influence for the intimidable, were able more than to hold their own.[31] The *laissez-faire* policy of their intellectuals alienated them from working-class opinion in the country, and in the towns they were destroyed as a party by the reaction of the middle-class electors against the revolutionary violence of Chartism and discredited by their alliance with the Irish leader, O'Connell, which the balance of parties imposed upon them in the House. After the Radicalism of the Dissenters had been placated by the removal of their religious and civil grievances, the Whigs and Tories held a strategical position.[32] The Radicals were not prepared to dismiss the Whigs when the alternative was a Tory Government. The Whigs were not prepared to unite with the Radicals in an attack on the House of Lords, where the Tories were securely entrenched. Greville wrote in 1842 " only the Tories can carry liberal measures. The Whigs' work prepares, but cannot accomplish them ; the Tories directly or indirectly thwart, discourage and oppose them until public opinion compels them to submit, and then they are obliged to take them up and to do that which they can do but the Whigs cannot do."[33]

Whether universal suffrage would have produced a better England it is impossible to say. It is unlikely that the rationalism of a Bentham would have recommended itself to the countryside, or the economics of his followers to the towns of the hungry 'forties. It is possible that an extended suffrage in 1832 would have given power to many an unscrupulous demagogue. A younger Disraeli might have bewitched a younger Queen, and England have produced her Jackson, or Napoleon the Third. It may be doubted whether, at this time, the essential conditions for successful representative government were developed. People were not in a condition to be persuaded by discussion. Economic hardship and religious bigotry—in the case of Ireland racial distrust based on economic fear and religious contempt—might have been fatal to the Mother of Parliaments. The Anti-Corn Law League of the 'forties showed both the power of the middle class and its limitations. The League was successful because it did not meddle with religious prejudice, because it did not relate to Ireland, because it touched none of the theoretical problems of government.[34] Cobden had succeeded in educating every section of English society in a common enthusiasm for a proposition in economics. A moral and religious spirit had been infused into a topic of bread and profit. But if the League was a success the Chartist Movement was a tragic failure. Universal suffrage in the 'thirties might have meant a struggle between those who could organize, as Cobden organized the League, and those who could manipulate the discontents voiced in the Charter. With the suffrage as it was Bright, in 1848, hoped that it would be possible to organize a party for political reform more formidable than the League. He did not succeed until 1860.[35]

The political ideas of the upper middle class were almost exhausted by 1846. " Their Nonconformist Liberalism, the cause and symbol of their rebellion against the landlord caste that had at once starved and insulted them, was now, in the more prosperous time of Free Trade, gradually giving way to Churchmanship in religion and Conservatism in politics."[36] They were prepared for no further attack on Church or land monopolies in Great Britain and Ireland, or on the aristocratic control of place and power.[37] " Politically," wrote Graham, " power is now vested in the hands of the middle classes ; transfer it again and it will pass into a divided empire between the aristocracy and the working classes which will bring town and country into hostile array . . . a war of classes and interests will commence, the end of which I cannot foresee."[38] Even the Duke of Bedford was persuaded " that if a successful attempt were made to retrace our free trade steps we should witness the commencement of a war of classes."[39] " A government of progress was indispensable," Aberdeen wrote to Princess Lieven ; " none can be too Liberal for me provided it does not abandon its Conservative character."[40] " Resistance to reform was not grounded on attachment to the old forms of the constitution . . . it rests mainly on fears of peril to property."[40A] In 1852 Gladstone was " on the Liberal side of the Conservative party rather than on the Conservative side of the Liberal party."[40B] In 1856 Gladstone wrote " for all purposes for which I value Liberalism the Liberal party is dead. It is held together by two bonds : one which is called the loaves and fishes, or the patronage of government ; the other, votes for the ballot and other such trash to which I am conscientiously opposed." But there was, he said, " a policy going begging, the general policy which Peel in 1841 took office to support—the policy of peace abroad, of economy, of financial equilibrium, of steady resistance to abuses, and promotion of practical improvements at home ; with a disinclination to questions of organic change gratuitously raised." To this he could add " happily, no longer a question of party—the accomplishment of what yet remains for the liberation of commerce from the shackles that it ought not to bear."[41]

His struggles for the liberation of commerce led Gladstone to the great Budget of 1860, and in 1861 to a tacit alliance with Bright. The latter wrote to him in 1861, " the past is well-nigh really past, and a new policy and a wiser and a higher morality are signed for by the best of our people, and there is a prevalent feeling that you are destined to guide that wiser policy and to teach that higher morality."[42] This alliance between Bright and Gladstone—between the popular forces which, after the collapse of Chartism, Bright had reawakened and trained in constitutional methods, and the driving force of Gladstone's parliamentary genius, developed during the stultifying ascendancy of Lord Palmerston—is a good example of the process of English political change. Gladstone, the pupil of Canning, and of Peel, the colleague of Palmerston, the representative of Oxford and of Lancashire, a vague philosopher and a meticulous accountant, was brought into alliance with all those interests the existing system of government ignored.

It is in this general background that we must see the changes in the art of government from the Reform Act of 1832 to that of 1867. It was the government of an oligarchy. The Reform Act had not weakened the hold of the governing families upon the Cabinet, and their younger members were still dedicated to the service of their country and their order, in the popular chamber. In the 'sixties a landed aristocracy of about 2,250 persons owned together nearly half the enclosed land of England and Wales, or nearly 15 million acres out of 33 million ; and 400 peers and peeresses owned nearly 6 million.[43] In 1848, out of a Cabinet of 14, four were united by the ties of the closest relationship.[44] Russell's Cabinet of 1852 was called the Dukery. In the Cabinet of 1859, which included three dukes and the brother of a fourth, Gladstone, Milner Gibson and Cardwell were the only three men without titles. It was felt to be " of great importance to the country and highly conducive to the working of the constitution that young men in high aristocratical positions should take part in the administration of public affairs and should not leave the working of our political machine to classes whose pursuits and interests are of a different kind."[45] This system of family alliances has its advantages. An oligarchy which is a real power and not merely the puppet of a despot is a very subtly organized party system within a miniature State. A healthy oligarchy is the seed of a Liberal democracy. Its members understand the distinction between laws and conventions, between principles and the exigencies of policy. Though balanced on the razor edge of privilege they can observe fine points of honour. A powerful oligarchy is a miniature State in which persuasion has taken the place of violence and broken friendship of broken heads. But this system also has its disadvantages ; and these are not merely that it is not a government of the people—for the people may not yet be fit to govern—but the disadvantages of its family character. Loyalty to persons seems more important than reasons of State. The curse of age is too often upon it. Palmerston, the Regency buck, survived to be the old and slippered pantaloon of 1860 ; Gladstone, the " young man with the black hair and the white face," survived to be the tragic octogenarian of the Cabinet of 1892. The Russell of 1845, who precipitated the crisis of the Corn Laws, survived to lose his political reputation in the 'sixties. In the formation of Cabinets, as in ancient China, the dead had more consideration than the living. Seniority was almost as fatal in the arts of peace as it was in the arts of war.

To the statesmen of 1832 the problem was whether or not the constitution could be worked at all. A constitution in any changing social order must provide for a change of government. The succession of governments " affects the sanity and health of the whole state." A king must choose his favourites in such a manner that he is neither made a puppet nor deposed ; an aristocracy must divide its spoils so that it is not dissolved in civil war ; a democracy must provide a mechanism by which the play of thought and the swing of opinion may be registered in political power. It must keep order while agreement to change is sought by debate. The advantage of the mixed constitution of England before 1832 was thought to be that it provided both for stability and change. It had allowed, as far as was possible, for the methods of government to approach the methods of thought. Governments have their roots in violence. How can they be pruned to flower into persuasion? The methods of power and the methods of reason are so different that the powers that be have rarely been the powers that think. Before 1832 the apologists of the constitution said that it operated at three levels : for the ordinary adjustments of policy there were the alternations of different groups within the governing class ; at longer intervals there were the elections in which the pulse of a wider social order could be felt ; while in times of emergency there was the monarchy to initiate change or to resist uncritical enthusiasm. King, parliament and people were supposed to be bound, each to each, by natural piety. The hereditary king was a barrier to despotism ; the " grave and thoughtful considerations " of the Lords a check to the intemperate vote of the Commons ; while the middle class was the conscience of the State, " the most disinterested, the most independent, and the most unprejudiced of all."[46] The bonds of natural piety had in fact been strengthened by more material cords. The King had bought his own retainers in the Commons, and the Lords were represented there by their nominees.

The Reform Act of 1832 made it impossible for the House of Lords to control a majority in the Commons. There were now two Houses and not two departments of a single House. Nor in time of crisis could the Minister chosen by the King be certain of a majority in the Commons. " How," asked Peel, " could the King hereafter change a

41

Ministry? How could he make a partial change in the administration in times of public excitement with any prospect that the ministers of his choice, unpopular, perhaps, from the strict performance of necessary duties, would be returned to Parliament?"[47] But if power no longer rested in a subtle trinity of King, Lords and Commons, where did it rest and through what channels did it flow?

In a civil government, Locke had written, the people must have power to cashier their rulers. But how, after 1832, was this to be done? If by the King, he might be brought in violent conflict with the people ; if by the people, there were the alternative dangers of the development of party groups, or of a despotism derived from a plebiscite. In 1841 Disraeli argued that Melbourne, defeated at the election, should have resigned. Melbourne said that it was not right " to judge what the conduct of the members may be by their declarations on the hustings."[48]

Members, then, were to be free to support or oppose whatever government seemed in their wisdom to be best. But who, then, was to decide when the House of Commons must be dissolved? Suppose such a confusion of parties that no government could remain in power ; suppose a crisis in which the government of the day was not prepared to accept the verdict of the House ; what then could be done ? It was here that the Crown was felt to be the lynch-pin of the constitution. It was the Crown which was to decide which Minister should be invited to conduct in the House of Commons the business of the State. It was the Crown which was to decide in consultation with the Minister of its choice the most suitable occasion for the dissolution of the House of Commons. But the position of the Crown was by the extension of the franchise made delicate indeed. It must accept a government which could control a majority in the House of Commons. If a government, defeated in the House, desired to appeal to the electorate, it was not clear whether or not the Crown need grant the dissolution required. So obscure was the position that it was believed by Melbourne that the Minister acceptable to the Crown ought not to dissolve unless there were a certainty of success, otherwise the prestige of the Crown would have been damaged by having a majority returned slap against it. If the position of the Crown were to depend upon its being able to choose, before an election, the party or group of parties which would therein succeed ; or if the electorate were always to support the Minister the Crown had deigned to choose, the constitution would have been odd indeed. The actual solution, by which the Crown came to accept the duty of inviting a Prime Minister to form a government, from that party or parties which could control a majority in the House of Commons, and to accept from that Prime Minister and his Cabinet advice as to when a dissolution was most desirable ; that a Minister defeated at an election should resign, the Crown sending for the leader of the party or parties which seemed to have been successful, was the subtle and complex discovery of half a century of anxious experiment. The interplay of tradition and experience, the moulding of a subtle constitution by the exigencies of new conditions are shown in the crises, grave and gay, of : the Dismissal of Melbourne, 1834 ; the Bedchamber Question, 1839 ; the Repeal of the Corn Laws, 1846.

In 1834 the dismissal of Melbourne showed that neither the King nor his Ministers had had time to appreciate the effect of the Reform of 1832. The elevation of Lord Althorp, a member of the Ministry, by the death of his father, to the House of Lords, gave the Prime Minister, Melbourne, a problem in Cabinet reconstruction. He proposed that Lord John Russell should be the new leader of the House of Commons. Russell was not acceptable to the King, who considered that he had the right and the opportunity to reconstruct the Government under a Minister of his own choice. Melbourne was not actually dismissed, but his veiled offer of resignation was accepted by the King as something he had a right to ask. The significance of the crisis lies in the sequel.

Peel, who took office in a minority, failed to secure a majority when he appealed to the new electorate as the King's Minister. In his Tamworth manifesto he said that " he had a firm belief that the people of this country will so far maintain the prerogative of the King, as to give to the Ministers of his choice not an implicit confidence, but a fair trial." Though defeated in the election he met Parliament, and only resigned when, after several months, it was obvious that the House of Commons would not support him. Then he gave as his reason for resignation that he saw " the greatest prejudice to the cause of good government and to the prerogative of the Crown " in " exhibiting the executive government without control over the House of Commons." The incident is significant for two reasons. Peel specifically accepted the responsibility for whatever part the King might have played in the dismissal of Melbourne. " I have been asked," he said, " whether I would impose on the King in his personal capacity the responsibility for the dismissal of the Government . . . I claim all the responsibility which properly belongs to me as a public man ; I am responsible for the assumption of the duty which I have undertaken and if you please, I am by my acceptance of office responsible for the removal of the late Government."[49] This was a somewhat Delphic utterance. The King could not in his personal capacity dismiss a Minister ; but could he dismiss a Minister whenever he could find someone prepared to take office and responsibility for his predecessor's dismissal even though he were in a minority? What would be the position of the Crown when the new Minister responsible for the dismissal of the old was defeated in the House and at the polls? If it were not to participate directly in party politics the Crown would have to accept the advice of its Ministers on its use of the prerogative of dissolution. The Crown might be free to choose a Minister, but it could not be free to decide when to change one.

The Bedchamber Comedy was produced in 1839. The Melbourne Cabinet, one of the weakest ever known, and entirely dependent upon the Radicals and O'Connell, was defeated on the Jamaica Bill. Melbourne advised the Queen to send for Wellington and, if he refused, for Peel. " Your Majesty appears to Lord Melbourne to have no other choice. The Radicals have neither ability, honesty nor numbers. They have no leaders of any character." When the Queen sent for Wellington, he explained " that he had no power whatever in the House of Commons, if he was to say black was black they would say it was not." Peel, who was next applied to, would not take office in a minority unless he might have such evidence of the Queen's confidence as would be given by her acceptance of his nomination of the ladies of her household. The Queen refused. " I replied that I never would consent and I never saw a man so frightened." The Melbourne Cabinet returned to office.

Peel was in a minority and knew also that with the existing registration he could not secure a majority. The conditions were unprecedented and never to be repeated. Neither Melbourne nor Peel wished to dissolve. The Queen was advised by Melbourne to do " everything to facilitate the formation of a government . . . we must not have the position they have in France of no party being able to form a government." She was to " urge this question of the household strongly as a matter due to yourself and your own wishes " and " not to give a promise that you will dissolve, nor to say positively that you will not." The Queen herself was triumphant, writing to Melbourne, " she must rejoice at having got out of the hands of people who would have sacrificed every personal feeling and instinct of the Queen's to their bad party purposes."[50]   To the King of the Belgians she wrote that she had acted " quite alone and shall be supported by my country who are very enthusiastic about it and loudly cheered me on going to church on Sunday." Until the verdict of the electorate on an existing Ministry should be taken as final, the Crown could not avoid a central responsibility in the procedure of forming a Government. When two parties were neither sure of the Commons or of the electorate, the fate of governments hung on the gossip of a household.

The underlying confusion of principle was clearly revealed two years later when the Melbourne Ministry, after a series of defeats in the House of Commons, did not offer to resign. Peel argued when moving a vote of no confidence that it was " at variance with the principles and the spirit of the constitution for a Ministry to continue in office without the confidence of the House." Russell and Macaulay in reply said that while inability to perform the administrative duties of the State was a ground for resignation, general support need not be given to a government's legislative programme. Peel made the significant retort that legislation and administration were " so interwoven as to render it utterly impossible to draw a line of distinction between them," and " the character of administration and the claims upon public confidence was infinitely stronger on account of their legislative measures than on account of their administrative acts." Recognition of the fact that administration is not enough did not mean the principle was accepted that that party should govern whose legislative programme was acceptable to the electorate. When Melbourne at last advised the Queen to dissolve, he misled her as to the significance of her act. He said that an unsuccessful dissolution would be a bad thing because defeat of her Ministers would be an affront to the Crown. The Queen came to think of a dissolution of Parliament, not as an appeal to the political sovereign people to select their government, but as " a valuable weapon in the hands of the Crown which should only be used with certainty of success."[51] Disraeli's insight was clearer and he urged that Melbourne should have resigned without meeting Parliament.

The crisis of the Corn Laws in 1846 revealed important problems in the nature of the constitution and in the very nature of government itself. The Conservative party had been formed from the alliance of a group of interests—sugar, cattle, and corn. Their leaders had begun the transmutation of " Old Corruption " into the efficient machine which was later to serve Gladstonian finance. They feared dependence upon the blackguard influence in the House of Commons, or such an extension of the suffrage as might threaten monarchy, property or their conception of public faith. A Conservative statesman was in a difficult position. In the House he would not displace a Whig Government if it meant his own dependence upon the Radical vote. In the country he feared the people even when they were on his own side. It required the genius of Disraeli to see that a Phillip drunk might be made a useful ally to a Percy sober.

The failure of the Irish potato crop presented Peel with a fundamental problem in the relation between the technique of politics and the necessities of government. Out of the crisis of 1846 was developed

45

the nineteenth-century conception of party government. It was a critical test of the issue whether, in a national crisis, party is enough.

The case made against Peel is simple. The leader of a party, with a majority in the House of Commons, he used his position as Prime Minister to betray his party that the country might be saved—his opponents add, by him and not by others.

When Peel became convinced that the Corn Laws must be repealed and was not supported by his Cabinet, he resigned, advising the Queen to send for Lord John Russell. When it was obvious that neither his own colleagues nor Lord John Russell could form a government, he announced that he was prepared to stand by the Queen, that he would undertake to deal with the difficulties and that he would serve the Queen if she called upon him to do so, and that those who would not go with him he would dismiss at once.[52] He claimed that " the real interests of the cause of constitutional government must be determined by the answer which the heart and conscience of a responsible Minister might give to the question ' What is the course which the public interest really demands? ' " " It was," he said, " no easy task to secure the united action of an ancient monarchy, a proud aristocracy and a reformed constituency." He carried repeal and disrupted his party. Was this as Melbourne said, " a damned dishonest act " or, as Aberdeen thought, " very noble " and of " great courage "?

It is said that he made " the higher obligation of preserving political good faith in political life subservient to the repeal of the Corn Laws " ; that, if their repeal was necessary to save the State, it was not for him to do it. There were other leaders, his critics said, with heart and conscience to secure the united action of an ancient monarchy, a proud aristocracy and a reformed constituency.

Whatever blame may be attached to Peel it is to misunderstand the constitution to regard him as false to the spirit of party. All statesmen of the time would have been prepared on various issues to serve the country against their party. The existing parties were based on an electorate which was far narrower than the middle class. Peel was not prepared to appeal to the uncertain verdict of an election if reform could otherwise be secured. " I thought," he said, " such an appeal would ensure a bitter conflict between the different classes of society and would preclude the possibility of dispassionate consideration by Parliament, a number of whom would probably have committed themselves by explicit declarations and pledges." Peel was in a false position. He regarded himself as the natural leader of the middle classes, but he thought they could only be led from within the Conservative party.

As Greville said, " he was the Liberal chief of a party in which the old anti-Liberal spirit was still rife ; they regarded with jealousy and fear the middle classes . . . with whom Peel was evidently anxious to ingratiate himself and whose support he considered his best alliance . . . there was an unexpressed but complete difference in their understanding and his of the obligations by which the Government and the party were mutually connected. They considered Peel to be not only the Minister, but the creature of the Conservative party, bound above all things to support and protect their special interest according to their own views and opinions. He considered himself the Minister of the nation." The tragedy of Peel was that he considered himself to be the Minister of a nation to which he dare not openly appeal. When, after the Corn Laws had been repealed, he was defeated by a combination of the Protectionists with the Whigs and Irish, Peel resigned rather than dissolve on the Irish question or Free Trade. " I am decidedly against dissolution," he wrote to Wellington, " on an Irish question, above all, on such a question as the Coercion Bill. Shall we dissolve on some other ground? . . . On what ground shall we appeal to the country? We must appeal to it on some principle. The natural one seems to be Free Trade and the destruction of Protection. If we are to succeed we shall succeed by an unnatural combination with those who agree with us in nothing but the principles of Free Trade. A short time only would pass before this combination would be dissolved and we should be at the mercy of our new allies."[53]

The period between the fall of Peel, in 1846, and the formation of the last government of Palmerston in 1859, shows the perils to which constitutional government, without party organizations with clear programmes and broad-based popular support, is liable. It was in this period that Disraeli learnt how to manipulate the Queen, and Gladstone the need for an extended suffrage. It was in this period that we drifted into our most shameful war and that Palmerston was for the middle class the politician it really deserved. It is in this period, too, that our political leaders " behaved so like children " that the Queen, advised and assisted by the Prince Consort, had to organize our Cabinets and direct their policies.

A brief summary of the different Cabinets and their character will give some idea of the anaemia of the constitution :—

The 1st Russell Cabinet, 1846-52. Russell took office on the resignation of Sir Robert Peel. At the dissolution of 1847, 325 Whigs and Liberals were returned, and 226 Tories and 105 Peelites. Russell in a minority had to rely on the antagonism of the Protectionists and the Peelites. In 1851 he was defeated and resigned, but no combination could be found either to form a government or to dissolve. He had to resume office, finally resigning in 1852.

1st Derby Cabinet, 1852. This was the weakest government which has ever tried to govern the country. Derby knew that if he taxed food he would have a rebellion, or as good, in the towns ; and that if he threw over Protectionist principles his party would do the same by him. The Queen wrote to Leopold, " in the present case our acquaintance is confined almost entirely to Lord Derby, but then he is the Government." Disraeli was, for the first time, Chancellor of the Exchequer. The election of 1852 returned 300 Conservatives, 270 Whigs and Liberals, 40 Peelites, and 40 Irish. The Government met the new Parliament, was defeated on Disraeli's Budget by 19 votes, and resigned.

The Aberdeen Coalition, 1852-55. The formation of this Cabinet of six Whigs, six Peelites and one Radical taxed the full resources of the Court. Would Johnny and Pam serve together? Would Aberdeen work with Russell? Could anyone persuade Johnny to serve under Aberdeen? Contemporaries called it a " tessellated pavement," " a clique of doctrinaires existing as a government by Court favour."[54] It was melancholy, they said, to see " how little fitness for office is regarded on all sides and how much the public employments are treated as booty to be divided among the successful combatants."[55] Graham said that " on the whole they were gentlemen and they have a perfect gentleman at their head." In 1855 this Cabinet collapsed from inability to conduct a war it had been unable to prevent. Albert complained that the parties then behaved a good deal like children. Derby refused to form a government, though his party was 250 strong. His error, Gladstone considered, was gross.[56] Disraeli was annoyed because, as he wrote at the time, " we had actually the Court with us, for the two Court favourites, Aberdeen of the Queen, is extinct, and Newcastle of the Prince, in hopeless condition ; and our rivals were Johnny, in disgrace, and Palmerston, ever detested." It was Palmerston who took office next.

Palmerston Cabinet, 1855-58. For a brief fortnight the Peelites, Graham, Gladstone and Herbert, were in his Government. The general election of 1857 was practically a plebiscite for Palmerston after he had dissolved on his China policy being censured in the Commons. In 1858 however he was defeated by a combination of the whole of the Conservative party, the Peelites, Lord John Russell and the Radicals.

His Cabinet unanimously resolved to resign. Palmerston declined to give the Queen any advice as to his successor, but laid before her the state of parties as it concerned Russell and Derby.[57] She sent for Derby. He, after his refusal in 1851 and 1855, had either to accept or to break his party for ever. With a majority of 2 to 1 against him in the Commons,

48

he asked if he would be allowed to dissolve? Aberdeen, who was privately consulted, said that if a Minister advised the Queen to dissolve she should certainly do so ; that while the sovereign might refuse a dissolution, whoever was sent for to succeed, must, with his appointment, assume the responsibility for that act ; that a government had the right to threaten dissolution, but that they would be wrong to join the Queen's name with it. So the Queen allowed Derby to know that a dissolution would not be refused him and trusted that her honour would be safe in his hands as to the use to be made of that knowledge. The Crown was now in the dangerous position of supporting a party in conflict with a majority in the House of Commons.[58] Derby, after a dissolution, was defeated in the House by 13 and resigned. The Queen sent for Granville, who opened delicate negotiations with Pam and Johnny. Granville could not be Prime Minister because if he had the first place either Johnny or Pam would have to take third.[59] These fine points of honour were bleeding privilege to death. The worst possible combination was made. Palmerston became Prime Minister, pledged to domestic sterility, and Russell Foreign Secretary, when his powers had failed. It was Gladstone's experience as Palmerston's Chancellor of the Exchequer in this Government which convinced him that the constitution must be revitalized by the touch of popular power. The real issue, as Disraeli saw in 1858, was " whether parliamentary government is compatible with our existing institutions. The House of Commons is broken into sections which, although they have no unity of purpose or policy, can always combine to overthrow the Queen's Government however formed."

The confusion of the Commons had reprieved the House of Lords. In the first session of the Reform Parliament, when there was a large Liberal majority in the Commons, the lords had acquiesced in the first part of the programme of radical reconstruction. When the division between the Radicals and the Whigs grew and the former were forced into alliance with the Irish, the courage of the peers revived. By 1835, the Lords " presented the appearance of a dominant party faction . . . too numerous to be affected by any constitutional process . . . too obstinate to be turned from its fixed purpose of opposing all measures which have a tendency to diminish the influence of the Conservative party."[60] Only through Wellington's support in the Lords could Peel carry the Repeal of the Corn Laws.

After 1846 the Lords, having no direct interest in factory organization, passed the Factory Bills sent up to them from the Commons. But they strenuously opposed the amelioration of the conditions of the Irish peasant, or the reduction of the privileges of the Established Church.

In 1856, they refused to admit life peers and " rejected the inestimable and unprecedented opportunity of being tacitly reformed " (Bagehot). The fact that the Prince Consort was believed to be in favour of the introduction of literary and scientific peers no doubt stimulated the Lords in the defence of their privileges. The Queen was of the opinion that an absolute duty devolved on her of requiring that peerages should not be conferred upon any person who did not possess, in addition to other qualifications, a good moral character.

Though they won the battle of privilege in 1856, the Lords lost the struggle with Gladstone in 1861. They rejected a measure which repealed the excise duty on paper, the last survivor of the taxes on knowledge. Lord Lyndhurst said : " I do not dispute . . . that we have no right whatsoever to amend what is called a Money Bill. We have no right to originate a Bill of that nature . . . but the principle does not apply to the rejection of Money Bills." The Lords had a good tactical case because their rejection of a Bill which repealed a tax, far from embarrassing the executive, gave it a large sum of money. The annual Budget then consisted of a number of separate Bills, and the Lords, by rejecting one, ran no risk of incommoding the Chancellor of the Exchequer. But Gladstone, who then held that office, retaliated first by securing the appointment of a Select Committee which examined the precedents, and confirmed that the Lords had not the right to amend a Money Bill, and showed that their power of rejection had never been exercised purely on financial grounds ; secondly, by persuading Palmerston to move resolutions asserting the financial privileges of the Commons and declaring that it had " in its own hands so to impose and remit taxes and to frame Bills of Supply that the right of the Commons as to manner, measure and time may be maintained inviolate " ; and thirdly, in 1861, he combined in one Bill the entire financial scheme of the year so that the Lords could neither amend nor reject the measure without directly challenging the Commons.

The last scene of this eventless history was the passing of the Second Reform Bill in 1867. The way it passed epitomizes the character of the period it was to supersede. Palmerston died in 1865 and Russell was again Premier. Though Parliament was against reform all the leaders were committed to it. Gladstone introduced a Reform measure which was defeated by a revolt of the Whig cave under Lowe. Russell had to choose between immediate resignation or dissolution. " To dissolve would have been a daring act and an appeal from a shuffling Parliament to an awakened people."[61] It was the course most conformable to the principles and spirit of the constitution.[62] Because there was a risk of war between Prussia and Austria, the Queen was not inclined to consent to a dissolution. Russell resigned and the Reform Bill was carried by a Conservative Government, by a government in a minority and through a Parliament elected to support Lord Palmerston, who detested reform. The new measure added a million voters, whereas the rejected measure of 1866 would have added only 400,000. Whether Disraeli's dishing the Whigs was the " half-accidental result of a balance of forces and of manœuvres of attack and defence prepared in swamp of expediency," a deep laid design, or the result of unprepared opportunism, we shall never know. But the shock to men's confidence in the political morality of English statesmen was severe. Three Conservative statesmen left Derby and Disraeli as a protest on behalf of political honour against mere party expediency.[63]

We have given a brief sketch of the conditions which determined the party and the strength of the governments between 1832 and 1867. How were they organized for the performance of their functions? Cabinets were dependent upon the House of Commons, but they were not yet prepared to appeal to the electorate to break a deadlock in the House. The conception was only slowly developed that the opposition was an alternative Cabinet prepared to take office when the one in power should fail. In 1831 Peel had written, " there are two parties which call themselves Conservatives : one which is ready to support monarchy, property and public faith ; there is another which is prepared to ally itself with Radicals if only it can turn out the Government." Experience taught that " it is safer and easier to displace a Ministry than to change and direct its policy by the active intervention of Parliament."[64] In 1859 Palmerston told the Queen that " those who unite to turn out a government ought to be prepared to unite to form a stronger government than that which is overthrown." In 1864 Disraeli complained to Derby that " the principle now conveniently assumed by our opponents that the Opposition is a body prepared to take office and therefore bound to give official opinion on the conduct of every department, seems to me to have no sound foundation."[65] But in spite of the broken state of parties, the changing character of government compelled the Government of the day to demand that it should be supported unless there were an alternative party prepared to take office. In 1840 Lord John Russell said " there has been, in the course of the last thirty years, very great changes made in the mode of conducting business . . . when I first entered Parliament it was not usual for governments to undertake generally all subjects of legislation. Since the Reform Bill it has been thought convenient that the Government should propose changes in the laws ; there is more discussion and more motions by more members."

The extension of the business of the State involved a modification of those ancient forms of Parliament procedure which, in 1832, were in essentials what they had been in the seventeenth century. They had been developed to defend the representative body against the over-whelming power and influence of a powerful executive. The rules of procedure were ramparts against corruption by an executive in the service of the Crown. With the coming of popular government the House had to be so organized that the Government could carry out the policies for which it had been elected.

Before 1832 the functions of a government were chiefly executive. Changes in the law were proposed by independent members and carried not as party questions, but by the combined action of both sides. After 1832 the business of the House was continually on the increase and the proportion of its time required for government business steadily increased too. If there was not to be chaos, the rules of procedure had to secure that there should be certainty, day by day, as to the business to be transacted. This could only be done by limiting the privileges of private members to move amendments at every stage of the consideration of legislation, or the grant of moneys for the business of the State. While unofficial members " endeavoured by cunningly-devised arrangements to entrench themselves against the superior power of the Government " the broad problems of parliamentary procedure were treated on a non-party basis. That there must be more certainty, and that the Government must have more time for essential business was recognized by all parties ; there was also general agreement " that the old rules and orders, when carefully considered and narrowly investigated," were " the safeguard of freedom of debate and a sure defence against the oppression of overpowering majorities."

A radical transformation of parliamentary procedure was not made until after the Reform Act of 1867 and the attack of the Irish party on the whole traditions of the House. But changes of some importance were made in the period 1832 to 1872. In 1833 committees were given power to meet from 10 a.m. to 5 p.m. and to sit during the sitting of the House. In 1835 the first printed questions appeared on the notice paper. In 1839 so great had been the flood of petitions that all debate was forbidden on their presentation. In 1849 it was settled that the first reading and printing of a Bill should be decided without debate or amendment moved. By the " rule of progress " the abuse was stopped of allowing the merits of a Bill to be debated each time the House went into committee for its discussion, although its principles had been debated and accepted upon its second reading. In 1846 Mondays and Thursdays were fixed as Government days and a third day was usually conceded towards the middle of the session. In 1852 the Committees of Supply and Ways and Means were fixed for Mondays and Thursdays and also for Wednesdays. This did not give the Government enough control over financial business, so in 1861 it was decided that the Committee of Ways and Means and the Committee of Supply might be fixed for every day upon which the House should meet for the dispatch of public business. Finally, in 1872, it was resolved that the " rule of progress " should be extended to the Committee of Supply. This meant that amendments on the occasion of going into such committee were only allowed on a day when a new division of the Estimates was being taken, and not at subsequent sittings. In 1879 the Government was secured one day a week for supply by making it impossible to move amendments on that day.[66]

The dependence of the Cabinet upon a House of Commons which neither the Crown nor the House of Lords could now control meant that a principle of collective responsibility was necessary, if the Cabinet were to be able to control the Commons in the carrying out of essential business, and if loyalty to party principles was to take the place of loyalty to the person of the Crown as the mainspring of political action. Wellington, an old Tory, saw " a great difference between willingness to serve the Crown if called upon " and " volunteering in a course of measures which are to have for their object to force the administration to resign, and the sovereign to call for the services of others, myself included " (1839). On the same occasion Graham, a Whig, wrote that " the possession of power in our popular government is the sole object of political warfare . . . it is not in human nature that a great party can be kept together by the abstract hope of checking the misconduct of a bad administration, in the absence of the fixed purpose of displacing them . . . Let it once transpire that you are afraid to take the government and your party is gone."[67] If power was to be respectable those who had it must share the principles which would control its use. Graham, when in 1835 he declined an invitation to join Peel, said that " the sudden conversion of long political opposition into the most intimate alliance—no general coincidence of principle, except upon one point, being proved to exist between us—would shock public opinion."[68] In an entirely different context Cobden made the same point when in 1859 he refused Palmerston's offer of the Board of Trade. He wrote to his wife that " to take office now, without a single declaration of change of view regarding my public conduct would be so monstrous a course that nothing on earth shall induce me to do it " (1859).[69] If honour required that you should agree with those you joined, solidarity was needed for efficiency among those in power. Openly avowed and tolerated differences of opinion upon matters standing for immediate action would kill a Cabinet. Diversity in consultation must be followed by unity in decision. A dissentient was expected to resign his office before he openly voted and spoke against the policy of the administration. " That which of course you will skilfully avoid," wrote Palmerston to Gladstone in 1862, " will be the appearance of proclaiming or divulging to the public differences of opinion which may have existed in Cabinet discussions, but which have been merged in an aggregate acquiescence." After 1846, when there were few deep cleavages of principle between the politicians of the day, their differences were drawn to fine threads of honour. Loyalty to Peel's memory kept the Peelites out of office from 1846-55. Party lines were then so indistinct that it could be seriously considered that Gladstone should be in the same Cabinet with Disraeli,[70] and Gladstone, who had considered Palmerston the worst possible Prime Minister, could serve with him as Chancellor of the Exchequer in 1859.

In the construction of his Cabinet, a Minister had a delicate task. There were two situations of influence in the general as distinguished from the departmental government of the country : the one that of the Prime Minister, the other that of the leader of the House. Whoever was Prime Minister with a colleague of equal political prestige would have to make him leader of the House. It was necessary to have powerful Ministers in the Lords and the holder of the Foreign Office had to placate the Queen. In the 'forties the Prime Minister needed a confidential friend at the Home Office. It was responsible for internal order and in particular had to deal with the disturbances that accompanied the Chartist movement.[71]

The office of the Prime Minister received its modern stamp from the capacity of Sir Robert Peel. Melbourne's Cabinet had been a mere government of departments without any centre of unity—" our Cabinet is a complete republic and Melbourne, their ostensible head, has no overruling authority " (Greville, August 24th, 1840). Peel's small Cabinet of twelve was a real unity. The problem of Cabinet organization was already acute. " I defy the Minister of this country to perform properly the duties of his office, to read all that he ought to read, including the whole foreign correspondence ; to keep up the constant communication with the Queen and the Prince ; to see whom he ought to see ; to superintend the grant of honours and the disposal of ecclesiastical patronage ; to write with his own hand to every person of note who chooses to write to me ; to be prepared for every debate, including the most trumpery concerns ; to do all these things, and also to sit in the House of Commons eight hours a day for 118 days." (Peel to Arbuthnot,

1854.) In the formation of a government " Nobody," he told Greville, " could form an idea of what he had to go through in the disposal of places, the adjustment of conflicting claims, and in answering particular applications, everybody thinking their own case the strongest in the world and that they alone ought to be exempted from the general rule . . . everybody . . . fancying that to any office they had ever held they had a sort of vested right and title, and forgetting that younger men must be brought forward."[72]

CHAPTER III

MACHINERY OF ADMINISTRATION, 1832-70

Administration and the Oligarchy—Development of Government Departments : War Office—Admiralty—Foreign Office—Board of Trade —Local Government Board—The Treasury—Civil Service Reform— The character of the Civil Service—Of the Judiciary—And of Local Government.

THE industrial revolution compelled the State to create a machinery of administration almost as complex as the new machinery of industry itself. The eighteenth-century conception of liberty, equality and justice had to be protected against the inequality and violence implicit in an uncontrolled industrial revolution. The growth of industry would have created a new and more unequal feudalism had not the democratic State produced administrative devices for the protection of the elements of social justice against the principalities and powers of greed.

But it was inevitable that a representative government should suffer from the defective planning of its administrative machinery. For, when government is based upon persuasion, continuity with the past is often a political duty when revolution is an administrative necessity. In England the history of every government department is almost as complex as the history of the constitution itself. In each department there have been revolutions, restorations, in a few cases almost civil war between conflicting personalities and policies, and an enveloping crust of custom.

Every department of the State has been profoundly affected by the circumstances of its origin. Some go back to the great offices of a feudal monarchy : the Lord High Treasurer, the Lord High Admiral, the Lord Chancellor ; others have derived from the peculiar development of the office of the Secretary of State in the struggle between Parliament and the King ; others have had their origin in committees of the Privy Council—which has been used as a kind of potting shed for new administrative plants. Even those which have been established by the legislation of the last hundred years bear in their powers and organization marks of the political conditions under which they were set up. Of the older departments only the research of scholars in dusty archives can trace the process by which they emerged ; of the more recent, while their legal framework may be found in statutes and official orders, their real working can be seen but darkly in the evidence produced before committees of enquiry and in the material scattered here and there in the biographies of statesmen.

The complex law of the prerogative, the exigencies of responsible government, the political tradition of *laissez-faire* have all left their mark upon our executive machinery. What the United States has suffered from the tyranny of a written constitution we have suffered from that burden of the past which so firmly rides many of our executive departments. " The rusty curb of old father antique, the law " is in the mouth of every bureaucrat. Our system of government is haunted by the ghosts of extinct offices and confused by a terminology which might have been deliberately designed to confuse appearance and reality. Our councils are not councils, our committees are not committees ; nor are our boards boards, or our commissioners commissioners. Every Minister presides not only over a part of the machinery of government of the modern state but also over a legal museum which illustrates the continuity of our constitutional development.

There was throughout the nineteenth century " an obstinate prejudice against the organization of a competent bureaucracy."[1] There was little progress in reconciling the compromise which government by discussion compels with the simplicity of form that technical development requires. Responsible government may require that any detail of administration may be made the occasion of a political battle, yet the stability of democracy depends on the development of a political sagacity that will not butcher an administration to make a party holiday.

The growth of English administrative machinery was stunted by the continuity of her political and legal tradition. We paid too big a price in administrative immaturity for our national tradition of gradualness. The drama of politics attracted much of the ability that should have gone to the drudgery of administration. The Henry Irving tradition in the drama had its political counterpart in the Prime Minister actor-manager. The allocation of political talent among the different departments was determined too much by the traditional prestige of the departments and too little by their real social and political importance. In the first half of the century it was almost an insult to offer an able statesman the Department of Education, the Colonial Office, or the Department of Woods and Forests which controlled our drains and health. Not until the 'nineties did our politicians begin to discover the importance of being earnest in such matters as the structure of Local

Government or the provision of higher education. In the first half of the century only the toughest eccentricity could secure serious administrative changes in the face of the tremendous complacency of the legal and political traditions. A man had to be obsessed with one idea or be a hardened egoist to break down the obstruction of the official world—a Brougham in law, an Owen in industry, a Chadwick in health, or a Wakefield in colonial affairs. A measure of efficiency in Local Government was only secured with the grim assistance of the cholera. If there were many who would rather see England free than sober, there were others who would rather see Englishmen dead than governed. Only the threat of German and American industrial supremacy and the fortunate accident that, in Morant, the Board of Education had a civil servant whose experience of the dynastic and religious feuds of Siam equipped him to understand the Anglican and Nonconformist minds, produced at long last the Education Act of 1902.

The development of our government departments in their modern form began in 1782, when the secretariat, which throughout the eighteenth century had been divided into a Northern and a Southern department, the one dealing with Northern Europe and the other with Southern Europe and a variety of miscellaneous duties, was reorganized. The Northern department became the Foreign Office, and the Southern the Home Office, with Irish and Colonial business attached. From the latter have been budded off the different Secretaries of State as the pressure of war and social change compelled.

In 1794 Pitt appointed a Secretary for War, but there was no clear definition of his duties. In 1798 he was made Secretary for War and Colonies because our army was mainly concerned with the capture of scattered colonies. His responsibilities were not clearly defined because there existed a Secretary at War with an undefined responsibility for finance, and a Commander-in-Chief who was the representative of the King as head of the Army. The War Office was, in fact, destined to suffer every ill that an administrative body can be heir to. In 1904 a committee reported that " its organization had been built up piecemeal as the result of constant changes and compromises while fundamental principles were subordinated to temporary exigencies or to personal and political considerations." Since the seventeenth century an efficient Army had been suspect as an instrument of despotism. What Army we had had to be organized, not for the protection of a land frontier, but for the defence of scattered possessions overseas. Confusion was confounded by the constitutional principle that the sovereign was head of the Army. This effectively prevented the development of the clear responsibility of a Secretary of State to Parliament for its efficiency. Instead of a Secretary *for* War there emerged in the eighteenth century a Secretary *at* War who, once the subordinate secretary to the Commander-in-Chief in the field, had acquired an anomalous and imperfectly defined responsibility for military questions in the House of Commons. So we began the nineteenth century with a Secretary *at* War who had an undefined responsibility for finance ; a Secretary *for* War who was also the Secretary for the Colonies ; and a Commander-in-Chief, whose relations to both no one could define. The Home Office was responsible for the relation between the military and the civilians.

After the Reform Act of 1832 the establishment of the clear responsibility of a Secretary for War to Parliament was opposed by Wellington as a dodge of the Whigs to destroy the Army and debase the Crown. He determined that the Whig dogs should get no military bones. Largely through his influence, the Commander-in-Chief retained control of patronage and discipline in the Army and when, in 1856, the Duke of Cambridge, cousin to the Queen, was made Commander-in-Chief and the obstinate personality of Queen Victoria enlisted in defence of his powers, a wisely-planned War Office became a political dream.

At the outbreak of the Crimean War the Army was managed by seven separate departments with sleepy inefficiency. For the War Office was " a very slow office, an enormously expensive office, a not very efficient office, and one in which the Minister's intentions can be entirely negatived by all his sub-departments and those of each of the sub-departments by every other."[2]

(1) The Secretary of State for War and Colonies was responsible for the general control of the Army. Though in time of peace responsibility for general control meant little more than responsibility for its size, in time of war it meant responsibility for major strategy. The staff of his office did not include a single soldier. (2) The Commander-in-Chief was responsible for the discipline of the Army, but he could take no action involving any cost without the Secretary for War, and had no control over the troops outside the United Kingdom. (3) The Secretary at War was responsible for the estimates and the protection of civilians from the military, but he had no control over the material of the Army. These were under (4) the Master General and the Board of Ordnance with a constitution going back to Queen Elizabeth. The Master General supplied material for the Army at the request of the Secretary for War, and for the Artillery and Engineers at the demand of the Chancellor of the Exchequer. The Board met without the Master being present and he could rescind all they did without discussion.

(5) The Commissariat Department was responsible for the provisioning of the Army abroad. It had its headquarters at the Treasury and its own officials abroad. Because during the Napoleonic wars financial experts had been necessary to stop undue competition for bills which officers then drew on the Treasury, it was now responsible for the health and feeding of the troops. " By sheer force of routine the troops abroad were fed chiefly upon salt meat."[3] (6) The Home Secretary was responsible for the use of the military in Great Britain because before 1846 the Army was the only effective police. Finally (7), the Board of General Officers clothed the cavalry and infantry of the Army. As Albert complained to Granville, " English statesmen never look at any subject as a part of a whole." Nobody ever asked themselves the question " Why we wanted an army? " and then " what that army should be."[4]

The Crimean War secured some reorganization. In 1854 the Secretary of State for the Colonies was separated from the Secretary of State for War. But though the Secretary of State for War was now free for new duties there was no thorough reorganization. Against the realization of a War Office dealing with the Army as a whole, there was a tacit combination of Court, Tory and bureaucratic influence, before which Parliament was helpless.[5] The Army Medical Board and the Board of General Officers passed under the control of the Secretary for War. The militia and yeomanry, which had been transferred to the Secretary at War from the Home Office in 1852, were transferred in 1855 to the Secretary for War.[6] In 1854, against the vigorous protest of Sir Charles Trevelyan, the Treasury was deprived of the Commissariat.[7] In May, 1855, the Letters Patent of the Board of Ordnance, which dated back to the fourteenth century, were revoked and its duties divided between the Commander-in-Chief and the Secretary for War. The Commander-in-Chief became responsible for the administration of the Artillery and the Engineers, while the Secretary of State undertook the supervision of the civil side of the Board's activities. The Secretary of State was given the office of Secretary of State at War until that office was abolished in 1863.[8] But no real effort was made to make the new office an organized whole and the real cause of the muddle, the dual control of the Secretary of State for War and the Commander-in-Chief remained.

When, in 1860, a Select Committee on Military Organization, presided over by Sir James Graham, examined their relation, neither of these two high officers could clearly explain their relations. But, in fact, the Commander-in-Chief was becoming gradually and imperceptibly more and more dependent upon the Secretary for War, as the Army could not exist without certain services which were entirely supervised by the Parliamentary head of the War Office.[9] The North-brook Committee recommended in 1869 that the War Office should be divided into three departments : (1) The Commander-in-Chief, who was to be the sole military adviser of the Secretary of State and in charge of the regular Army and auxiliary forces ; (2) the Surveyor-General of Ordnance, who was to be responsible for supply, transport, clothing and munitions of war, including the purchase, construction and charge of material ; and (3) the Financial Secretary, who was to control all the financial business of the Army. The Committee also considered it was essential that the Commander-in-Chief should be under the same roof as the Secretary of State for War.[10] At the same time Cardwell, Secretary of State for War in the Gladstone Cabinet of 1868-74, claimed full responsibility for the Secretary of State.[11] By the War Office Act of 1870 the Secretary of State became responsible for Army business as a whole, and his duties were defined in an Order in Council of June 4th 1870 which placed the Commander-in-Chief in a position of complete subordination to the political head of the department.[12] The War Office was divided into three departments of the Commander-in-Chief, the Surveyor-General of Ordnance and the Financial Secretary.[13] But though the offices of the Commander-in-Chief were removed from the Horse Guards to Whitehall, in loyalty to his spiritual home he continued to write his letters under the address " Horse Guards, Pall Mall."[14]

Compared with the War Office the Admiralty in the nineteenth century seemed a model department. The basis of its organization was laid down by Sir James Graham in 1832. He reformed a dual organization which, inherited from Elizabeth, was not working without friction. There were two departments : the Admiralty Office and the Naval Board. The Admiralty Office was the department of the Lord High Admiral which, since 1708, had been put in commission and dealt with appointments, promotions, the movement of ships and the control of general policy. The Navy Board, subordinate to the Admiralty Office, dealt with the management of ships, dockyard accounts, stores, victualling and transport. Graham transferred the duties of the Navy Board to five principal officers, under the direct control of the Board of Admiralty, each department being placed under a superintending Lord, who represented it at the Admiralty.

This concentration of power on the grounds of efficiency and economy was open to serious criticism. Even in the eighteenth century the Board of Admiralty had had too much to do. Its administrative duties had interfered with its consideration of higher problems of policy in the preparation and conduct of war. Graham's centralization abolished the

A HUNDRED YEARS OF ENGLISH GOVERNMENT

Admiralty Board as an independent, superior Board, concerned primarily with the function of command, undisturbed by details of management. " It was apparently supposed . . . that the work of planning and conducting war could be performed simultaneously with the departmental duties."[15] The Board in fact suffered severely from undue centralization and from confusion between its powers as a whole and those of the individual members. The Board met daily and almost all the business of the Admiralty was brought before it by the several Lords for decision and consideration. By 1861 the Lords were working at least ten hours a day.[16] As the powers of the Lord High Admiral were vested in the Board, the First Lord had no authority to give orders alone.[17] The exact powers of the Board were by no means clear, because they were derived from a patent which referred their powers to the Lord High Admiral, and his powers had depended largely on usage. Graham, examined by a Committee in 1861, thought that no new " patent would carry all the powers which by usage, prescription and former patents have been exercised and any omission might be fatal at a moment of extreme urgency."[18] The First Lord was specially concerned with the efficiency and strength of the fleet. But no Lord was specially charged with responsibility for finance. The position of the Controller of the Navy was anomalous, for he conducted the work of the dockyards outside the Board acting under the First Lord, but with no civilian to control his expenditure. Absorption in administrative business not only took the Board's attention away from the problem of strategy but also from those of tactics.[19] By Order in Council, in 1869, the Board was extensively reorganized. The First Lord was made responsible for all the business of the Admiralty and the others were to be his assistants. The duties of the Board were divided into three branches : material, personnel and finance.

In the organization and work of the Foreign Office there has been a continuous, if slow, progress towards greater representation and greater efficiency.[20] The existence . of constitutional government made it necessary that English statesmen should put more truths on paper than those of other countries, so that as early as 1815 documents were more carefully kept and the organization of the office was in advance of that of other countries.[21] The establishment of a modernized procedure and rules of business dates from Canning (1820-27), [22] and from his time the diplomacy of the nineteenth century was carried on by what was, for the times, a highly-organized machine.[23] For though a powerful Foreign Secretary might master every detail of the office, yet the policy which he directed was the product of a number of different processes, carried out by an office machine increasing rapidly in size. In 1828 the

Foreign Office sent out 5,000 dispatches; in 1853 the number was 35,000; in 1854, 49,000.[24] When in 1851 the Queen required that Lord Palmerston should take no action of importance before her pleasure had been consulted she was asking an administrative impossibility. The battle which Palmerston then lost was gradually won by the growing complexity of the business of the Office.[25] In the 'sixties the hierarchy of the Foreign Office consisted of the Secretary of State, the permanent Under-Secretary and the transitory Parliamentary Secretary; an Assistant Under-Secretary had been added in 1858; below them were the Chief Clerk and three others to deal with audit, estimates and accounts. Eight Senior Clerks, each with an assistant, had charge of one of the eight divisions under which, for Foreign Office business, the countries of the world were grouped.[26] In the 'seventies the Foreign Office was composed of four departments : the Political Department, which alone dealt with policy; the Librarian's Department; the Treaty Department; and the Chief Clerk's Department, which was purely financial.

In the staffing of the office a revolution was begun in 1856 when Clarendon introduced a qualifying entrance examination. This was not severe, but a nomination from the Secretary of State was required first and after appointment there was a probationary period, which was exacting and effective. Granville stiffened the examination so that only those who had spent at least four years swallowing languages abroad, and many months being crammed with geographical minutiæ, could hope to succeed. The essential principles of Foreign Office appointments were a desire to eliminate patronage, because it imposed on the Foreign Secretary the invidious task of both remembering his relations and not forgetting his friends, and a determination to admit only gentlemen to the competitive field. In the diplomatic world a wide gulf was thought to yawn between the mere expert and the accomplished man of the world. It was said that a hundred spies could not ascertain so much as an English gentleman, whom princes and ministers believed that they could safely trust.[27] Not until 1822 was the first attempt made to create a salaried diplomatic service responsible to the State and not a mere part of the Ambassador's family circle. But the idea of the Ambassador's " family " remained throughout the nineteenth century and not until after the war of 1914-18 was the diplomatic service assimilated to that of the Foreign Office. In the Foreign Office itself the system of nomination, while it secured that the Secretary of State felt the same responsibility for the efficiency of his office that a colonel of a crack regiment may feel for the warlike and social qualities of his officers, had the disadvantage that gilded youth, however intelligent, was wasted on routine work that could as well have been performed by competent clerks. But the closeness of its relations with the Queen and the prestige which it derived from its responsibility for affairs of blood and State prolonged, for the Foreign Office, the period of class-conscious puerilities. It is significant that the able Secretaries of State for Foreign Affairs were often exasperated by the inefficiency of its gilded youths and dusty seniors.

The Board of Trade is an excellent example of the fortunes which shape and warp an English Department of State. In the eighteenth century there had been a Committee of the Privy Council—" the Lord Commissioners for promoting the trade of our Kingdom and for inspecting and improving our plantations in America and elsewhere." It had only advisory powers, and action wanted the instrumentality of a Secretary of State. With the industrial revolution its influence declined. In its offices Gibbon enjoyed his " days and weeks of repose without being called from the library to the office." In 1784 Pitt established a Consultative Committee and in 1786 a board, intended to be a permanent part of the machinery of government, dealing with problems of trade. " The original idea of the Board of Trade was that it was a board composed of men whose opinions and judgment upon all commercial questions submitted to them was of a kind to carry great weight with the public and the Government . . . (its reports) became State papers and the ground work for the Imperial policy of the State upon commercial questions." But the collective authority of the Board of Trade as a deliberative committee did not survive the Napoleonic Wars. It became a mere meeting of the President and Vice-President, and two secretaries. In 1853 its minute-book was discontinued and a departmental register substituted. Its powers were entirely transformed by the development of free trade and the industrial revolution. For free trade meant that tariffs were regarded merely as a matter of revenue to be decided by the Treasury, while commercial policy became an appendage to the system of power and prestige controlled by the Foreign Office. In Palmerston's time negotiations for commercial treaties were referred to the Board of Trade.[28] In the 'fifties Cardwell was of the opinion that it should only advise on matters which came specially under its cognizance in connection with its executive duties.[29] In the 'sixties the Treasury did not consult it on tariff changes,[30] nor was it consulted by the India Office and but seldom by the Colonial Office.[31] But while the Board of Trade was losing its significance as a department for the determination of commercial policy, its executive functions were rapidly and confusingly growing as the State became responsible for conditions of industry and trade. From the 'forties it was entrusted with the administration of various statutes regulating railways, shipping and company organization. A report of 1854 said that fresh business had been heaped upon it without reorganization. It was divided into four distinct departments, each with a separate class of clerks and a separate class of messengers. There was no security that correspondence would not be carried on by two departments on one and the same subject, each ignorant of what the other was doing. After 1870 we shall see it develop into a complex structure, a federation of departments, whose separate technical and executive duties over-shadowed its consultative functions as a whole.

In 1782, when the old Board of Trade was abolished, Colonial business was entrusted to the Home Secretary, assisted, after 1786, by a Committee of the Privy Council. In 1801 the Secretary for War and Colonies was made responsible for both war and colonies. By him they, too, were shamefully neglected. " Colonial Governors reported crises, complained of their wrongs and even died without the Minister seeming to be aware of the fact."[32] But in 1812, with Bathurst and Goulburn as Under-Secretaries, the nucleus of a true Colonial Office came into being. It had the disadvantage that its Secretaries of State rarely remained more than three years in office ; but it enjoyed the advantage of a succession of able and long-serving permanent secretaries. Its work was inevitably complex, for our colonial territory, after the disruption of the first British Empire by the Declaration of Independence, was a thing of shreds and patches. It must often have seemed to the permanent secretary that his was the head upon which all " the ends of the world are come " and to his critics he seemed a little weary. " One day the Colonial Secretary is in Ceylon a financial and religious reformer promoting the interests of the planters and casting discredit on the religion of Bhudda, the next day he is in the West Indies teaching the economical manufacture of sugar, or in Van Diemens striving to reform the fiends that he has transplanted to that pandemonium ; now he is in Canada dealing with a war of races ; at the Cape of Good Hope dancing a war dance with his Kaffir subjects ; or in New Zealand an unsuccessful Lycurgus."[33] When, in 1854, it was made a separate department it had to fight hard to establish its claim to have the final decision in all matters except those involving important foreign or financial policy. The delays for which it was often blamed were due as much to the procrastination of other departments, which it had to consult, and the niggardliness of the Treasury, as to its own short-comings. A question about the transportation of convicts would involve the Treasury, the Home Office, the Ordnance Department, the Inspector of Prisons, and the agent of the colony. All financial dispatches had to be referred to the Treasury; all tariff dispatches to the Treasury or the Board of Trade; all convict dispatches to the Home Office; and all the question of land and immigration to the Commissioners concerned. The Treasury and the Board of Trade were at loggerheads about the limits of their jurisdiction and " while adjusting between themselves points of etiquette " the two boards agreed in the leaving the business undone. Correspondence was " uselessly and idly protracted by certain departmental feelings of dignity or independence indulged in on all sides at the expense of the public services." The transfer of Malaya from the India to the Colonial Office took seven years to effect, mainly because of the wrangles between the India and the War Office.[34]

But it is the development of the Poor Law and Public Health Departments that best illustrates the interplay of experience and theory and the pressure of casual emergencies.

The administrative machinery of the new Poor Law in 1834 was the outcome of a national emergency and a political philosophy. The administration of the new scheme was given to three commissioners who were not members of Parliament; the policy of the new code was based on a simple faith that if the market for labour were uncorrupted by charity, private or public, the labourer would be found worthy of a hire ample to maintain a citizen and his family. Both the policy of the new Poor Law and the administrative machinery for its application were severely modified by experience. From the deterrent Poor Law was to develop a system of State control of public health, and the organization of the labour market. From the three commissioners of 1834 was to descend the Ministry of Health of 1919.

The administrative device of conducting a public department by an authority independent of Parliament broke down. " Parliament poked at it until it made it impossible . . . the House of Commons would not let the Commissioners alone. For a long time it was defended because the Whig Lords had made the Commission and felt bound, as a party, to protect it . . . but afterwards the Commissioners were left to their intrinsic weakness . . . the Commission had to be dissolved and a Parliamentary head was added." The three kings of Somerset House, as the Commissioners had been derisively called, were superseded by a Poor Law Board—though why a Board has never been explained. But with due solemnity a collegiate authority was established—the Minister even being endowed with a casting vote in case his fictitious colleagues should prove to be equally divided in opinion. In practice the civil servants took the place of the Poor Law Commissioners. The lucid and didactic reports of the latter gave place to the dull and colourless effusions which are a department's protective colouring against possible Parliamentary attack. They must be dull enough to be above suspicion.

In the meantime the early reports of the Commissioners had laid bare the relation between poverty and ill-health. If the Englishman's home was his castle he could not defend it against disease. Chadwick, in 1848, secured the appointment of a Board of Health for five years, with himself as one of the Commissioners. The Board, like the Poor Law Commission, was not responsible to Parliament, though one of its members was a Government representative. It consisted of the Head of the Office of Woods and Forests, an unpaid member, and two paid members. When cholera was about, Chadwick was tolerated, but without the cholera he was not to be endured. In 1854 the Board was reformed, Chadwick and Southwood Smith being deposed, and made to consist of a President and ex-officio members, i.e., the President and Vice-President of the Board of Trade and the Principal Secretary of State. Internal disagreements followed between the ex-officio members and the working members ; antagonism was aroused in the engineering profession, and resentment in the localities. In 1858 the Board was abolished. Its scientific and medical functions went to the public health branch of the Privy Council ; its local government powers to the local government section of the Home Office ; while the Admiralty and War Office were appropriately selected for the control of contagious diseases. For some decades the countryside was in the happy position that a complaint as to the condition of privies would go to the Home Office, while the fever they had caused might be studied by the Privy Council.

The result of this interplay of new theories, tactless administrators and cautious politicians was revealed by the Royal Sanitary Commission of 1871. It reported that a single and powerful Ministry was necessary " not to centralize authority but to set local life in motion." Economy and efficiency demanded that there should be a single authority for two subjects so necessarily cognate as public health and the relief of destitution. " Sanitary laws must bear a constant ratio to Poor Law, the one making provision for health, while Poor Laws are necessary for the relief of destitution of which sickness is both cause and effect ; so that Local Government . . . seems most capable of being arranged into two departments under one common head." A timid and unconvinced Cabinet merged three scattered departments : the Public Health branch of the Privy Council, the Local Authorities branch of the Home Office, and the Poor Law Board itself into a new Ministry, the Local Government Board of 1871.

How has the technique of co-operation between the Treasury and the other departments been secured? Its achievement was one of the triumphs of Victorian bureaucracy. The foundation was laid by the Exchequer and Audit Act of 1866. Before that the Treasury was both ignorant and despotic. In 1853 Northcote and Trevelyan reported that " at the Treasury neither the political nor the permanent officers . . . possess . . . personal knowledge of any portion of that vast extent of civil and military business which they have to control . . . the internal arrangements and regulations of the different departments are very imperfectly understood at the Treasury and the general supervision with which that office is charged on behalf of the public is either entirely omitted or performed in . . . a loose, superficial and perfunctory manner." The reason for its inefficiency was that, though since the revolution of 1688 Parliament had controlled expenditure by appropriating annual grants to specific purposes, it had not provided for any clear accounts of the way in which, in fact, they might be spent. The only information available as to the way the money had been expended was that given by the Chancellor of the Exchequer in his annual Budget speech. Even the finance accounts which were begun in 1802 were ineffective because they gave only the issues from the Exchequer to the departments with no details as to how the money had actually been spent. " It somehow escaped the financial genius of Pitt and Peel that control of the Estimates was ineffective unless the House of Commons also knew how its grants had been expended—Chancellors of the Exchequer, their advisers and Parliament itself were still under the illusion that Parliamentary control over expenditure could be effectively secured by safeguards in the issue of money from the Exchequer without following the expenditure further." Although in 1831 Sir J. Graham, at the Admiralty, began the reform by securing that an annual balance sheet should be laid before the House of Commons, based on an audited account and showing the actual expenditure under each head of service, down to 1854 the cost of collecting the public revenue was defrayed out of the gross revenue and was not specially voted by the House ; nor were the accounts of the Treasury itself subject to an outside audit. In 1857 a powerful committee recommended that the appropriation check applied to the Navy in 1832 should be extended to all departments and that " these audited accounts be annually submitted to the revision of a committee of the House of Commons nominated by the Speaker." In 1861 Gladstone moved and carried the appointment of a Public Accounts Committee, and in 1866 the Exchequer and Audit Act replaced the separate controller of the Exchequer and the Board of Audit by a single officer, the Controller and Auditor-General. He, though appointed by the Chancellor of the Exchequer, was to hold his office like a judge, independently of the executive. This secured the formal safeguards for the control of public expenditure. Money was voted only on a vote moved by a member of the Government ; the monies granted had to be specifically accounted for to an independent official ; and he made a report to a special committee of the House of Commons—the Public Accounts Committee.

The position of the Treasury was transformed. Before 1866 " Parliament not knowing anything about audited accounts, the Treasury was absolutely autocratic ; it could allow or disallow expenditure and there was nobody to check it. The audited accounts came before the Treasury, and if the auditors objected the Treasury might pass them over. At the same time the Treasury—although it was autocratic as far as the control by Parliament went—could not exercise that control beneficially because it did not know what the other departments were doing." After 1866 the reports of the Comptroller and Auditor-General told the Treasury what the departments were doing and subjected the Treasury itself to the same supervision as was applied to them. The Treasury was now informed, controlled and responsible. The co-operation of the Public Accounts Committee, the Comptroller and Auditor-General and the Treasury secured the development of an efficient code of financial procedure. The Public Accounts Committee never considered that the Controller and Auditor-General should limit his reports merely to the points he was specifically bound by the terms of his appointment to bring to the notice of Parliament. He brought to the notice of Parliament any facts found in the course of his audit which might indicate improper expenditure or waste. At the close of the South African War, he drew attention to the dual system of contracts by which large sales of surplus stock were made to contractors, concurrently with the purchase of similar stock from the same gentlemen at an enhanced cost.[35]

After 1832 it was impossible that the old system by which the public services were the outdoor-relief department of the aristocracy should long continue. When the scale of government was small the skilled assistance required by a Pitt or a Canning could be found among their private friends, while the routine work could be left to the attentions of party patronage. But the scale of government changed. The kindness of patrons to incompetence had been partly responsible for the loss of America. Was the second British Empire to be lost for the same cause? The administration of Ireland had taught Sir Robert Peel the necessity for integrity in the public service. The revolution of 1848 gave everyone a shock and created a disposition to put their house in order. The

Crimean War suggested that if Britons had never yet been slaves, their freedom was due more to geography and luck than to the efficiency of the War Office. In India it was becoming obvious that while empires might be won by adventure they could only be kept by competent administration. Organization and integrity could alone retain what genius and luck had won. At home the advance of industry and science meant that the traditional governing class had to fortify themselves with technical and professional advisers in matters strange and new, like factory legislation and sanitation. The State had to take over the elements of the new knowledge that was being won in the factory and the laboratory. The period following the industrial revolution was an age of tough and eccentric reforms. A sensitive statesman or head of a department may well have desired skilled assistance to meet the trenchant criticisms of a Wakefield or a Chadwick.

The growth of industry would have destroyed the State, created a new and more unequal feudalism, had there not been developed a new science of administration to be the servant of representative government. The development of the Civil Service was contemporaneous with the reorganization of the learned professions, medicine, engineering, and even the law. The development of organized professions in all branches of knowledge compelled the professionalizing of the ancient craft of ruling men. This raised new and subtle questions as to the nature of political freedom which we can even now only dimly see. But it was fortunate for our political life, that the first steps to provide professional knowledge and trained ability at the service of the State, should have taken place under favourable conditions.

The very slowness with which, in England, democratic government was substituted for aristocratic privilege made possible the success of our Civil Service. It was rescued from private patronage without becoming public spoils. Had there been a revolution in England in 1848 the organization of the public service might have been determined on the basis of abstract political principles popular at the time. The Civil Service might have been made a crazy monument to a fanatical misunderstanding of the doctrine of the equality of man. Some uncultured Benthamite might have imposed an organization based on the cruder ideas of Gradgrind. A sudden introduction of universal suffrage might have caused the public service to be enrolled as one of the battalions in the battle between the Ins and the Outs of party warfare. It happened otherwise. An aristocracy was on the defensive and compelled to improve its efficiency if it were to survive. Instead of a sweeping change which might have left the new organization open to the destructive influence of all those forces in a nascent popular government

70

which may cause despotism or corruption, the changes in the English political system and its administrative machinery were slow enough to secure the best of both worlds—the dying *noblesse oblige* and the disinterested scientific service struggling to be born. To say this is not to claim that the course of administrative change in England in the nineteenth century might not have been swifter and more thorough than it was, but merely to emphasize the blessings that were in fact secured and the possible dangers avoided.

It is against this background that we should set the report of a Treasury committee (the Northcote and Trevelyan report of 1853) which thoroughly examined the staffing and organization of the existing Government departments. It is one of the most important State papers ever published. " When," the authors said, " we came to make our general report we had arrived at an ample induction and our premises were so large and we had gone with such detail into the state of the different establishments that the conclusions arrived at in our report were the necessary logical inference of what had preceded." They made three fundamental proposals : (1) that clerks should be selected by open competitive examination ; (2) that in all public offices intellectual work should be separated from the merely routine and mechanical ; (3) that the examination for the admission to the public services should be conducted by an authority independent of the particular department that was to employ them. The brilliant Trevelyan and the wise Northcote saw the need for the State to adhere to three important principles of a democratic, industrial and scientific age : the career open to talents ; the division of labour ; and the acceptance of the judgment of professional organizations on matters coming within their special competence—the professors were to decide who could serve the State.

Their proposals were acutely and bitterly discussed. Civil Service reform, and particularly the competitive system, was exceedingly unpopular in the House because it would deprive members of the advantage of putting their friends and relations into public offices.[36] But in their defence of the interests of their class, politicians and administrators and others of contemporary eminence in educational theory and practice brought forward arguments which are still relevant to some problems in administration. The report had said that government " could not be carried on without men possessing sufficient independence, character, ability and experience to be able to advise, assist and to some extent influence those who are from time to time set over them." They had found that Government service, far from being the prize of the strong, was the refuge of the weak. The absence of any test of capacity plus the certainty of provision in the case of sickness had furnished a strong inducement to the parents of sickly youths to obtain appointments for them. Admission to the public service was eagerly sought after by the " unambitious, the indolent or the incapable." While no pains were taken in the first instance to secure a good man for the office nothing was done after a clerk's appointment to turn his abilities, whatever they might be, to the best account. Ability might be passed over to satisfy the whim of a patron. Thus a vicious circle had been set up. " Civil servants were habitually superseded because they were incompetent and were incompetent because they were superseded." Northcote and Trevelyan proposed to harness to the services of the State the strongest of all motives, the desire to excel. They were for the full rigour of the game of competitive examinations both as a safeguard against patronage and as an incentive to ambition. A mere qualifying examination, they said, would repudiate all ideas of excellence and make possible the return of patronage in the method of selecting from among those who were qualified. The examination they said " should be in all cases a competitive literary examination." They saw no other mode by which (in the case of inferior no less than superior offices) the double object could be attained of electing the fittest person, and of avoiding the evils of patronage. " The examination should be based on the subjects studied at the universities and not any technical knowledge that might afterwards be required by the successful candidate in his work. Only by throwing the examination entirely open could the proper class of candidate be attracted." Proficiency in " history, jurisprudence, political economy, modern languages, political and physical geography, besides the staple of classics and mathematics, should be made directly conducive to the success of young men desirous of entering into public service." " We believe that men who have been engaged up to two or one and twenty with studies which have no immediate connection with the business of any profession, of which the immediate effect is merely to open, to invigorate and to enrich the mind will generally be found in the business of every profession superior to men who have at eighteen or nineteen devoted themselves to the special duties of their calling." This judgment, though it might in the then educational organization of England make the public service the monopoly of a privileged class, was certainly true and was particularly valuable in defending a tradition of general culture against the narrow specialism that a desire for economy and the coarser tradition of the competitive industry might have imposed.

To these proposals the men most experienced in the public service offered criticisms which were some of them foolish and some of them shrewd. As they were Englishmen defending a privilege they wrote many high-sounding phrases about character.

Sir G. C. Lewis said that men of intellectual ability were not necessarily trustworthy. James Booth, Secretary to the Board of Trade, thought that " the lower you descend in the social scale the less probability was there that the candidate would possess the moral qualities which are more important than the intellectual in the important business of life." Nineteenth-century Christians may have believed that it was difficult for a rich man to enter the kingdom of heaven, but they found it difficult to believe that the poor could deserve to. Inspired as many of them were by the Puritan conception of a calling, they could not avoid confusing it with a sense of social distinction. Unto him that had social standing had been given the virtue that deserved it. Stephen thought that competition would not secure that " strange faculty of dominance which seems to stand apart from other powers of the mind and is not increased by polished cultivation." Others suggested that no " man of ability would submit himself to an arduous examination in order to earn a post so ill-paid, obscure, and subordinate " as that of a Government clerk. What young man crowned with the highest Oxford or Cambridge honours would enter a calling that would at the best make him a chief clerk the day that his friend became a bishop or a judge?

Hammond, of the Foreign Office, thought that all his clerks ought to come from the same social class. Addington went so far as to claim that in the Foreign Office, by every clerk entering as a copying clerk and working his way up, an office had been developed unsurpassed if not unequalled in its working power. Romilly feared the democratization of the Civil Service, while the legislature remained aristocratic. Graham, a timid constitutional purist, wrote to Gladstone, " It is clear that if this measure be adopted the reign of patronage is at an end... I am not certain that parliamentary government can be conducted on such principles of purity . . . It leaves the House of Commons, . . . that mighty engine, without its accustomed regulator at the very moment when you are about to increase its powers." He thought that " jobbing was a part, though an ugly part of the price a free people pay for constitutional liberty." Others protested that the competitive system was too high a code for a lax world ; that it was too uncharitable, leaving no shelter for the weak and helpless. Others feared that to abolish patronage in the State would mean that it would be attacked in the Church with results good Churchmen might boggle to consider. The heads of the departments were, of course, in favour of selecting their own recruits for their particular department whether a test were imposed or not. In short, most of the arguments showed the naiveté and the shrewdness found in club and counting-house with here and there a touch of common-room facetiousness.[37]

J. S. Mill thought that " open competition would be one of the great public improvements, the adoption of which would form an epoch in history. The knowledge that the Government would bestow its gifts according to merit and not according to favour would be a moral revolution in the lowest classes." This, the essential principle of the Northcote and Trevelyan report was not fully applied until 1870. In 1854, in the Queen's Speech, the Aberdeen Government expressed its intention to reform the Civil Service, but was replaced by the Government of Lord Palmerston which was not quite so convinced of the evils of patronage. However, in 1855, three Civil Service Commissioners were appointed to conduct the " examination of the young men proposed to be appointed to any of the junior situations in the civil establishments." New appointments to the junior ranks might be made from among those pronounced qualified by an authority independent of the authority appointing them. But the heads of departments were not compelled to use the new method, though the Superannuation Act of 1859 brought pressure to bear by providing that no one should be eligible for a pension unless they possessed the certificate of the Civil Service Commissioners. A mere qualifying test was found to be worse than useless. It stereotyped mediocrity and concealed bad appointments. The device of a limited competition was no better, for it enabled the Minister to retain in practice his power of nomination while relieved of any sense of responsibility. It was quite possible for an unreal competitive test to be held between the nominee it was intended to appoint and two gentlemen (sometimes known as the Treasury idiots), who could be relied upon to be beaten however weak their opponent might be. The Civil Service secured neither the advantages of competition nor those of patronage. A committee of 1860, fearful of offending vested interests, contented themselves with insisting that there should be a real, though limited, competition. For ten years the Civil Service was recruited from among nominated candidates who had passed a qualifying test of fitness. In 1870 there was a vital change. An Order in Council made a competitive test obligatory for certain departmental posts. The power of the head of the department (under the Order in Council of 1855) to dispense with the certificate of the Civil Service Commissioners was withdrawn. The Civil Service Commissioners alone might dispense with it when moved by the head of the department and the Treasury. The power of the Treasury was extended from the region of finance into the conditions of departmental administration, for they were to approve the rules about admission that the Civil Service Commissioners and the departments might frame. Henceforward the civil servant was to be under three masters :—The Civil Service Commissioners, who held the key to the entrance to the public service and were the St. Peter of the bureaucratic heaven ; the Treasury, who decided the general conditions of service to be enjoyed by those who passed the scrutiny of St. Peter ; and the heads of the departments, who remained responsible for the particular careers of their staffs.

The Order in Council allowed for important exceptions to the competitive principle. A certificate of the Civil Service Commissioners was not necessary in the case of certain offices held directly from the Crown, in the case of Section IV of the Superannuation Act of 1859, in the case of promotions from officers already within the departments, nor in the case of menial and temporary posts.

The conventions which govern the relation between the civil servants and the Minister were first clearly developed after 1832, when the new administrative technique and the financial probity, required by an industrial and trading community, were developed by a series of great Ministers from Peel to Asquith. It was during this period that the technique of Treasury control, which was the administrative counterpart of middle-class policy and the elimination of patronage, were carried through. But to develop a scientifically planned bureaucracy was impossible because of the opposition of aristocratic prejudice and middle-class parsimony. We were governed by brilliant amateurs with aristocratic prejudices and middle-class paymasters.

In spite of the abolition of patronage the leading civil servants were drawn from the same social class and often from the same families as the great political figures they served. " Ministers preferred to have as the permanent chiefs of their departments men of the same social standing as themselves, whom they had known at Eton or other great public schools or at Oxford or Cambridge and who, by kinship or marriage, belonged to their world." Temperament or the wealth and influence they could command led some to politics and others to the Civil Service, where power could be had without fame. However they might differ in their views, politicians and civil servants were rarely incomprehensible to one another. One political chief might see the world of politics as an exclusive society which it flattered his vanity to enter ; another as a stage on which to show his parts ; some administrators might regard their departments as a kind of club which they could run in the service of the State ; others as a field for their missionary efforts. But the relations of both were governed by a tradition as strong and uniform as that which ruled in the clubs to which they both belonged. The effect of these old traditions has lingered on though the conditions which gave them birth have passed away. The Civil Service still has something of the traditions of the common-room and the country house.

In the eighteenth century the permanent officials had been little more than the clerks of their political chiefs. Chatham allowed no one but himself to take any responsibility. It was considered a peculiarity in Mr. Pitt that he used to take a Treasury clerk into his confidence. In 1812 an Under-Secretary in the Foreign Office was little more than a private secretary. Palmerston told Queen Victoria that a Minister should conduct and direct the details of his department himself.[38] Lord Salisbury was to define bureaucracy as " allowing your civil servants to think instead of doing the work yourself." At the Foreign Office he kept the large political questions in his own hands, and with his Civil Service " the asking or receiving of advice, the taking of council together did not form recognizable elements in their relations."[39] This tradition of supreme subordination was peculiar to the Foreign Office, which worked under the eye of the Queen and under therefore several pressures of the normal Victorian atmosphere of deference. In the Colonial Office the tradition was rather different. There the political head was often transitory and undistinguished, while the permanent secretaries were of long service—Stephen eleven years, Merivale and Rogers twelve years each, Herbert twenty-one years—and of exceptional ability. " I never," wrote Sir J. Stephen " served but one man (Mr. Huskisson), who extorted the concession that his was a dominant understanding ; nor but one (Lord John Russell) who compelled us to feel that his was a dominant soul. The rest were throwings up of the tide of life ; complacent men in high station or at best dramatists, I should say actors." At the Treasury the prestige of station in the Minister might be mitigated by intelligence in the officials. We have the testimony of Lord Welby, who served no less than twelve Chancellors of the Exchequer, that " while Mr. Gladstone was always ready to deal with questions submitted to him . . Lord Beaconsfield never cared for Treasury business." " Sir Charles Wood had the reputation of taking kindly to Treasury papers " but " Sir G. Lewis preferred a classic, though ready to deal with what came before him."[40] In new departments like the Local Government Board and the Committee of the Privy Council on Education, as also in older departments like the Home Office and the Board of Trade which had to venture into new and technical problems of administrative control, the influence of the civil servants might be far greater, especially when these departments did not secure the best Cabinet talent. Occasionally there is evidence of friction and discontent. According to Greville, " nothing ever equalled the detestation " with which Palmerston was regarded at the Foreign Office, though they did " justice to his ability and to his indefatigable industry."[41] Despatches drafted by Hammond, the Permanent Secretary, were often redrafted by Palmerston.[42] At the Board of Trade, Gladstone considered that he had a very bad adviser in the secretary Macgregor.[43] In the 'seventies Disraeli made sweeping and unfair judgments on the Foreign Office and our diplomatic representatives abroad.[44]

Gradually the gulf between the statesman and the civil servant was to be widened. In old times, wrote Bagehot, " men like Lord Liverpool, Sir G. Rose and Mr. Huskisson were found eminent in the public offices, and in consequence of that eminence were brought into Parliament. Now permanent heads never think of changing places any more than a Hindoo thinks of becoming an Englishman." The abolition of patronage did much to promote the separation. There has been too a steady change in the scope of the problems with which politicians and civil servants have had to deal. Before 1870 the life of politics was to be found more in the struggle to change the common opinions of men than in attempts to mould the world in which they lived. A great leader could guide and educate a small electorate because he felt and knew in himself the emotions and the thoughts which were also theirs.

> . . . I only speak right on ;
> I tell you that which you yourselves do know.

His followers could see in him themselves writ large. It was not yet the function of the politician to persuade and the bureaucracy to perform. The ability by which the leader got his power was often the same ability needed to perform what he had promised. The politician had to apply to politics the accepted principles of the family and business life of an age of peace and plenty. The problems of politics were comfortably contained within the scope of common morality and the common sense of business.

In the administration of justice we find in a concentrated form all the virtues and defects of our administrative system—insight and tenacity within an accepted tradition, allied with a readiness to produce the most fantastic theories, in defence of vested interests challenged by experience or thought. Nor is it surprising that the shadow of their glorious past should have eclipsed the reforming vigour of our legal minds. In English history the artificial reason of the law has been a weapon to hack down the divinity which might have hedged a king. Small wonder that lawyers sometimes think their profession more an art to be exercised to the glory of God than a technique in the service of man. There is a less romantic cause. The nature of their work produces a profound belief in the value of certainty even if it is certainly wrong and a respect amounting to awe for the rights of property. Everything in their experience tends to stress the value of certainty. They see the application of general rules in the most concrete way— to the determination of disputes that go to the heart of individual lives and fortunes. Except for the preservation of order in which they are the servants of the State, the services of lawyers have been mainly required by the rich. And in England, where the judges are selected from among the most successful advocates, there is little to modify the general tone of a profession whose highest skill must be mainly in the service of the rich. There is nothing in the legal profession to correspond to the hospital service of the great physicians.

Judges are trained to the most rigorous examination of the facts that are brought before them. But to what end? To determine whether they are such as to bring the case within a given rule. They have no responsibility except for the determination of the facts, the application of the rule and the development of its implications. They do not have to consider consequences save as a particular decision may imply the illogical or confused interpretation of a rule. They are concerned only with the rule and not with those to whom the rule must apply. Their training forbids them to consider the hardship of individual cases, and if they accumulate a sense of the injustice of a given rule they have no responsibility for its reform. They see the social order only through the medium of individual cases of dispute, and there is little in their work to produce the administrators' sense of the need for continuous change.

But whatever the explanation, the facts are plain and startling. " Scarcely ever has any occupant of the bench led the way to reform. Seldom, if ever, has the bench collectively asked for or initiated reform."[45] When in 1730 English took the place of Latin in judicial proceedings, Lord Raymond considered the innovation dangerous. In 1810 the proposal to abolish the death penalty for stealing seemed to Lord Ellenborough a " measure pregnant with danger to the security of property." Drawing and quartering in 1814 was, the Attorney-General considered, a bulwark of the constitution not hastily to be removed.[46] In 1847 some of our most eminent judges were consulted on the problem of juvenile crime, and they gave it as their opinion that reform and imprisonment were utterly irreconcilable. The introduction of County Courts in 1846—without which the enforcement of his contracts by the small man was impossible—the legal profession strenuously opposed. The reform of the administration of justice in

1873 was nearly wrecked by the opposition of the Inns of Court. Neither Bentham, Brougham, Selborne nor Haldane could induce the acceptance of a Ministry of Justice.

A hundred years ago the judicial system was so centralized that " it is almost true that he who had aught against his neighbour had to seek his remedy in Westminster Hall."[47] In 1800 almost all the judicial work of the kingdom was done by fourteen men. " If the administration of the common law was centralized, the administration of the supplemental law called equity was still more centralized ; it was all centre ; the two Chancery judges never sat out of London."[48] Centralization was perhaps the least of the evils. On the substance of the law " the dust of antique time " lay so unswept that " mountainous error " was " too highly heaped for truth to o'er peer." The Common Law Courts were distinct from Chancery. Instead of a reasonable division of labour with the Court of Chancery providing the more flexible and discretionary services which the rules of Common Law did not permit, the two systems " applied different notions of right and wrong to the same matters." " The Common Law treated as untenable claims and defence which equity allowed and one side of Westminster Hall gave judgment which the other restrained the successful party from enforcing . . . the bewildered litigant was driven backward and forward from law to equity and from equity to law. The conflict between the two systems was one which, if it had not been popularly supposed to derive a sanction from the wisdom of our forefathers, might have been deemed by an impartial observer to be expressly devised for the purpose of producing delay, uncertainty and untold expense."[49] The three Common Law tribunals : Queen's Bench, Common Pleas and the Court of Exchequer had each a different history and different functions, but were alike in having a procedure, " antiquated, technical and obscure."[50] Of the Chancery side it was said by Dickens that it " had its decaying houses and its blighted lands in every shire, its worn-out lunatic in every workhouse, and its dead in every churchyard " ; and in 1839 by a legal expert that " no one could enter into a suit in chancery with any reasonable hope of being alive at the termination if he had a determined adversary." In early days the Lord Chancellor had sat alone as Judge of First Instance ; alone on appeal from the Master of the Rolls and from the Vice-Chancellor ; alone in the House of Lords as a Court of Appeal from himself or a writ of error from the Common Law Courts, except when assisted by a few peers. Even when in 1840 the judicial staff of the Court of Chancery was seven, the state of business was scandalous.[51]

To substitute for this chaos a single supreme court, each department of which should administer the same principles of equity and law and guided by a common and swift code of procedure, had been the dream of Bentham and the aim of Brougham. Not until 1873 was Lord Selborne able to bring forward and carry through Parliament the Judicature Act of 1873 which brought together in one Supreme Court divided into two branches, the one of original and the other of appellate jurisdiction, all the judicial powers of the previously existing Superior Courts of England.[52] Even then the bill was nearly shipwrecked on the question of appellate jurisdiction.[53] Selborne wished " to put an end to the expense and delay incident to the system of double appeals ; and for that purpose to concentrate in one Court of Final Appeal all the judicial power which was or could be made available for that purpose ; abolishing the intermediate jurisdictions of the Exchequer Chamber and the Court of Appeal in Chancery."[54] He considered that the appellate jurisdiction of the House of Lords ought not to stand in the way of the establishment of the best possible court of final appeal for England. But such a final court of appeal raised the question as to whether or not it should hear Scottish and Irish appeals. Uncertainty over this lasted until a new Government under Disraeli was in power, with the result that in 1876 the jurisdiction of the House of Lords, strengthened by the addition of salaried life peers, was restored. " The system of double appeal . . . was brought back without check or restraint."[55] There was now a Supreme Court which was not supreme ; and the Court of Appeal was a mere court of appeal.

During the eighteenth century and the earlier part of the nineteenth century " the pressing demand for cheap and local justice was staved off by the occasional and sporadic creation of little courts, *courts of conscience,* or *courts of request.* About a hundred of these were erected as now this town, now that, made its voice heard. In general a body of unpaid commissioners, of local tradesmen or the like, was empowered to adjudicate without a jury upon very small debts. Not until 1846 was the serious step taken of creating a new system of courts throughout the land, though already in 1830 Brougham, inspired by Bentham, had proposed the plan which in main was at last adopted."[56] During a seventeen years' struggle the Bar opposed the scheme. The limit of the competence of the new courts was fixed first at £20, but in 1850 it was raised to £50 and in 1903 to £100. Though every session of Parliament has witnessed an extension of their powers, in 1933 the Bar Council still felt obliged to " view with grave concern " any extension of County Court Jurisdiction.[57]

The needs of commerce imposed a reformation of the jurisdiction of the courts. For Criminal Justice and Police the problem was quite as bad. The social and political importance of the office of justice of the peace to the ruling classes prevented the development of a paid and trained magistracy. The English labourer was denied the justice that was given to the Indian ryot. When, in 1842, the Cabinet considered employing assistant barristers in aid of the unpaid magistrates at Quarter Sessions, Peel said that on the one hand it would conduce to a speedier and better administration of justice, civil and criminal, in several districts ; but on the other " it will strike a severe blow against the useful influence of the best part of the local and provincial aristocracy of the country." While Wellington said more bluntly that " it would destroy the influence of the landed gentry and of persons of education and good social manners and habits." Whatever their influence on social manners and habits in 1837 " over a considerable portion of England, property was less secure than in any great European country, excepting only Italy and Spain." Commercial travellers were loth to travel after dark—property was safe neither on the river nor on the canal, nor upon the turnpike road,[58] while rural crime went unprevented, undetected and unprosecuted. In 1839 there were upwards of 500 voluntary associations for promoting the apprehension and prosecution of felons—for performing in fact by individuals the first duty of a civilized government.[59] In 1829 the Metropolitan police had been established for the capital ; in 1839 and 1840 Parliament enabled police forces to be established in the country. But not until 1856 was their establishment made compulsory.

In 1832 the organization of local government carried a greater burden of the past than even that of the central government. In the following century it was the local authorities who first felt the impact of the forces released by the industrial revolutions. It is in local administration that the outlines of any Utopia have to be filled in. Only from the experience of local authorities can the evidence for or against a particular scheme of reorganization of the structure and policy of the central government be collected. Only when there is life at the extremities can there be reason at the head. This, of course, is true whether or not the local administration is representative or not. If there is a completely centralized government it must act through local officials who are given wide discretionary powers. But if the central government is to be representative—to depend for its efficiency on the willing co-operation of its subjects—some form of local representative government will be advisable. The existence of local representative and responsible councils will bring home to the people the nature of the process of government— the subtle interaction of law and convention, of logic and of experience, of reason and of character. They provide for experiments in policy and method and a training ground for political skill. By making possible local variations in policy and law they help to maintain a habit of obedience to the law which a centralized system might destroy. The maintenance or creation of a system of local government is a searching test of the political genius of a people and its leaders. It involves continuous compromise on, and a succession of decisions in, matters which are dull in detail but in bulk the very basis of the State. It is a search for a living unity when the development of technical services—in health, in education, and in transport—threaten a mechanical specialization. To say this is not to prejudge the question whether a system of territorial decentralization will be appropriate to the conditions which the transport developments of the twentieth century may impose. But it is to say that the vital problem of local government has been to secure a compromise between the tradition of different local areas and the revolutionary changes in areas and policy science demands. On the success with which that is done at every stage depends the real health of the body politic whatever physical unity of its people science may hereafter provide.

In England local government has had to be adapted to great changes : the redistribution of the population caused by the revolution in industry after 1750 ; the changes in methods of transport, particularly the development of the bicycle and the motor at the end of the nineteenth century, which made speed a necessity and a sport ; the development first of sanitary science and then of preventive medicine, which meant that a government which had performed its first duty of securing order had now the power and duty to secure health.

The method of adaptation was determined partly by the development of the franchise. The great changes in English local government have followed closely on the Reform Bills of 1832, 1867, 1884 and 1918. The winning of the franchise by the middle class in 1832 was followed by the Poor Law Act of 1834 and the Municipal Corporations Act of 1835 ; the winning of the franchise by the industrial worker, in 1867, was followed by the creation, in 1871, of an efficient central authority for the supervision of local government and by the organization of an ordered system of local sanitary administration ; the grant of the franchise in 1884 to the agricultural labourer was followed in 1888 by the democratization of county government ; and the coming of universal suffrage after 1914-18 produced the radical reconstruction of the Acts of 1929 and 1933. Our local government has been entirely remade by Parliament during the last hundred years. For the most part those Parliaments were fearful of popular power. It is to be noted also that nearly fifty years separate the three great reforms 1835, 1888 and 1929 one from the other ; that the principle on which our local councils are organized was laid down in the Municipal Corporations Act of 1835, and was extended to the counties in 1888 ; while the areas and particularly the relation between urban and rural authorities was determined in 1888 before the motor car had begun to replace the world of Dickens by the world of H. G. Wells. Government departments concerned with local authorities have been given wide powers to adjust the local machinery to a shifting population and changing needs.

CHAPTER IV

THE STATE AND SOCIETY, 1870-1914

The economic condition of England after 1870—The action of the State which it required—To civilize where Industry had barbarized—To secure and to supplement the working of the market—The case of Land and Ireland—Capital, the Foreign Office and the Bank of England—The organization of the labour market—The provision of health, factory and educational services—Philosophical and popular ideas—Bradley and Herbert Spencer—The Empire in trust and the Empire in partnership— The foreign scene—Statesmen not at ease.

BY 1870 the people of the United Kingdom seemed to be on the road to an abundant though dingy Utopia. The population had increased from about 21,000,000 in 1821 to more than 31,000,000 in 1870. This increase in population had been compatible with a fall in the price of food which had not been offset by a fall in wages. Men may not live by bread alone, but a larger loaf had secured the political support of the working class for Free Trade. In place of the despairing violence of Chartism it had concentrated on limited and specific reforms. The Reform Act of 1867, enfranchising the urban working class, was a tribute of the middle class to the economic and moral progress of the " responsible working man." Having made God in its own image the middle class hoped that He would help them to make all men in that image as well.

This prevailing optimism was not very well grounded. The position of England in 1870 was the result of special conditions which were soon to pass away. A variety of causes had contributed to the development of the industrial revolution in these islands. England's prosperity and political security were due to conditions as unique as those which produced the glory that was Greece, and time was to show that they were less stable than the grandeurs of Rome. Wool had given us cotton ; cotton gave us factories ; factories gave us foreign trade ; and foreign trade brought more cotton.[1] For the application of science to industry fate had given us suitable climatic conditions, a fortunate distribution of coal and iron in relation to a then incomparable means of com- munication—a network of rivers navigable to an all surrounding sea. England's previous economic development had provided her with a machinery of capital investment, a market in land, and a mobility of labour which, on the Continent, had been delayed by feudal traditions or destroyed by war. Her previous political history had given her a unity and a social order favourable to the development of a vigorous economic life. " In the first half of the nineteenth century the industries of England present a picture of increasing production, rapid increase in the number of single undertakings and in each separate area of production the keenest competition between the various manufacturers, only giving way occasionally and under pressure of certain exceptional conditions to monopolistic organization."[2] Her island position had enabled her to develop almost unhindered by war and revolution her special advantages for supplying the world with manufactured goods. In a generation from 1850 she had become the forge of the world, the world's carrier, the world's banker, the world's workshop, the world's clearing-house and the world's *entrepôt*.[3] Fortune had given to the British people the conditions necessary to the wealth of nations which Adam Smith had specified in 1776.

But with all these advantages there were circumstances in the position of this country before 1870, which might have given warning of difficulties to come. The world now well knows that improved communications may bring different cultures into such sudden contact that all of them may be destroyed ; it knows too well the barbarizing effect of pioneering conditions on a migrant population, and the bloodshed and corruption which may come when an economic order outgrows its political framework. Catastrophies must ensue when the tortoise of political wisdom and social tolerance fails to keep pace with the hare of economic development. Division of labour does not necessarily produce the intelligence its co-operation requires. The forces which had produced the American Civil War and were later to produce the World War—the struggle of different political, social and cultural traditions to maintain themselves in an economic environment they could not control—were present in England before 1870. Though the repeal of the Corn Laws had not destroyed the prosperity of agriculture, the struggle to secure that repeal had come near to disrupting our political system. Had the ownership of land not been concentrated in comparatively few families united by ties of blood with the rising manufacturing interests ; if the struggle over the Corn Laws had been a struggle, not between cousins but between separate geographical areas and different cultural traditions, our political structure might not have survived. Had our peasantry not already been destroyed and our proletarians not yet enfranchised English Liberalism might never have been born. The case of Ireland shows on a small scale the problem which has since shaken the world. England's industrial development produced a problem of mobility of labour from Ireland which under-mined the system of local government in many English cities, nearly ruined our relations with the United States, shattered the great Liberal party led by Gladstone from 1868-85, nearly destroyed the procedure of the Mother of Parliaments and was ended only by civil war in the twentieth century. The Irish Free State, which may yet prove the Achilles heel of the British Empire, was 'he outcome of a comparatively simple problem of the relation between an economic order and its political framework. In Ireland an Englishman has a clue both to the political problems of the United States and the foreign policies of Balkan States.

Within Great Britain there were no separate nationalities which preferred poverty and their own political and social order, to plenty and the political and social order of an alien culture. Nor should it be forgotten that in the 'eighties the whole foreign-born population of the United Kingdom did not equal its emigration for a single year. Had all the Welsh been Roman Catholics, or had all our Nonconformists lived in Scotland, the problem of minorities might have made democracy in Britain the hazard it has been in Europe.

The nationalism of Ireland, and the reduction almost to barbarism of the populations on the new industrial frontiers, should have given warning before 1870 of problems to come. The prophetic eye of Disraeli had seen a problem of two nations, and the essence of his Conservatism was not to secure the abolition of rich and poor, but to reconcile the hierarchical landed order and the anarchical industrial frontiers in a nation state. Had this country not already become the centre of an international economic order Disraeli might have anticipated our contemporary autarchies. As it was, he was reduced to a spurious imperialism. The problem of Ireland and the problem of industrialism were to break the Liberal Party, to produce a Conservatism unable to think clearly about economics and, in the fullness of time, a Labour Party whose inspiration was more the memory of past wrongs than an understanding of the nature of politics.

After 1870 the real difficulties of this country began. The overthrow of France by Germany in 1871 was a heavy setback to European Liberalism. The political unity, secured by the United States through civil war, and the political unity of Germany, secured by wars of aggression, prepared the way for the decline of English agriculture and the loss of her supremacy in iron and steel. The depression of 1874 revealed the special vulnerability of the English economic order. Specializing for a world market they had given hostages to a fortune they were powerless to control. The opening of the American West found English farmers unprepared to meet the competition of wheat mined from the virgin prairies. In 1870 the United Kingdom provided half the pig-iron of the world. By 1913 the U.S.A. provided three times, and Germany half as much again as we did. In 1890 the United States and in 1893 Germany passed this country in the production of steel. By 1913 the German production was twice and the American four times that of the United Kingdom. Britain's percentage of the world's international commerce dropped from nearly 22 per cent. in 1871-75 to little more than 15 per cent. in 1913. The loss of her supremacy in iron and steel and a decline in her percentage of world trade were inevitable as the industrial and commercial revolution spread round the world. The real grounds for anxiety were more subtle than a mere reduction in her share of world production and trade. They lay in the hesitancy with which she made adjustments which were forced upon her, and in the fact that future industrial conditions would favour great Continental land powers more than an island empire.

English agriculture had been the best in the world but the land had not been wisely used. The tenure of agricultural land designed to protect the social interests of the landed aristocracy had meant that in a country overflowing with capital, there had been little investment in the soil, because there was no security of tenure which would warrant men of capital investing their money in it.[4] There was a political factor in the prosperity of agriculture ; and when after 1886 the supremacy of landed wealth was lost, their leaders gone, the smaller men and the farm labourers had neither the political influence nor the commercial and financial experience to secure the organization which was best for themselves in a competitive world. In the new age of steel which followed the inventions of Bessemer in 1858, and Thomas in 1878, Britain enjoyed no natural advantages. England had been the pioneer in almost every phase of the industrial evolution based on iron and coal. But whenever a great change in technique or organization occurs, the older seat of an industry has difficulty in maintaining its position. England was to find herself severely handicapped in the later revolution based on steel, electricity and the research chemist. The production of wrought iron depended on the skill of experienced workers ; steel on the scale of the producing units and the skill of metallurgists.[5] With the discovery of aniline dyes in 1866 the chemist made his first effective entrance into the field of industry. The invention of the internal combustion engine in 1876 made possible the first motor car in 1887. In the 'eighties the hunting of the microbe began the opening of the tropics. In 1894 Niagara would be harnessed to the service of electricity. The English discoveries in science and technology, 1800-70, had been made by self-taught men who owed little to universities.[6] The new chemical and electrical trades required technicians who could only be produced by an efficient system of secondary education, possessed by Germany but not by us.[7] In the United States not only was there a more open career to talent, but a large home market offered every inducement to the development of large-scale industry. In this country old established firms had old plants, nepotism in their management and a disinclination to hustle for new inventions.[8]

The volume of British foreign trade continued to increase up to 1913. But there was real ground for anxiety in the fact that in that increase the basic industries of coal, textiles and metals played the major part.[9] In the half-century before the war of 1914-18 our output of coal was more than trebled. In the same period following the opening of the Suez Canal and the substitution of iron and steel for wood in the construction of ships, we secured the supremacy of our Merchant Navy. But that supremacy was dangerously linked with the increasing part played by coal in our exports. The export of coal was the basis of competitive power of our ships as carriers of the world's commerce. In this we had given two hostages to fortune : the demand for coal depended upon technological conditions which might swiftly change ; and the volume of trade depended on the political stability of the pre-war order.

What did these changes mean for the problem of government ? The economists, we have seen, tended to assume that there would be little difficulty in providing just that amount of government control and no more, which was necessary to secure the material advantages of specialization and exchange. If there were some unbalanced enthusiasts who were prepared to say that all goes best when nothing is regulated, saner minds demanded " as much individual freedom as is consistent with the welfare of an organized society and the performance of self-imposed obligations." But this and similar formulæ assumed that there was agreement as to the nature of welfare and the conditions under which obligations could rightly be deemed to be self-imposed. The problem of serving Mammon and whatever gods there be is more subtle than at first sight may appear. Economic science derived its prestige from its discovery that there was an order in society which was due, not to the decision and power of an authority, but to the co-operation through the market of individual wills. This economic order seemed to be the result of those natural laws which theology and reason had always assumed Nature to observe. The economists had shown how it was possible for there to be an ordered production and distribution of goods and services when individual choice was not politically dictated, and when the means of satisfaction for every individual were not unlimited. The laws of the economists were nothing more than the logical implications of certain assumptions as to the relation between means which were available and scarce, and the alternative uses to which they might be put. In so far as they are correctly formulated these laws are never broken. Whether a community is tottering on the verge of starvation or lolling in the lap of luxury economic law will be satisfied, as the law of gravity is satisfied, whether an economist speaks in comfort from a platform or dangles at peace from the lamp-post to which an ill-judged taste for abstract speculation may have brought him. But, of course, any system of production and distribution with which we have to deal only works because it satisfies other laws besides those which the economists have so subtly abstracted. The market of economic analysis assumes contract, and the idea of contract is only possible in a certain kind of society. If there is to be contract violence must be taught its place. And for violence to be taught its place the fundamental problem of politics—the right use of force—must also be solved.

And so we may say that the economists assumed an ideal State. They assumed that it was possible to know and to secure just that amount of Government control which was necessary to secure the desired advantages of specialization and exchange. They assumed that it was possible to secure, within a given state, that there should be no manipulation of governmental machinery in the interests of particular economic groups, and they assumed that the social and administrative conditions could be provided to supply that mobility of labour and of capital, which the application of science to industry requires. In a word they tended to assume that whatever the proportions in which the factors of production were combined, and whatever the speed at which those proportions might be changed, the political skill required would unfailingly arrive. The magnitude of these assumptions was hidden by the tacit alliance between economics and utilitarianism. The latter, by its confused assumptions that men both should and did pursue courses which would maximize their pleasures, provided just the political thought the early industrial revolution required.

In the period after 1870 the importance of the social order which the economist had assumed was to be startlingly revealed. The application of science to industry meant a rapid speeding up of the process of division of labour and of exchange. At first this was of enormous benefit to the particular area within which it occurred. But even in the area of a single State it meant the degradation of large classes of labour whose wits and sinews could not adapt themselves to the conditions of the market. For why should the rhythm of economic change harmonize with the rhythm of man's life ? How can a man know that the change in demand for his skill may not occur when he is too old to learn afresh? What guarantee could there be that the mobility of labour which industrial progress requires can be harmonized with the social framework of the family? These difficulties were hidden for a time because the structure of industry was decentralized and the process of change still slow enough for the common virtues of honesty and frugality to secure their reward. At every point there was expansion. The structure of industry might be described as a system in which the centre was everywhere and the circumference nowhere. Still it was obvious that technological advance resulted in the sacrifice of one district or one class of labour to the benefit of the whole. Within a given country this sacrifice could be mitigated by private charity or a State Poor Law. But what would be the position where technological advance required the sacrifice of one country to the economic benefit of the world?[10] It may be true that " there is no possibility of a world-wide arrangement of production or of a division of labour other than natural causes or chance dictates."[11] But it is too much to expect that every individual and every area will accept the fate which chance or nature dictate to them without themselves attempting to play the part of Fate. And how do they play the part of Fate? By the well-known political device of Protection. " In its essence Protection is the effort to maintain the *status quo* even at the sacrifice of the greater wealth which might be secured by readjustment."[12] When in the period of 1800-50 there seemed to be developing a division of the world into new countries producing raw materials and old countries manufacturing them, the United States of America took steps to see that she was not limited to the production of raw materials. As early as 1834 Germany took steps to secure that England should not be the only industrial country in Europe. When, after 1870, the new wheat-growing areas of the American middle west were being developed, the agricultural groups in Europe took steps to protect themselves against the flow of wheat. And when after the war of 1914-18 the dislocation of European trade and industry threatened a large emigration to the United States, that country took steps to prevent the social consequence of too free a market in labour. If the distribution of specialization is due to chance and natural causes why should the cultural and political systems submit to the dictates of chance? Within a single political system it may be possible to persuade the threatened group that it is for the general interest that they should give way. Within a single political system it is possible to secure that a threatened group which prefers not to give way shall not be in a position to organize a damaging resistance to the force of change. A common political loyalty will facilitate a healthy economic differentiation and provide the basis for the stresses and strains of continuous adjustment in the ways of work and life. The proper functioning of the market requires the supervision of the subtlest political skill. But if the economist can assume a State he cannot assume a world State. In the absence of a world state the development of Protection, when the rate of economic change is too severe for the cultural and political traditions concerned, is inevitable.

By 1870 it was becoming clear that the new forces of industry were not necessarily in harmony with the national traditions on which the political systems of Europe were based. In the United States the economic exploitation of a continent was providing the material basis for her industrial supremacy ; but in Europe it was not so easy to serve two masters—nationalism and plenty. To many nations Cobden's tidings of great joy that commerce was " a grand panacea which like a beneficent medical discovery will serve to inoculate with the healthy and saving taste for civilization all the nations of the world " was a message of political and social conflict. For it was not every country that could, like England, follow Cobden for its daily bread and Palmerston for its national pride. And even in England by the end of the century Chamberlain—a commercial Palmerston—was to feel " that the tendency of the times is to throw all power into the hands of the greater empires, and the minor kingdoms—those which are non-progressive—seemed to be destined to fall into a secondary and subordinate place."

These conflicts between national cultures were only in their beginnings. Within the United Kingdom fresh and urgent aspects of the problem of the relation between the economic and the political order were being revealed. Originally *laissez-faire* had been a claim by pioneers for freedom to shape a new society unhampered by a corrupt and meddling political machine. New powers could only be put at the service of mankind if the dead hand of a tradition and the curse of privilege were removed. It promised a policy of plenty in place of a *politique* of power. This new freedom in the economic world had been enormously successful. But as the standard of living rose and the scale of the new industrial order swiftly grew, the political problem took on a new urgency. A privileged aristocracy lost its responsibility ; power was less mitigated by tradition ; and the prosperous middle class were free to make a society in their own image. To Cobden this English " shopocracy " seemed to glory in being " the toadies of a clodpole aristocracy, only less enlightened than themselves." To Matthew

Arnold, of the three things necessary to civilization : a love of industry, of the things of the mind, and of beauty, it seemed that the new middle class only understood the first. Its freedom to get rich had produced neither right reason nor fine culture. If there was to be a rallying point for the intelligence, and for the best instincts of the community, it would have to be provided by the State. In the 'eighties William Morris was writing that " the present lower middle class are almost the worst in the community. They ape the bad habits of their betters and they despise those below them. Though they live in a kind of swinging comfort . . . they are ill housed, ill educated, crushed by grovelling superstition, lacking reasonable pleasures and entirely devoid of any sense of beauty." The combination of the vulgarity of a new rich with the traditional servilities of a deeply class-conscious society, had produced a snobbery and a vulgarity probably unparalleled in social history. If, on the Continent, an Englishman was a synonym for a gentleman, it was because the nobility had been the only Englishmen who travelled. Had foreigners visited England in any numbers the blackguardism of the lower classes in this country would have been notorious throughout Europe. In 1878 W. S. Jevons, one of the soberest writers and observers of the nineteenth century with no æsthetic axe to grind, said that while no Englishman was surprised when " a Frenchman surpassed us in politeness, and a German in profundity, and an American in ingenuity and affability," we ought to feel ashamed that the Scandinavians " far surpass us as regards the good breeding and the general culture of the mass of the people."[13] The American rowdy might be more dangerous with his bowie knife, but compared with the English black-guard he was a man of refinement.[14] The reason was that " the amusements of the masses . . . have been frowned upon and condemned and eventually suppressed by a dominant aristocracy . . . . It seems to be thought that the end of life is accomplished if there be bread and beef to eat, beer to drink, beds to sleep in, and chapels to attend on Sunday."[15] In the past the rich had excluded the mass of the people even from the natural enjoyments of the air and sun that they might enjoy their shooting and other forms of sport. " It is hardly too much to say that the right to dwell freely in a grimy street, to drink freely in the neighbouring public house, and to walk freely between the high-walled parks and the jealously-preserved estates of our landowners, is all that the just and equal laws of England secure to the mass of the people."[16] J. S. Mill's essay on *Liberty* in 1859 was an attempt to demonstrate to the many-headed multitude that the idiosyncrasies of the highbrow might mitigate the miseries of the low.

The vulgarity of the middle and the blackguardism of the lower class were only a symptom of an underlying economic problem. Bagehot, one of the wisest of the Victorians, had realized that economists need not be opposed to the " legislative promotion of those industrial habits which conduce to the attainment of national morality or national happiness at a sacrifice of national wealth ; to efforts at national education or compulsory sanitary reform ; to all national aid from England towards the starving peasantry of Ireland ; to every measure for the improvement of that peasantry which would not be the spontaneous choice of the profit-making capitalist." Where there was no effective demand—that is to say a demand which it would be profitable to business men to meet—for some of the vital conditions of a healthy social life, those conditions would have to be provided by the use of political power. Just as J. S. Mill realized that political democracy was unworkable unless its members had reached a stage of development in which they were prepared to be persuaded by discussion,[17] so a free market in all things material and mental required that, in things essential, those who bought should understand their real needs. Those who had been excluded by a landowning oligarchy from the conditions necessary to their physical and mental development, suffered all the barbarizing influences of pioneering industrialism, in which the conditions of the cities had the squalor and brutality of the camps of a barbarian and undisciplined soldiery, and could not be expected to make a civilized society by the exercise of their freedom to buy and to sell. Another and more threatening problem loomed. The greater the success of industry the greater might be the specialization it might demand. What was to prevent the development of an industrial order in which the workers would be merely living tools? The economists replied that the rising standard of living would more than offset the disadvantages of increased specialization. They tacitly assumed that if each were for himself, the magic of the market would place even the hindmost beyond the devil's reach. This optimism was unfounded. Living tools cannot be scrapped save by the hand of death ; and the lingering taboos of Christian cult would not allow even the painless extinction of those who might miscalculate the demand for their particular kind of skill. The more intricate the web of industry, the more difficult it became for any one individual or family to determine how best to prepare themselves to earn enough to live. Those who were fortunate enough to be employed in industries in which they could combine to control the market value of their labour, merely made more severe the pressure upon those who were not. The development of the great Trade Unions indirectly increased the degradation of the unskilled labourer and the horrors of the sweated trades. An even more radical problem has since been understood—there is nothing in the theory of wages to suggest that in a free market every worker can earn sufficient for his needs as a citizen.

Herbert Spencer lamented that the artisan was able to obtain " from a fund raised by taxes certain benefits beyond those which the sum secured by his labour enabled him to purchase." But is there any reason to suppose that the market value of any individual's services in a system of complex division of labour will be sufficient to secure for him the goods and services which his development as a citizen requires? The inequalities of income which the development of division of labour produces may even undermine the social unity on which a peaceful development depends. The inequalities which are the product of freedom may destroy freedom itself. Whether this should be dealt with by a system of minimum wage legislation, or by progressively raising the standard of those who are permitted to compete in the labour market, cannot here be discussed. It is sufficient to note that the problem is implicitly present wherever there is production for more than subsistence. Another question raises even more delicate political problems. Individuals may earn enough, if those earnings are rightly spent, to provide for themselves and their children the necessary conditions of freemen. But what they earn may not be rightly spent. It is here that we touch the heart of the problem of individualism. It is doubtful whether anyone would maintain that he has a duty never to interfere with another individual for that individual's own good. If anyone does seriously feel bound by that fearful duty it is extremely unlikely that the frailty of human sympathy will permit him to fulfil it. Such quixotic indifference will only be possible when, a glorious angel in his own unique universe, he can contemplate his neighbours each in theirs, moving to God or going to the devil as they shall freely choose.

The fact that we consider it our duty to interfere forcibly with children for their own good makes it difficult to be sure that it is our duty never forcibly to interfere with an adult for his own good. And our doubt is strengthened when we remember that the principle that we learn best by going wrong is not applied by an advanced community to a backward one. If this admission of the responsibility of the more developed, or the more experienced, individual or community for the less developed or experienced, is felt to be an invitation to the bludgeoning of despotically disposed cultural despots, it may be pointed out that the avoidance of such responsibility by those on whom it rests, will give great power to the unscrupulous.

However we may decide the difficult question of when we ought

94

to interfere with others for their own good, we must always be interfering with them for the good of others and our own. Education, health, insurance, safety regulations, must be imposed by some on others as the only way of avoiding their brutality, infection, or their clamorous demands for sympathy and help. The greater the division of labour in a community and the more complex its organizations, the more often will such regulations be required. In some cases it is impossible for anyone to enjoy the results of his own care unless others are restrained—health ; in others it is impossible to provide a service for some without its being available to all—beauty of the countryside. These are obvious enough. But there are a vast number of others where experience has shown that, either because most do not possess the means, or because the service is not easily controlled by the demands of consumers in a market, public provision is desirable.

There is really nothing to prevent a society based upon freedom of contract producing a hierarchy more deeply divided than any in the past. Only an unfounded prejudice in the equal value of men as tools could lead anyone to suppose that each can earn what a man and a citizen requires to live. In 1886 Booth reported that " 32 per cent. of the population were living in a state of chronic poverty . . . incompatible with physical health and industrial efficiency." Whether this was due to the fact that freedom of contract had not been properly secured—that there were forces of coercion on the side of the masters—or whether they were due to the market for labour being so well organized that it reflected only too truly the value of each man's work, a vital problem for the State was revealed. If the degradation were due to the existence of force and fraud the State must discover the legal and administrative machinery which freedom of contract requires. If it were due to the precision with which the markets sorted the productive sheep from the unproductive goats, the State had to decide how far payments according to the value of their work should be supplemented by payment according not only to the needs of individuals but according to the need of their fellow citizens that their sickness and indigence should not poison the whole social order.

After 1870 the State in England became more and more concerned with two main tasks : where there was reason to believe that the free play of individual choice and judgment would be of benefit to society, it had to secure that the law would provide that there should be neither force, fraud, nor the obstruction caused by obscure and dilatory legal forms, to hamper the creative urge of individual self-help ; where the free play of individual choice and judgment in the market did not produce those things which individual choice and judgment outside the market, and in its considered political judgment, thought both necessary and possible, the State tried to discover administrative methods for their production and control. For those things which the market could provide, a market had to be organized. For those things necessary to society, which the market did not provide, provision had to be made. Broadly speaking we may say that neither for the ownership and use of land, nor the accumulation and application of capital, nor for the sale of labour was the market properly organized. And experience suggested that it was unlikely that either education, health or safety or the provision of the statistics and fundamental research on which the life of industry depend, would be produced by those who live by persuading others to buy.

Before passing to a brief consideration of some of these problems of the State an obvious point must be mentioned. The first condition of an intelligent individualism was lacking when the existing law, whatever its content, was in form so complex as to be unintelligible even to the expert. In the middle of last century not only was the statute law of great bulk, but in the ordinary edition the contents formed one mass without any systematic arrangement. There was no thorough severance of effective from non-effective enactments, nor did there exist in a complete form any authoritative index or other guide by which they might be distinguished. The judicial dicta and decisions were dispersed through upwards of 1,300 volumes comprising nearly 10,000 cases, exclusive of 150 volumes of Irish reports. Well might Sir Henry Maine write, " Such a system in the end beats all but the experts ; and we, accordingly, have turned our laws over to experts, to attorneys and solicitors, to barristers above them and to judges in the last resort."[18] He added, " that the very small place filled by our own English law in our thoughts and conversation is a phenomenon absolutely confined to these islands."[19] In 1878 there began the revised edition of the statutes and Westbury began the authorized series of law reports.[20]

In 1829 the Real Property Commissioners had reported that " the law of England, except in a few comparatively unimportant particulars, appears to come almost as near perfection as can be expected in any human institution." That they were wrong is now generally admitted.[21] The Land Law of England was in fact the law appropriate to an aristo-cratic state.[22] The landowners constituted a powerful trade union able to enforce their rules of apprenticeship, rate of work and oppor-tunities for leisure and amusement, through their control of the machinery of Parliament. In their development of the land, economic advantage was subordinated to questions of political and social prestige. A scheme of settlements which had been devised by certain ingenious lawyers at the Restoration had passed into the category of things immemorial and become one of the sacred bulwarks of Church and State.[23] The defectiveness of the rules of Land Law had far-reaching effects. It prevented the proper utilization of the land by discouraging investment. It made the Parliamentary franchise incomprehensible to the layman. " It may have been supposed," wrote Maitland, " that one part at least of our law would be plain, the law relating to the Parliamentary franchise. But it never will be plain so long as it depends on a real property law essentially nonsensical."[24] Proposals to establish a registry of titles were useless so long as the actual rules of the Land Law were themselves defective. It is impossible to register what cannot be determined. The depression of the 'eighties in agriculture, and the change in its science, compelled the landowners to abandon privileges which as a powerful trade union they had held at the expense of the community. During the period of agricultural prosperity 1860-74 tenant-farmers had been discouraged from investment in improvements because of the fear of eviction. In 1875 they were protected by the Agricultural Holdings Act. In the 'eighties, there was a popular outcry against settlements and the Settled Land Act of 1882 was passed. In 1880 the Ground Game Act entitled farmers to kill hares and rabbits. In 1906 the Agricultural Holdings Act gave compensation for damage by game and freedom to determine the choice of crops and the disposal of produce. But not until after the War of 1914-18 during which the Lands Requisition Committee had had brought home to them " the expense and delays of land transfer in this country as compared with Continental countries "[25] was some of the dust of antique time on an English title to landed property hoovered away.

In 1870 there began in Ireland a grimmer struggle than in England over the relation between contract and civilization. The creation of a peasant proprietorship in Ireland was begun in that year. It was to be a magnificent lesson for English statesmen in the relation of the State to the economic order. In Ireland " all the circumstances, all the associations and all the accretions " which had grown around the naked idea of contract were different from England.[26] As about half the country was owned by 700 persons,[27] the landlord was in essence a monopolist. But he was a monopolist who differed in religion from his tenant ; who, dwelling out of the country, had little or no idea of social obligations ; and who before 1874 was the only part of Ireland represented in the British Parliament. The Act of 1870 tried to make by law a partnership which in England existed by custom.[28] It gave compensation for disturbances, for improvements, and it legalized the Ulster tenant right custom.

It failed because of the great variety of its exceptions, the lowness of the compensation and the tenants' insecurity of tenure.[29] When prices rose, as they did until 1878, the farmer preferred to pay the increased rent his landlord demanded rather than be evicted and take his compensation. After 1878 when prices fell and evictions grew the agrarian question was amalgamated with a national movement and developed into a national and class war. By 1881 Mr. Gladstone was convinced that a " further degree of State intervention with the holding of land was the only solution. When her institutions permitted it Ireland would doubtless benefit by a system of free contract, but the conditions then existing did not allow it."[30] The Act of 1881 carried further the experiment of 1870. The Ashbourne Act of 1885 made the first real attempt to settle the land question in Ireland by creating a peasant proprietorship. It enabled the entire purchase money of a holding to be advanced by the State.[31] By this time the Irish had their war chest in the United States and could buy arms, men, dynamite and assassins.[32] In 1891 Balfour introduced a new system under which the landlord or vendor was paid in a specially-created Guaranteed Stock. In 1903 Wyndham's Act, and in 1904 Birrell's, laid the foundation for the complete abolition of landlordism in Ireland.[33]

We have seen in Chapter I the difficulty which the principle of limited liability had to overcome. From 1872 the spread of the company system took about thirty years to complete.[34] In the nineteenth century each unit of British industry was on a comparatively small scale. " Its basis was in the main a family basis ; its capital was provided privately and it was built up and extended out of profits ; in so far as it required banking facilities, it found them from independent banks, often family banks, which in general had their headquarters in the provinces, and particularly in the Midlands and the North, where the new industries flourished."[35] In Germany, the great industrial developments after 1870 were due in a large measure to the assistance of the banks ; in France the individual investor, being very small, relied almost entirely on the investments suggested to him by the big banks ; and in the United States the banks devoted themselves to the development of American industry rather than to international finance ; in this country London's financial organization adapted itself to the needs of a world-wide commerce, but industry maintained its independence of financial control.[36] And here, by the end of the century in the sphere of foreign investment the demand for political aid was felt. It had been assumed that the industrial structure might be left to individual foresight. The structure of industry was left to the individual judgment and the savings of innumerable small capitalists. In the case of foreign investments, though the machinery was separate and specialized, there was no formal regulation of capital investments, except to prevent fraud and to prevent activities judged socially unwholesome.[37] The savings of the *rentier* and professional classes were invested through the London market in foreign enterprises and Government stocks.[38]

The power to act without complications of official formality was considered to be one of the secrets of our financial supremacy.[39] The State was reluctant to interfere. It wished neither to check investment operations nor to call on banking institutions to give assistance to some governmental purpose.[40] But in the small circle of the ruling minds, financial was united with political power in a community of similar ideas.[41] Towards the end of the nineteenth century our rulers had not only an estate in the country but also investments in the wide-wide world. The Government was pressed and yielded to the demand that it should aid British industry to secure openings and contracts abroad.[42] With the development of German competition, the Foreign Office became more active in the promotion of the interests of commerce. In 1897, Great Britain denounced the commercial treaties which prevented her from granting imperial preferences. In 1898, the Imperial Department of Agriculture, and in 1899, a School of Tropical Medicine was opened. In 1899, also, the first development loans were given to the Colonies. In 1900 the Colonial Stocks Act was passed. Fortunately for the peace of Europe the important objects of British policy usually lay outside Europe. But when they were touched, the British Government renounced its attitude of non-interference between itself and the financial forces of the country.[43] There was developed a powerful and subtle tradition of co-operation between them and a " skilful and determined combination of self-interest and national interest secured."[44]

In every advanced financial organization there is a market in which funds available only for very short periods are lent out. This market for short period loans—the call loan market—was provided by the ordinary commercial banks. The capital market dealt with the supply and demand for long period loans. The Stock Exchange dealt with the transfer of rights in already existing securities. Savings of a special character were dealt with by insurance companies, savings banks, and agricultural mortgage banks. Given a sufficiently long period and given an international gold standard, harmony between these diverse forces might be secured by the rate of interest. But by the middle of the nineteenth century it was clear that there " resided in the financial structure a tendency not only to harmony but also to disharmony." The necessity " was gradually realized for some agency capable of acting as a brake upon the system." This was the Bank of England acting as a central bank. That there is a distinction between the code of behaviour appropriate to a commercial bank, and that appropriate to a central bank, was recognized as early as 1797. It was a bone of contention between practical authorities for nearly three-quarters of a century afterwards, and was finally established by Walter Bagehot in 1873.[45] Whereas the object of a commercial bank is to make a profit, a central bank must when necessary incur losses for the safety of the financial system and the economic welfare of the country. It must hold the account of the Government, because the latter's financial operations are conducted on such a scale, that, unless special measures are taken, they may seriously derange the money market. It is responsible for the management of the monetary system of the country.

The Bank of England was almost unique as a central bank, in that it was a private institution practically independent of any form of legal control, save in regard to its power of issuing banknotes and granting loans to the State. It was practically free to do whatever it liked except that in order not to oppress His Majesty's subjects, it was debarred, by the Tonnage Act of 1694, for all time from using any of its funds in dealing in merchandise or wares of any description. Independent of political influence, yet functioning solely in the public interest, it showed the knowledge, judgment and authority of individuals placed in a position of unchallengeable independence, with great resources and every technical device at their disposition. Before 1914, as London was the most powerful financial centre in the world, the automatic operation of the gold standard, under the supervision of the Bank of England, was comparatively satisfactory.[46]

After 1870 the problem of the proper organization of the labour market was to grow and grow until it became the major problem of government. The dominant opinion before 1870 was that any tendency to destroy the freedom of individual action was " directly contrary to the undoubted truths of economical science " which must be " unflinchingly upheld at the peril of unmeasured evils."[47] It was recognized that true freedom of action could only exist, if individuals were free to combine to secure those things which apart they never could. " The workman has a right to guard his own health, convenience, comfort and safety, and this he cannot effectively do while he remains an isolated individual. The reason is evident : the employers form a small class, between whom communication and concert are much more easy than between their men, and who have usually a strong disinclination to alter, for the benefit of their men, any custom or regulation which seems to be for their own advantage. The single workman, dependent for his living upon his week's wages, is utterly incompetent to enforce any concession from his wealthy employer. Union is the natural remedy."[48] But if collective bargaining was desirable in order to secure conditions of safety, leisure and health, collective bargaining for the raising of wages was condemned as either futile or immoral. Futile, because it was extremely unlikely that, with their comparatively small numbers, they could have any permanent effect on the rate of wages, "The most that could be done was to moderate or delay the adjustment of wages to conditions of bad trade by the enforcement of standard rates."[49] Immoral because a union could only succeed in maintaining a high rate of wages by PROTECTION, that is by levying contributions from other classes of labourers and from the population in general.[50]

This appeal to the altruistic sentiments of Trade Unions was open to the fatal retort which laid bare the radical confusion at the heart of all individualism, that the effect on others was no concern of theirs. How could any person make any contract with an easy conscience if it was his duty to consider whether his gain was not another's loss. "If," wrote Edgeworth in a famous pamphlet, "it is attempted to enforce the argument against Trade Unionism by the consideration that it tends to diminish the total national produce, the obvious answer is that unionists, as ' economic men,' are not concerned with the *total produce*. Because the total produce is diminished, it does not follow that the labourer's share is diminished."[51] In this matter "the untutored mind of the workman had gone more straight to the point than economic intelligence *misled by a bad method*, reasoning without mathematics upon a mathematical subject."[52] Trade Unionism in so far as it spread a knowledge of the conditions of the market and tended to break down the pools of labour bargaining in isolated ignorance, would make competition nearer the perfection which economists assumed in their analysis of its benefits. But in so far as there were undoubtedly combinations of employers enjoying advantages of wealth and knowledge which gave them a superiority of bargaining power, and combinations of workers which gave them a temporary monopoly as compared with the unorganized workers, there was no reason to suppose that the actual contracts made were in the interests of the community as a whole. It was theoretically tenable that there was "an adjustment of contracts more beneficial than that which the mechanical play of competition tends to establish." In so far as competition was perfect it might be to the advantage of all. But in so far as competition was imperfect, because of monopolies on either side, there was no reason to accept its result. It was extremely unlikely that in a community, in which "the whole structure of our wealth and refined civilization " was " built upon a basis of ignorance and pauperism and vice," that mathematically-perfect competition would exist.

Before 1870 the Legislature and the Courts, in so far as they were not defending the privileges of the owners, were wrestling with the problem of reducing the element of coercion in the making of contracts. They were opposed to the use of violence by strikers against blacklegs but they could not ignore the opportunities for victimization and fraud which the masters enjoyed. If, as Jevons admitted, the collective bargaining of the Trade Unions was a more flexible and subtle instrument, than the use of paternal legislation, for securing health, safety and leisure, they might also prevent intimidation and fraud.

Whether Trade Unions were attacked as creating monopolies of particular kinds of labour skill which could be exploited at the expense of the rest of the community ; or defended as securing a closer approximation to a properly organized market for labour, it was clearly revealed by the Poor Law Commission of 1905-9, that the market for labour was so defective that it was one of the main causes of pauperism. " The system of odd jobs was the most certain, the most extensive, cause or condition predisposing to pauperism."[53] The significance of the unorganized nature of the labour market was revealed in the study of Unemployment, first published by Sir William Beveridge in 1908. He showed that " while the teaching of Adam Smith had secured the abolition of the visible and legal obstacles to the mobility of labour, such as laws of settlement and of apprenticeship, nothing had been done to remove the impalpable but no less real barriers of ignorance, poverty and custom."[54] While it had been assumed that the demand for labour was single and concentrated and the supply of labour infinitely mobile and adaptable, investigation showed that while the markets for other commodities were increasingly organized that for labour was still left to ill-informed individual action.[55] The prevailing method of obtaining employment was still that of personal application at the works. The way to sell labour was to hawk it from door to door.[56] The consequence of this dispersal of demand in a variety of local places, and the lack of knowledge on the part of the individuals composing the supply, was that making a livelihood was a gamble. In all trades, in proportion as the market was unorganized and labour immobile, there was a tendency for fresh men to enter under the influence of local developments at one place, though men of the same trade were standing idle elsewhere.[57] This unorganized condition of the labour market resulted in (1) each employer or small district contriving to maintain a separate reserve of labour ;[58] (2) the recruitment of trades not in accordance with their real growth, but by local accidents ;[59] (3) the longer men were in one occupation the less they would know how to find work outside ;[60] and (4) a swelling of the casual labour market by every form of human weakness and misfortune and from every point of industrial unrest.[61] The increasing pace of industrial change required that the market for labour should be so organized that changes in demand for different forms of labour, due either to changes in demand for goods and services or in the methods by which they were produced, should be made known to those concerned. The spread of information was a matter which cried out for organized rather than for individual action.[62] Only by such an organization of the labour market could boys and girls be guided in their choice of a career or educational authorities plan the technical training which they would require.[63] The beginnings of such an organized market for labour was provided in 1909 by the Labour Exchange Act. In 1911 a scheme for compulsory insurance against unemployment was begun. It was seen that a flexible industrial structure involved an incidence of unemployment on individuals for which they could not be fairly held responsible. Unemployment which was due to the mobility of labour industrial efficiency required, could be fairly charged to the working cost of industry itself.

An essential condition for the development of a market in commodities is the provision of statistics. The census had been established in 1801 ; a census of production was commenced in 1906. In 1886 a voluntary system under the Board of Trade was begun for the collection of annual returns of acreage, cropping and livestock, but compulsion was resisted by the agricultural community because it might be made the basis for increased taxation. Not until 1917, when the Corn Production Act passed in the emergency of War offered a subsidy for certain crops, was it possible to secure the inclusion of agriculture in the census of production. In 1882 the word " Unemployed " first appears as a noun and in 1886 there is the beginning of a systematic collection of labour statistics. In the same year the Board of Trade began to supply traders with an account of the movements of overseas trade and tariff changes, extracts from consular reports and information about openings for British trade and industry abroad.

The development of our public health services, bewildering in detail, is simple in principle. Attempts to reduce the cost of pauperism in the 'thirties led to an investigation into the prevalence of epidemic disease and its relation to poverty. In 1843 a Royal Commission had recommended legislative and administrative action to deal with the serious national evil of bad sanitation and ill-health. In 1869 the Royal Sanitary Commission summarized the minimum sanitary conditions necessary for civilized social life. The driving force in this early period was the dread of the spread of infection.[64] Later a motive of economy was added to the fear of infection. Sickness was found to be a heavy hidden charge on industry. The ignorance and ill-health of the England of the pioneering industrial revolution could not be afforded by an England in competition with the vigour of the United States and Germany after 1870. The development of medical science after 1850 brought a vision of a preventative medicine concerned not merely with the unseen drains beneath the house but with an " understanding of those unseen processes of attack and defence which find their sphere in the cells and fluids of the body, and their influence upon the infecting or disturbing agent."[65] From the vision and technique of Pasteur's work on the causes of fermentation in 1858 there followed between 1871 and 1894 the discovery of the bacilli of leprosy, typhoid, tuberculosis, cholera, diphtheria, tetanus and plague. From the discovery of the unseen bacilli research passed to the discovery of its agent, the toxin and the antitoxin by which it could be met.[66] With the hunting of the microbe the doctor took his place beside the engineer in questions of health adminis-tration. Whereas in 1869 water supply, sewerage, streets and highways, housing, the removal of refuse, consumption of smoke, public lighting, inspection of food, provision for the burial of the dead, registration of death and sickness were recognized as necessities for a civilized life, a generation later the study of animal and vegetable parasites, infection by bacteria, disinfection and causes of specific diseases were equally necessary. In the twentieth century infantile mortality, school hygiene, tropical medicine, tropical disease, industrial hygiene, and venereal disease were vital parts of the work of public health authorities. Pre-ventive medicine entered a biological setting which comprehends the nature of the organisms, the nature of their environment and their inter-relation[67] In 1908 the systematic examination of school children was begun. In 1911 the National Insurance Act provided a system of insurance against ill-health for all employed persons between certain ages and with certain financial limitations. Ten million persons in England became eligible for the care of over 10,000 doctors. These panel patients could seek medical advice as soon as they felt the need ; and a doctor could multiply his attentions without fear that his motive would be misunderstood. Disease could be studied from the beginning and treatment continued until it was effective.[68] This change was largely the result of the Poor Law Commission of 1905-9, which had laid bare the contradictions of the existing system. " While poor law principles might approve a generous establishment of sanitary provision for the prevention of disease and destitution, on the other hand, medical relief for the individual, as a form of relief, had to be grudging or even deterrent in order to avoid pauperization, and it thus deprived itself of effectiveness . . . . So long as it dealt only with sickness as an outcome of economic destitution, it was obviously debarred from affording medical treatment as a *preventative* measure against potential destitution." The National Insurance Act of 1911 brought the great mass of the less obtrusive forms of sickness into prominence, and showed them to be a field of public health activity.

As early as 1833 the supervision of some of the conditions of industrial employment had been made part of the business of government. The Factory Act of that year began an important development by providing that there should be four paid inspectors responsible for the policy it imposed. Until the registration of births was made compulsory in 1837, these inspectors did not know the age of the children whose conditions of work they were supposed to control. At first they had power to make " such rules, regulations and orders as may be necessary for the due execution of the Act " and power to try offenders, impose fines and in default to commit to prison. Such a combination of legislative executive and judicial powers was not then to be endured. In 1844 the rule-making powers were transferred to a Government department. By 1878 the whole manufacturing field had been brought under control. The staff was organized into districts with district inspectors and grouped into divisions each under a superintending inspector and the whole staff placed under a chief inspector at the Home Office. After 1890 there was a rapid improvement. In 1891 it was made compulsory to give particulars of earnings to all piece workers in textile factories ; in 1895 the Home Office secured power to apply special rules to dangerous trades. Four industrial diseases were made notifiable by employers or by doctors who learnt of their existence. A reasonable temperature was for the first time required in the factory. In 1901 it was decided that ventilation must be satisfactory. When Asquith was at the Home Office special medical engineering and electrical branches were added to the inspectorate and women inspectors were appointed for the first time.[69]

The development of our public health services most clearly shows the intricacy of the relations between the individual and the community. In so far as Christian tradition imposes upon the State the duty to strive officiously to keep alive any member of the community who might otherwise die, the State finds itself involved in a responsibility for an understanding and an application of the forces which determine life and death. In 1801 the first census, and in 1836 the registration of births and deaths, put the State upon a course which may only end with the supervision over the exits and entrances of life and death that

Plato proposed for his guardians. The privilege of procreation may yet have to be controlled—for if it may be made a crime to make two blades of grass grow where one had grown before it is difficult to see why it should not be made a crime to make two mouths be where one had been before. Nor can the State rest content with its control of the size of the population. It may be immediately concerned with the age distribution of whatever population it decides upon. As the expectation of life increases and the proportion of the population over working age increases, the ceremony of making way[70] may become a part of our national pageantry. The anthropologists have shown us that primitive man was so often right where the godly thought him wrong, that his prescriptions for senility may come to enjoy the same prestige as his prescriptions for puberty. In any case the possible fusion of Eastern indifference to death with the Western technique of experiment and investigation may produce startling results. The partnership of the living with the dead and those yet to be born may grow closer than even Burke could wish.

Down to 1870 schools in England were provided by private persons, endowments or joint stock companies. The assistance of the State was limited to the meagre grants which Parliament gave to be administered by religious bodies. By 1870 it was clear that private enterprise had failed to provide the elements of education for even half the children of the country. A census report of 1851 put the number of children in England between three and fifteen years at 5,000,000, of whom only 2,046,848 were at school, 49 per cent. staying till eleven and 28 per cent. till thirteen. In 1869 two-fifths only of the children of the working classes between the age of six and ten were on the register of Government aided schools and only one-third of those aged ten to twelve. In the private schools, with a few brilliant exceptions, the quality of the teaching was almost worthless. In London a Royal Commission had found that in the uninspected schools among the teachers " none are too old, too poor, too ignorant, too feeble, too sickly, too unqualified in one or every way, to regard themselves, and to be regarded by others, as unfit for school-keeping."[71] No fundamental improvement was possible before 1870 because, as Cobden wrote in 1850, " the Liberal party, the soul of which is Dissent, are torn to pieces by the question, and it is not easy to heal a religious feud. The Tories, whatever they may say to the contrary, are opposed to the enlightenment of the people. They are naturally so from an instinct of self-preservation."[72] After the Reform Act of 1867, which enfranchised the sceptical and thinking artisans, the Government in 1870 said that in areas where the religious denominations had specifically failed, a local school board was to be

106

elected. These school boards might compel attendance if they wished and pay the fees of necessitous children. The aim of the Education Act of 1870, " was to complete the present voluntary system, to fill up the gaps, sparing the public money where it can be done without, procuring as much as we can the assistance of the parents and welcoming as much as we rightly can the co-operation and aid of those benevolent men who desire to assist their neighbours."[73] In 1873 the children of parents receiving poor relief were obliged to go to school. In 1876 a motive for absence was removed by forbidding the employment of children under ten. In 1880 attendance was made universally compulsory up to ten. In 1891 school fees were abolished in most schools. But not until 1918 was universal full-time attendance up to fourteen and the abolition of all fees secured.[74] It had been recognized, as Lowe put it, that we must educate our masters ; it was soon obvious that we must train our workers and educate our industrial leaders. As Forster said, when introducing the Bill of 1870, despite their powerful sinews and determined energy our uneducated labourers were in danger of being overmatched by the well-taught workers of other countries.[75] In the 'nineties it was clear that " Englishmen must take business as seriously as their grandfathers had done, and as their American and German rivals were doing : that their training for business must be methodical like that of their new rivals and not merely practical on lines that had sufficed for the simpler world of two generations ago."[76] To meet this need for technicians, chairs in the older universities were provided for the natural sciences, provincial universities were developed, and the new County and County Borough Councils were empowered to develop technical education. In 1899 the Board of Education was created, and in 1902 the skill and cunning of Morant and Balfour secured the abolition of the school boards, a compromise on the question of religious teaching in schools, and the responsibility of local authorities under the supervision of the State for the development of both elementary and secondary education.

As the need to co-ordinate the complex specializations of industry compelled the abandonment of *laissez-faire*, the political problem was made more difficult by the varieties of intellectual experience which science brought to the different social classes. As the contradictions latent in the seeming simplicity of the utilitarian creed were revealed, academic minds were encouraged to examine with some Socratic skill the nature of society. In his *Ethical Studies* Bradley gave to Utilitarianism a mortal wound from which it has never recovered. He once more united England with the Continental thought from which it had so long been sundered. He showed that there is a reason in morality which

107

is something more than calculus of pleasures. What Bradley taught with one of the finest English metaphysical minds, in some of the most lucid of English prose, T. H. Green persuasively lectured, though with theological presuppositions which made his exposition needlessly obscure. The best philosophical minds were driven to consider once again that the social order was a moral order, and that the problem of politics was not a simple antagonism between a party of persuasion and a party of coercion, but the discovery of those institutions which should lessen our fears and make possible our loves.

If philosophers had their intimations of developments to come, the general public was hopelessly bewildered by the impact of the new science of biology on their dying creeds and common-sense morality. In 1859 Darwin's *Origin of Species* came to convince the world of two propositions : that the origin of man himself was of the same nature as that of all other living things ; that the varieties of living things could be explained without the assumption of a miraculous and incomprehensible design. To many his work was the occasion for confusing every political and moral issue of which they had heard. They must have known even before 1859 that babies were neither moral nor rational ; yet Darwin's evidence that morals and reason had a natural history nearly sent them to the dogs. A return to the jungle was thought by many to be the only way to keep their present freedom from it. For a time a barbarous conception of self-help was reinforced by the belief that science showed mutual aid to be the enemy of progress. Darwin himself in the *Descent of Man* repudiated these puerile vulgarities. He wrote : " Important as the struggle for existence has been and even still is, yet as far as the higher parts of man's nature is concerned there are other agents more important. For the moral qualities are advanced either directly or indirectly much more through the effect of habit, the reasoning powers, instruction, religion, etc., than through natural selection : though to the latter agency we owe the social instincts which afford the basis for the development of the moral sense." The conception of evolution, carefully studied, imposed in fact a duty on each individual to consider how he himself in his intimate life might serve his kind, and a duty in fellowship with others to control the environment they shared.

The real significance of Darwin's vision was largely lost because the English middle class paid for its contempt for things of the mind by its acceptance of Herbert Spencer's confused ideas about evolution and the nature of society. He tried to reconcile a conception of evolution with a conception of rights. The former owed more to engineering than to biology ; the latter derived from Thomas Hodgkin's conception of society as a natural phenomena to which the universal spirit had assigned natural laws. He seems to have believed with the Utilitarians that pleasure is the sole good, and that to consider the direction of evolution is by far the best criterion of the way in which we shall get most of it. For a generation he prevented clear thinking by his followers about the interdependence of living things and their environment, or about the nature of duty. This was particularly unfortunate at the time. The new contacts and the conflicts of culture, which the swift development of communications was producing, required the most careful philosophical criticism and control. Seeley's *Expansion of England*, which showed the development of the Empire in a fit of absence of mind, gave to the English doctrine of muddling through an almost cosmic significance. If an empire could be built up in this mindless way could not a society be created in the same way? Here were symptoms of that attack on reason which on the Continent was later to have such devastating effects. But it was in England that the bewilderment caused by the impact of science on ancient customs was first severely felt. In the nineties there were many who, like Lord Salisbury, " had never known what it was to doubt the truth of Christian doctrine " but " had all his life found a difficulty in accepting the moral teaching of the gospel." This must have produced in others as in him " a very profound sense of the obscurity of things."[77]

The importance of religion waned, as more and more of the sceptical and thinking artisans became a political power, but Protestant bigotry was replaced by a nationalism so virulent and pervasive that it could destroy nearly every gift which science offered to man. In England it had been possible to believe that there was no essential conflict between the development of Free Trade, the growth of Liberalism and the sense of national unity. England was to save Europe by her example of freedom broadening slowly down from precedent to precedent. Our politics were the dispute of a family over individual morals, and individual shares in one increasing revenue. The Irish troubles could be put down to the Papist aberrations of the bad boy of the family. But in the third quarter of the century the force of nationalism was to show itself in disturbing ways. Instead of a cultural and spiritual tradition, nationality became a self-conscious pose. A spiritual heritage became a creed to be taught; to some a business to be developed. Beginning with Seeley's *Expansion of England* there was steadily developed a new and vulgar imperialism which hoped to see the frontiers of suburbia advance to the equator. To Chamberlain our tropical possessions were England's undeveloped estates, which could never be developed without imperial assistance. It was to seem to Kipling that

" God has arranged that a clean run youth of British middle class shall, in the matter of backbone, brains and bowels, surpass all other youths."

The worst ravages of this racial megalomania were prevented by the traditions of the Colonial Office itself, the integrity of all those who were capable of sustained economic analysis, and the national tradition which was firmly opposed to military adventures.[78] Before 1871 three Permanent Secretaries of State for the Colonies had expressed separatist views—Stephen, Merivale, Blatchford. If they were retained it was because " the authority of the British Crown " was " the most powerful instrument under Providence of maintaining peace and order in extensive regions of the earth and . . . in diffusing amongst many millions of the human race the blessings of Christianity and civilization."[79] When in 1872 Disraeli was saying in his grandiloquent way that " the colonies have decided that the Empire shall not be destroyed ; and in my opinion no Minister in this country will do his duty who neglects any opportunity of reconstructing as much as possible of our Colonial Empire,"[80] the structure of that Empire had so developed that we were saved from the dangers of pursuing an imperial will-o'-the-wisp. It had already split into the Empire in partnership and the Empire in trust. Between 1837 and 1867 over three-quarters of a million had left Great Britain and Ireland for British North America and nearly another million for Australia and New Zealand. In Canada in the critical period between 1839 and 1854 a silent revolution had taken place. It was carried out by mere instructions from the Crown, conveyed by dispatches to the Governor. Whereas in 1839 Lord John Russell, as Colonial Secretary, could hold that responsible government—the acceptance by the Governor of such policy as a colonial cabinet responsible to a colonial legislature might produce—was " entirely incompatible with the relations between the mother country and the colony," in 1846 the Colonial Secretary, Lord Grey, was writing that " it cannot be too distinctly acknowledged that it is neither possible nor desirable to carry on the government of any of the British possessions in America in opposition to the opinion of the inhabitants."[81] The powers of the Crown were never formally abolished. But by the growth of con-stitutional conventions there was a progressive expansion of the sphere of colonial self-government from limited autonomy to the complete self-determination of the present Dominion status.[82] Responsible government once established in British North America was extended to Australia and New Zealand. In 1852 the colonies were allowed to devise their own constitutions. In 1859 the Government of Canada asserted its right to " adjust the taxation of the people in the way they deem best, even if it should unfortunately happen to meet with the disapproval of the Imperial Ministry." Dominion tariffs were to grow unpruned by any imperial or Free Trade hand. In 1867 the British North America Act was the legal embodiment of a federal constitution devised by the self-governing colonies of British North America for the conduct of their national affairs. From that time on the rapid evolution of the Overseas Dominions involved many complicated adjustments of old political machinery to changing conditions. The tendency to equality of status was both right and inevitable. Geographical and other conditions made this impossible by the way of federation. The only alternative was by the way of autonomy ; and along that road it was steadily sought.

The more or less casual meetings of the self-governing colonies at the Jubilees of 1887 and 1897 and the Coronation in 1902 developed into an Imperial Conference with rules of procedure and a regular constitution. In 1907 Imperial Federation was specifically rejected and a formal constitution was drawn up. " It will be to the advantage of the Empire if a conference to be called the Imperial Conference is held every four years, at which questions of common interest may be discussed and considered as between his Majesty's Government and his Governments of the self-governing dominions beyond the seas." By 1926 every self-governing member of the Empire was master of its destiny. In fact if not always in form it was subject to no compulsion whatever.[83]

Entirely different from the Empire in partnership was the development of the Empire in trust. The opening of the Suez Canal in 1869, the final triumph in 1875 of the steamship over sail, the rapid development of railways with the new forms of steel, the discovery of the microbe, made the partition of Africa by the European Powers as inevitable as the early stages of the industrial revolution had made the occupation of the Mississippi Valley. When science had removed the barriers of disease to the course of trade, either the existing political organization had to accept responsibility for the control of the racial and cultural conflicts which inevitably ensued or they would see the establishment of a black feudalism ravaged by greed, superstition and lust. With what skill the delicate task of the partition of Africa was carried out by a Europe, which possessed no central authority, the diplomatic records now show. A divided continent had to partition a new world on pain of seeing the re-establishment of slavery, and the extinction of the small tapers of culture it had painfully kept alight on the edge of a dark abyss.

In Canada the presence within a British colony of a politically conscious alien community, French and Catholic, and the existence on its borders of the powerful influence of the Republican institutions of the United States had hastened the development of responsible government. So far as the white colonies were concerned, their eventual independence was considered desirable and inevitable. In 1836, Cobden had regarded the colonies as but an accessory to those unjust privileges of aristocracy, the army, navy, the church and the Corn Laws. In 1841 Sir G. C. Lewis in a classic discussion had argued that neither for tribute or military assistance, for trade facilities or as outlets for immigration, or as penal settlements, were the colonies of any possible value as possessions. In 1860 Cairnes wrote that " in commercial policy, in territorial policy, in military defence, the colonies, in the teeth of example, advice and remonstrance, have pursued their own way. We have abandoned all the objects for the sake of which our colonial empire was founded. We are unable to impress our will upon our colonies in any particular, however in itself reasonable or just or apparently necessary for their safety or ours. We retain the privilege of spending yearly £4.5 millions on their protection and receive in requital prohibitive tariffs and ironical allegiance." An English colony was not worth the sacrifice of a single American contract. In 1861, when a powerful committee inquired into the existing system of colonial defence, the outlook was so dominated by the idea of colonial self-reliance that it was sometimes difficult to differentiate those who favoured imperial co-operation from those who looked forward to imperial disintegration.[84] Godley, the Assistant Under-Secretary for War, considered that the presence of the British flag all over the world added very much to our weakness.[85] Lowe, the Chancellor of the Exchequer, considered that as the thirteen colonies had once revolted from *us*, so we because we were taxed for their benefit might separate from *them*.

Outside Canada, Australia and New Zealand we had in fact incurred commitments which it would have been morally shameful and psychologically impossible to abandon. As Sir J. Stephen had once said we had become responsible for many " detached islands with heterogeneous populations—wretched burdens to this country which in an evil hour we assumed, but which we have no right to lay down."[86]

The experience and responsibility of the Colonial Office had grown in many " repulsive controversies " to which no member of the Cabinet but the head of the Colonial Office could ever be persuaded to devote any time.[87] The abolition of the slave trade had made it responsible for the re-creation of a society in the West Indies. For the first five years after its annexation New Zealand had been the scene of an important experiment in the art of native government. In 1830 the term

" Crown Colony " was for the first time applied to the tropical possessions under the direct control of the home Government. The retention of the Cape of Good Hope had embarked us in a continent where no frontiers could be drawn, and in contact with the Boers, whose native policy would make either withdrawal or peaceful settlement impossible.[88] In West Africa small forts retained to suppress the slave trade provided the starting-point for a commercial and political expansion once the economic value of the tropics was realized. In India the mutiny of 1857 had led to the inauguration of a new era of public works undertaken by the central or provincial governments, which was profoundly to modify the *laissez-faire* tradition. As soon as inland penetration became possible the policing of coastal districts by a navy was no longer sufficient. If the natives were to be protected at all the Government had to become a road maker, a railway builder, and a constructor of ports. For it was only by the development of a commerce in tropical products, such as palm-oil, rubber, cotton and gum that the trade in men or slavery could be suppressed. The Congo showed the danger of shirking Empire when trade had already connected two unequal civilizations.[89]

This interplay of economic and political factors is clearly shown in the work of Salisbury. Speaking in the House of Lords in 1890 he said, " Up to ten years ago we remained masters of Africa, practically, or the greater part of it, without being put to the inconvenience of protectorate or anything of that sort, by the simple fact that we were masters of the sea and that we have had considerable experience in dealing with native races. So much was that the case that we left enormous stretches of coast to the native rulers in the full confidence that they would go on under native rulers, and in the hope that they would gradually acquire their own proper civilization without any interference on our part. Then suddenly we found out that that position, however convenient, had no foundation whatever in international law. We had no rights over all those vast stretches of coast—we had no power of preventing any other nation from coming in and seizing any portion of them."[90] Was he to allow a struggle for supremacy between white traders of different nationalities, with the degradation of the natives which must ensue and the possibility of national sentiment provoking war? He decided that a selective regulation of the British advance, the transmutation of independent movements into an expansion of Empire was to be preferred. " The rights of the black man that he recognized were : the right to a rescue from the curse of the slave trade ; the black man's right to share in the religion and civilization of which the white races were the trustees ; the right to be well governed. But there was no questioning of the right of European absorption and no idea of a right to independence or sovereignty. And for the reason that his generation had knowledge of what Africa for Africans meant. Their dilemma was, were they justified in placing fresh burdens of cost and responsibility upon their own people at home? "[89] When chartered companies were resorted to—the Niger Company in 1886, the East African Company in 1888 and the Rhodes South Africa Company in 1889—though they received monopolistic rights in trade and administration, their fiscal powers were limited; the Imperial Government reserved the right to supervise their native policy; exclusive control over their foreign policy and the right to withdraw their charter. Before 1870 a harder, more emotional generation had believed either in extermination by the sword and natural causes, or assimilation by the gospel. After 1870 neither assimilation nor extermination were feasible. It was now a question of the technique of control. Where there was to be indirect rule, the Government and not the trader had to take the responsibility. In 1869 the Suez Canal altered the trade routes of the world. In 1870 the cheapening of railways by Bessemer steel, made possible the penetration of the Continent; in the 'eighties the chartered companies offered profitable investments; in 1897 the mosquito was discovered to be the cause of malaria. At the same time a new conception of the duties of government emerged. The colonial authorities became responsible for the economic as well as the political welfare of the lands they governed.[91] Lord Harcourt, when Colonial Secretary, said that " the position of the Colonial Secretary on the Crown Colony side of his department carried with it the powers, duties, responsibilities and anxieties of a practical and laborious despot controlled only by the forces of nature, by his own discretion and by the sporadic curiosity at question time of friends or opponents, inspired either by imagination or information."[92] It had to provide a policy with regard to vacant lands, irrigation, methods of cultivation, transport, health. It had to experiment in a variety of political methods.[93]

The essential element in all this was the need for the State to keep pace with the development of trade, if only to prevent the bloodshed and degradation of uncontrolled private traders, and the exclusion of the area from Free Trade should other countries have got control. To preserve the open door for all comers was after the 'fifties the aim of policy of Great Britain, and one great motive of her expansion was to prevent her own commercial exclusion.

After 1870 in foreign relations English statesmen had to consider that the absolute supremacy of the British navy was threatened by the potential power of any industrial power, with access to the sea, to challenge it with the new weapons science was producing. Russia in the Black Sea, France in the Mediterranean and the new Germany in the North Sea were all potential rivals. Though the two-power standard at sea was proclaimed in 1889, it had to be recognized that it was impossible to increase our army proportionally to those of the great land powers, nationalism and the industrial revolution had produced. There was an almost universal conviction that for Constantinople to pass into the hands of Russia would be a disaster for the British Empire. It was also the conviction of English statesmen that it was futile to spend any more English blood in sustaining the Turkish Empire. She was too feeble for independence and her vassalage to Russia would be too dangerous for our route to India. And if she were eliminated as a sovereign power, government of some kind would have to be found for the wretchedly oppressed multitudes of European Turkey. The Balkans could not be left as a no-man's-land. " But," wrote Salisbury in 1876, " division of that kind of jetsam is peculiarly difficult. If the Powers quarrel over it, the calamities of a gigantic war must be undergone. If they agree people call it partition and denounce it as immoral."[94] If the approaching demise of Turkey threatened the European balance of power that balance had been even more profoundly disturbed by the Prussian defeat of Austria and of France. " Austria's existence," wrote Salisbury, " is no longer of the importance to us that it was in former times. Her vocation in Europe has gone. She was a counterpoise to France and barrier against Russia : but France is gone, and the development of Russia is chiefly in regions where Austria could not, and if she could would not, help us to check it."[95]

It seemed in fact that in 1870 the only political structure on the Continent was the league of the three Emperors of Russia, Prussia and Austria, while as a threat to the Mediterranean route to India there was the possibility of an alliance of France and Russia. Such was the general background of the diplomatic drama which culminated in the Congress of Berlin. Beaconsfield succeeded in driving a wedge between the three emperors, whose autocracy was incompatible with British Liberalism and strategically a threat to British imperialism. " Next to making a tolerable settlement for the Porte " our great object at the Congress of Berlin " was to break up and permanently prevent, the alliance of the three Empires."[96] The breach thus opened between Germany and Russia by this masterpiece of diplomacy was never again completely closed.[97] But if England had divided her enemies, her system of responsible government made it impossible for her to make sure of the support of possible friends. While she wished to assure herself of the armed assistance of Germany against Russia, she was not prepared to support Germany in the event of a second Franco-German war.[98]

115

Bismarck always thought that serious negotiations with England were dangerous because they were impossible without secrecy, and if secret the absence of Parliamentary sanction would make them worthless.[99]

To the difficulties of the shifting balance of power on the continent of Europe between the great land powers, was added in the 'eighties the triple drama of the continent of Africa. (1) In the south it was not possible to draw any settled boundary between the crumbling native states and the British and Boer colonists with their conflicting native policies. In 1880 Black Michael complained that in Africa many thought that Zululand should not be a border at all, but should be included in His Majesty's possessions. " But if Zululand, why not Swaziland and so on northward to the Equator? . . . I don't think it is for our interest to continue this kind of advance, while we are responsible for the cost of it."[100] Thus spoke the voice of mid-Victorian finance before the problems of economic imperialism silenced it perhaps for ever. (2) In 1882 the Gladstone Government began our long occupation of Egypt " from a love of peace and on the principle of peace "[101] with the hope and intention of withdrawal provided only that " the order of things to be established shall be of a satisfactory character and possess the elements of stability and permanence."[102] (3) In 1885 French rivalry in Egypt and West Africa together with the Russian threat in Central Asia compelled England to recognize Germany's right to colonization in Africa.[103] In these complexities the policy of splendid isolation was pursued by Lord Salisbury. Although in 1898 Chamberlain, supported by Lansdowne and Devonshire, was in favour of an Anglo-German alliance openly sanctioned by Parliament as opposed to an alliance with France or Russia, Salisbury felt equally little confidence in Russia, Germany or France.[104] By 1900 the position of Britain might well seem precarious. " Your Majesty," wrote Bulow, " is quite right in feeling that the British must come to us. They have just lost a good deal of hair in Africa ; America is uncertain ; Japan is not to be depended upon ; France is filled with hate ; Russia is perfidious ; public opinion is hostile in all countries. . . . At present it is beginning to dawn gradually on the minds of the British that they will not be able to hold their world empire merely by their own power against so many opponents."[105]

In 1894 Britain had already moved towards Japan as the one Power capable of holding Russia in check.[106] In 1902 the Conservative Government made a treaty with Japan, though it involved a surrender of the tradition of the constitution that the British Government would not pledge itself to take part in war before public opinion had decided for itself.[107] In Manchuria, Russia was seeking to extend her authority, while in the Yangtse valley England was using her influence to exploit her commercial interests.[108] Russia's tightening political and economic hold over Persia provoked a statement from the British Foreign Secretary in the House of Lords in 1903 that there must be no foreign naval base in the Persian Gulf.[109] In 1904 the Tangier crisis between France and Germany produced the *entente cordiale*, which though for Lansdowne it was a mere colonial agreement having no threat for Germany,[110] laid the basis for a working partnership which the German naval threat to British sea power ripened to an alliance in war. From 1902 it was necessary that England should win France, hold Russia, agree with Italy, and prevent the German naval menace and the threat of her strategic railways in Asia Minor.[111] In this task her diplomatic brains were " far superior to those of Germany, both in the clearness with which they perceived their goal, and the logical accuracy with which they carried on their negotiations."[112] By 1907, the opinion in the inner English political circles was that Germany was going to contest with us the command of the sea and our commercial position.[113] Though this may have been a delusion of some courtiers and bureaucrats, it should be recorded that in 1908 Asquith told Balfour that " the Government could form no theory of the German policy which fitted all the known facts except that they wanted war."[114]

What effect had the changing face of industry and trade, the new worlds of science, and the mutations of society upon the art of politics? The diaries and speeches of the traditional leaders are eloquent with their growing distress. In 1884 Hardy is writing of the " revolutionary race which Gladstone has started and Chamberlain will run."[115] Goschen tells the Eighty Club that " the dethronement of orthodox political economy seemed likely to be signalized by the appearance of a swarm of quacks."[116] To Selborne, in 1886, it seemed that we were approaching a time " when the real contest will be between revolution and the English Constitution such as we have known it."[117] In the 'nineties, Chamberlain is demanding a Red Cross service for the competitive industrial system.[118] The eternal laws of supply and demand and the sanctity of private right in property are mere phrases, " the conventional cant of selfish wealth."[119] In 1895, Salisbury writes despairingly " Governments can do so little and prevent so little nowadays. Power has passed from the hands of statesmen, but I should be very much puzzled to say into whose hands it has passed. It is all pure drifting."[120] And the true full note of a dying age in Rosebery's speech at Glasgow in 1909. " In my opinion the deep, subtle, insidious danger which underlies all is the danger of Socialism . . . . I may think Tariff Reform or Protection an evil, but Socialism is the end of

117

all, the negation of faith, of family, of property, of monarchy, of empire."[121]

We may sympathize with these masterful administrators of the unforeseen. For, by 1880, human affairs had reached such a state of complexity that they required the aid of mathematical analysis. " The lights of unaided reason—though sparkling with eloquence and glowing with public spirit—are but a precarious guide unless a sterner science fortify the way."[122] In Government departments the simple decimal dots which dukes had sometimes damned, gave place to formulæ, rich and strange. But statistics' artful aid and mathematics' magic spells, though they might reveal, could not solve the problems of the State. To the extensive but backward view of history, the importance of the period 1870-1914 might seem to lie in the attempts, made by a growing democracy, to master the plutocratic powers which held it in thrall. It might seem to be an attempt by publicity and measurement to cure the sickness of an acquisitive society. But the contemporary politician could enjoy no such simplicity of vision. For he had not merely to decide on which side he stood in some dispute ; but which disputes would justify his leaving colleagues with whom, in other things, he was agreed. The more numerous and more urgent the issues which arose, the more had he to strive to retain the method of persuasion in conditions which threatened force.

Was the conflict between rich and poor to be solved as Disraeli had flamboyantly proposed by securing a " union of the cottage and the throne," or as Gladstone had so often preached, by developing in the unprivileged the moral integrity he assumed the privileged to possess ? Or must it, as the Radicals proposed, be slowly mitigated by the growth of reason and measurement in State affairs at the expense of tradition and privilege ? And how was this domestic problem related to the changing balance of power in Europe, and the spreading network of a closely woven world economic order, in which it seemed that markets might not open to the merely " economic man," but only to be the Machiavellian use of political power? And how again was it related to those religious issues which to some statesmen were of equal importance with the quantitative economic adjustments they were called upon to make? In 1868 Disraeli had made his main appeal to the Protestantism of the nation. " The ultimate triumph, were our Church to fall, would be to that power which would substitute for the authority of our Sovereign the supremacy of a foreign prince."[123] The youthful Esher shrewdly remarked in 1880 " if the Irish were Mahommedan or Hindus we should have no difficulty with them. Every consideration would be then shown to their religious prejudices. Because they are Catholics they have been treated like dogs and are borne down by the vulgar bigotry of English Evangelicalism."[124] " I should consider," wrote Selborne in 1885, " the maintenance of the Established Church of much greater importance that the predominance of my own or the defeat of any other political party."[125]

By the middle of the 'eighties, the traditional Conservatism was facing the destruction of the economic basis of its order. The vision of a Tory democracy based on a union of the cottage and the throne, was already the baseless fabric of a dream. It had had to yield to the realities of an industrial order in which wealth could no longer be held merely on the understanding that traditional obligations would be gracefully performed, but by its power to manipulate the springs of human action in a still imperfectly educated electorate, and its willingness to serve when it could not cajole. It was saved partly by the fact that the world-sweep of the industrial revolution already gave indications of its challenge to the splendid isolation in which the English economic heritage had been so shrewdly developed. Salisbury's policy of splendid isolation anticipated in the sphere of foreign affairs a desire which was steadily to grow in all cultural groups, until, in the decades after the War of 1914-18, it destroyed the economic order the nineteenth century had achieved. It was saved also by the fact that the Irish question disrupted the Liberal Party by raising the ghost of all those questions, religious and national, it was their belief that peace and plenty had for ever laid. In these circumstances it was understandable that the new and most vital political movement at the end of the nineteenth century should have been the rise of the new Labour Party. Its leaders turned their backs on all the mighty issues which were preparing a challenge to the world, and sought, in the domestic morality of their countrymen and their common-sense capacity in common tasks, to develop a simple form of economic Nonconformity. It had its origin in three main sources : the new professional classes which the growth of science and the increased functions of the State had called into being ; the humanitarianism which, with the decay of traditional Christianity, now sought to save the slums as it had once sought to save the world ; and the unions of organized labour whose leaders desired something more than to be the mere promoters of collective bargains. The professional classes who were not entirely specialized in the natural sciences had intimations of the challenge which science offered to the traditional art of politics. It was only by research, and above all by quantitative measurements, that the problems of society could be solved. They realized that only the educated classes could lead a peaceful revolution. They recognized that " the middle and upper classes are the revolutionary element in

119

society ; the proletariat element is the Conservative element as Disraeli well knew."[126] Their humanitarianism was Puritan and peaceful. It was Bernard Shaw who made the Puritan in the Englishman face the question of the real place of property in the social order. Suppose that private property was demonstrably not reliable evidence that its owner possessed the Christian virtues of thrift and honesty, but only of the uncertain operation of economic forces, natural, amoral and capricious. Suppose that it could be shown that it was as difficult for a poor man in an industrial society to be a good citizen as for a rich man to enter into the Kingdom of Heaven. If these things were so, then the humanitarianism which had had its Radicalism mitigated by religious faith would, with the decay of that faith, be faced with an absolute obligation to abolish inequalities which were no longer justified by any spiritual law. It was peaceful because they realized the " ordinary citizen's desire for gradual and peaceful change as against revolution, conflict with the army and police, and martyrdom."[127]

CHAPTER V

GOVERNMENT AND PARTIES, 1868-1914

The effects of the Reform Acts, 1867 and 1884—In the constituencies—
In the House of Commons—On Political Leadership and Party Organization—The development of the Cabinet system in 1868-80; 1880-1906;
1906-14—The general character of each period—The conventions
determining the selection of the Prime Minister and the changing of a
Government—The formation of Cabinets—Their work and organization.

THE Reform Bill of 1867 gave to the working men a pre-
ponderance of voting power. " Will they," asked Lord
Cranborne, " do that which no class armed with power has
hitherto done in the history of the world "[1] *not* use their new-found
power to further their own interests? " What an unknown world we
are to enter," Gathorne Hardy wrote in his diary. " If the gentry
will take their part they will be adopted as leaders. If we are left to
the demagogues, God help us ! "[2] Goschen wrote, " we believe that
the new electorate will . . . attribute an importance to sentimental
questions which these questions have not hitherto been able to secure
. . . that in social questions they will require more vigorous action, a
fiercer warfare against abuses, more Government intervention; that
in economical matters they will be less faithful to political economy . . .
and that there may even be a tendency to take a somewhat different
view of the right definition of national prosperity."[3] He said that the
classes who had hitherto exclusively wielded political power " will
retain ample strength to prevent their being overwhelmed by numbers
on questions where they have a right and justice on their side."
Humpty Dumpty had had a great fall, but the frying-pan might be
avoided. He was broken but not yet scrambled.

The classes which had wielded political power hitherto were not
left defenceless. In the boroughs the new Reform Act provided a
lodger franchise. But in the counties it added to the existing £50
rental qualification a new occupational franchise for tenants of property
rated at £12, and it reduced the yearly values of the qualifying tenement
in estates for life, copyhold estates and long leaseholds from £10 to
£5. These changes secured great indirect influence to the large
landowners. Politically, there were now two Englands : a democratic

England of the cities and an aristocratic England of the shires. In the boroughs the number of electors was more than doubled. In Birmingham it was tripled, in Leeds, Blackburn and Bolton, quadrupled.[4] But, save in London, the difficulties of registration prevented the lodger franchise from having any influence upon the election. In the counties neither the small tradesman, nor the miner, nor the peasant had the vote. Conservatism was further strengthened by the very unequal distribution of seats. Even though the Redistribution Act of 1868 disfranchised 52 seats, the small rural boroughs with an aggregate population of 500,000 were of greater weight than the 10,000,000 of the Metropolitan, Midland and Northern boroughs. The Lake District had a representation in the House of Commons equal to six times that of the mining and shipping North-East.[5]

Such confusion and complexity could not continue, however subtly defended. In 1872 the Ballot Act was passed in spite of the hostility of the House of Lords and the secret disapproval of the House of Commons. The secret ballot it provided was opposed by Disraeli as a retrograde step, divorcing political life from publicity.[6] It had been opposed on similar grounds by many Liberals. But the power which the open ballot gave to the larger land-owners to exercise compulsion on their tenants, and the more physical compulsions employed in the towns, made reform inevitable. Of the election of 1868, Bright wrote " . . . the corruption, bribery, compulsion, tumult of this General Election have probably never been exceeded—the whole country is disgraced and ought to be shocked, and no man who has no other remedy to offer can with any show of reason resist the ballot."[7] The blow given by the Ballot Act to the indirect influence of the landowners made possible the development of the Nationalist Party in Ireland.

The distinction between the urban and rural franchise of 1867 could not long survive. Selborne might argue that there were natural differences between rural and urban communities justifying and making expedient a difference in their franchise : that the first was dependent upon territorial ownership and the possession of land ; the second an organized unity with an opinion of its own.[8] But every year the distinction became more arbitrary and unreal. Areas entirely urban in character were treated as though they were rural. Towns more flourishing and populous than neighbouring boroughs were denied representation. By 1884 there was no one to oppose the principle of extending to the counties the £10 occupation franchise, the leasehold qualification, and the lodger qualification which had been introduced into the boroughs in 1867, and the third Reform Bill was passed. The real fight was over distribution. The House of Lords feared that if distribution were not settled by the existing Parliament, a new Parliament with a Radical majority might create equal electoral districts, so they refused to pass the Franchise Bill until redistribution had been agreed upon. Gladstone declared that he would not dissolve on the issue of the Franchise Bill, but that if forced to dissolve, he would raise the question of the position of the House of Lords in the Constitution. By the influence of the Queen, the party leaders were brought together and " with incredible facility and rapidity " they produced a " larger, more symmetrical and consistent scheme for a rearrangement of all the electoral districts in the United Kingdom than had before been thought of by any practical statesman."[9] The essence of the scheme was that all cities and towns with less than 15,000 inhabitants were thrown into the counties ; and the counties and the big towns were broken up into single-member constituencies.[10] The Conservative principle of the representation of communities was replaced by the Radical principle of the representation of majorities. The redistribution seemed to Gathorne Hardy a revolution, while Goschen and Sir Henry Maine were plunged in gloom.[11]

What was the effect of these changes in the franchise ? It is difficult to say because the problems of government are determined by the course of industry, the march of science, and the decay of religion as much as by the extension of the franchise. Education, health, and social legislation would have had to be developed by any Government whether or not there had been an extension of the franchise. One vital effect of the extension of the franchise was to alter the whole machinery of government and to provide a new environment to which the subtle mutations of party leadership and constitutional practice had to be adapted.

It seemed to Goschen that " the whole centre of gravity of the Constitution had been displaced " by the Act of 1867. Mill had pointed out that, before 1867, the interests of the working classes could not be represented or understood in the House of Commons.[12] Bright said that our defective representation let " the scandalous abuse " of the Church of England put on the character of a national and useful institution, though five-sixths of Ireland and two-thirds of Scotland, and 14,000 chapels in England and Wales were Dissenting.

The reforms of 1867 and 1884 did not suddenly transform the House of Commons. The number of members who could claim close relations with peers and baronets gradually diminished ; the number of those concerned with industry and commerce gradually increased. In 1860, 108 Members of the House of Commons were either sons of peers or heirs to the peerages ; in 1897, 51. In 1865, 90 Members of the House were engaged in manufacturing and mercantile operations ; in 1880, 112. From 1874 to 1900 the number of brewers, ironmasters, armament makers and manufacturers increased from 61 to 120. Both in 1865 and 1880 there were 80 Members who had served in the Army or Navy, 250 had attended one of the great public schools or gone up to Oxford or Cambridge. Not until the rise of the Labour Party and the Liberal victory of 1906 was there a drastic change in the character of the House.

The enlarged electorate caused an entirely new technique of political leadership. The Constitution now required a Prime Minister and a leader of the Opposition who could touch the springs of action in the common man. Persuasion and propaganda were to replace patronage and corruption. Appeals to the new and many-headed Cæsar were repugnant to statesmen of the old school. In 1868 Derby is writing of the " balderdash and braggadocio in which Gladstone has been indulging on his stumping tour."[13] In 1874 Selborne is perturbed that Gladstone as Prime Minister should propound in an election address a popular budget.[14] The Midlothian campaign of 1879 seemed to him " a precedent tending in its results to the degradation of British politics, by bringing in a system of perpetual canvass, and removing the political centre of gravity from Parliament to the platform."[15] By 1880 Gladstone is uneasy at the use made of his own technique by the Radical Chamberlain. In the 'nineties Rosebery will shock the Queen by addressing a popular meeting on a policy not previously discussed with herself. In 1900 an election will be fought on the initiative of a Minister—Chamberlain—not the Prime Minister, and in a manner to make a fitting prologue to this century of propaganda ; while in 1910 where Gladstone had sowed and Chamberlain watered, Lloyd George will reap and glean the increase. By then a General Election will be considered by a large proportion of the electorate as practically a referendum on the question which of two Governments shall be returned to power.[16]

A doctrine of the mandate was gradually developed. In 1868 when Gladstone carried resolutions against the Church of England in Ireland, Disraeli claimed that the House of Commons had no right to deal with a question undiscussed at the previous election. In 1886 Hartington writes " although no principle of the mandate may exist there are certain limits which Parliament is morally bound to observe. . . . The House of Commons has no right to initiate legislation especially immediately upon its first meeting of which the constituencies were not informed and of which they might have been informed."[17]

The swing of the pendulum became a cliché of the politicians' vocabulary. The electorate seemed to show a preference for the party whose defects it had had most time to forget. For a time, too, its verdict promised to be decisive. Before 1867 Cabinets had depended on the subtle calculations of groups and were defeated or successful by very small margins. Peel, in 1841, had turned out the Whigs by one ; Russell, in 1852 was displaced by nine ; Derby in the same year by nineteen. In 1866 the second reading of Russell's Reform Bill had been carried by five and Ministers were afterwards defeated by eleven. Then Gladstone in 1868 carried the Irish Church Bill by 118 and this majority was the sign of a new political era. Governments could now look to majorities of a hundred and more. The number of constituencies which were contested at a General Election was greatly increased. Before 1867 it was common for half the seats to be uncontested.[18] In 1859, 101 constituencies were fought ; in 1865, 204 ; in 1868, 277 ; in 1880, 352.[19]

In the period 1868 to 1880 there were two great ministries : the Gladstone Ministry, 1868-74, with a majority of over 100, followed by the Disraeli Ministry of 1874-80. The swing of the pendulum in 1874 might be ascribed to the fact that all the powerful interests affected by five years of legislation, the landed interest, the Church of England and those who desired religious education in elementary schools, the brewers and licensed victuallers, went over to the Conservatives. As Disraeli put it, with his artist's insight into the coming technique of propaganda : the Ministry had " harassed every trade, worried every profession, and assailed or menaced every class institution and species of property in the country." The electorate were invited to close " this career of plundering and blundering."[20] In more concrete terms the public houses were mobilized against the chapels and the Government " borne down in a torrent of gin and beer."[21] In 1880 it was the Conservative turn to be borne down by a torrent—this time of Gladstone's Midlothian denunciation—" from day to day, under a Ministry, called, as if in mockery, Conservative, the nation is perplexed with fear of change."[22]

A simple alternation of Liberal kettle and Conservative pot did not continue. The Gladstone Government of 1880-85 marked the transition to a new era, for it was hopelessly divided between the Old Whigs under Hartington and the new Radicalism of Chamberlain. A peaceful substitution of Radicalism for Whiggery was not to be. In 1886 when Gladstone dissolved after the rejection of his first Home Rule Bill, 316 Conservatives, 74 Liberal Unionists, 195 Liberals and 85 Nationalists were returned. The Home Rule issue helped the Conservatives to hold office—except for the short Gladstone-Rosebery

Administration 1892-95—until 1906. The House of Lords could avoid the adjustment of its powers to a changed political and social era, until the split of the Conservatives themselves over the mirage of imperial economic unity, enabled the Irish Party and the new industrial democracy educated by the Independent Labour Party since 1893, to demand the passage of the Parliament Act in 1911.

An analysis of the election results from 1885 to 1910 reveals some of the forces which were shaping the political scene. Ireland was committed to the continuous return of her eighty unchanging patriots—until the Home Rule issue should be solved they were simply a weapon of Nationalism and not a possible instrument of government. Liberalism of the Gladstone tradition was only firmly secured in the Celtic fringe of Wales and Scotland. The south-east of England was almost overwhelmingly Conservative except at the election of 1906. The industrial north was mainly Liberal, London, on the whole, Conservative, while the full swing of the pendulum was to be seen in the Midlands and the West. With the rise of the Labour Party we can trace the disintegration of the older political traditions, and the emergence of new political forces. From 1874 the public house was an important election agency for the Conservatives and the chapel for the Liberals. By 1900 the inspiration of Nonconformity and temperance are finally exhausted and the Liberal Party draws deeply upon Fabian springs. Meanwhile the Conservative Party has lost the battle for the unity of the United Kingdom and has failed to agree or persuade to an imperial unity.

The enlargement of the electorate altered the relation of the member to his constituency and the party machinery had to be reorganized. After 1835 the Carlton Club for the Conservatives had provided the initiative in scrutinizing the electoral rolls, but the connection between the central organization and the local party committees was very loose.[23] Elections to the Tories, when they took place, were little more than an unseemly though necessary formality to enable the natural leaders to assume control.[24] After the Conservative defeat of 1852 Disraeli had employed a solicitor, Rose, to undertake a revision of the party organization. The Central Conservative Office in Whitehall kept a register of approved candidates and tried to get the local people to make their own selection from among them. In 1868 these local associations were affiliated to a National Union.[25] In 1873, for every borough election, Disraeli had " an expert to visit the scene of action and prepare a confidential report so that he might as far as possible be acquainted with the facts."[26] But in 1880 the Central Office seems to have been quite ignorant of the mind of the electorate.[27] Later under

Akers-Douglas as Whip and Captain Middleton as chief agent its organization seems to have given satisfaction.[28] The Conservative Central Office remained " handmaid to the party " and was never allowed to usurp the functions of leadership. Neither the Union nor its council had any executive power. In the last resort power lay with the leader of the party and his self-selected committee of M.P.s called the central committee.[29]

After 1867 the organization of the Liberal Party, too, was changed. In Birmingham Schnadhorst organized the New Model for Chamberlain. This became the inspiration of the National Liberal Federation. " The Birmingham plan is perhaps the only one on which the Liberal Party can be sufficiently organized in a great constituency," wrote Harting-ton, in 1877.[30] But the Whig leader feared that a federation of such local organizations would put the management into the hands of the most advanced men. And indeed by 1877 the Federation was a Liberal Parliament outside Parliament, a weapon of Radicalism providing for the direct participation of all members of the party in the determination of policy. Local associations chose their candidates on condition that they adopted the party programme determined by the periodical meetings of the Federation. The power of the Liberal machine severely taxed the Liberal leaders. In 1891 Schnadhorst had to point out that delegates attended, not to express opinions, but to hear what measures the leaders of the party could adopt with reasonable hope of remaining a united party.[31] Hartington felt that Chamberlain had organized an outside power to the belittlement of Parliament. Harcourt wrote to Morley that it was " absurd that we should leave the Federation to formulate a creed and then go down to swear to all its articles."[32] The machine, complained Rosebery, was a permanent force jealous of and a enemy to whatever was extraneous to it.[33]

After the passing of Sir Henry James's Corrupt Practices Act, 1883, the cost of a contest for almost any seat was within the means of men with moderate means, or no means at all, if they represented a cause for which subscriptions could be raised.[34] In 1885 Joseph Arch secured a 600 majority over the Duke of Portland's brother.[35] Rosebery subscribed £50 to this election because it seemed to him a farce to give the agricultural labourer the vote and then not to allow their chief representative to sit in Parliament.[36]

On the nature and source of party funds the biographies of statesmen are usually discreet. We catch occasional glimpses of collecting activities. " What we want," Disraeli wrote to Stanley in 1868, " is to raise one hundred thousand, which it is believed will secure the result. It can be done if the Cabinet sets a good example." He induced his colleagues in the Cabinet to subscribe a minimum of £10,000.[37] In 1879 Esher tells us " we made out a list of peers and M.P.s who may be asked to subscribe to a General Election fund. There are 114 of them. An average of £500 a piece would, Harcourt thinks, enable us to win twenty county seats."[38] With the development of the large federations the money affairs of the party funds were supposed to be entirely in the hands of the Chief Whip, the Prime Minister knowing nothing of them unless in some particular case the facts came out.[39] Sometimes they did. In 1891 Rhodes gave Schnadhorst £5,000 ; later, alarmed at certain speeches of Gladstone and Labouchere, he asked him to divert the money to charity. Schnadhorst exceeded his functions and reassured him. By 1901 the *Spectator* was suggesting that Rhodes had given £5,000 to the Liberal Party in return for a promise that Egypt should not be evacuated.[40]

After 1832 some progress had been made with the task of adapting and modifying the procedure of the House of Commons for its new work as a legislative machine controlled by an executive based on popular power. Between 1840 and 1870 the average length of a session had actually declined from 131 to 115 days.[41] Procedure had been simplified and an increasing control by the Government secured. Further tightening of the Government's control of the procedure of the House would in any case have been necessary with the great increase of legislation that came with the growth of collectivism after 1870, but the first important changes were the result of Irish obstruction in 1880. The Ballot Act of 1872 made possible the return in 1874 of fifty-nine Home Rulers. In 1875 Parnell, their leader, began a policy of systematic obstruction, not as a method of debate, but as a weapon to destroy the Parliament of the United Kingdom as a constitutional assembly.[42] He intended to destroy the Union by paralysing its political organ. The Speaker and the Government had to raise a state of siege. In 1881, after a sitting lasting forty-one and a half hours, the Speaker announced that he considered that he would best carry out the will of the House and might rely upon its support if he declined to call upon any more members to speak, and at once put the question from the chair.[43] This emergency use of the prestige of the Chair could not be a permanent solution. In 1882 an autumn session of six months was devoted to the reform of the rules.[44] It produced the closure by which on the initiative of the Speaker, 200 members agreeing, the question under debate could be at once put to the vote. This was useful enough to stop obstruction on a particular question, or to prevent a Bill from being talked out, but was little use for controlling full and informed debate on the details of a Bill.[45] The Guillotine (first used as an expedient in 1881 and 1887), by which a certain number of days is allotted to each of the remaining stages of a Bill, was a brutally efficient weapon for carrying legislation, but clumsy and unsatisfactory for the improvement of debate.[46] It tended not to hasten Parliamentary debate but merely to dispense with it.[47] In 1909 the Speaker was first given the power to select amendments so that time might be spent on ones the House wished to consider. The " Kangeroo " was made an inherent instead of an occasional power in 1919. Its disadvantage was that it added " omniscience to the many qualities already demanded of the Chair."[48] In 1902 Balfour had laid a complete scheme of reforms before the House of which the parts adopted secured the application of closure to Supply, a fixed distribution of the time of the session between the Government and private members, and the allocation to the Government business of the earlier part of each day's sitting. Rules which had once been framed to " promote a fertilizing flow of eloquence " had now been modified " to dam up its vast and destructive floods and keep them within reasonable limits."[49]

By 1910 the average length of a session had increased to 140 days. Of these finance took 38 ; another 25 went to debates on the Address, various motions and formal business, leaving only 77 for legislation. Allowing 14 days for private members, little more than 60 were available for Government legislation. During the ten years ending 1909, 388 Government Bills passed the House in 483 days. The ten most important occupied 207 days leaving 276 for the remaining 378. In the same period the average time in general debate each session was 24 for English supply services and procedure ; 19 for the Empire, including the Army and Navy ; 16 for finance (exclusive of supply and consolidated fund) ; nine for Ireland ; two for Scotland ; one for Wales.[50]

In this general background it will be convenient to consider the development of the Cabinet system and the subtle conventions by which it is governed in the three periods, 1868-1880, 1880-1906, 1906-1914.

1868-1880 : It is not easy to recapture the inner spirit of these strange politics. We should be nearer doing so if we could understand the technique by which Disraeli led simple squires in their halting quest of democratic power. With no science (he was " on the side of the angels "), with exotic morals (" the man," said Gladstone, " is falser than his doctrines ") Disraeli had an artist's insight into the problems of political power. " In legislation," he wrote, " it is not merely reason and propriety which are to be considered, but the temper of the times."[51] But what to him was the spirit of the times ? He made Sidonia say " the tendency of advancing civilization is in truth towards pure monarchy. Monarchy is indeed a government which requires a

129

high degree of civilization for its full development. It needs the support of free laws and manners and of a widely diffused intelligence. Your House of Commons that has absorbed all other power in the State will in all probability fall more rapidly than it rose. Public opinion has a more direct, a more comprehensive, a more efficient organ for its utterance than a body of men sectionally chosen. The printing press absorbs in a great degree the duties of the Sovereign, the priest and Parliament ; it controls, it educates, it discusses. That public opinion when its acts would appear in the form of one who has no class interest." This adumbration of the totalitarian state within the chaos of Victorian economic plenty and spiritual poverty should warn us on what depths the frail bark of the democratic state is launched. In 1873, when Disraeli was seriously considering the future of the Conservative Party, he said, " all the questions of trade and navigation, of the incidence of taxation and public economy are settled. But there are other questions not less important and of deeper and higher reach and range which must soon engage the attention of the country—the attributes of a constitutional monarchy, whether aristocratical principles should be recognized in our Constitution, and if so in what form, whether the Commons of England shall remain an estate of the realm, numerous but privileged and powerful, or whether they should degenerate into an indiscriminate multitude."[52]   When in office he secured an influence over the Queen and used the monarchical tradition for party ends. " I do think Dizzy has worked the idea of personal government to its logical conclusion," wrote Lady Ponsonby to her husband.[53]   And she continued, " that superstition . . . can be worked by an unscrupulous Minister to his advantage and the country's ruin."

It was Gladstone's opinion that since 1874 the Queen's " mind and opinion had been seriously warped."   That she had been deliberately misled by a mind more powerful than her own and by one who " owed everything to woman "[54] cannot be doubted. In 1867 when the Queen was trying to settle the Reform Bill dispute Disraeli wrote to Northcote, " the Royal project of interposition with our rivals is a mere phantom, it pleases the vanity of a court deprived of substantial power."[55]   But in 1872 he is saying that " the principles of the English Constitution do not contemplate the absence of personal influence on the part of Sovereign, and if they did the principles of human nature would prevent the fulfilment of such a theory."[56]   In 1881 he told the Queen " that the speech of the Sovereign is only the speech of the Ministers is a principle not known to the British Constitution. It is only a piece of Parliamentary gossip."[57]   His influence with the Queen led her to the constitutionally perilous experiment of continuing a correspondence with him after his resignation. Did not the Queen express the hope and belief " that this shameful heterogeneous union—out of mere folly —will separate into many parts very soon and that the Conservatives will come in stronger than ever in a short time—the sort of mad and unreasoning flow of Liberal success is so unnatural that I feel certain it can't last."[58]   It may be argued that Disraeli merely lied to the Queen for the good of his country ; that his flattery was like the courtesy of the barrister to a prejudiced and incompetent judge. In the time of Gladstone and Disraeli not to be a gentleman was a ground for political criticism.   The aristocracy said Albert was no gentleman ; Albert said it of Disraeli ; Disraeli said it of Gladstone.[59]   Gladstone considered that a gentleman was necessary at the War Office to deal with the Commander-in-Chief.   In 1878 Disraeli, attacked separately from his colleagues, said that in the old days such efforts at dividing a Prime Minister from his colleagues were "not only deemed unfair and unjust and unconstitutional, but ungentlemanlike."[60]   In 1874 Disraeli told Lady Bradford that he had broken the Irish ranks " by keeping my temper and treating Butt and his intimate colleagues as gentlemen, which they certainly are not ; but their vanity is insatiable."[61]   To prove the Liberal Party gentlemen Granville in 1874 challenged the Tories to a race across country.[62]   Attacked by Chamberlain in 1876 Disraeli described the attacked as " one of the coarsest and stupidest assaults I well remember.   No intellect, no sarcasm or satire or even invective : coarse and commonplace abuse such as you might expect from a cad on an omnibus."[63]   To Derby he wrote that Gladstone was an " unprincipled maniac . . . extraordinary mixture of envy, vindictiveness, hypocrisy and superstition ; and with one commanding characteristic—whether Prime Minister or leader of the opposition, whether preaching, praying, speechifying or scribbling, never a gentleman."[64]   Gladstone, he told Lady Bradford, was a " vindictive fiend."[65] Gladstone considered that Disraeli " demoralized public opinion, bargained with diseased appetites, stimulated passions, prejudices and selfish desires that he might maintain his influence."[66]   Without venturing to understand the code of a gentleman in those exacting days the student may feel that it did not cover the writing of some of the letters by which Disraeli fooled the Queen.

If Disraeli stooped as no gentleman should to lead a Queen by the nose, Gladstone, with the greatest respect for the Constitution as he had been trained to understand it by Peel and by Palmerston, was driven after 1874 into violent opposition to the Queen, the House of Lords and the power of aristocracy. His position as a popular leader was clearly revealed when, though he had retired from the leadership of the Liberal Party in 1874, it was found impossible for any other Liberal to accept office while he should remain in politics. "There is not room for argument about the proposition that the man who leads the Liberal Party out of doors ought to lead it in Parliament," wrote Hartington, who had borne the burden of the leadership in Opposition of the Liberals in the Commons, to Granville, who had carried the same burden in the Lords. "It is only fair to the Queen, to the country, to the party, that this should be acknowledged at once."[67]   And so in 1880 the Queen had to accept Gladstone as Prime Minister with a Cabinet which in her view contained "all the worst men who had no respect for kings and princes or any of the landmarks of the Constitution."[68]

In considering the working of the Cabinet system we must note the procedure by which a change of Government was brought about—for this is a vital test of the efficiency of a political system, the forces which determined the choice of Prime Minister, and the organization and working of individual Cabinets. In the period 1868-80 there was an important modification of the method by which the Government was changed. It was established that a Government would be acting in the spirit of the Constitution if after a defeat in the Commons it asked for a dissolution, and if after a defeat at a General Election it resigned without meeting Parliament. It is important to see the way in which the problem appeared to the Ministers concerned ; for it is not the conventions of the Constitution at any given point of time which are so important as the process by which the conventions come to be changed.

When in 1868 Disraeli was defeated on the Irish Church resolutions put forward by Gladstone, the Queen would not hear of his resigning. Gladstone was of the opinion that the Cabinet ought not to dissolve without a reasonable chance of success. Disraeli argued that the House had no right to deal with a question which had not been discussed at the previous election. He said that he would "indicate what I think is the duty of the Cabinet as regards themselves and their party and then by Her Majesty's special desire I shall refer their duty under the circumstances to the Queen personally."[69]   Having secured his Cabinet's consent to a dissolution he went to the Queen ten days later without again consulting his colleagues because he felt that their resolution to dissolve might have weakened.[70]   This was resented as a departure from precedent. Defeated at the election he immediately resigned, putting into practice the theory he had stated in 1841. His real reasons for resignation at the time are not clear. The Queen was anxious to get the business over before December 14th.[71]   Disraeli talked the matter over with Stanley, Cairns and Hardy, and the Cabinet agreed, though with some fear that the Conservative Party would be offended and alienated.[72] In 1873 there was a complicated exercise in Constitutional niceties. The Gladstone Government (1868-74), with a normal majority of ninety, was defeated by three votes on an Irish Universities Bill which had offended the Protestants, the Irish Roman Catholics and the educationalists—a Cerberus snarling in the road to knowledge. Gladstone was for dissolution. Hartington, the Whig leader, was not, thinking a change of Government would be bad for Irish administration. After two Cabinet meetings it was decided to resign.[73] Disraeli then declined to take office. Gladstone held that by defeating a Government you lay under an obligation to replace it ; Disraeli that because a Minister has a majority which can prevent another parliamentary leader from forming an administration likely to stand he did not " thereby acquire the right to call on Parliament to pass whatever measures he and his colleagues think fit." It was, the Conservatives considered, neither their duty nor their interest to dissolve Parliament for Gladstone. They would not admit the right of any Government " to make any question they please vital, and if a combination negatives it force upon one portion of it all responsibility."[74] Gladstone was in fact compelled to take office again. The crisis revealed on what nice agreement and complex understandings the seeming simple two-party alternation depends.

The Gladstone Government impulsively dissolved in 1874. Defeated at the election Gladstone like Disraeli in 1868 resigned without meeting Parliament. He was careful to state that such a resignation was not always proper. He considered it " more agreeable to usage that the expiring Government should await its sentence from Parliament by meeting it while in possession of office."[75] He wrote to Granville " it is Parliament not the constituencies that ought to dismiss the Government and the proper function of the House of Commons cannot be taken away from it without diminishing somewhat its dignity and authority." This time he resigned for reasons of convenience.

In 1878 the Disraeli Cabinet (1874-80), in spite of the peace with honour their leader had brought back from the Berlin Congress, decided that, possessed of a good majority, they would not dissolve.[76] By 1880 the persistent obstruction of the Irish under Parnell was making the conduct of necessary business difficult. The Queen, anxious for the continuance of a Conservative Government and alarmed at Gladstone's Midlothian oratory, proposed that Beaconsfield should come to some agreement with " some of the sensible and reasonable and not violent men on the other side." Disraeli tactfully replied " that there were no sensible and reasonable men to appeal to." " The nominal leaders have no authority; and the mass . . . are animated by an avidity for office such as Lord Beaconsfield after more than forty years' experience cannot recall." But the time would come " when the interposition and personal influence of Your Majesty may most beneficially be exercised in bringing about a more satisfactory state of the House of Commons than now prevails. "[77] In March, misled by by-elections in Liverpool and Southwark and by rumours of Whig secession he dissolved. Before the decision was taken the Cabinet sat two and a half hours and every member of it was required to give his opinion, the members of the House of Commons having the priority.[78] Defeated, he resigned without meeting Parliament.

How had the Gladstone and Disraeli Cabinets been formed and worked? Great informality marked the method by which a political leader was then selected. Disraeli said " the leader of a party in a House of Parliament is never nominated : the selection is always the spontaneous act of the party in the House in which he sits. Lord Derby never appointed me to the leadership, but the party chose to follow me and the rest ensued."[79] The Queen, it was recognized, could exercise her discretion as to which of the possible leaders she would invite to form a Ministry. When Derby had resigned in 1868 he " ventured to submit that as there is no question of political change Your Majesty should apply to the Chancellor of the Exchequer."[80] She could have sent for Richmond or for Stanley instead of sending as she did for Disraeli.[81]

When Disraeli resigned the same year, 1868, the Queen had no hesitation in sending for Mr. Gladstone. She recorded of their first interview, after he had consented to form a Government, that " he was most cordial and kind in his manner, and nothing could be more satisfactory than the whole interview."[82] There were certain difficulties to be adjusted about the Cabinet which Mr. Gladstone proposed. Lord Clarendon as Foreign Secretary—with " his temper, his manner, his want of discretion, etc.," could not Mr. Gladstone by dwelling upon his bad health get him, without compromising her, to take any other office ? Lord Russell, the Queen said, " ought surely not to be thought of," and Mr. Gladstone felt that " he had for the last few years done nothing but injure a brilliant reputation." The rather peculiar person, Mr. Lowe, " of a very angular mind," might be difficult to manage. Should the kind and genial Mr. Bright be included (and Gladstone thought India would do for him) as he and Bright disliked each other.[83] The Cabinet was formed without much difficulty.

Clarendon went to the Foreign Office ; Russell gracefully declined office, and Bright became President of the Board of Trade.

Gladstone considered that his Cabinet of 1868-74 was " one of the finest instruments of Government that ever were constructed." It was really a working Cabinet and not an assemblage of departmental Ministers.[84] It seemed to him to approach closest to the perfection once achieved by Peel. Gladstone had serious limitations as a Prime Minister. He was utterly unlike the colleagues with whom he had to work and his own supporters in Parliament. No one, it was said, ever knew quite what he meant.[85] His fullest statements were to some uniformly obscure.[86] The chiefs of the Liberal Party had hitherto been either pure Whigs with Liberal or even Radical leanings, or Canningite converts whose Liberalism was more in foreign than in home affairs. Lord Russell was a type of the first and Lord Palmerston of the second.[87] In Gladstone all the contradictory elements seemed to move together with equal power.[88] His combination of a belief in political liberty and High Church principles was a mystery to the Tories, and his belief that to our system of landed property we owed the kindly and intimate relations between our higher and lower classes an exasperation to the Radicals.[89] His appreciation of working men puzzled the patrician Whigs. In 1878 Granville was astonished to meet him in Regent Street coming from a meeting of working men.[90] In the 'seventies the landed magnates and the leaders of commerce and industry were with the middle classes prepared to support the Liberal Party. But beneath the surface there were serious divisions. On Dis-establishment, household suffrage in the counties, education, and the land laws the Whigs and the Radicals were completely divided. When Gladstone temporarily retired in 1874 the Whigs would follow one leader, the Radicals another and the Irish a third.[91]

Gladstone was better in his influence on legislation than in the executive part of his work. The only departments of State in which he was naturally interested were the Treasury and the Board of Trade. The Foreign Office he regarded as task work, and he was only interested in the Army and Navy in so far as they affected the Estimates. He was " disposed to regard the heads of departments as to a great degree autonomous in their own provinces, and entertained great doubts as to the right of a Prime Minister to require a Cabinet Minister to resign.[92] He denied the right of the Queen to know what were the individual opinions of members of the Cabinet. He did not stoop to manipulate the Queen for his party's power, nor did he, as he might, make party capital out of his knowledge of her political bias and petty obstructions.

Disraeli's Cabinet of 1874-80 was a masterpiece of a different political art. He adopted with the Queen a combination of deference and *camaraderie* which served to make her a tool to his designs while she felt herself to be his partner in the highest problems of the State. While forming his Cabinet he prayed Her Majesty " to permit him to observe that in forming an administration, it is necessary to make some offers, which you are almost certain will not be accepted. Powerful personages are conciliated by the offers of great posts, and might be estranged were they not made, even though it may be impossible that they should be accepted."[93] His Cabinet was a small Cabinet. He " proposed having only twelve in the Cabinet—six in each House." Pursuing his intention of changing back the oligarchy into a " generous aristocracy round a real throne " he placed round the person of his Sovereign the heads of the house of Cecil, Seymour, Bridgeman and Lygon, the heir of the Percies, a Wellesley, a Somerset ; while in the Cabinet and in important positions outside there were the representatives of the Stanleys, Hamiltons, Lennoxes, Herberts and Cecils, besides a Manners, a Lowther, a Bentinck and a Bourke.[94] He recognized the Conservative debt to Lancashire by putting R. A. Cross, the director of a Lancashire bank, at the Treasury and " he recommended very highly a Mr. Smith of Westminster, a rich and most respectable clever man who always maintained that the working classes were not Republican."[95] When in 1878 the resignation of Derby over the Eastern question imperilled the Government, Disraeli secured both the confidence of Lancashire and the adhesion of the House of Stanley by promoting Derby's brother and heir to be Secretary for War,[96] while Northumberland, the head of the Percies, was taken into the Cabinet as Lord Privy Seal.[97] It was not fitting to Disraeli's mind that a Tory Cabinet should lack on its front bench in the Lords a due representation of the old families.[98] Whereas Gladstone denied the right of the Queen to know what were the individual opinions of members of the Cabinet, Disraeli made her feel that she was its most important member. On the Eastern crisis he kept her accurately acquainted " with the views and feelings of the various members of the Cabinet." At one time he said the views were seven, and the seventh was " the policy of Your Majesty which will be introduced and enforced to the utmost by the Prime Minister."[99] Though he might control the Queen with unscrupulous ease Disraeli, in Salisbury's opinion, as head of a Cabinet lacked firmness. " The chiefs of departments got their own way too much, the Cabinet as a whole got it too little . . . with all his great abilities he was unable to decide a general principle of action . . . his final political principle of action was that the party must on no account be broken."[100]   He could not in office, as he had in Opposition, skate so boldly over the thin ice between his own reforming ideas and the property interests of those who had made him their champion.[101] He adopted the practice of leaving his colleagues to manage by themselves the conduct of Bills affecting their own departments and only intervened himself at critical moments.[102] The Cabinet decided that the invasion of Afghanistan should take place through only one pass. Lytton objected, because Lytton did Gathorne Hardy did, because Gathorne Hardy did Disraeli did.[103] Determined not to lose Hardy, the representative of the Oxford clergy, a Bill for consolidating the Burial Acts was lost.[104] The decision to purchase the Suez Canal shares (1875) was Disraeli's own, carried in the Cabinet against strong opposition.[105] The decision to stand by Frere in South Africa, who had committed the country to war not only without leave but contrary to his instructions, was Disraeli's supported by Hicks-Beach in the Cabinet and the Queen outside.[106] In the Eastern crisis he stood between the Queen eager for war and a divided Cabinet unable to realize that firmness was the only way to peace.[107]

1880-1906 : To the Conservatives the Liberal victory of 1880 seemed portentous. " The hurricane that has swept us away is so strange and new a phenomenon that we shall not for some time understand its real meaning . . . it seems to me to be inspired by some definite desire for change and means business. It may disappear as rapidly as it came or it may be the beginning of a serious war of classes," wrote Salisbury.[108] The Radical programme sponsored by Chamberlain in 1880 was to sound the death knell of the *laissez-faire* system and the intervention of the State on behalf of the weak versus the strong, in the interest of Labour versus Capital, of want and suffering versus luxury and ease.[109] The predominance of the Radicals made the " Whig Party a mere survival kept alive by tradition after its true functions and significance have passed away."[110] Halifax wrote to Goschen that " it used to be an article of the Liberal creed to get rid of all legislative interference with what men did in the way of business, with two exceptions only : (1) if it was injurious to the public ; (2) to protect those who could not protect themselves. All the Bills introduced by the present Government run counter to this principle."[111]

The Gladstone Cabinet of 1880-85 was a bridge between two political worlds. The conflict between the pretensions of the Crown and the power of a popular leader could no longer be concealed ; the Irish question was threatening the very basis of peaceful government ; Gladstone stood out as the popular leader, but, in him, the new leader was shackled by the old priest. His ecclesiastical mind could not reach down to "the sceptical and thinking race of artisans" whose present discontents must be the basis of reform. With a passion for justice and financial purity he could not see that the financial technique of government was only a means to the necessary conditions of social justice, inquiry might lay bare. He could see that the condition of Ireland was incompatible with both the religious and economic assumptions of the English middle class ; he did not realize that the condition of the English working class was incompatible with freedom and personal dignity.

The Constitutional crisis had been clearly revealed when Disraeli resigned. During Gladstone's retirement, Granville in the Lords, and Hartington in the Commons, had borne the dust and heat of Opposition. The Queen, who considered that Gladstone's "whole conduct, since 1876, had been one of violent, passionate, invective against and abuse of Lord Beaconsfield,"[112] was anxious that anyone but he should be Prime Minister. It had to be explained to her that Gladstone, as the leader of the Liberal Party in the Country, should lead it in the House ; that he would be more dangerous outside the Cabinet than as its leader. "If the Government were overthrown by him he would come to power, relying on the more advanced section of the party, whereas if called upon by the Queen now it would be necessary for him to obtain the support of as large a number as possible of its more moderate members."[113] As Hartington said, "the spirit of the Constitution is that the ablest and most powerful member of the Opposition should be called on to take the position of the retiring Government."[114] Because neither Granville, the leader in the Lords, nor Hartington, who had been chosen leader in the Commons, could form a Government with safety to their party or without danger to the Crown the Queen acquiesced. Disraeli advised her how to behave. He suggested she might in her interview with Gladstone say : "the Opposition having succeeded in defeating my Government, I have in the spirit of the Constitution sent for their leaders, who have confessed their inability to form a Ministry and have advised me to send for you. I wish, therefore, to know whether you are prepared to form an administration." Characteristically, he added, "Mr. Gladstone will probably be diffuse in his reply, which will give Your Majesty an advantage in ascertaining his real intentions."[115]

This Gladstone Cabinet (1880-85), was to be shattered by internal dissensions and the tragedy of Gordon. With a majority of twelve in the Commons and defeated in the Lords, it debated the question of resignation at one of the longest Cabinets ever held. Granville was for resignation, but Bright persuaded Gladstone against.[116] In 1883

Granville had written to Hartington " that it would be a great responsibility to turn Gladstone out and destroy the coherence of the Liberal Party. The effect upon the position of the aristocracy and the richer classes may be very great."[117] In 1884, the Government finally resigned after a defeat on their own Budget, caused by a combination of Tories and Irish. There was a prolonged crisis. Dissolution was impossible, because the old constituences had by the Act of 1884 ceased to exist, and the new ones were not yet created. For some time Salisbury refused to take office until assured by the Queen that Gladstone's guarantees for the conduct of Parliamentary business until the election were satisfactory. When, in 1886, 249 Conservatives, 335 Liberals and 86 Parnellites were returned, Randolph Churchill, Smith and Hicks-Beach were for resignation, but Salisbury decided to meet Parliament, compelling the Opposition to combine for his defeat.[118] The political situation was unparalleled. Lord Carnarvon on behalf of Salisbury had secretly negotiated with Parnell, and Parnell, through Mrs. O'Shea, with Gladstone. The latter had been converted to Home Rule and, pondering the precedents of 1827 (Catholic Emancipation), 1846 (Corn Laws) and 1867 (Reform), was prepared to support a Conservative leader who would carry it through. Parnell did not care with whom the deal was made, but ordered the Irish vote in English cities to be given to the Tories, as they controlled the House of Lords, and he did not know of Gladstone's conversion until too late. The electorate in the counties supported the Liberals in return for the Reform Act of 1884. So, although the Irish vote in the cities had given some twenty to forty seats to the Tories,[119] Parnell allied himself with Gladstone. It was this complex of circumstances which led Salisbury to meet Parliament (January, 1886) before he resigned. Gladstone took office and was defeated on his Home Rule Bill. He dissolved and, beaten at the election, he resigned without meeting Parliament, holding that it was best for Ireland that the strongest party should at once face its responsibilities.

The Queen now vigorously intrigued to secure a Government composed of all those most opposed to Gladstone. There was little she could do. When she urged Hartington to support Salisbury that the country might not be exposed to perpetual changes of Government, he tactfully replied that " . . . there remains on the part of the large majority of the constituencies as strong an attachment to party organization and associations, that no such fusion of parties could at present take place."[120] The new Prime Minister, Salisbury, had succeeded to the leadership of the Conservatives in the Lords, on the death of Beaconsfield, in 1881. He held that it was for the Queen to choose between him and Northcote, the leader in the Commons.[121] His Cabinet was in office until 1892. There is a unique record of his decision to dissolve in 1892 ;[122] 269 Conservatives were returned, 46 Liberal Unionists, 81 Irish and 273 Liberals. Meeting Parliament the Government fell to a vote of no confidence, moved by Mr. Asquith. Once again the Queen had to accept Mr. Gladstone, and he, when the Lords rejected the Home Rule Bill of 1893, would have dissolved on the issue of the position of the House of Lords in the Constitution, but his colleagues were not to be persuaded. In 1894, blind and deaf, and at odds with his Cabinet over Naval Estimates, he resigned for the last time and his successor, Rosebery, was the Queen's choice. In 1895, after two Cabinet meetings, and much difference of opinion, the Rosebery Government decided on resignation. Lord Salisbury held that it ought to dissolve. But Rosebery, while admitting " that it may be unusual that the same House of Commons should declare a want of confidence in two successive administrations " refused.[123]

The dissolution of the Salisbury Government in 1900, marks the beginning of a new political age. Disraeli had shown what a little unscrupulousness could do with a Queen ; there were many who thought that Gladstone repaid the lesson by showing how unconscious hypocrisy might secure the devotion of a people. Chamberlain was to show the power which was latent in the exercise by a powerful Minister of the prerogative of dissolution. He had worked out a style between the old rhetoric and the new colloquialism. His speech had been so direct that the Queen had said that unless it were modified he could not remain in the Cabinet. Now, in 1900, though not Prime Minister, he was the most powerful member of the Cabinet and determined to capitalize success in war as a party majority. He did not feel inclined to undertake the responsibility of a settlement without a popular mandate.[124] A General Election was to turn on the personality of a single Minister, who was not the Prime Minister.[125] Salisbury came round with reluctance to the opinion that it was expedient and necessary to do what he disliked. Chamberlain's word to the nation on the eve of the polls was " patriotism before politics."[126] The implied antithesis was ominous for representative Government in the new century.

We have considered in some detail how governments were changed between 1880 and 1906. The working of the Cabinets in the same period must be briefly considered. In 1880, Gladstone was no longer the law-giver of an obedient Cabinet, but the moderator between forces that clashed violently on nearly every issue of politics. The Queen looked to the Whigs, Granville and Hartington, to blanket his fires. Gladstone himself understood little more than the Queen, the basis of

140

the electoral verdict. He formed his Cabinet, three-fourths of Whigs and one-fourth of Radicals, while the Liberal Party in the country was three-fourths Radical and one-fourth Whig. Hartington, the Whig leader, only held on at the War Office because he felt that his resignation would mean Radical leadership. He was " terribly sick of office and seldom found himself in real agreement with his colleagues."[127] Granville was intriguing with the Queen as to the best moment to turn Gladstone out. On the other side were the Radical twins, Dilke and Chamberlain. Gladstone was, with great difficulty, persuaded that he must admit Chamberlain (aged forty-two). Dilke was not included, but was kept informed by Chamberlain of everything that went on. " In the matter of leakages," wrote Gladstone, " our State is little short of disgraceful." Had not Chamberlain and Dilke had an unusual influence with the Press, and, behind them, the power of the Radical caucus, they could not have held their own for five years against a Cabinet of peers. After the passage of the Reform Bill in 1884, this Cabinet was in dissolution. It seemed like a man afflicted with epilepsy, and each fit was worse than the last.

The Salisbury Cabinet, 1886-92, taxed the resources of its Premier. In the formation of their Cabinets, Prime Ministers must play a subtle part. They must note the exacting sense of political proprieties ruling in the small world of clubs, deal with voracious appetites for power— when a Government was being formed the Carlton Club resembled the Zoo at feeding-time[128]—placate the prejudices of the Queen, political and personal, and adjust an unwritten constitution without disaster to a changing social order. For Salisbury the problems were more than usually complex. He felt that the country was " on the inclined plane leading from the position of Lord Hartington to that of Mr. Chamberlain, and so to the depths over which Mr. Henry George rules supreme."[129] Gladstone's conversion to Home Rule had lost him and secured to Salisbury, the Queen, society, the great Whig families, and the Radical Chamberlain. Salisbury thought that the Government should have been formed by Hartington. This leader of the Liberal Unionists, a sportsman whose leisure was mostly spent in the hunting-field, at his club, or on the racecourse, embodied for a time the feeling that justice to Ireland must not mean injustice to one-third of her population.[130] But Hartington would not form a Government, nor would he join the Cabinet, because to have done so would have left Chamberlain with so small a following, that he might have slid back into Gladstonianism.[131] The conflicting claims of his aged and shakey team forced Salisbury to take the double burden of the Foreign Office and the Premiership, so that the Government suffered by having a peer

141

Prime Minister absorbed in foreign affairs, while Smith, its leader in the Commons, was unable to control a distracted party. The revolt and resignation of Randolph Churchill, who as leader of the Tory democrats was as much a thorn in the side of Salisbury as Chamberlain had been to Gladstone, opened a place for Goschen as the accredited representative of Liberal Unionist opinion.

Salisbury himself " was by temperament and opinion, incapable of becoming a great law-maker. He did not believe in any good to be effected by inspired ventures in legislation. Legal provision had to be made for the accommodation of existing institutions to the constantly changing social conditions of the people ; practical evils had to be remedied as they appeared."[132] " To those who know English politics well," he wrote, " they are not attractive " ; their highest rewards confer no real power. Their strongest men have to carry out ideas that are not their own."[133] In 1886 Hicks-Beach wrote to him, " I confess much doubt whether the country can be governed nowadays by persons holding opinions which you and I should call even moderately Conservative. But I feel pretty certain that the only chance of its being so governed is by those who hold such opinions combining to do so."[134] So we find the Salisbury Government under the influence of Chamberlain carrying out much of the Radical legislation which Gladstone had regarded with distrust : the extension of local government to counties and free education, and measures to keep agricultural workers on the land.[135]

The Gladstone Cabinet of 1892 was one of the strangest in English history. The Queen accepted him as Prime Minister for a refusal might have increased his power. But the Grand Old Man was, at eighty-two, " a very alarming outlook." She would, she said, in no way " interfere in the formation of this iniquitous " Government. Through the Prince of Wales, she persuaded Rosebery to take the Foreign Office and vetoed the inclusion of either Dilke or Labouchere. The Cabinet included Morley as Chief Secretary for Ireland, Campbell-Bannerman as Secretary of State for War, Asquith at the Home Office and Sir Edward Grey as Under-Secretary for Foreign Affairs. In his diary, Sir Algernon West has left us a picture of this Cabinet, Gladstone with the doors of the senses gradually closing, Rosebery, incapable of co-operating with anyone, Harcourt, rowdy and quarrelsome. In the Commons, even with the support of the Irish—who were now divided into two groups—it had a bare majority of forty. In the Lords there was an overwhelming majority against it. When the Home Rule Bill arrived there, though the shooting season was in full swing, 419 peers were present to defeat its forty-one supporters.

Patriotism was more than grouse.

In 1892 Gladstone had sent the Queen a memorandum on the House of Lords which she had found " very curious." He pointed out that on the three previous occasions he had been in Office his party had been largely, though unequally, represented in all orders of the community ; that now, though Liberal views were supported by a majority of the English-speaking people, they were hardly at all represented, and were imperfectly known in the powerful circles with which the Queen had personal intercourse. There was a widening gap between the upper and more numerous classes. The present Government had a bare tenth of the membership of the Lords and possessed not one acre in fifty.[136]

Rosebery, who was sent for by the Queen on her own iniative to succeed Gladstone, described his own difficulties in a letter to the Queen. " He has inherited from his predecessor a policy, a Cabinet and a Parliament, besides a party of groups one of which is aimed against himself. All this is kept in existence by a narrow majority which may at any moment break away. He, himself, is only able to guide this tumultuous party through a leader, bitterly hostile to himself and ostensibly indifferent to the fate of the Government. Lord Rosebery in the meantime is shut up in a House almost unanimously opposed to his Ministry and for all political purposes might as well be in the Tower of London."[137] The relations between Harcourt and Rosebery were so strained that in the end they only communicated through a third party. Harcourt complained that he was expected to accept beforehand and defend a policy of the Prime Minister and Foreign Secretary in the Lords without having been consulted beforehand ;[138] that the situation of a leader of the House of Commons called upon to defend appointments of which he knew nothing and did not approve was impossible.[139] He told Rosebery that the Secretary for Foreign Affairs ought to be in the House of Commons and that the leader of the House of Commons should have constant opportunity of communication with him. He complained that all those on whom depended the issue of peace or war—the Prime Minister, the Foreign Secretary, the Admiralty and the Colonies were in the Lords.[140] Rosebery as Prime Minister, was not pleased when Harcourt asked that he should be able to make independent decisions in the House of Commons, see all official despatches, have some control over patronage, and that a Cabinet should be called at his request.[141] Rosebery and Harcourt, being poles asunder on the fundamentals of government, could not make the adjustments that Disraeli and Northcote, and to a less extent Salisbury and Smith, had achieved. The days of a peer Prime Minister were numbered.

143

Imprisoned in the Lords, Rosebery was plagued by the Queen. She had her own views "as to the Constitution that was fifty-seven years ago delivered into her hands" and found some of Lord Rosebery's views " Radical to a degree, almost Communistic." At one time he had respectfully to refuse to admit the need for the Queen's sanction before submitting a question to a popular audience, for " such a principle would tend to make the Sovereign a party in all the controversies of the hour and would compromise its neutrality."[142]

In the Salisbury Cabinet of 1895 the Conservatives, old Whigs, and Radical imperialists formally coalesced. What in 1885 seemed impossible—Salisbury, Goschen and Chamberlain in the same Cabinet —was secured. But Cabinet making was a delicate task. The high Tories complained that deserving Conservatives were sent empty away, while Liberal Unionists and the Birmingham gang seized the loaves and fishes.[143] Devonshire was offered the Foreign Office, but preferred to be Lord President of the Council; Chamberlain, invited to be Chancellor of the Exchequer, preferred the Colonial Office; Goschen went to the Admiralty; Hicks-Beach became Chancellor of the Exchequer because he was, after Balfour, the only debater fitted for the House of Commons; Lansdowne was made Secretary for War because he had served under Cardwell; James wanted to be Lord Chancellor, but because of Halsbury's claims he had to be content with the Chancellorship of the Duchy. The Cabinet contained eight peers, three of them the heads of great families, but its inner life was determined by Salisbury, Balfour and Chamberlain.[144] Salisbury, aloof in the Lords, " did not exercise the control over his colleagues either in or out of the Cabinet that Beaconsfield did " ; he " frequently allowed important matters to be decided by a small majority of votes, even against his own opinion " and " left his colleagues very much to themselves unless they consulted him."[145]

The development of imperialism and the course of the South African War made Chamberlain by 1899 stronger than the Prime Minister and probably stronger than all his colleagues together.[146] He was able to secure the Khaki election of 1900. In 1902 Salisbury resigned and Hicks-Beach decided to leave office with him. The Duke of Devonshire, who had three times been offered the Premiership, was now passed over because he was a Liberal Unionist. Chamberlain was laid up by a serious cab accident and the King sent for Balfour.[147] It required all the powers of his office for Balfour to get changes he thought essential against the opposition of his colleagues on the one hand and before the return of the Liberals on the other. Coached by Morant he secured the compromise of the Education Act of 1902; he supported the

Irish Land Purchase Scheme of 1903 and the Licensing Act of 1904; he was responsible for the Committee of Imperial Defence; backed Lansdowne at the Foreign Office when he concluded an alliance with Japan and the Anglo-French Convention of 1904. It was Balfour's concern for the reorganization of the military and naval forces and for an understanding with France and Japan which led him to remain in office long after a dissolution had become necessary. The centrifugal nationalism of the colonies had thrown Chamberlain back on Imperial preference.[148] By 1903 the Cabinet was divided between the Free Trade policy of Ritchie, the Chancellor of the Exchequer, and the Chamberlain programme of Tariff Reform. In his situation Balfour defended a policy of agreement to differ so long as party convenience required. Though Hicks-Beach said that Chamberlain's tariff proposals had divided, and if persisted in would destroy the Unionist Party,[149] Balfour claimed the right to an open mind. " I should consider that I was ill performing my duty, I will not say to my party, but to the House and to the country if I were to profess a settled conviction where no settled conviction exists."[150] He wrote to Devonshire, " whatever be the merits of the questions . . . why should the fact that some of us differ and many of us hesitate about it, break up or tend to break up the present Cabinet . . . our resignations must produce an immediate dissolution and this is not a felicitious moment for putting the party fortunes to the hazard. . . . I think in this connection we ought to bear in mind that through many Parliaments Catholic Emancipation was an open question in the Tory Party; and a generation later the same was true of Free Trade. I suppose that Dis-establishment occupies at the present moment a similar position among the Radicals. I cannot conceive why we are not to allow ourselves a liberty of difference which we allow to our opponents and which is in strict conformity with constitutional tradition. . . . It should be agreed that the question is an open one; that we should be allowed officially to collect information upon the effects of the proposed policy, that we should discourage explicit statements of individual opinion."[151] In September, 1903, he summarily dismissed Balfour of Burleigh and Ritchie, though he had, unknown to the Cabinet, Chamberlain's offer of resignation in his pocket. The next day two other Free Traders, Hamilton and the Duke of Devonshire also resigned. Balfour then accepted Chamberlain's resignation and persuaded the Duke of Devonshire to withdraw his. But later, when Chamberlain and the Free Traders complained not unnaturally that they had been tricked, Devonshire felt compelled to resign.[152] Balfour was determined to hold power until the treaty with Japan was signed. He was determined to reorganize the War

Office and to establish the Committee of Imperial Defence before Campbell-Bannerman should take office. So he carried out the " fine idea of Joe freely operating outside, Arthur sympathizing with him and co-operating inside and Mr. Austen holding the keys of the safe."[153]

By December, 1905, Balfour could no longer avoid resignation or dissolution. He resigned hoping that the dissensions of the Liberals would be their destruction. Most of the constitutional experts were agreed that precedents were against the formation of a Government by an Opposition in the last months of an expiring Parliament. But Campbell-Bannerman accepted office. " Personally," he said, " I am strongly against refusing office ; it would be ascribed to divisions or to cowardice . . . refusal is not in keeping with the clamour we have made for the last year or two."[154] At the election of 1906 the long Conservative reign was ended. In the next eight years the Constitution was to be tested to the verge of civil war as a political order nursed in tradition but apt for every revolution reason might commend.

1906-14 : It is impossible to give even in outline the political events which tested and moulded the pre-war constitution between 1906 and 1914. For the first time since Napoleon the condition of foreign affairs imposed on those responsible for defence preparations for a war which might involve the life of the English political and economic system. A Foreign Secretary had to negotiate in a European anarchy for a democracy which could only decide for peace or war on the very eve of Armageddon. The Ministers for the Army and Navy had to secure the essential minimum for safety from a Parliament preoccupied with problems of social reconstruction. For the first time since the hungry 'forties there was a failure of real wages to rise. With the collapse of the landed aristocracy the issue between competitive industrialism and the elements of social justice was clearly set. But the issues of war or peace and of social reform or social revolution could not be squarely faced until the Irish questions had been dealt with. A political history would have to lay bare the interplay between the problem of the Lords and Ireland and the political education of an industrial proletariat under the shadow of a deepening European crisis. Here we can only consider the nature of the Constitution as shown by the crisis of the Parliament Act, of the Home Rule Bill which followed, and the difficulties of a democracy in the issue of war or peace.

The formation of the Campbell-Bannerman Government in 1905 was a fine example of the complexities of that art. Balfour had no doubt that the King would send for Campbell-Bannerman as the recognized leader of the Liberal Party since 1898[155] in the Commons. Spencer, the leader in the Lords, was followed by only about twenty peers.[156] Edward VII had already established friendly personal relations with the Premier-to-be.[157] In forming his Cabinet Campbell-Bannerman had to harmonize a diversity of creatures. Grey, Asquith and Haldane considered that effective government required that Campbell-Bannerman himself should not lead in the Commons. Campbell-Bannerman had mentioned to Asquith that " that ingenious person R. B. Haldane proposed to dump him on the Upper House."[158] When he refused this courteous elimination there was a possibility that Grey, Asquith and Haldane might refuse office. But Asquith wrote to Haldane, " Grey is resolved to refuse office. I have come to the conclusion that it is my duty to accept. If I refuse to go in, either the attempt to form a Government fails or a weak Government would be formed entirely or almost entirely of our colour." Grey's real difficulty was to join a Government in which Rosebery was not included. But he was persuaded by Acland that he ought not to imperil the whole Liberal cause.[159] With the Foreign Office (Grey) and the War Office (Haldane) held in suspense Cabinet making " was attended with more than ordinary difficulties. Alternative plans had to be made on the assumption that the two recalcitrants would come in or that they would stay out."[160] Campbell-Bannerman remained in the Commons, but with Asquith at the Treasury, Haldane at the War Office and Grey at the Foreign Office the Liberal Imperialists were strongly entrenched. Among the new men were Lloyd George, who as the President of the Board of Trade was to vivify that office as Chamberlain had vivified the Colonial Office ; Birrell at the Board of Education ; Sidney Buxton at the Post Office. Outside the Cabinet as Under-Secretaries of State were McKenna, Winston Churchill and Herbert Samuel.

The election of 1906, on the surface a victory for Free Trade and Nonconformity, was at bottom a victory for a new industrial democracy.[161] " Unless I am greatly mistaken," wrote Balfour to Knollys, " the election of 1906 inaugurates a new era."[162] " Something more than the ordinary party change is going on before our eyes, and I do not think the full significance of the drama can be understood without reference to the Labour and Socialist movements on the Continent."[163] The new Government did not singe a king's beard, but they caused his eyebrows to rise when they " ' presented him ' with a gracious speech promising twenty-two Bills in the new session."[164] To its three most contentious Bills—Education, Trade Unions, Plural Voting—the Government added a Merchant Shipping Bill and private members a dozen more, of which some, like the Land Tenure Bill, were adopted and pushed forward by the Government. Innumerable committees and commissions were appointed to explore Canals and Waterways, the Feeding of School Children, the Miners' Eight-Hour Day, Metropolitan Police, Vivisection, the Welsh Church and Small Holdings.[165] For a long time it was unusual to meet anyone in London who was not a member of some committee of investigation. But Governments do not live by research alone. And Oppositions also serve who only stand and wait. For the Unionists the resources of the Constitution were not yet exhausted. " There has certainly never been a period in our history in which the House of Lords will be called upon to play a part at once so important, so delicate and so difficult," wrote Balfour to Lansdowne.[166] The Government " will bring in Bills in a much more extreme form than the moderate members of their Cabinet probably approve : the moderate members will trust to the House of Lords cutting or modifying the most outrageous provisions; the left wing of the Cabinet, on the other hand . . . will be consoled by the reflection that they will be gradually accumulating a case against the upper house." And so it came to pass. But the ultimate results of this cool advice to exploit the Constitution were to be a transformation Mr. Balfour did not foresee. The Lords were led to challenge the new democracy and its leaders on ground where the challenger was certain to be destroyed. Campbell-Bannerman said that Balfour's course " left no room for doubt . . . that the second chamber was being utilized as a mere annexe of the Unionist Party."[167] It was said that Balfour signalled to it to come to his rescue, not on great emergencies affecting national interest, but on measures which touched only the ordinary interests of the Unionist Party.[168] Lloyd George said it was not the watchdog of the Constitution but Mr. Balfour's poodle. For a time the poodle could bite. In a Cabinet which contained the Catholic Lord Ripon and the Nonconformist Lloyd George unanimity on educational policy was not possible.[169] Lloyd George spoke of the Education Act of 1902 as " riveting the clerical yoke on thousands of parishes."[170] As English opinion was not ripe for the abolition of State religious instruction, and as provision for all the sects was not possible because they were so numerous, the Government's Education Bill in 1906 was its most difficult task. The House of Lords so transformed the Bill that for the Commons to have recovered its original form would have been a labour of weeks.[171] The Lords were persuaded that the Cabinet dare not dissolve when the issue might be made one of Church versus Chapel instead of Lords versus People. Though Campbell-Bannerman was for dissolution the majority of the Government were against risking their majority.

148

The Lords destroyed the Education Bill but they passed the Trades Dispute Bill of 1906, though it was a private members' bill which the Government accepted in place of one prepared by their own advisers. The new bill gave clearer recognition to the right of combination and the liberty to strike. The Lords rejected a Plural Voting Bill, a Land Valuation Bill and a Licensing Bill, in spite of the intercession of the King and Lord Milner. They accepted from Asquith and Lloyd George a Workmen's Compensation, the Eight-Hour Day, Trade Boards and Labour Exchanges.

Asquith had been summoned by the King to succeed Campbell-Bannerman in 1908. Lloyd George took Asquith's place as Chancellor of the Exchequer. Court circles felt that they were at last over-whelmed by the middle classes.[172] By the end of 1908 Asquith felt that the Lords had effectively blocked the road in education, temperance and land reform, Welsh Disestablishment and Irish Home Rule. Then the Lloyd George Budget of 1909 tempted the Lords to their destruction. Its provision for a more steeply graded income tax and for taxing the landlords was necessitated by the needs of the Navy. But because the former might remove the revenue motive of a tariff and the Land Value Duties would require a complete survey and valuation of their land the peers, who were more property-minded than politically inspired, opposed it.[173] In vain their intellectual leaders counselled caution. Hicks-Beach, Cromer and Balfour of Burleigh because they were Free Traders were not listened to.[174] In vain the latter pointed out that though they had an abstract right to reject a Budget, " usage, precedent, national convenience were arrayed against its exercise." " Finance," he told them, " differs from all other legislation in this respect. If a Bill is rejected either by the Lords or by disagreement the *status quo* remains and survives . . . it is not so in finance. A referendum in finance would destroy the control of the House of Commons over the Government." The Lords, blind to the fact that their rejection of the Budget would enable Lloyd George to pillory them as rich and selfish irresponsibles, rejected the Budget by 350 to 75 (30th November, 1909). The Constitution was now to be tested for its capacity for fundamental self-amendment. It fell to the Prime Minister Asquith to manipulate the complex conventions of the Constitution so that neither Edward VII in the Court, nor Lloyd George in the constituencies should strain the delicate fabric to collapse.

Before the rejection of the Budget by the Lords Edward VII had seen the Opposition peers with the agreement of Asquith. So anxious was the King that the Budget should pass that he asked Asquith to sanction his promising them a dissolution in January, 1910. This would have given away the principle at stake and Asquith refused.[175] After the rejection Parliament was dissolved, and at the election in January the Liberals lost a hundred seats, but the Government, so long as it was supported by the forty Labour and eighty-two Irish members, had a majority of 124. The Government was now dependent for its existence on the Irish and they were determined to destroy the power of the Lords to veto Home Rule. What followed is a classic example of the complex working of Constitutional niceties in time of crisis and of the underlying forces which may destroy a State.

Before the election Asquith knew that Edward VII considered that he would not be justified in creating new peers until after a second General Election. To pledge himself to create peers to pass a Bill dealing with the House of Lords, a Bill which had not even received the assent of the House of Commons, would be a breach of his duty. That the King should place permanently in the hands of the Prime Minister of the day the prerogative to create peers was considered in Court circles to be an outrage.[176] According to Esher, Balfour was of the opinion that as Lansdowne, the leader in the Lords, was pledged to pass the Budget if the Liberals were returned there was no crisis. Asquith knew before the first election that two elections would be necessary if the Lords were to be reformed. The passing of resolutions limiting the Lords veto was the first business of the new session. Asquith had to explain to his followers that he had received no guarantee that the Royal prerogative for the creation of peers to pass a Bill for the reform of the Lords had been given. When the resolutions were passed, he told his followers that " if we do not find ourselves in a position to ensure that that statutory effect will be given to this policy in this Parliament we shall then either resign our offices or recommend a dissolution of Parliament," and he added, " that in no case would we recommend dissolution except under such conditions as will secure that in the new Parliament the judgment of the people as expressed in the election will be carried into law." Asquith was striving to keep the King's name out of politics. At the height of the struggle Edward VII died, and his death was followed by a conference between the parties to find a compromise. But this failed, as it was bound to do. The vital issue was Home Rule, and this could not be settled by any adoption of joint sessions between the two houses, nor were the leaders prepared to settle the Home Rule issue separately by referendum. With the failure of the conference Asquith decided that for the sake of the Monarchy itself a dissolution must take place at once. Had he resigned the Opposition could not have lasted, and a dissolution granted to them would have brought the King into politics. The King was between the devil of the Tory Party who considered him to be their natural head, and the deep sea of the Radical press. On November 11th Asquith saw George V, explaining that he could not advise a second dissolution unless he had reasonable assurance that the King would use his prerogative if the Government secured a sufficient majority. He secured not a guarantee but a hypothetical understanding.[177] Asquith's view of the functions of the Crown were clearly stated. " It is to act upon the advice of the Ministers . . . whether the advice does or does not conform to the private and personal judgment of the Sovereign. . . . It is not the function of a Constitutional Sovereign to act as arbitrator or mediator between rival parties and policies ; still less to take advice from the leaders of both sides with a view to forming a conclusion of his own."

At the election the position of the Government was practically unchanged. The Government was returned with a majority of 126, Labour providing forty-two and the Irish eighty-four. In July, 1911, the Cabinet submitted a Minute to the King that it would be their duty to advise the Crown to exercise its prerogative for the creation of peers. Asquith insisted that he himself and not the King should inform the Opposition, so that there might be no doubt that the responsibility was the Government's. There was a real danger that the Tory Party might regard the King as their natural ally who was deserting them in a crisis.

The Parliament Act was finally passed by the Lords in spite of the efforts of Halsbury, F. E. Smith and Lord Willoughby de Broke to secure its rejection. But it seemed to many of the Conservatives that single chamber Government had been imposed upon England by pressure from Ireland.

The Parliament Act of 1911 provided a temporary settlement of a conflict within the Constitution which had been steadily increasing since 1868. When the Conservative Party realized that the Liberal Party under Gladstone was a trinity of three unequal parts—old Whig, new Radical and Irish patriots—they naturally developed the idea of demanding a dissolution whenever their views and those of the House of Commons conflicted. In the absence of a written constitution embodying a theory of democratic government they had a plausible case. For the vital problem of all constitutions is the procedure to be adopted for securing a peaceful change in the policy or membership of whatever body exercises the supreme power in the State. In the British Constitution, once it became impossible for the Monarch to exercise his or her discretion as to who should be entrusted with the formulation of the policy of the State, the problem was acute. Was the only check to the policy favoured by a majority of the elected House of Commons to be their interpretation of the public mind and their fear of punishment for any indiscretions at a possibly remote election, the very date of which they themselves could determine ? How was the power of the people to cashier their rulers to be secured ? The people elects the legislature ; a majority of the legislature empower some of their number to exercise every power of the State subject only to the limitation that they, the majority, do not object and that the people do not rebel. Further, as the power of the legislature extended to the very framework and fundamental principles of the Constitution itself, it could transform the organs through which the people's will was expressed. This difficulty could be met in part by the theory of the mandate. But there could be no provision that a mandate would be sought on any issue except that which seemed desirable to the party which was seeking a majority when an election did occur. Without a non-elected power in the State the mandate might establish a dictatorship.

In 1868 the House of Lords passed the Irish Church Bill because its principles had been approved by the country at the polls. But their amendments led to a protracted deadlock broken only by negotiations between the two parties, aided by the personal influence of the Queen. In their first use of their newly-discovered weapon the Lords were advised by the skilful Disraeli. After his death in 1881 and the succession of Lord Salisbury the relations between the two houses deteriorated. Even before 1867 Granville, then the Whig leader in the Lords, had found them as hostile to a Liberal policy abroad as to reforms at home. During the Gladstone Government, 1868-74, he had had to recommend an Education Bill and the abolition of university tests in an assembly hostile to any religious equality, the Irish Land Act of 1870, a great scheme of Army reform to those who considered that the military forces of the Crown were the natural preserves of the Upper classes. He had had to justify the abolition of purchase by warrant, secret voting, the legal status of Trade Unions and the complete alteration of the structure of the Supreme Court.[178] Over the Reform Bill of 1884 the Lords had hoped to force a dissolution, but Gladstone had refused to dissolve except on their own position in the Constitution.

It was the split on Home Rule in 1886 which made the position of the House of Lords impossible. The number of Liberals in the Lords shrank to pitiable proportions. Not merely was the great majority of the lords opposed to Home Rule. In that they might have claimed to be expressing a national will as opposed to a passing combination of petty interests. But the development of the need for social legislation after 1886 coincided with the development of the House of Commons as a legislative machine that could not endure the brake of privilege the Lords applied.

A new machinery of party organization had been made to meet the new political conditions which the enlargement of the electorate and the spread of popular education produced. Disraeli had some insight into the new art of leadership which was required. Gladstone with conscious skill or unconscious cunning had achieved the arts which leadership requires. But the general attitude of the aristocracy to the new electorate was to be fatal to their order.

A study of the elections which followed the third Reform Bill of 1884 shows that the doctrine of the swing of the pendulum was little more than a comforting superstition held by the Opposition and a bogey by which a Government could discipline rebellious back benchers. The real problem was much more subtle and complex.

It was true that a Government which relied entirely on its record in office to secure the support of the electorate at its next appeal would be likely to suffer disappointment. Benefits conferred would not mean power renewed. It was not the record of the Government, but the occasion of the election which would determine the result. When Disraeli in 1878 did not resign and fight while Peace with Honour still echoed in the public ear, he went down two years later to surprised defeat. Chamberlain, by forcing an election in 1900 while the passions of war were still stirred, secured a second term of office for the Salisbury Government. The most subtle example of this skill in seeking the right moment for electoral victory was the dissolution of 1886. For the Gladstone Government, by refusing to dissolve in 1885 on the technical ground that the constituences were not yet in existence and resigning office to Lord Salisbury, deprived the latter of the advantage of being the Opposition and yet secured the support of the agricultural labourers whom they had enfranchised in 1884. Not only was the occasion for dissolution of the utmost importance ; the nature of the issues and their presentation were found to be all-important. The issues must be simple and as little complicated by detail as possible. Careful preparation of the public for the acceptance of new ideas, and on the other hand sudden appeals to old prejudices in conditions making it difficult for your opponent to mobilize an appeal to reason, were the arts to be mastered by the party agents. In 1886 Gladstone failed because the issue of Home Rule was presented before it had had time to be developed ; in 1906 the Liberal case against Tariff Reform succeeded because it had had full time to be developed. The same election provided a perfect example of the use of political prejudice. Not only was the Conservative Party hampered by a confused presentation of the case for Tariff Reform while the Liberal opposition had ample

153

time to develop the logical appeal of the Cobdenite case ; it also had the misfortune to have arrayed against it the instinctive fears of the populace. The education policy of 1902 had " stirred into life one of the fundamental fears of Protestant England : was ' Rome to be on the rates ? ' " Balfour's Licensing Act of 1904 enabled beery " Mr. Bung the Brewer " to leer from Liberal posters ; prejudice and virtue thus enlisted, Imperial Preference was attacked as threatening a " Dear Loaf " and a return to " the Hungry Forties.' " Finally, as a crowning mercy to the Liberal cause, the introduction of indentured Chinese labour on the Rand gave their supporters a chance to denounce a threatened slavery.

CHAPTER VI

MACHINERY OF ADMINISTRATION, 1870-1914

Efforts of the departments concerned with Defence, Health, Home, Trade and others to adjust themselves—Politics and administration—The Treasury—Tradition—The problems of Civil Service recruitment and promotion—The development of delegated legislation.

THE problem of the organization of the defence departments was radically changed by the shift in the economic forces which pressed upon the world and by the changes in the political and social structure of England at which we have glanced. In the Army the anomaly of a royal claim to more than titular supremacy, the anachronism of ranks recruited from criminals and officers too gentlemanly to acquire professional skill, could not remain. But the changes could only be brought about by the methods which the Constitution provided, and in the spirit which inspired the political parties and their leaders.

The swiftness and precision of the Prussian victories of 1866 over Austria and in 1870 over France produced sufficient anxiety about army administration to secure that the Cardwell reforms were carried through. By the War Office Act of 1870 the Secretary of State for War secured formal recognition of his responsibility for all aspects of army administration. The Army Enlistment Act of 1870 introduced a " system of short service with the colours, followed by a period in the reserve, which provided the army with a pool of trained men, who could be recalled for service at any moment."[1] Humanity had first appeared in the treatment of soldiers after the Crimean War, when the Prince Consort secured separate quarters for wives and children of common soldiers in barracks.[2] In 1871 the enlistment of criminals was forbidden and the discharge of men of bad character authorized ; the abolition of the system of purchase of commissions killed the conception that only those who were possessed of property could be trusted to defend the honour and liberty of those who had none.

The struggle over the Army Regulation Bill which proposed the abolition of purchase shows the obstacle which constitutional niceties and political prejudice might oppose to administrative reform. The Commander-in-Chief in the Lords was opposed to the course

155

recommended by the Secretary of State for War in the Commons. The delaying action of the Lords was met by Gladstone advising the Queen to cancel the warrant under which purchase had been made legal. The Lords were then compelled to pass the Bill in order to secure for the officers concerned the compensation which it provided. The struggle had a wider significance than its bearing on army reform. The opposition of a group of colonels in the Commons led them to try to baffle the majority by mere consumption of time—an early experiment in parliamentary obstruction; while the Peers were brought sharply into conflict with the Commons on an almost naked class issue.[3] The discipline of the Army, Gladstone said, was " a subject so grave, so delicate and associated at such a multitude of points with the interests and feelings of the governing class, that it should be as little as possible exposed to the influence of parliamentary pressure."[4]

The root difficulty of the division of power between the Commander-in-Chief as representative of the Crown, and the Secretary of State responsible to Parliament, was not fully resolved. " You cannot," wrote Disraeli in 1879, " get a Secretary of War to resist the cousin of the Sovereign with whom he is placed in daily and hourly communication. I tremble when I think what may be the fate of this country if, as is not unlikely, a great struggle occur with the Duke of Cambridge's generals."[5] In 1881 a claim by the Duke of Cambridge that " the command of the Army rested with the Commander-in-Chief as representing the Sovereign," and that he could not be " merged in the Secretary of State " drew from Childers, the Secretary of State for War, a clear statement that the latter was responsible for the exercise of the Queen's prerogative and not a mere financial officer who had " gradually intruded on the province of the Crown by means of the power of the purse."[6] By an Order in Council, February 21st, 1888, the work of the War Office was distributed between a military division under the Commander-in-Chief, responsible for everything connected with the efficiency of the soldier, and a civil division under the Financial Secretary, responsible for expenditure and the control of the manufacturing departments.[7] This intense centralization of responsibility by which the Commander-in-Chief alone " would be accountable to the Secretary of State, even for such a matter as the defective design of a heavy gun," could not lead to efficiency,[8] and the Hartington Commission proposed that the War Office be remodelled on the lines of the Board of Admiralty. They wanted the Secretary of State advised by a War Office Council consisting of the heads of the various departments, individually answerable to him for their administrative work; the office of Commander-in-Chief abolished and replaced by a general officer responsible for the command of troops stationed at home, and a Chief of Staff to advise on the fundamentals of military policy as a whole.[9]

To the Queen these " reckless changes and incredibly thoughtless proposals were ' really abominable.' " The evidence given before the Hartington Commission was suppressed " because the difference of opinion in high quarters was so acute as to render publication indiscreet."[10] When the Duke of Cambridge was finally induced to retire in 1895 the new scheme retained the Office of Commander-in-Chief, though with altered duties and responsibilities. Instead of an Army Council as the Hartington Commission had recommended, the Secretary of State was to preside over a War Office Consultative Council composed of the Commander-in-Chief, the Adjutant-General, the Quartermaster-General and the Inspectors-General of Fortifications and Ordnance. The Commander-in-Chief was made the principal adviser of the Secretary of State on all military questions, and military opinion was to be focused by means of an Army Board, presided over by the Commander-in-Chief.

This scheme, for which Campbell-Bannerman was mainly responsible, was an unfortunate compromise. It involved the simultaneous responsibility of the heads of departments to both the Parliamentary and military heads ; the Commander-in-Chief was in an anomalous position, not having full authority over the heads of the military branches for which he was responsible.[11] As neither the Council nor the Army Board had clearly defined responsibilities, it is not surprising that in 1899 Chamberlain dreaded our War Office more than the Boers,[12] or that "military calculations of requirements proved utterly inadequate to meet grossly misjudged situations and betrayed also in their detail a lack of coherent organization or forethought."[13] The Esher Committee of 1904 pointed out that the War Office had been administered from the point of view of peace, and that it was necessary " to make a complete break with the past, and to endeavour to reconstitute the War Office with a single eye to the effective training and preparation of the Military Forces of the Crown for war."[14] The Committee recommended the establishment of an Army Council on similar lines to the Board of Admiralty, but modified to meet the special conditions of the Army ; the creation of a Chief of Staff; and the abolition of the Office of Commander-in-Chief. In 1904 an Army Council was established consisting of seven members (four military and three civilian) with the Secretary of State answerable to Parliament for everything connected with the Army. The Commander-in-Chief was bowed off a scene which he had confused for over half a century and the

Army was at last controlled by a responsible statesman, advised by soldiers.[15]

Compared with the War Office, the Esher Committee thought the Admiralty an administrative paragon. " The Admiralty system is sound in principle. It has been handed down without material change from the period of the great naval wars. It may be said to have been founded on the proved requirements of war. . . . It conforms closely to the arrangements under which the largest private industries are conducted."[16] The Board had been extensively reorganized in 1869, and after some minor changes in 1887 consisted of a First Lord; four Naval Lords (one being controller); the Civil Lord, the Financial and Parliamentary Secretaries, and the Permanent Secretary. The First Lord was head of the department and directly responsible to Parliament. With the coming of steam and steel, even for the Admiralty events took a questionable shape. Naval supremacy in wooden ships, " which took a long time to build; which no Power had the materials to multiply indefinitely, and which once built were serviceable for sixty years," could not suddenly be lost.[17] Steel, steam and many inventions enabled foreign Powers to build on level terms. Great Britain did not originate the important nineteenth-century naval changes. Neither armour nor turrets, or breech-loaders, neither mines nor torpedoes, or submarines were British ideas. The service did not favour inventions.[18] Perhaps their inventiveness was damped by the rigours of Treasury control. The Gladstonian tradition that the cost of a service should be the decisive factor in deciding upon its desirability was there firmly enshrined. Intelligence in experts was not encouraged by politicians. " If soldiers were allowed full scope they would insist on the importance of garrisoning the moon in order to protect us from Mars," said Salisbury.[19] Of the Admiralty Hicks-Beach said, " their experts' way of dealing with subjects deprived me of all confidence in them. . . . I believed their demands were based, not on what was really needed, but upon what they thought they could get us to give."[20] The pressure of Treasury control caused a wasteful struggle for pence when there should have been an expense of thought. " More than half the difficulty between the Admiralty and the War Office arises from personal feelings, distrust and jealousy where there ought to be hearty co-operation and this is really a serious mischief . . . the Admiralty say almost in as many words that the War Department want to do them out of stores."[21] Neither the Army nor the Navy had any organs of thought to relate and co-ordinate their demands on the public purse to the public needs.

After 1870 the self-governing colonies were partly responsible for their own defence, and the development of the steamship by changing conditions for moving troops had altered the basis of strategy.[22] In 1885 a Colonial Defence Committee was organized. In 1890 the Hartington Committee advocated "the formation of a Naval and Military Council which should probably be presided over by the Prime Minister, and consist of the Parliamentary heads of the two services and their principal professional advisers." Campbell-Bannerman was not prepared for a thinking and planning war machine, holding that in this country there was no room for general military policy in the larger and more ambitious Continental sense.[23] In 1894 a conference was held in Downing Street on the co-ordination of the fighting services—Spencer from the Admiralty, Campbell-Bannerman from the War Office and Rosebery, at which the latter introduced what he afterwards considered to have been the germ of the Committee of Imperial Defence.[24] In 1895 Devonshire was asked by Salisbury to preside over a Defence Committee of the Cabinet. The scope of this committee was "ill-defined and uncertain. The War Office and Admiralty and other departments were inclined to refer questions to it as little as possible. . . . It did not often meet, had no permanent secretariat and kept no records. Its functions consisted in settling now and then controversies between the War Office, the Admiralty and the Treasury, which would formerly have led to interminable correspondence or would have been brought before the Cabinet as a whole."[25] In the South African as in the Crimean War the Cabinet had no means of obtaining a reasoned opinion on which to base its policy. In 1901 Balfour established the Committee of Imperial Defence. It consisted of the Prime Minister, the Secretary of State for War, the First Lord of the Admiralty, the Secretary of State for India, the Chancellor of the Exchequer and such persons including the Dominion Prime Ministers —as from time to time the Prime Minister chose to summon. To this fluidity in its composition much of its efficiency and usefulness was due. It was, and remained, not an executive but a consultative body. But it was provided with a secretariat and considered strategical schemes affecting every aspect of imperial defence.[26] It was a committee of this C.I.D., appointed in 1911, which produced the famous war book in which there was worked out for each department every detail of what they must do in the event of war.[27]

The Royal Sanitary Commission of 1869 had urged the need for a strong Government department to deal with Public Health. A timid and unconvinced Cabinet decided to create a new Ministry, the Local Government Board, containing the Public Health powers of the Privy Council, the Local Government Act department of the Home Office and the Poor Law Board itself. " Whether the Government ever intended, as the sanitary enthusiasts were led to believe, to establish a sort of twin Ministry with separate departments for Public Health and Poor Relief under a single political chief cannot now be determined." " The Bill for the constitution of the new authority was originally in the hands of W. E. Forster, Vice-President of the Committee of the Privy Council for Education . . . but education was competing with public health for the attention of the Minister most competent to deal with both." Goschen was promoted to the Admiralty before the measure could be got through Parliament. A weaker and less experienced administrator, J. J. Stansfield, brought in and carried a weaker Bill and became the first President of the Local Government Board. An internecine feud followed between the civil servants of the Poor Law Board interested in Poor Law and those interested in Public Health, in which the latter were worsted.[27a]

There were two functions warring within the bosom of a single department. Sir J. Simon has described how from being an executive officer of the Privy Council he became a mere advisory officer, who could do little or nothing without the sanction of the Secretary of the Board. The Minister backed the Secretary, and the medical adviser went to the wall. In 1876 his branch, " the Medical Department," was broken up and dispersed among the branches of the former Poor Law Board. For nearly half a century the Poor Law side of the Local Government Board maintained its predominance. The Public Health services of the more enterprising local authorities were developed by local Acts, by successive Public Health Acts, Isolation Hospital Acts, Artisans' Dwellings Acts, Sale of Food and Drugs Acts. When, in 1913, the Board of Control succeeded the Lunacy Commissioners in the supervision of persons of unsound mind, they brought out the Public Health aspect of this service and were brought into closer relation with the Local Government Board. From 1911 there was the vast new system of Public Health Insurance under separate Boards of Commissioners for England, Scotland, Ireland and Wales. The Royal Commission on the Poor Law, in 1909, proposed that the Boards of Guardians should be abolished; that the conception of a deterrent Poor Law should be abandoned; and proposed a " vast extension of the best possible provision for the sick from whatever disease they might be suffering; the removal from the Poor Law of all kinds of mental deficiency, from the dangerous lunatic to the feeble-minded." It approved the provision of Employment Exchanges, national pensions for the aged and unemployment insurance.[28] As the new science of medicine and the new demands of a democracy for social services developed, expert medical staffs were attached to many Government departments. The Local Government Board as the department administering the Poor Law was responsible for " a composite system embracing the care of the destitute of all categories, including sick persons, mothers and infants, lunatics, mental defectives, children of school age, and aged persons so far as any of these may happen to be destitute."[29] The National Health Insurance organization supervised the administration of medical and sanatorium benefits, of cash benefits in the form of sickness, disablement and maternity benefits; there was a division of authority between the Board of Education and the Local Government Board in maternity and child welfare. The Privy Council under the Midwives Act, 1902, was responsible for the approval of the rules of the Central Midwives' Board governing the qualification and conduct of midwives. The Home Office supervised the administration of Part I of the Children's Act, 1908, which related to infant life protection. Such a system could not be economical and had an obvious tendency towards departmental rivalry and friction. With the development of public health services in various directions —nursing, diagnosis of disease, medical treatment—it was of great importance that they should be controlled by a single Minister.

The War Office and the departments concerned with health—the lords of death and life—are excellent examples of the way in which the functions of the State in the nineteenth century attached " themselves to the office in which the need for them happened to be first imperatively felt, or which had to provide money for them, or which was the department of the Prime Minister or the Court or whatever power in the State had dealt with them before they were regularly organized." At any time we shall find that some departments will have outgrown the purpose for which they were originally established, while others will have been established hurriedly to meet some passing emergency, without due regard to their permanent duties, or to the relation which those duties might bear to those of existing departments.[30]

The Privy Council, formally the most important, is in practice the least differentiated of the organs of the executive.[31] By 1880 its functions could only be classified alphabetically. It was responsible for assizes, burial boards, charters of boroughs, clergy returns, coinage currency, contagious diseases of animals, convocation, county courts, Dentistry Acts, Education Acts, gas company amalgamations, etc., etc., to the end of the alphabet. The Home Office was the residuary legatee of the departments which had branched off from the original office of the Secretary of State. With the development of the groping collectivism of State legislation after 1870 it was loaded with many cares. Harcourt, in 1883, said that its work had increased five times in twenty years.[32] Early State regulation of industry had been reconciled with individualism on the ground that the powers exercised were merely police powers— the protectors of innocence or the enemies of vice. So the Home Office. was made responsible for the early Factory Acts, the safety and hours of work of women and young persons in factories, industrial diseases, manufacture of explosives, safety in mines. After 1870 it began to be consulted on industrial questions other than safety. It was made responsible for the Workmen's Compensation Act, 1906, the Shop Acts and the Employment of Children Acts. Before 1914 it had acquired responsibility for the protection of wild flowers, advertisements and money lenders. Since 1918 it has acquired Northern Ireland and the tote. The Office of Works was the Cinderella of the Government departments, performing the menial services for all the rest. Rosebery in 1884 refused the Commissionership of Works as he considered it " the least of all the offices, being only a sort of football for contending connoisseurs."[33] This snobbery of office had bad effects on the appearance of London. In 1912 the Office of Works had so over-ridden and ignored the London local authorities that relations between them were practically non-existent.[34] For constitutional reasons the Office of Works was not allowed undivided control of the public estates : the property of the Government was managed by the Office of Works at a dead loss defrayed out of the general pool of taxation and the Crown Lands were managed like any private estate by trustees for the Crown.

The development of the Board of Trade most clearly marks the growth of Government action. Deprived by the triumph of free trade of its powers over commercial policy it became the instrument for whatever regulation of industry the State might undertake. Its growth was swift but unplanned. In 1786 it had seven clerks ; in 1840, thirty ; in 1853, sixty, and by 1914 there were over three thousand. In 1851 the powers of the abortive Railroad Commission 1846-51, were trans-ferred to the Board of Trade. When a large proportion of our merchant ships were found to be " commanded and navigated in a manner reflect-ing discredit on our national intelligence and injurious to the interest of Great Britain " it acquired multifarious duties under the Merchant Shipping Acts (1854). In 1866 the administration of fisheries was transferred to it from the Office of Works. In 1872 it received from the Emigration Commissioners the duty to administer the Passenger Acts. By 1880 it was clear that the Bankruptcy Acts had failed to distinguish between the judicial and administrative aspects of the control of bankruptcy, and in consequence the law's delays had prompted private arrangements in which collusion and fraud were alarmingly prevalent. In 1883 the control of the administrative side of this vital part of a competitive and changing social order was transferred from the courts to the Board of Trade. In the first half of the nineteenth century the method of granting letters patent for inventions and manufactures did not differ from the procedure in other kinds of patents, such as grants for nobility. As late as 1852 every application " passed through nine stages in seven separate offices situated in different parts of the town at a distance from one another, and in all these stages fees were exacted." In 1852 the first Patents Commissioners were appointed ; in 1883 they were swept away and replaced by a Comptroller-General.[35]

As late as 1890 the President of the Board of Trade did not have a leading position in the Cabinet. The Board was an abode of peace for Hicks-Beach when he was too sick to take the Irish Office.[36] After 1886 it became more and more involved in vital issues of industrial organization. In that year the House of Commons adopted a resolution on the motion of Charles Bradlaugh that labour statistics should be collected and published. The same year also the Board of Trade Journal commenced a system of commercial intelligence. The department was well-nourished by statistics, for its statistical branch had been organized by Porter (1832-76), and after 1876 by Giffen. When after 1900 the hitherto steady advance of real wages was stayed, and the social reconstruction of the country after its headlong rush to wealth and power began, the Board of Trade under Lloyd George became one of the most important departments of the State.

Like the Board of Trade the Board of Education too had its origin in a Committee of the Privy Council. The distribution of the first meagre grants in aid of education was given to a committee of the Privy Council appointed in 1839 by Order in Council to avoid discussion in Parliament. By 1847 the " business of the Education committee had absorbed the greater part of the staff of the Privy Council Office."[37] In 1848 although Kay Shuttleworth, the assistant secretary, was really doing the work of an Under-Secretary of State, the members of his department still regarded the clerk to the council as their official head. In 1853 the Northcote and Trevelyan Report remarked of the Education Department of the Privy Council that " to bring together under the charge of a single establishment business of a wholly incongruous character tends not to efficiency but to confusion." In 1865 Lingen, the Permanent Secretary, said that the Council except as a merely consultative body was of no account. Full parliamentary responsibility rested on the Lord President and the Vice-President. The usual practice of the office was that the committee was only convened to ratify what the President and Vice-President had prepared before-hand. But the passion for phantom committees or boards arose from the desire of Governments to avoid awkward questions about the prestige and possible cost of a new department. *Laissez-faire* morality saw to it that any new department of State was only a little one. To grow and blush unseen was the only way to escape a Treasury massacre. In education policy, so great were the passions latent in religious rivalries that it was thought best not to define too closely the character of the Committee of the Council. Although a Department of Education had been advocated by Disraeli in 1855[38] Lowe justified the retention of the Committee on the ground that it was a check against individual corruption or indiscretion. Minutes upon which public money was to be distributed should not, he thought, be left entirely to one Minister. He did not think that the office required a Minister of high rank. " It is not analogous to the Secretary of State's Office ; we do not administer important affairs ; we merely follow the public where it leads and pay out money. That is a much lower occupation altogether than the administration of great transactions which is vested in every Secretary of State."[39] It was convenient too that while the Lord President of the Council could answer for the Committee in the House of Lords the Vice-President could answer in the Commons. Although W. E. Forster, nominally Vice-President, was a real Minister of Education inspiring the great increase of work after the Education Act of 1870, it was not until 1899 that the Department was cut adrift from the Privy Council and set up as an independent Board. This was made possible by the urgent need to bring into some organized relation the shreds and patches of our education system. The Act of 1870 had been passed to remedy the failures of the voluntary system. It seemed that the decay of religion was necessary for the growth of education. An effective compromise between the State and the religious bodies was not secured until 1902. Meanwhile, religion apart, the relation in the curriculum between the rudiments to prevent barbarism and the essentials to make efficient workers and trained industrial leaders had to be decided. In 1886-87 the Education Department laid down that " the course suited to an elementary school is practically determined by the limit of fourteen years of age and may properly include whatever subjects can be effectively taught within that limit." Following this lead many School Boards developed a " higher elementary " education which overlapped with the secondary education provided after 1888 by the new County Councils. The Bryce Commission found that for education other than elementary there were two authorities : the Department of Education, the central authority responsible for the work of the local School Boards ; the Science and Art Department, which financed the technical education provided by the County Councils. It recommended the formation of a " Department of the executive Government presided over by a Minister responsible to Parliament who would obviously be the same Minister to whom the charge of elementary education would be entrusted." This was secured in 1899.

The Treasury was the centre of the administrative machine. The system of audited accounts inaugurated by the Act of 1866 had taken away the unlimited discretion which the Treasury had in the past enjoyed and blindly used. An enlightened tyrant replaced a capricious despot. For the system of reports, prepared by the Comptroller and Auditor-General and considered by the Public Accounts Committee of the House of Commons, not only told the Treasury what the departments were doing, but subjected the Treasury itself to the discipline of impartial audit. But the traditional antagonism between the Treasury and the departments was not removed until after 1914-18.

In 1887 Sir R. E. Welby, then Permanent Secretary to the Treasury, considered that " the theory of the control exercised by the Treasury was complete." He did not know " in what sense it could be improved by formal power or by any formal document."[40] The essence of the theory lay in the distinction drawn between policy and finance. The Treasury was " responsible for financial order throughout the service " . . . it had " to give its assent to every measure . . . of every kind which was proposed and which had for result the increase or tendency to increase the public expenditure."[41] This right of the Treasury to determine what the departments of State might spend rested upon an unbroken principle which had the force of law. By that principle the Treasury possessed the power to determine by what means the controlling authority of the Crown over the public expenditure could best be maintained, and its decision as to what expenditure was or was not sufficiently authorized was final and without appeal.[42] But this power of the Treasury was purely financial. " From the moment it interfered in any shape or kind with policy it was departing from its proper sphere."[43] The Treasury could compel a department to state a prima facie case for any proposed change which involved an increase of expenditure and if that case were unsatisfactory the Treasury could compel reference to the Chancellor of the Exchequer and through him to the Cabinet.[44] This power of the Treasury by which " all acts of administration requiring money " came before the Treasury " as a sort of shadow " gave it control also over all questions as to the staff required to carry out the work of the departments.[45]

165

It is obvious that skill and patience were needed to divide the substance of policy from its financial shadow. Unless there was the closest co-operation between the departments and the Treasury, they would fail to agree where the division lay. The officials responsible for advising the Chancellor of the Exchequer on the financial aspects of proposed policy, were also responsible for advising him in his criticisms of the policy of his colleagues in relation to the general financial policy of the country. Antagonism between the Treasury and the departments existed throughout the nineteenth century. The struggle of Peel to prune away the vested inefficiencies of eighteenth-century departments had passed into the Gladstonian tradition that to take care of the pence was policy enough. This was a mere shadow of the underlying conflict between the technique of business with its preoccupation with costs, and the eighteenth-century tradition that the patronage of gentlemen was at once the defence of the privileges of their order and of the liberties of common men. After 1870 this contest between patronage and efficiency became a contest between the policy of *laissez-faire* and a new collectivism.

The antagonism between the Treasury and the departments caused serious inefficiency. For the Treasury " did not interpose their veto at the beginning of a policy when they might prevent it, but at the tail of the policy when they can only spoil it."[46] So long as there was no close co-operation between the Treasury and the departments the former could not initiate reforms ; it could only criticize reforms which involved increased expenditure. It adopted the policy of automatically reducing the estimates of a department as a blind way to encourage economy. It used to cut down the education estimates by £10,000.[47] This irritating hint to departments to think again led them to think ahead, asking more than they need and not reducing expenditure when they might. The Treasury could not resist an application for expenditure from a powerful administrative department strongly represented in the Cabinet. It was forced to secure economies by resisting administrative reforms which involved an initial cost, by cheese-paring on the salaries of civil servants, particularly the lower grades, and by resisting the development of new departments. It was the constant business of the Treasury when any new proposal was made " to see if they could not suggest something else which was cheaper."[48]

So long as policy and finance were regarded as two antagonistic powers, two incompatible loyalties, there could be no sound finance. The special difficulties of army finance brought the clearest statement of the principles involved. " There are two totally different conceptions of financial control . . . the first and more or less traditional one, based on constitutional analogies, is that administrative departments are to be distrusted, watched, and checked, and the function of finance . . . is confined to watching, criticizing and checking their expenditure. . . ." This means the " creation of two twin antagonistic powers . . . the expenditure which should be directed solely to secure efficiency tends to degenerate into extravagance, and economy which should check waste to result in incomplete efficiency. . . . The second, and more modern notion of financial control, means the union of finance and administration so that financial consideration may attend and determine administrative policy from its inception as well as control it during its progress, and review it in anticipation of each new financial year. The latter theory . . . attributes higher functions and a more real and profitable control to finance than the older and more limited theory of its functions appropriate to times of imperfect administrative organization. . . . The one would make finance a mere critical division of . . . administration the other recognizes the function of finance as that of governing the whole policy of administration."[49] This policy of co-operation between the Treasury and the departments in the common and related duties of efficiency and economy was reaffirmed by the Haldane Report of 1918. It said that " the superiority of the spending departments in knowing what is required for the execution of their several services, in accordance with the policy with regard to them which has been determined by Parliament or the Government, must necessarily limit the scope of any useful exercise of the restrictive authority of the Chancellor of the Exchequer. On the other hand, the wider experience and expert knowledge which his department should possess, not of all the details of each particular service, but of all its financial incidents and implications, and of the methods by which administrative efficiency can be ensured and increased will enable the department of finance usefully to criticize the methods of other departments."[50]

The decision to recruit the Civil Service by competitive examination was the start of its reorganization. In 1854 it was a fragmentary and disjointed service of some 16,000 officials distributed among departments whose relations to one another were as remote and prickly as those of separate States. Over this Balkanized service the Treasury exercised only an uneasy suzerainty. The confusion was due to the needs of an oligarchic constitution in a changing world. Aristocracies often retain an administrative confusion as a tribute to their own antiquity and a defence against the probe of vulgar curiosity. Many nineteenth-century administrators took the same pleasure in the nebulosities of their departments that a second-rate lawyer takes in obscurity of the law by which his own importance is magnified and his

167

pay increased. To the confusion inherited from a past unswept by revolution, there was added the chaos of rapid and unco-ordinated growth due to the creation of departments in response to casual emergencies, when neither political principles nor financial policy would permit a systematic plan.

The essential problem of staffing was to decide whether the Civil Service should be one or many. Was the Civil Service to be made into a unit so that the separate departments might think themselves to be merely sections of a single service, or were the critics of the Northcote and Trevelyan Report right when they claimed that the Civil Service " was a thing so heterogeneous in its nature that it required the application of special rules and principles suitable to its different parts ?" Was each department to have its own system of recruitment or was there to be a system common to the whole Civil Service ?

Owing to the independent action of the different departments there was by 1874 a chaos of functions, a chaos of grades and a chaos of rates of pay among the personnel of the service. " There were utterly incongruous arrangements as to number, classes, rates of pay and prospects of promotion in the several departments and in the various offices within the same department. The advancement of any particular member of the service was governed not so much by his ability or conduct as by the accidental circumstances of his having originally entered in one office rather than in another." Instead of the two classes of civil servants, those responsible for policy and those trained for routine work common to the whole service, which the report of 1853 had proposed, there had developed a litter of shattered grading schemes. A continuous struggle was necessary if the ideal of the service as a profession with definite prospects was to be retained against the tendency to vary the conditions of work and rates of pay in every department. For this tendency there were obvious reasons rooted in the nature of Government service.

The report of 1853 had argued that only by having two separate and distinct schemes of examination, for two separate and distinct grades of clerk, could the State offer a definite career and avoid the waste of using men of ability on the drudgery of the routine work of an office. This principle of separate recruitment for policy and routine work, was bound up with another, namely, that the State should gather the fruits of the educational system as they matured. Such were the imperfections of the English educational system that the Government, by its competitive examinations, recruited men whose potential capacity was greater than they had had any opportunity to develop at the age when economic necessity compelled them to sit. Boys were taken into the service for routine work who, but for the imperfections of the educational system might a few years later have competed for entrance to the policy-forming grade. In private enterprise the handicap of an imperfect educational opportunity may disappear in the rough and tumble of competition. But the State was pledged to offer a career with definite prospects to the recruits into each grade. So the method of recruitment by competitive examination raised the awkward problem, how to provide for promotion within the service from a class recruited at one stage of the educational system to a class recruited at another, without either damaging the attractiveness of the higher grades to the best minds that the universities could produce, and without giving such discretion to the heads of departments as might threaten once more a development of patronage.

It was not merely a question of providing for the recruitment of the right proportion of entrants to two grades and their subsequent relations within the service. The Civil Service quickly became an organization too complex to be run by a simple division of labour between a policy and a routine grade of clerks. As the functions of the State were extended the structure of the service became more complex. Between the civil servant responsible for policy and those who did the routine work, there was inserted an Intermediate grade who did the executive and audit work required in the new departments set up to run complex social services ; and below the routine grade boy and girl clerks were recruited in increasing numbers to do the manipulative work of the departments. This changing character of Civil Service work interacted in a complex way with the changes which were taking place in the educational system.

The first demand for a division of the service into policy-forming and routine grades was met by a classification of the service into First and Second division clerks. But by 1890 the State was recruiting from the elementary schools a group of boy clerks below the Second division to do the increased routine work of the State, though in so doing they were creating blind-alley occupations. By 1912 the development of the new social services created a demand for executive officers and to secure them, an Intermediate class was inserted between the First and Second divisions, recruited from among the ablest pupils of the secondary schools who, for economic reasons, could not go to a university. Further, while it has been held desirable to use general classes common to the whole service in all departments wherever possible, so that the conditions of pay and the prospects of promotion might be as clear and wide as possible, such simplification had not been possible. Of the three classes into which Civil Service work came to be divided—

administrative, executive, and clerical—the proportions in which they were required varies widely in different departments. In some there was no place for administrative grades, in others no place for executive. Special departmental classes were created because in some branches of clerical work a supervisory grade was required at a lower point in the organization than in others. Complications were caused by the sudden creation of new departments. This often meant the recruiting of staff outside the normal examination system and the assimilation afterwards of some of the recruits surprisingly high in the service. Further, there was a steady mutation of grades due to the action of the Treasury. For the Treasury was often tempted to press for a departmental class (paid on a lower scale) for new duties. The temporary economy could cause discontent in the service because it obstructed the channels of promotion and made it difficult for new entrants to estimate their prospects.

From the very beginning of the competitive system there was no shortage of candidates for Government service. But once a man was in the service he found that he had given hostages to fortune because there might be little demand for his services in the open market. The conditions of their service might be modified and it might not pay them to protest. Until the development of Whitleyism after the war of 1914-18, all negotiations could only take place through the head of their department. The Treasury was not prepared to recognize a trade union structure or the technique of collective bargaining. It exercised a steady pressure for economy in administration. The principles of permanence and pensions designed to secure the freedom of the Civil Service from patronage made it chary of " establishing " more civil servants than was absolutely necessary. It secured the recruitment of temporary or unestablished civil servants for work which was not clearly permanent. These were often kept on as temporaries long after they should have been established. By 1914 nearly 50 per cent. of the Civil Service consisted of unestablished grades. The chaotic organization of the service made it difficult for the Treasury, even had it wished to do so, to secure any precise relation between remuneration and service. In the lower grades the wage paid barely reached subsistence level. In the higher grades, in return for undoubted privileges of security and a pension, the civil servant was expected to forego claims for overtime which would have been given in private enterprise. However pressing the grievance of a particular grade the Treasury was reluctant to remove it because of the possible demand for proportional changes from the other grades. As the scale of State activity grew the Treasury was forced more and more to make the conditions of pay and service follow those of commerce. It could not allow the conditions within the service to differ too widely from those prevailing in private enterprise. As the Civil Service was neither a caste above suspicion nor an order which had renounced the world ; as it did not live of its own nor by the proceeds of private charity but by those of compulsory taxation, a relativity (blessed word) had to be maintained between its conditions and those of the outside world. The Treasury had the difficult task of holding the balance between the conditions of an order in the service of the State and the employees of a private enterprise. It did not wish the service to adopt the methods of collective bargaining and the strikes common in private enterprise ; it did not wish the worker in competitive industry or the public to attack those privileges of the public servant which were the safeguards of its purity. The civil servants on their side, regarding themselves as a public profession, strove to secure a fairness in promotion that no trade union in competitive industry would have attempted to demand. As the conditions of recruitment and promotion were determined by general rules laid down and applied by the Treasury, the civil servant was immune from the direct operation of the forces which in private enterprise determine the wages and conditions of service, but they were not immune from the sporadic demands of Parliament for economy.

The new bureaucracy was developed to carry out the policies which Parliament approved. This it could not do unless it exercised wide discretionary powers. The problem of the scope and control of " delegated legislation " now appears. Delegated legislation, it has been said, is a " natural reflection, in the sphere of constitutional law, of changes in our ideas of government which have resulted from changes in political, social and economic ideas, and of changes in the circumstances of our lives which have resulted from scientific discoveries."[51] Delegated legislation is only a special aspect of the problem of the relation between the tradition of democracy and the scientific spirit. " Behind all delegation of legislative power lies the desire to reconcile democracy and despatch, the interested but always illuminated innovation of the amateur with the disinterested research of the expert."[52]

Two factors may be distinguished as responsible for the confused development of our delegated legislation : (1) the *laissez-faire* tradition of the reforming politicians before 1870 with lack of any urgency in the need for administrative and legal reform because of our political isolation and industrial supremacy ; (2) the powerful and subtle traditions of the Constitution.

(1) Before 1870 reformers were mainly concerned with the promotion of humanitarianism, the extension of individual liberty and the reform

171

of a fantastic legal procedure. They were more concerned to remove the evils of a bad Government than to consider the planning of a good. Their theory of democracy was astonishingly naive. In its classic statement by Mill it is assumed that if all interests were represented in a legislature the balance of power would be held by the intelligent and disinterested minority. Parliament was simply the common room and the club writ large. Fortunately they were never called upon to apply in practice this theory of conflicting interests harmonized or subdued by common sense. Until 1867 political power was limited to an electorate supposed to be large and intelligent enough to identify its own interests with the interests of the greatest number without the latter being troubled formally to vote their approval. Except for the legal reforms needed by the business world, the reorganization of Government came from the pressure of casual emergencies. Factory legislation was due partly to humanitarianism and the political antagonism of the agricultural and manufacturing wings of the governing class. The control of shipping and railways was due to a seeming failure of the principles of *laissez-faire* in a key position of the economic order. Civil Service reform was due to the shock of 1848 ; War Office reform to the disgrace of the Crimea and the rise of Prussia ; while in the Colonial Office there was a confused interaction between economic theory, humanitarianism and the recognition that in dealing with diverse civilizations the technique of each for himself and the devil take the hindmost was not enough. Even after 1870 when the extension of the suffrage to include all householders, the rise of organized labour, and the growing competition of foreign States with large, trained bureaucracies, compelled the State to provide elementary education, to investigate the root-causes of poverty and disease which threatened public order and health—even then the continuance of sectarian passions, the inherited cancer of Anglo-Irish hostility, the passions of the South African War, and the muddled struggle over the tariff, prevented any systematic reorganization of the machinery of Government.

(2) The influence of the traditions of the Constitution has affected every detail of the machinery of Government. The innate conservatism of English political practice has been as mixed a blessing as the legal rigidity of the constitution of the United States. Clouds of antique statutes and the dust of out-moded forms have obscured the majesty of the law. The position of the Prime Minister would have been very different but for the lingering death of effective monarchy ; the procedure of the House of Commons has been as much a pageant of the past as a code of rule for effective debate ; that there is no Civil Service but only servants of the Crown has had far-reaching effect on the

structure of our Civil Service ; and the " rusty curb of old father antique the law " has prevented the development of our administrative law. In no other country are lawyers more powerful and in no other is the law less understood by the ordinary citizen.

It is not therefore surprising that the last Committee on Ministers' powers reported that " the system of delegated legislation has been built up haphazard without plan or logic, and that the extent and limits of delegation have been determined by accident and expediency and not upon any system." Political and legal tradition have prevented a clear recognition of what was really being done. As Parliament became responsible for what had previously been done or left undone by local agencies, it had to provide some method by which its general rules could be adapted to local conditions. As Parliament came to deal with subjects which involved a technical and scientific knowledge it had to recognize its own incapacity to deal with the details ; finally, as Parliament passed from merely laying down the conditions of competition to an attempt to determine the purpose and the methods of co-operation, it has had to provide a machinery by which schemes may be prepared, developed and enforced. The advance of science has increased the number of problems which are best dealt with by fashioning a remedy and then applying it where experience dictates. The increasing unity of the community compels in time of crisis an ever-increasing delegation of power to the executive.

Only after 1850 was there any great increase in delegated legislation. It was a necessary instrument for carrying out the collectivist policy which industrial progress and scientific knowledge made inevitable. The development of large business corporations made the old procedure of control by the criminal law or the common informer inadequate, because a corporation could not go to gaol and financial penalties might be less than the cost of complying with the regulations. The new codes of health and safety could only be applied by employing inspectors, analysts, and in the last resort by the power of Government departments themselves to act in default. The great development of delegated legislation begins with the establishment of the Board of Agriculture in 1889 and the Board of Education in 1899, and takes on something of its modern scope with the social legislation of the Liberal Government 1906-14, which provided Old Age Pensions, National Health Insurance, Labour Exchanges, and the germ of a Ministry of Transport and a Department of Scientific and Industrial Research.

CHAPTER VII

1914-18

The three problems of war: Constitutional; Political; and Administrative—The development of the War Cabinet—Its organization—The unsolved problem of leadership in war—Some examples of State control: Man-power—Munitions—Food—Shipping—The Air Ministry—The general character of Government control in time of war—Elasticity and decentralization—The real root of power—Problems of democracy in war.

THE power of a Government in war is dependent upon resources accumulated in peace. Representative Governments have the advantage of an agreement that the war is just and should be pursued. Their disadvantage is that the machinery they must use to make the vital decisions war demands will be geared to party groups and loyalties irrelevant in a state of war. Representative Governments will be unskilled in the use of ruthless means to a limited and specific end. In time of peace they are organized to discuss policy until little opposition remains to what they do. Every detail of their machinery of Government will bear the marks of the compromise which is the spirit of the whole. In peace the politican has a loyalty to his party as the means by which society may be improved; the Civil Service has a duty to run that part of the machinery of Government which is outside party politics and to give to the party in power the best service it can. In peace Government is partly technical routine and partly an education of the people in a way of life. But in war policy cannot be adapted to an intellectual condition of the people; it has to be adapted to a physical condition at the front of war.

For the performance of our traditional rôle in a European war the political organization of the Cabinet and the machinery of the Civil Service had been effective. " The Committee of Imperial Defence had elaborated a war book which set forth the emergency legislation needed and the action required of every Government department. All this stood well the test of experience."[1] But as the nature of the struggle was revealed the machinery of Government had radically to be transformed. In a few months we can see changes in the spirit and the machinery of Government which normally would have taken many years. They provide overwhelming evidence that the health of political

174

institutions depends upon the existence of tolerated differences of opinion as to the ends as well as to the means which society should pursue. The war reveals a sickening of the State because all its institutions had to be adapted to a purpose which was imposed—though the compulsion came not from a despot but from an enemy in arms.

It was impossible to combine rapid and effective action in the various theatres of war with the peace-time conditions of Cabinet responsibility and control. The Cabinet was deposed in favour of a small and select group of its own members based on the political support of a coalition; this new body had to find the principles and the machinery which should determine the relation between politicians and soldiers in war. To the solution of this the central problem of Government in war, the Committee of Imperial Defence had made no advance.[2] Whatever the supreme authority might be it had to administer materials, men and services with which in peace the state had no concern. Three problems emerged in war : the Constitutional, which required a modification of the law and the conventions of Cabinet responsibility; the problem of leadership, which required that the relation between soldiers and politicians should be determined; and the administrative, which required that the life of the country should be administered for the needs of war. It is significant that a healthy popular Government found little difficulty in solving the first and the third. But the second remained to the end insoluble; and it did so because of a fundamental incompatibility between the disease of war and the life of democratic States.

The first pressure of the business of war was dealt with by the time-honoured precedent of a committee of the Cabinet. The Prime Minister and those heads of departments who were responsible for the day to day operations of war consulted with the Committee of Imperial Defence on serious questions involving new departures in policy or joint strategical operations. But the force of constitutional tradition made it impossible without serious friction to draw a hard and fast line between an inner and an outer Cabinet.[3]

By November 1914 a special committee of the Cabinet, a War Council for the conduct of the war, was established. This absorbed the Committee of Imperial Defence. But the Cabinet as a whole did not abdicate its authority. All important steps were reported to it and at times it took an active part and asserted its overruling authority.[4] By this time the need for drastic changes was becoming clear. Asquith, the Prime Minister, was a great parliamentarian, who had shown in his handling of the Parliament Act all the gifts that peace could demand of a Constitutional statesman. These same gifts had secured that we entered the war united and not divided. He had realized " that the break-up of the Cabinet involving his own resignation," would have meant " a war conducted by a Conservative Government . . . the country divided . . . an unknown number of people determined to stop the war at the earliest possible moment."[5] But for him the war would have found us divided, with a Cabinet in disorder or dissolution and impotent to take any decision.[6] But the qualities which could launch us smoothly into war could not teach us to weather its storms. In the Cabinet " he waited on others. He no doubt often averted conflict but he never contributed a suggestion."[7] It was not simply that Asquith was not a man born to lead in war. The principle of a responsible Cabinet drawn from one party was itself unworkable in war. In a few months the opposition found that their position was intolerable. If they criticized the Government they were thought to be unpatriotic ; if they did not it was assumed that they shared with the Government responsibility for what was done.[8] The graceful party minuet of peace could not be danced to the drums of war. The first coalition was formed on May 26th, 1915. This was an unwieldy body of twelve Liberals, eight Conservatives, one Labour, and Lord Kitchener, twenty-two in all. Asquith said that its formation was one of the most uncongenial jobs that he had ever had to carry through.[9] It was made especially unpleasant because the Unionists had pegged out their claims, and already suffering from that terror of the mob and its leaders which was later to destroy the peace which war secured, had compelled the omission of Lord Haldane.

This first coalition did little to solve the problem of creating an inner Cabinet, and even less to determine the right relation between civilian and military spheres. In June, 1915, the inner War Cabinet was replaced by the Dardanelles Committee. The latter was a dropsical body consisting of the Prime Minister, the First Lord of the Admiralty, Churchill, Sir Edward Carson, Bonar Law, Lord Crewe, Lord Curzon and Lord Lansdowne, and such experts as they might consult. Whereas in the War Cabinet all important matters connected with the war had been dealt with by four or five Ministers, now at least a dozen powerful, capable and distinguished persons who were in a position to assert themselves had to be consulted. "At least five or six opinions prevailed on every topic and every operative decision was obtained only by prolonged discursive and exhaustive discussions."[10] The decisions of the Dardanelles Committee had often to be re-debated in the Cabinet.[11] As the operation in the Dardanelles developed to include the many operations undertaken in the Near East, the Dardanelles Committee developed into the War Committee. Its defects were ineradicable. It was too large ; it was overcharged with duties and it was often kept in ignorance of essential and vital information of a technical kind upon the problems which came before it. There was delay, evasion and obstruction in giving effect to its decisions.[12] It was hampered by the necessity of obtaining Cabinet approval, while the Cabinet was responsible for what it could not really control.[13]

It is not possible here even to outline the process by which Lloyd George displaced Asquith in December, 1916. " In the preparation of the ground, the gradual marshalling of forces, the swift changes of front, the handling of the Press and all else that goes to the make-up of modern political strategy " it " stands as the classic example of this kind of warfare."[14] Without attempting to judge the fairness of the actions taken it is possible to see the problem which was involved. Asquith was not temperamentally fitted for the conduct of the war. He was the embodiment of a peace-time tradition which had to be transformed for the war and perhaps for ever. The peace-time processes for securing a change of government were unthinkable in war. There could be no appeal to an electorate.[15] Political leaders were like an advance guard which, cut off from the main body, must act as best they can. It was a tide in the affairs of men for which no pilot could be found save among those already on the bridge. Lloyd George (1) felt that Asquith seemed to be wedded to a tradition and a technique that could only bring disaster ; (2) knew that Bonar Law, the leader of the Unionists, would regard any coalition as a temporary co-operation of parties which left unprejudiced the position of the leaders of the separate forces.[16] With Carson, Beaverbrook and Northcliffe to assist him Lloyd George detached the Unionists from Asquith and forced them to co-operate with himself. The usual Constitutional devices for a change of Government not being available, he had to use intrigue and the barons of the Press, as dictators have since had to use prison and the assassin. According to Chamberlain the Unionists desired to work with Asquith, distrusted Lloyd George, and believed that Asquith's influence with the Liberals, the Irish and the Labour Party was necessary.[17] They had little confidence in Bonar Law's judgment and none in his strength of character.[18] It seems that Asquith was misled by Bonar Law as to the attitude of the Unionists. When Asquith resigned the King sent for Bonar Law and when he failed to secure the support of either Lloyd George or Asquith (whom he consulted in that order) the King sent for Lloyd George.[19] Before the latter accepted office the King invited Asquith, Bonar Law, Lloyd George, Balfour and Henderson to confer with him and with each other at Buckingham Palace.[20] It is said that Lloyd George became Prime Minister because inquiry had elicited that a Ministry under Bonar Law would not be sustained on a division.[21]

Lloyd George was not free to choose his Cabinet without reference to party politics,[22] and to politics which could not be modified by an appeal to the electorate. He had not that freedom of choice which belongs to the leader of a united political party. Out of 260 Liberals only 136 were prepared to support him. The majority of the Tories in Asquith's Cabinet was opposed to his premiership. Bonar Law insisted that his political colleagues should have posts in the Cabinet, posts which Lloyd George would have preferred to give to men of business. Only the refusal of the Liberal Ministers to join his Cabinet enabled him to include a few non-political men—Sir Joseph Maclay as Shipping Director; Lord Devonport for Food; Prothero as Minister of Agriculture; Lord Cowdray as Chairman of the Air Board and Fisher at the Board of Education.[23] The Tories would have neither Churchill nor Lord Curzon.[24]

Lloyd George as Prime Minister was clear about two things : that a Cabinet of twenty or more was a futile instrument for the conduct of business which required immediate action[25]; and that no Prime Minister could possibly undertake the task of running Parliament as well as running the war.[26] The Parliamentary Constitution would have to go into cold storage for the duration, where it was to be hoped that it would not decay. In December he formed his War Cabinet of five, the central organ for the direction of the war. Other Ministers attended when required and brought their expert advisers if they wished. In practice the Cabinet room was often overcrowded with Ministers and their officials.[27] With the representatives of the Dominions and of India included, the War Cabinet became the Imperial War Cabinet. In May, 1917, General Smuts was made a member. The Constitution had produced a Public Safety Committee.

The War Cabinet was only the nerve centre of an elaborate organization. Individual Ministers were made responsible for specific interdepartmental administrative problems, e.g., Lord Curzon for the provision of unsinkable ships. *Ad hoc* committees were detailed to report on specific problems to the Cabinet, e.g., man power and food production. Standing Committees were appointed on special problems such as War Priorities, Easter Affairs, Economic Development, Home Affairs and Demobilization. These standing committees enabled Ministers who were not members of the War Cabinet regularly to meet.[28] The Economic Committee had ten Ministers and met at least once a week ; the Committee for Home Affairs had nine.

So complex a system could not be run with the informality of a Gladstonian Cabinet. An agenda, a time-table, and some method for recording decisions and communicating them to the people concerned were now essential. These were provided by the Cabinet Secretariat, which was a small staff of civil servants, and an extension of the Secretariat to the Committee of Imperial Defence. " The subjects " for the War Cabinet " were placed on the agenda by the Prime Minister or by any member of the War Cabinet or at the request of any Minister or department concerned. . . . At the beginning of each week a list of the outstanding subjects ripe for consideration and awaiting decision were circulated by the Secretariat and this list was usually worked off in the first two or three days of the week."[29] An elaborate time-table was prepared and Ministers were summoned by special telephone to the Cabinet. Where Ministers disagreed they could circulate in advance a statement of their cases. The Secretariat had its own conventions. It did not consider it the duty of its members to initiate or to perform administrative acts. It avoided any interference with the responsibility of the departments. It dealt direct with the Minister and left it to him to decide whether his business should be brought before the Cabinet or not. In practice Ministers who were concerned with problems of national policy, such as India, not directly relevant to the immediate problem of war found it difficult to secure the attention of the War Cabinet.

So far the Constitution had shewn a flexibility adequate to the stresses of the war. The War Cabinet solved the problem of adjusting an executive rooted in party politics, and whose life in time of peace was shaped by its relation to the House of Commons, to the unity required by war. But the War Cabinet did not really solve the problem of leadership in war. The unsolved problem of the relation between the politician and the soldier remained.

Asquith had only with extreme reluctance crossed the boundary between the civilian and the military spheres.[30] He would not play the part of an amateur strategist or foist his opinions upon men who had made soldiering the study of their lives.[31] But Lloyd George knew that a man who had made a life's study of anything might hug his own opinion in the face of new and bitter truth. " In an emergency the able but unimaginative expert is a public danger. On the one hand their thorough knowledge of the details of the business, and their high reputation, give them an authority which it is difficult for the amateur to set aside. While in a situation for which there is no precedent experience often entangles the expert."[32]

In all human affairs there is a sharp conflict between the knowledge of the expert and the wisdom of common sense. " When questions are submitted to deliberation, scientific thinking is in constant demand :

but in the last resort we come to issues that cannot be scientifically settled or the parties would agree; these are matters we say for judgment; and the wise counsellor is the man of good judgment." Of matters for judgment there are two main sorts: there may be agreement as to the result desired, but deliberation as to the means, e.g., will a strike produce the desired rise in wages? There may be a dispute as to whether the result which can be achieved is worth securing, e.g., is the successful strike worth the suffering involved?[33] These difficulties are well known in peace and can be mastered if the civil servants and the political heads of the great departments know their job. But the practices of peace give little guidance in war. For war involves the direction for a special purpose of the whole power of the nation, and the statesman must ultimately be responsible. The supreme command of the nation in arms must be in the Cabinet, the supreme authority in the State. "It is for the statesmen, with such advice as they can command, to survey the battle area as a whole on land and sea, to examine the needs and possibilities, to make their plans and to dispose of their resources to the best advantage."[34] The handling of armies and navies must be left to professional experts.[35] And they are experts very different from the kind the statesman uses in time of peace.[36] "The civil servant can be trusted to carry on the plan of the Government even when he does not agree with them . . . but a soldier in war cannot do the same."[37] The advice of the expert soldier and sailor, unlike the advice of the expert financier, involves action which they alone can take.[38] What then should be the relation between the statesman who must make vital decisions and their experts who alone can carry out the policy decided? It has been suggested that it should be of "the nature of a partnership, in which the statesman becomes the senior partner."[39] But the terms of that partnership in arms and battles had not been considered before the war.[40] Churchill held it was part of the business of a civilian Minister to prepare plans of campaign. Kitchener the expert was not only Secretary of State for War, but also the chief military adviser of the Government, and to a great extent his own Chief of Staff.[41] A military view detached from all political considerations was never available for the civilian Cabinet.[42] The experts "did not conceive it their business to inform the War Council of the Cabinet where and why they differed from their civilian chiefs."[43]

In December, 1915, Sir William Robertson was made Chief of the Imperial General Staff. He proceeded to define the respective functions of Ministers and soldiers in war. The War Council, composed exclusively of civilian Ministers, was to be the supreme directing authority in the position of the Commander-in-Chief of the imperial land forces. But it was to receive all advice on matters concerning military operations through one authoritative channel only. That channel was to be the Chief of the Imperial General Staff. Robertson secured that " all military operations required to put into execution the policy approved by the War Council should be issued and signed by the Chief of the Imperial General Staff under the authority of the Secretary of State for War, *not* under that of the Army Council." The Cabinet could not act through the Army Council without the knowledge of the General Staff.[44] The effect of these changes was " to bring about an immediate improvement in the business of conducting the war."[45]

But the problem of the terms of the partnership between statesmen and soldiers was not thereby solved. Lloyd George has made the specific charge that Sir William Robertson signally failed to realize what his duty as an independent adviser to the Imperial Cabinet on military matters required.[46] He withheld from the Cabinet essential facts about policies he supported but believed they would oppose.[47] " The truth that mattered was wilfully and skilfully kept from their cognisance."[48] Nor were the statesmen in a position to compel their experts to co-operate. " On land the High Command had its way. As far as the general strategy of the land fighting was concerned it was their policy. The only exception was the campaign in Palestine, which they deprecated."[49] At sea, the Government compelled the Admirals to take measures necessary to meet the submarine menace. " Had they not overruled the Sea Lords the submarines would have won and the Allies would have been beaten."[50]

Not only was the British Government at the mercy of their Commanders-in-Chief, whose ability and prestige were far greater than that of the military advisers attached to its War Ministries, but every Allied Government was in the same predicament. It has been said that an Allied strategy did not exist. " Instead of one great war with a united front there were at least six separate and distinct wars with a separate, distinct, and independent strategy for each."[51] The only way out of this impasse was to set up an authoritative inter-Allied body with its own staff and its own intelligence department who, working together, would review the battlefield as a whole and select the most promising sector for concerted action.[52] When the disasters of 1917 secured the Allied Supreme War Council in November of that year the military experts were merely advisory. The proper relations between the military and the civilians remained to the end undiscovered.

Behind the front line of strategy the record of the Government was good. As the nature of the struggle was at first understood by none there was unavoidable delay in getting the machinery of government which the war required. But as soon as a policy was determined the administrative skill for its application was quickly forthcoming. Some of the problems to be solved must be briefly glanced at.

As the whole idea of conscription was alien to our political tradition and its necessity not realized there was from the first a fatal misdirection of our man-power. So long as voluntary enlistment continued men left industries, where later they were to be desperately wanted, to join the ranks. The essential interdependence of the army and the factory was not recognized. There was a false distinction between the home front and the front of war. Psychologically this may have been valuable. The war was always kept at a distance. But it seriously impeded the proper organization of the country's strength. Trade Unionists who would themselves have gladly fought in the trenches would not allow changes in their working rules which might have saved those already there. The very emotions which steeled the country to war supported this obstruction. The war was a war for freedom and freedom involves the right of a man to work at the conditions he can secure by contract. In demanding higher wages and in resisting the rationalization of industrial processes the worker felt he was fighting the same battle as his military brother. A country of industrial *laissez-faire* in conflict with a country despotically organized is here at a disadvantage. There is a vital psychological and administrative problem for democracies to solve. How are they to extend to the whole of their industrial order the military psychology of discipline—the humorous acceptance of the fact that the Army has the whip-hand. The Army is psychologically a totalitarian state. Does its *morale* depend upon there being in the background a civilian population that is free to enjoy advantages even at the expense of those who are in the Army itself ?

A Government whose political tradition was Free Trade and individualism realized that industry must be deliberately organized for war production only under the pressure of startling events and dangerous crises.[53] No scheme had been prepared to settle the order in which men should be withdrawn from industry.[54] In 1914 there was no central State machine fully equipped with experience, knowledge or power for the organization of labour in a national emergency. The three departments then concerned with the organization of labour—the Local Government Board, the Home Office and the Board of Trade—had little control over or relations with the recruiting departments of the War Office or the Admiralty.[55] Few could realize the length of the struggle that was before them ; even those who did could hardly realize that the demand for men for the Army would be so great, that it would need careful husbanding of the civilians left to supply the essential needs of the Army in the field and the civilian population at home. In the United Kingdom out of an estimated male population of 14,350,000, some 5,500,000 were finally serving with the armed forces. The larger the army in the field grew, the larger was the number of men and women at home required to equip them. Nor was it merely a question of providing the man-power for the supply of the armies, but of supplying the labour required to feed the civilians and to produce those exports on the sale of which our financial security was dependent.[56] None of these problems could be dealt with at once. The nation was not willing to submit to unquestioning discipline. The authorities had no machinery with which to handle the problems. It was impossible to estimate " during the astonishments of war " what was the degree of importance to be attached to each of the different demands. Only gradually was the authority necessary created[57]—through the various stages of a Man-Power Board, the Ministry of Munitions, the Department of the Director-General of National Service to, in August, 1917, a Ministry of National Service.[58] The Ministry of Labour created in 1916 provided the basis for the whole supply of labour. It was deliberately removed from the immediate executive responsibilities involved in the administration of the Munitions Acts and made as far as war would permit neutral in labour matters. It was principally occupied in preparations for peace.[59] It was the Government's main instrument for conciliation.

The demand for munitions combined with the rush of skilled workmen to the colours created by March, 1915, a situation in which firms were living mainly by taking in one another's employees.[60] The Government was faced with the problems of limiting the movement of workmen, making one workman do the work of one and a half and preventing by persuasion or coercion industrial strife. The foundations of labour regulation were laid down by the Munitions of War Act of July 2nd, 1915. Faced with the industrial traditions of masters and men, the psychology of war which " with magnificent impartiality stirred up the best and the worst human passions,"[61] and with the limitations imposed upon swift and dramatic changes by the actual structure of industry,[62] the Government by this act laid the foundations of labour control. The fundamental principle of the Bill was that while the worker remained a civilian, with all the rights and privileges of civil law, his industrial rights were severely limited. In those controlled establishments where the worker was required to surrender some of his industrial rights the profits of the employer were also limited. Lockouts were made crimes and arbitration compulsory.[63] The Act, which was the culmination of a long period of negotiations commencing in November, 1914, provided a definite statutory basis for the development of a dilution programme.[64] Dilution was not secured by persuading the skilled man to let the unskilled take his job—because the unskilled could not do the work. It had to be divided into its component parts and fool-proof machines introduced.[65] Before long " the ugly shape of war was to intrude into every part of the workman's life."[66] His freedom of movement was checked, his wages controlled, strikes forbidden and his work defined. His recreation was limited, his consumption of liquor and the building of his home curtailed.[67] In August 1917, the struggle between workers and fighters was composed by bringing recruiting for both services under a common control.[68] The Ministry of National Service (August, 1917) was told by the War Cabinet it must be able to give the meaning in terms of man-power of all department proposals ; to make arrangements for transfers from the civilian to fighting and vice versa when necessary. A War Priorities Committee of the Cabinet was to decide what were the most pressing industrial needs and to tell the Ministry of National Service the channels into which labour was to be directed.[69]

Before 1914 the function of the Army Contracts Department (which had been reorganized before 1907) was to break up munition rings. Army factories were only allowed to produce one third of Government guns and ammunition and half the army clothing, so that a prosperous private enterprise might be a vital part of our defence.[70] The War Office machinery was adjusted to the needs of peace ; the resilience of private industry, it was believed, would meet the needs of war. By October, 1914, the buying machinery of the Army was paralysed. It was easier for manufacturers to do business with our Allies indirectly through the Board of Trade than with the War Office.[71] In November, 1914, Mr. Wintour of the Board of Trade, was made Director of Army Contracts. By his efforts the Army was secured its essential supplies of beef, jute, food, textiles and leather. But by May, 1915, it was clear that essential supplies would not be forthcoming merely from the incentives provided by rising prices. National factories were built ; raw materials were monopolized and distributed by the Government at fixed prices and manufacturers were required to produce shells at prices based on an analysis of cost.[72] By requisitioning practically the whole output of the engineering industry and making use of nearly all the iron and steel available, the Government virtually suppressed private trade and ignored civilian needs.[73] But in the case of textiles and foodstuffs civilian needs could not be ignored. The intervention of the War Office to meet the needs of the troops led inevitably to the development of a Ministry of Food. Starting with an effort to protect the Government against high charges, the stage was finally reached of a national and international organization to secure supplies at reasonable prices for the whole nation.

There was no general food problem until the end of 1916. The policy of the Government had been to trust as far as possible to private enterprise for the maintenance of civilian supplies.[74] Since 1870 our farming technique had been based on the assumption that transport had made available cheap corn for the towns, cheap manures for the land and cheap feeding stuffs for livestock.[75] Whereas Germany could feed her whole population for six out of seven days in the week we could only feed ourselves from Friday night until Monday morning. We could feed fifteen out of our forty-seven millions, or all of them for 125 days out of 365. In the spring of 1915, the difficulties of the Government over munitions led to the first Coalition ; in the autumn of 1916 the problem of food control helped the fall of Asquith. On October 10th Runciman explained that the importation of wheat into the United Kingdom would have to be undertaken by a Royal Commission, of which the chairman would be the Minister of Agriculture.[76] The idea of a Food Controller was even then a pleasant jest, but in November it was admitted that we " had been driven bit by bit against our will . . . to suspend the easy flow of purely voluntary action." In the House of Commons Churchill made a prophetic speech. " I believe that before the end of this war . . . all shipping will certainly be taken over by the Government and regulated in one form or another. . . . I believe that all important employment will be regulated by the State for the purposes of war. I believe that ration tickets for everything that matters will be served out to every one of us. I believe that prices will have to be fixed so as to secure to the poorest people in this country . . . the power of buying a certain modicum of food sufficient to keep up physical war-making efficiency at prices which are not outside the scope of the wages they receive. . . . I am sure that we shall come to a national organization of agriculture like there is a national organization of munitions."[77] When the Government failed to find and appoint a Food Controller it fell. When the new Lloyd George Government was formed in December Lord Devonport was made Controller. On December 2nd, 1916, the New Ministries and Secretaries Act gave statutory authority for the creation of three new Ministries—Labour, Food and Shipping.

So great was Lord Devonport's appetite for work and belief in his knowledge of food that Lord Rhondda, who took over in June, 1917, had to create a Ministry of Food out of a one-man business.[78] " The

Ministry of Munitions were then in charge of oils and fats, including the materials for margarine. The Board of Trade controlled the import of meat and cheese and had made a beginning with frozen fish . . . the Admiralty, the War Office and the Navy and Army Canteen Board obtained most of their supplies independently. The War Savings Committee undertook a large part of the Food Economy campaign. The Board of Agriculture undertook food preservation, and the control of oats was shared between the Board of Trade and the War Office.''[79]

All these powers (except the importation of refrigerated meat from South America, Australia and New Zealand, which remained with the Board of Trade) were taken over by the Ministry of Food or the Wheat and Sugar Commissions. Wintour, a former official of the Board of Trade, became Rhondda's right-hand man. The Ministry had not only to buy, sell, transport and distribute on the largest scale, they had to secure fair distribution at fair prices to ten million separate households. For the first they secured men with the widest experience of the special trades concerned. For the second they created a special staff with an interest in economic laws and experience in the arts of public administration. The genius of Rhondda organized an administrative machine which was centralized for thought but decentralized for action.[80] He saw that freedom from detailed Treasury control was necessary and that the Minister must give to publicity what in peace he would have given to parliamentary duties.[81] He fully used the knowledge of the physiologists. Calories were counted as carefully as rifles and shells. Every million calories represented the food required by one person for a year, every billion saved reduced by some 500,000 tons the demands made on our shipping ; and that meant in 1918, 100,000 additional American troops on the Western Front.[82] To reach the homes and daily lives of forty million people there were two administrative organs. In each of the fifteen areas into which Great Britain was divided there was placed a Food Controller, the representative of a central executive department. In nearly 2,000 separate areas there were established representative Food Control Committees. Finally a National Food Council run by a competent journalist showed that it was more blessed to persuade than to command.

By respect for scientific advice, by combining the traditions of the Civil Service with the experience of business experts, by decentralization of machinery and by a scrupulous attention to fairness in distribution the Ministry of Food was able to secure both peace and plenty.[83]

Shipping of all industries was the one in which the success of the ordinary machinery of commerce had been most conspicuous. Although the State had been forced to undertake the protection of the sailors in the signing of their contracts, the control of safety conditions, and although there was a strong case for further State intervention to secure a humanitarian minimum in shipping conditions, yet the free play of economic forces " with their ruthless automatic checks on inefficiency and error " had secured an elastic and responsive system among the various organizations responsible for the purchase, finance, transport and marketing and consumption of goods which entered into international trade. But as it was the system most subtly organized so it was the system in which, once State control was introduced, it would have to go the furthest. For " control of shipping depends upon control of commodities and must be international in character. Unless the State is to decide what is to be imported and the priority in which different cargoes are to be shipped it will be compelled to leave a free freight market in operation, for it is impossible for the shipowner himself to exercise an arbitrary selection . . . for shipping is the handmaid of commerce and unless the commercial interests are allowed to make known their requirements in the ordinary way the requirements must be fixed by the State itself."[84]   It was the effect of a partial State control of tonnage on the freight rates of that part which it did not control, which was the cause of the demand for a Ministry of Shipping. " The task of the Ministry of Shipping and Allied Maritime Transport Council was to concentrate the available tonnage on the shortest route as a corollary to the purchase of supplies on the credit of the State, in the nearest markets." The necessary concentration would not have been accomplished without an extension and centralization of control. It was a last expedient and was possible only through the financial assistance of the United States. It enabled the necessary minimum of supplies essential for war purpose to be maintained, but at a price in adverse exchanges, indebtedness and commercial dislocation which added immensely to the burden of war.[85] It would have been impossible without international control. No single State could fix the freights on cargoes carried under foreign flags and dictate the movements of foreign tonnage. As it was, with their overwhelming strength the Allies had to pay neutral shipowners rates three or four times as great as those allowed to British owners.[86]

In the early stages of the war the introduction of State control was opposed by the greater part of the shipping industry, on the grounds that it would imperil the flow of essential supplies. It was the effect of partial control on shipping rates for those who were uncontrolled, and the growing pressure for the allocation of essential supplies, which forced the creation at the end of 1916 of a Controller of Shipping. By that time there was a chaos of authorities in which order could only be introduced by a concentration and extension of power. In 1916, the Admiralty Transport Department was responsible for providing ships for naval and military service, tonnage and space for the Wheat Authority, and the carriage of a large proportion of British and Allied imports. But the Admiralty " had no definite power to criticize or refuse the demands of any of the departments or to limit the allocation of tonnage. The Board of Trade was responsible for the employment of all insulated space in liners with a modified right of diverting the ships themselves." A Ship Licensing Committee controlled, on the instruction of the Board of Trade on very broad lines, the employment of all ships not in full requisition. Various committees set up by the Board of Trade controlled the running of all British ships in the French and Italian coal trade. " The official ore broker chartered for the Ministry of Munitions British and neutral tonnage to bring ore from Spain and the Mediterranean." The Port and Transport Executive Committee appointed at the joint instance of the Board of Trade, Admiralty and War Office was responsible for all measures necessary to improve the turn-round of shipping at all ports.[87] The problem of the turn-round was at least as important as the problem of tonnage itself.[88] The whole shipbuilding resources of the country were subject to an absolute Admiralty priority. The Board of Trade issued under the Munitions of War Acts certificates for such ships as it desired to see completed, but it had no power to obtain the necessary allocation of labour and material for their completion. Over the whole field a Shipping Control Committee " exercised a general supervision, but possessed neither an administrative staff nor direct executive powers, though they were generally able to obtain Cabinet backing for their more important decisions."[89]

The Shipping Controller, when he was at last appointed, was a shipowner. He had not only to coerce those who put profits before patriotism, he had to command the support of those who distrusted the extension of State control.[90] Close association of shipowners and the Ministry was needed for success. Not only was " their knowledge and experience required in the practical work of the Ministry, but their services were of the utmost importance in conducting negotiations with their fellow shipowners."[91] The rapid extension of Government requisition of tonnage was followed by a decision to build and run ships on Government account. With the Admiralty, War Office and Ministry of Munitions freely competing for the material available, merchant shipbuilding received in practice only what was left over after their claims had been satisfied.[92] Only a strong department definitely responsible for building merchant ships could secure the materials required. When in three months, February to April, 1917, the submarine campaign sank 1,200,000 tons, which equalled the Controller's estimate of the largest output he could secure in a year, and the Admiralty could hold out little hope of a substantial reduction in the sinkings, the situation was so desperate that the Government in May transferred the control of Merchant Shipbuilding to the Admiralty.[93] But the problem of men and materials was not yet solved. There were five overlapping authorities : the Shipyards Labour Department at the Admiralty, the Labour Department of the Ministry of Munitions, the Ministry of National Service, the War Cabinet Labour Department and the Ministry of Labour.[94] On the one hand the War Office refused to release skilled men ; on the other organized labour was opposed to dilution until they were released.[95] For steel the War Office and the Ministry of Munitions and the Allies had claims which none of them would reduce.[96] In May, 1918, therefore, the Department of Ship-building was transferred to Lord Pirrie, an experienced shipbuilder, with the title of Controller-General of Merchant Shipping, a seat on the Board of Admiralty and the right of direct access to the Cabinet.[97]

In the development of the Air Ministry we have an excellent example of the interplay between technical, administrative and constitutional forces. In the stress of war the new department passed rapidly through stages which in peace would have taken decades. In 1912 the establish-ment of a permanent consultative committee called the Air Committee, with the duty of co-ordinating the efforts of the Admiralty and the War Office formed the nucleus of the future Air Ministry.[98] But there was no central policy for air. Fisher and Churchill at the Admiralty might have their vision of aerial navies fighting in the central blue, but the War Office could only think of aircraft as aids to reconnaissance —a not quite gentlemanly Pegasus. In July, 1914, the separate existence of a Naval Air Force was recognized.

In the early days of the war there was no clearly defined policy for air. It was undecided whether the naval or the military planes should be responsible for defence against Zeppelins. The development of a separate Air Ministry was the result of the technical problems con-nected with the supply of aero engines and aircraft. The equipment of an air force could not be organized on mass production lines along with the ordinary munitions and instruments of war. In February, 1916, Lord Derby's Air Committee was appointed to collaborate in arranging the supply and design for the material of the Naval and Military Air Services upon such points as might be referred to them by the War Committee, the Admiralty, the War Office or any other department of State. With no executive powers and no authority to override

Admiralty obstruction, the Derby Committee collapsed within two months. In the spring of 1916, Lord Curzon, the Lord President of the Council, was exploring the possibilities of reorganization and suggesting an Air Board as a step to an Air Ministry. Mr. Balfour, for the Admiralty, conducted the opposition. On May 11th the War Committee decided to establish an Air Board consisting of Lord Curzon as Chairman, two naval and two military representatives, Lord Sydenham as independent expert and Major Baird as Parliamentary Secretary. But the Air Board, like the Committee, was without executive powers and, though charged with the duty of organizing the supply of material and preventing competition, possessed no authority to determine a policy for the placing of orders. Lord Curzon claimed for the Air Board the control in both the air services, of invention, research, experiment, design, production and finance. Balfour claimed for the Admiralty the separate control of these functions as far as the Naval Air Force was concerned, while the Ministry of Munitions wished to undertake the design and supply of aeroplanes for both Army and Naval Air Forces. This was one of the grandest departmental disputes of all time, drowned only by the noise of battle itself. In December the War Cabinet decided that the powers of the Air Board should be enlarged. The New Ministries and Secretaries Act provided that the President of the Air Board should be deemed to be a Minister and the Board a Ministry. In relation to aircraft the Board was to have such powers and duties of any Government Department in authority, whether conferred by statute or otherwise as His Majesty may by Order in Council transfer to the Board or authorize the Board to exercise or perform concurrently with or in consultation with the Government Department or authority concerned.[99] The Ministry of Munitions was to undertake the design and supply of aeroplanes for both the Army and the Navy. The Air Board was to be responsible for allocating the available resources between the Admiralty and the War Office. This division of responsibility for design and responsibility for supply between the Air Board and the Ministry of Munitions might have been fatal had they not both been housed in the Hotel Cecil.[100] Propinquity secured what politics could not.

In August, 1917, the Smuts Committee pointed out that the Board was more a conference than a Board, that with no technical and advisory personnel of its own it could never form an independent air policy, and said that in their " opinion there is no reason why the Air Board should any longer continue in its present form as practically no more than a conference room between the older services, and there is every reason why it should be raised to the status of an independent Ministry in control of its own war services." On November 29th, 1917, the Royal Assent was given to the Bill creating an Air Ministry. Miraculously Admiralty and War Office agreed to its terms. The new Air Council, was based on the organization of the Army Council.

Three things clearly emerge from the experience of the State in the administrative problems of the war : (1) that the Government would have been powerless without the co-operation of representatives of the industrial and commercial interests with which they were concerned ; (2) that their legal powers were a matter of slight importance compared with the force of the opinion of the general public and the groups concerned that co-operation was a duty ; (3) that the conditions of war throw little light on the problem of State control of the life of a community in time of peace save that they bring out clearly the difficulty of combining a policy of plan with one of no plan.

In agriculture the Food Controller was "a constitutional monarch who could only govern with the support and approval of the majority in any particular trade. The voluntary co-operation of traders and manufacturers was at least as important as the compulsory powers conferred by D.O.R.A." All the innumerable Boards, Councils, Associations and Advisory Committees were associated with the work of the controlling departments and functioned to some extent as representative governing bodies of the trade or industry concerned.[100a]

In the first week of the war the President of the Board of Agriculture and Fisheries had set up a consultative committee of experts—agriculturalists drawn from all parts of the country and in touch with local opinion.[101] When in January, 1917, a Food Production Department was created with power, in consultation with the Food Controller, to make orders bearing on the better cultivation of agricultural land, England and Wales were devided into twenty areas, for each of which a local Commissioner was appointed as the Food Production Department's representative on the committee for that area. These Agricultural Executive Committees were given a free hand. The department said, " this is what we want done ; you know how it can be done." To this policy much of the success achieved was due.[102]

In the case of industry problems of man-power, production, exports and imports were so closely connected that they could be dealt with by industries as a unit. It was essential for the State to have the closest co-operation with all the interests concerned.[103] In the case of shipping the Ministry of Shipping looked to the liner companies to run their vessels with the same zeal and efficiency as if they retained a pecuniary interest in the success of the voyages. This trust would have been impossible had not the terms of requisition been arranged with bodies which were fully representative of the industry and organized strongly to speak for it.[104]

In all problems of industrial labour the Government relied upon the co-operation of the employers and the Trade Unions. In March, 1915, letters were sent to the Trade Unions asking them to consult with the Chancellor of the Exchequer and the President of the Board of Trade.[105] When the immense discouragements and disarrangement of war caused the inevitable industrial unrest the Government could only show its willingness to deal with remediable grievances and trust to the will to win.[106]

In spite of the wide powers conferred by D.O.R.A. (August, 1914) to make regulations for the public safety and, defence of the realm, the Government had no power to exercise a complete control of trade, to regulate dealings and to prescribe maximum prices.[107] It was only by the use of the absolutist theory of the Royal Prerogative that the subject has no legal right to compensation against the Crown that the tyranny of the market prices was overthrown. " It was because compensation for property requisitioned need only be made *ex gratia* that the costing system could be and was legally enforced." The principle that no compensation was payable for losses inflicted by measures which were of general application alone made a regime of maximum prices and the prohibition of private dealings possible.[108] But in the great majority of cases what was lawful and what was not did not matter. What mattered was the extent to which any measure commanded general support and was applied impartially all round. Measures of State intervention which went beyond what the best opinion in any particular trade regarded as necessary and possible were practically certain to fail, however valid their legal sanction.[109] The control of shipping was carried on largely by and through the leading representatives of the industry itself and rested at bottom on a basis of agreement.[110] In one case the shipowners, having established in court that a liner requisition scheme which was the pivot of the whole supply system of the country was *ultra vires*,[111] did not press their advantage, desiring only recognition of the fact that their co-operation was voluntary and not enforced.[112] " There was a strong feeling that the Government should not be hampered in the prosecution of the war by too close an inquiry into the strict legality of its administrative action." And of course a well-founded legal objection could be overridden by an Amending Act.[113]

The development of war-time control of the economic life of the nation was due almost entirely to the pressure of emergencies and " hardly at all to a deliberate policy of State intervention consciously thought out and consistently pursued."[114] With the outbreak of war certain interests saw their only salvation in the assistance of the State. In their case there was no conflict between the particular and the general interests. The Government guaranteed the solvency of the banks and discount houses by placing the credit of the nation behind approved commercial bills payable by debtors who could not meet their obligations.[115] Where the military necessity was obvious the Government took over the railways of the country by an agreement which guaranteed their pre-war dividend. As the refiners were paralysed by the failure of sugar imports from Central Europe, the Government took control of the purchase and importation of sugar.   When it became necessary for the Government to fix prices, control and centralized purchase had to be extended from the finished article back to the raw material. From the devising of machinery for the purchase of raw materials it was driven to experiment with the control of the production of essential foodstuffs.[116] Its control of commodities drove it to the control of shipping.[117] And in shipping at least it was clear " that it must be all or nothing ; . . . private trading actuated solely by economic motives and State trading liable to be deflected by political considerations could not exist side by side."[118]

The extension during the war of State control in every aspect of the national life provides certain simple lessons in the nature of government and the technique of administration. In the first place the whole party system was practically suspended. In so far as it existed, it existed rather as an embarrassment to the development of policy and the discovery of talent. Yet but for the party system the spirit and the talent which were available would not have been there at all. It is doubtful whether democracy could wage war for any length of time without a serious impairment of its political life. The attempt of the English aristocracy to resist the domination of Napoleon was paid for by a degradation of our political life for twenty years after the Battle of Waterloo. It is in the hour of victory that the most serious blow is likely to be struck at the life of the party system. The Liberal Party, which alone could secure unanimity for our entrance into the war, was destroyed by the peace it had made possible. Secondly, the control of the State was more successful in those spheres where publicity and measurement could give the results which were required. Given the simple problem of rationing and the control and purchase of raw materials, we had only to give the available experts a free hand to get what was required. An enormous new sphere was discovered for the use of statistics and the use of publicity where co-operation of the public was essential. Where they could be told what it was they were required to do, and where what was required could be related to some dominant emotional aim common honesty and technical skill were enough. This does not mean that the arts of administration were not taxed to their utmost. Never was it more clearly demonstrated that the success of administration lies in the centralization of knowledge and the decentralization of power. Elasticity and decentralization were the secrets of success.

In the case of wool purchase and meat control uniformity and a common policy were secured as much by periodical meeting between subordinate officers as by central direction.[119] Every controlling department had its advisory committees of expert and forceful critics. It was found possible to combine the expert experience of those trained in competitive industry and bargaining with the control and planning of the civil servants. " The initiation and direction of schemes rested with the permanent officials, who had no previous experience of commercial affairs . . . the execution, the technical capacity and the personal influence . . . were the contribution of business men."[120] But it was in the realm of business where results are measurable that the most success was achieved. " Elasticity and decentralization are easier to introduce in business administration than in the administration of law . . . business looks forward, law books backwards . . . though fairness demands similar treatment for similar cases at any one time, completely new principles may be followed at different times without injustice."[121] From this judgment it may be inferred by those who consider that the domination of the material environment is now a limited and calculable problem that it is possible to secure an administrative technique which shall secure the abolition of scarcity, though it may involve an abrogation of the traditional legal rights of liberty and property. Were the four years of war a rehearsal for a future five years' economic plan ? Fundamentally the answer is that the coercion necessary was provided by the enemy. The whole system of co-operation was a product of the feat of defeat. If it ever should be possible for men to feel for an idea as they felt for the complex of national feeling in the war, then the same degree of control would be possible ; only the battle front would be within the State against all those who were not converted to the ideal held by the dominant group. Nor should the enormous inefficiency, viewed over a period, of the methods used be forgotten. A scale of priorities was given by the dictates of the enemy. That shells might be made the whole equipment of our industries was distorted ; it was found impossible to impose the cost in any equitable way. What men could see and feel that had to be fairly divided ; but the unseen costs could be allowed to accumulate as they would.

Nor must the peculiar exaltation of spirit and steady degradation of morale be forgotten. The existence of the army in the field and the threat of death in nearly every home provided a stimulus and an emotional appeal in time of crisis which was very real even among those who would have been careful to disguise its presence. But it is equally true that there was a steady degradation in the character of our public men throughout the period. No human being could stand up to the ordeal of responsibility and keep his sense of proportion. The Lloyd George who drove Asquith from office for his country's good was mightier in power, but small in essential political stature when he called the General Election of 1918. If the experts and the professional civil servants escaped this corrupting breath of power and responsibility the whole of the ordinary population were deprived of any essential education in political realities. For they had not to choose the way that they would live, but only to lend a hand in whatever way they could to a common cause.

CHAPTER VIII

THE STATE AND SOCIETY, 1918-39

The influence of the war in the post-war World—The new economic
functions of the State—Currency and the Bank of England—Trade and
overseas investments—The abandonment of Free Trade—The problem of
the labour market—Theories of the relation of the State and industry—
The pressure of emergencies in Coal; Iron and Steel; Agriculture—
Some aspects of State action in relation to the standard of living—The
organization of Education—Public Health—And Police.

MANY of the problems of democratic government in 1918-39
would have existed had there been no world war in 1914-18.
Without the war the development of Free Trade, which is an
attempt to make use of the maximum territorial divisions of labour,
would have led to a conflict between the economic and all the other
aspects of man's estate. In particular the division of labour which the
progressive application of science to industry requires would have
conflicted with the psychological forces of nationalism. In the nineteenth century the largest Free Trade area in the world, the United
States of America, was only created by the destruction in civil war of
the slave-owning South. Nor would the wounds of that conflict have
been healed had there not been a territory as large as the Roman Empire
west of the Mississippi empty for occupation by victor and vanquished
alike. In Central Europe a political system which was to be the framework of the most powerful European industrial power was only created
by a policy of blood and iron. Not one of the colonies settled by
Englishmen failed to develop a system of tariffs for the development
of their political and social life. If the early stages of the industrial
revolution produced in England, which had boasted a cultural unity
since the Conquest, the Luddites and the Chartists, it was hardly to be
expected that on the world stage it would not produce convulsions of
enormous violence. Had there been no war the United States would
still have closed her paradise to the hungry hordes of Europe. Textiles
too, because they are one of the simplest forms of manufacture, catering
for an almost universal demand, would have been developed in the
East. The revolution in agriculture, which must have such far-reaching
consequence for the political and social structure of the future, destroying

as it does the traditional framework in which civilization—the life of cities—has hitherto been set, was inevitable. Nor was the war responsible for the demands made on the art of politics and the science of administration, when specialization of labour made the market value of most workers less than the minimum income they would need for the performance of their civic duties. Finally, the war did not create the conditions, strategic and economic, which are so much more favourable to the great land powers than they are to a democratic island empire.

All these conditions were however modified by the effects of the war. Possessing " the most delicate and most elaborate trade system," we offered " the largest possible target to dislocation because it sprawled all over the world."[1] We were an octopus in a sea of sharks. The war had been won by the world's two great sea powers blockading the most formidable land power. The Allied blockade and control of shipping acted as a tariff wall, and behind it infant industries grew to such maturity that, when peace was signed, they sought tariffs and subsidies in place of the shelter of war. The great trade routes of the Pacific had been open to the competition of the Americans and Japanese. Scandinavian countries had learnt to build their own ships. The political disturbances of China and of India injured British trade. The reduction in the volume of the world trade by the dislocations of war, and the fears and passions of the peace, struck an almost mortal blow to British shipbuilding.

The interplay between the growing sweep of the industrial revolution in the world and the particular dislocations of the war cannot be given here. The ultimate effect of their joint forces on the future of this country we can only surmise. After the Napoleonic wars it took twenty years for this country to recover its political and economic stride. The chaos and misery of the period after Waterloo to the hungry 'forties was a prelude to the complacent 'sixties and not to a second world war. In the early nineteenth century one thing was sure. The Napoleonic war and a combination of geographical and economic factors had thrust the industrial leadership of the world upon us. The political dislocation caused by the misery of the war, and the uncertainties of peace were mitigated by a rapid economic advance which brought a new plenty and a chance to live in peace. Moreover as the expedient of popular government had not then been tried the weaknesses of our political system could be envigorated by extensions of the suffrage. Not new parties only, but new political forces, could be called to the service of the State. The anæmia of aristocracy could be remedied by a transfusion of blood from the rising middle class.

So long as the goal of manhood suffrage lay ahead political deadlocks could be broken by an extension of the suffrage. In our relations with foreign powers we could plausibly argue that our own profits were the world's gain.

Underlying all the activities of the State in this country in 1918-39 were two anxieties : first, that the standard of living possible before 1914 might no longer be possible, while the insistence of a newly enfranchised people that it should, might destroy the recuperative powers of the economic system ; second, to prevent such a decline in our economic strength in relation to the world as would cause the collapse of the political and administrative orders for which we were responsible. If the general set of industrial and financial forces was against the continued supremacy of these islands what was to become of the political arch of which they were the keystone ? It was clear even then, that the despotic system of government might prevail if the democratic experiment of the British Commonwealth of Nations were to fail ; that neither the Scandinavian democracies nor the democracy of France nor even that of the United States could survive the confusions which would follow the struggle for China, India and Africa should the British political order collapse. To say this is to claim no superiority for the British in the art of politics. A system of constitutional and administrative devices had been developed with their centre in these islands and the collapse of that system would shake the world. It may be that it would be better for the world that the English political tradition should live hereafter only in her political literature— a word without the sword. But the end of that political system would be a turning-point in the history of the world. In the world's five continents it would mean that the application of natural science to the life of man would be made by force and not by persuasion.

Some of broader outlines of the economic context of State activity in 1918-39 must here be given. In 1913 about 30 per cent. of our industrial population was engaged directly or indirectly in the production of goods and services for sale outside Great Britain. British coal mines exported 40 per cent. of their output ; the cotton trade sent more than half of its exports to Asia. About 60 per cent. of all our foodstuffs were imported. Great Britain built 60 per cent. of the world's ships ; while British ships carried 50 per cent. in volume of the entire sea-borne trade of the world.[2] Shipping and other services to the value of £129 millions, together with an income from overseas investments of £210 millions, converted an excess of imports of £158 millions into a balance of £181 millions available for overseas investments.[3] In the five years 1907-11 of the total loans raised, about 20 per cent. had been for home investment, 35 per cent. for investment in the Empire, and 45 per cent. for investment in foreign countries.[4] London was the undisputed monetary and financial capital of the world, enjoying an almost effortless superiority needing no State-controlled machinery for its exercise. Britain's power had been attained " not by the pursuit of any preconceived plan, but by a process of almost unhampered evolution based on trial and error and aided by the practical aptitudes and instincts of our race, as well as by certain fortunate accidents in the way of natural resources and geographical position."[5]

The war and the increasing impetus of the industrial revolution throughout the world transformed the economic scene. In finance our previous effortless supremacy passed for ever ; in commerce the principle of free trade proved far more fleeting than the peace of Rome ; in the organization of industry, the distortions of war and the technical revolutions which followed, set a problem of reorganization which could not be solved without the help of the State. Whereas before 1914 the mean figure, round which unemployment moved, was in the neighbourhood of $4\frac{1}{2}$ per cent., after 1918 it was only once less than 10 per cent. (in 1927) and was at times more than 21 per cent.[6]

We may briefly consider the problems of the State in relation to (1) prices, (2) trade and commerce and (3) industrial organization.

All economic activity is carried on in an environment of law which imposes conditions on the manner in which all the factors of production become available.[7] The central function of any economic system that is based upon individual judgment and choice of occupation and enjoyment is " the continuous comparison of all sorts of prices and rewards for service including the profits of enterprise."[8] The State had to help to keep the movement of prices within the limits to which industry and the social order could be adjusted without collapse. " To allow prices to fall, whilst social forces maintain wage costs, obliterates profit, and the attempt to reduce contractual incomes without power to abate contractual incomes immediately jeopardizes both nationally and internationally the sanctity of contracts."[9] The maintenance of the sanctity of contracts recognized by the most ardent individualist as a function of the State, involves the solution by the State of the most intricate problem of applied economics—the control of the price level. Because the seamless web of pre-1914 finance had been rent first by the war, then by the burden of war debts, and again by the protective policies of national cultures threatened by industrial revolutions, Government action in the monetary field had by 1934-35 developed to an unprecedented scale.[10] After 1918 " a very violent depreciation of money in the immediate post-war period destroyed over a large part of the continent of Europe all rational calculation and all orderly social and economic development. This was followed by a period of relative stability in which material well-being progressed markedly. This was followed by a violent turn-down of prices . . . the problems thus raised transcend in importance any others of our time and generation."[11]

In this country the control of our currency was exclusively a matter for the Bank of England. In determining its policy it had to weigh the interests of group against group in relation to the interests of the country as a whole. It had been held that it should not be required to submit to political pressure and that economic analysis should not be distorted by party obligations.[12] It remained an autonomous regulator of one of the most vital conditions upon which economic activity depends. So far as civilization depended upon " the expectation of normal profits to individual concerns and the sanctity of contracts " the banks after 1918 had the care of civilization thrust upon them. The Bank of England developed an inner Cabinet—the Committee of Treasury, consisting of the Governor and seven other directors elected by secret ballot of the whole court.[13] The need for continuous consultation with other foreign banks led to the growth within the bank of a higher Civil Service.[14] The pre-1914 supremacy of London was replaced partly by co-operation between the central banks of the world and partly by conflicting national policies about the objects and methods of an international monetary system.[15]

The Government decided on April 28th, 1925, to return to the Gold Standard. Severely criticized by many experts at the time and disappointing in its subsequent results the decision was forced upon the Government by the expiry of the Act which then forbade the export of gold. The Government considered a renewal of the Act would have " destroyed our rising credit in every country of the world."[16] The pound was overvalued by about 10 per cent., causing a decline in Britain's share of world exports in the period 1925-29. The Balfour Committee of 1929 said it was " unthinkable that any appreciable body of opinion would favour a fresh departure from the Gold Standard " ; and three months before the country did come off gold the Macmillan Committee recommended " that this country should continue to adhere to the International Gold Standard at the existing parity."[17] After September, 1931, when the Gold Standard was suspended, the relationship between the Treasury and the Bank of England became closer than ever. The management of sterling was discussed continuously between the representatives of the Treasury and the representatives of the Bank of England.[18] In 1932 the Finance Act created an Exchange Equalization Account of £150 millions to be operated secretly for the protection of the sterling exchange against seasonal fluctuations, speculative operations and the movements of refugee capital. This account involved a further extension of Government responsibility for the monetary policy of the country which was, however, still regulated by the Bank of England.[19] The destructive speculative attacks on currencies which developed after 1929 was beaten off by defensive measures undertaken by central banks which raised their discount rates and limited credit for speculative purposes.

Down to 1925 there was no real cause for pessimism about the position of British trade. It seemed that the recovery of world trade from the impediments of war would restore our prosperity. We should enjoy an increasing proportion of one increasing trade. Though aground we were not yet on the rocks and would be floated off by the returning tide. But after the return to gold in 1925 there was no substantial diminution of unemployment and our export trade failed to maintain its progress and lost ground to its competitors.[20] The year 1927, which was the nearest approach to normal in the inter-war years, brought to light problems which were not merely the residual difficulties of the 1914-18 war but symptoms of a new industrial and commercial era. In 1929 we suffered from trade depression in many of our great industries at a time when other countries were enjoying a considerable degree of prosperity.[21] Between 1929 and 1934 when the volume of world trade shrank by nearly a quarter the share of the United Kingdom slightly rose (from 13.03 per cent. to 13.85 per cent.), but this was partly due to a temporary improvement of the terms of trade. Owing to the collapse of the price of raw materials, a bale of exports bought nearly 23 per cent. more in 1933 than it would in 1929. This advantage was not permanent. The labour and equipment set free by the improvement in the terms of trade were not transferred into other forms of production for the home market. The internal organization of finance and industry were not flexible enough to meet the changes in the markets of the world.

Before 1914 there had been available for overseas investment a surplus of between 130 and 180 million pounds. In 1913 an income of over £200 millions from overseas investments, and £130 millions from shipping and commissions had not only paid for the importation of some 60 per cent. of our food supply but had left £180 millions for investment abroad. By 1926 that surplus had been nearly wiped out. By 1929 it had recovered to £139 millions, but in 1931 it had become once more an adverse balance of £104 millions. In these conditions of violent variations it was impossible that the British Government, alone of the great Governments of the world, should renounce the use of tariffs as a defensive weapon or a constructive tool.

In the immediate post-war years of optimism, Mr. Keynes had written " we must hold to free trade in its widest interpretation as an inflexible dogma to which no exception is admitted. We must hold to it even when we receive no reciprocity of treatment and even in those rare cases when by infringing it we could obtain a direct economic advantage."[22] Although the war of 1914-18 had made the first breach in our Free Trade policy with the McKenna Duties which were continued after it, and although the post-war years produced a mild imperial preference and the safeguarding of key industries, in 1927 only 2 to 3 per cent. of British imports were liable to safeguarding or other protective duties and only one out of every 200 British workers was employed in safeguarded industries.[23] But in 1930 the Manchester Chamber of Commerce and the Economic Committee of the Trade Union Council both declared for the abandonment of our traditional policy. In November, 1931, the Abnormal Importations Bill was passed by the House of Commons in three days and in February, 1932, the Imports Duties Bill in six.[24]

The former was a temporary measure giving to the President of the Board of Trade power to impose duties to check an abnormal stream of imports. The latter was the real foundation of a new Protectionism. It gave Protection to home industries, provided a basis for preference within the Empire and for reciprocal agreements with or retaliation against foreign countries.[25] To a basic 10 per cent. *ad valorem* tariff on imports the Treasury were empowered to make additions on the recommendation of an Import Duties Advisory Committee.[26] In the summer of 1932 the Ottawa Agreement widely extended the principle of Imperial Preference. At the World Economic Conference of 1933 the representative of the British Government held that tariffs might be imposed for revenue, the maintenance of a country's standard of living, and the encouragement of forms of industry and production regarded as essential to the economic life of a country.[27] The Government had embarked on the difficult task of co-ordinating the threefold policy of Protection to British agriculture, trade agreements with countries in the sterling area, and Imperial Preference.

The regulation of trade thus imposed upon this country by the planning policies of the countries of the world involved also the control of external investments. Before the 1914-18 war 20 per cent. of new capital raised was for home and 80 per cent. for foreign investment. In 1928 the proportions were 60 per cent. and 40 per cent. respectively. After 1931 foreign lending came almost to a standstill. Restrictions were adopted as a deliberate policy. In 1935 of £182 millions raised nearly 89 per cent. were for home, about 9 per cent. for the Empire, and less than 2 per cent. for foreign countries. The State was becoming responsible for the deliberate allocation of British capital resources.

In 1907 Campbell-Bannerman could claim that the sea-power of this country implied no challenge to any single State, because our adherence to the principles of independence for all nations, and freedom of trade, made our fleet a messenger of good will and not a threat of violence.[28] In 1860 the whole Empire had been thrown open to world trade. In 1897 the British Government withdrew its opposition to the preference policies of those colonies which had full responsible government. Though by 1907 these had all developed a policy of Imperial Preference, the open door was maintained in the colonial empire. In 1917 a Royal Commission on the natural resources, trade and legislation of certain parts of His Majesty's Dominions, concluded that it was vital that the Empire should be in a position to resist any pressure which foreign powers might exercise through their control of raw materials and commodities essential to our well-being.[29] In 1919 Great Britain began to grant preferential rates in her tariff for the products both of the Dominions and the Empire and through the Colonial Office to secure preferences for British goods in the non-self-governing colonies and protectorates. By 1936 only in a small part of these was the open door still maintained.[30] These colonial agreements were among the most successful attempts to expand trade within a given area. Between 1929 and 1936 the " whole structure of British finance had been transformed." Free Trade, no taxation except for revenue, lowering the cost of living by every means ; the gold standard, the enormous sinking fund, the strict and punctual discharge of international obligations all had gone.[31]

In 1840 the revenue was about £52 millions, and almost exactly three-fourths was derived from customs and excise. Tea, sugar, tobacco, spirits and corn produced two-thirds of this customs revenue. From 1842 the income tax was developed as an instrument to make the reform of the tariff possible. In 1853 Gladstone proposed to secure the extinction of the income tax by 1860. But the Crimean War disposed that it should be raised from 7d. to 1s. 4d. in the pound. It was maintained at 10d. in 1860 in order to secure the revision of the tariff. In 1865, on the eve of the General Election, it had been reduced to 4d. In 1874 Gladstone again offered to abolish it.[32] In 1890 72 per cent. of our national tax revenue was obtained from indirect taxation.[33] In 1894 the reorganization of Death Duties—the graduation of the main tax according to the amount in the pool and not to sums drawn by particular beneficiaries—gave a great new direct tax comparable to the income tax and yet independent of it.[34]   In 1907 Asquith's Budget differentiated for the first time between earned and unearned income, levying 1s. for the latter and 9d. for the former on those with less than £2,000 a year.[35]   By 1913-14 46 per cent. of our tax revenue was indirect.

A total expenditure of about £50 millions in the eighteen-thirties had risen to £90 in the 'nineties and to nearly £200 in 1913-14.   In 1932-33 expenditure was £859 millions.   In 1914 the highest rate of income tax was 1s. 2d. in the £ and supertax was 1s. 4d.   In 1932-33 the figures were 5s. and 8s. 3d.   Before 1914 the richest taxpayer was not called to pay more than 1s. 8d. of his income to the State ; in 1933 he might pay as much as two-thirds.[36]   Indirect taxation provided about 39.8 per cent. of our national tax revenue.[37]

We have considered some of the facts which deepened Government responsibility for currency as the life-blood of a competitive system and compelled a reversal of its traditional policy of Free Trade.   It is possible to argue that the decline in our exports, as it was due to a change in our favour of the terms of trade, was a matter for congratulation.   Our daily bread could be earned by brows which sweated less. But this is to ignore the necessity of transferring the resources so released to the provision of other needs. We can now see that after 1918 our task was to transfer our energies to meet the changing needs of a dissolving world.   But the problem was difficult and its real character obscure.   The political forces of nationalism, the technological forces of scientific research and the economic problems inherent in the changing scale of industrial production presented to the business man uncertainties he had never known, and to the State administrative problems of an entirely new scale.

In the early nineteenth century it had seemed to Malthus that the root problem of human organization—the flaming sword that barred the gate of any earthly paradise—was the tendency of any easing of the task of filling stomachs to encourage also an increase in their number. Priapus would always outstrip Ceres.   This Malthusian fear was exorcized by the discovery that the fruit of men's labour and the fruit of their loins might be varied independently.   Nature ploughed by science might become more fertile in goods than man had been in his own image.   Solomon in all his glory could not multiply as fast as a machine.   But in place of the old problem of subsistence now resolved a new problem of organization had appeared.   Increasing supplies of goods depended upon a division of labour, and the greater the supplies the more various they were and the more various the more subtle the division of labour required. The assembling of the factors of production began to overshadow all other human problems. The problems of the organization of the labour market began to overshadow all others.

In this country before 1914 our labour had been trained and our capital sunk in old industries ; our population was clustered at the mines, at the shipyards, or in Lancashire. Our whole industrial life had grown into a mould.[38] We were specialists in the job of supplying the world with coal, textiles and other manufactured articles. The supremacy of our shipping was dependent partly on the fact that as great coal exporters we had the economic advantage of possessing a saleable ballast for out-going ships in search of foreign trade. When, after 1918, oil and electric power were developed as alternatives to coal, the cotton industry made rapid strides in the Far East, and the shrinking volume of world trade withered the shipyards, the problem of unemployment was most menacing precisely in those industries where our development had been greatest in the past. From 1923 to 1935, though the number of persons insured in the coal industry had decreased by 22 per cent., the unemployment figure was in the latter year 32 per cent. ; in shipbuilding, in spite of a contraction of numbers employed by 40 per cent. unemployment was 42 per cent. ; in cotton a shrinkage of 21 per cent. had still left 22.2 per cent. unemployed.[39]

Fundamentally the policy of economic nationalism was a " protest against interdependence and an attempt to protect group interests in each country from the disturbing effects of external change."[40] It was the policy of trusts and trade unions which could command the powers of the State. It has been stigmatized as " a flight from reality " on the ground " that every improvement in communications makes the interdependence of the world more real."[41] It would, however, be a flight from reality to ignore the fact that by 1934, as a consequence of the depression which began in 1929, " never before had so many Governments intervened so actively to protect particular producers or to regulate the functioning of the price system."[42] The essence of the matters would seem to lie in the fact that to make use of the maximum territorial division of labour would have imposed on particular groups a flexibility which they were not prepared to endure. In the case of the industrial revolution in this country an expanding population and a rising standard of living had only imposed on labour the mobility required by such methods as the Combination Acts and the Poor Law Act of 1834. When the first primitive suppression of combinations had been abandoned the complex legal and political adjustments of the laws relating to Trade Unions had to be worked out. Even then within our homogeneous community State action had to complete the organization of the labour market which the Trade Unions and employers' organization had only raggedly secured. It was necessary to provide for changes in occupation too sudden to be met by individual judgment. Those who protest against the madness which drove the world from freedom of trade ignore the forces which in fact determine industrial and commercial organization. In this country it is admitted that powerful Trade Unions and price-fixing associations with their multitude of contractual obligations made the problem of " wage adjustment capable of no obvious solution."[43] There were wide diversities in the relative position of workers in different industries and occupations.[44] The heavy fall in world prices imposed a particularly heavy burden on the wage earners in the export industries.[45] There was after 1918 a shift in demand from productive activities to services. The numbers of employed in the South increased 28 per cent. and in the North there was a decline of 3 per cent. But the proportion of unemployment was four times as great in the North as in the South of England.[46]

The relation of the State to industry after 1918 was one of the greatest confusion. Roughly there were three phases of the discussion and practice : (1) in the first five years after the 1914-18 war discussion was dominated by the influence of the experience of State control during the war and by some naive theories of nationalization and of industrial democracy. This country had had no experience of universal suffrage, but in the cause of social justice she was prepared to consider the possibility of the application of democracy to industry. The tendency was further strengthened by the facts that the country was highly industrialized, that the railways, miners, and transport workers seemed to hold a dominating position, while the employers' side was admittedly chaotic because the structure of industry before 1914 had been individualistic. During the 1914-18 war the Trade Unions had been taken into partnership by the State ; and after 1918 the leaders of industry were misled by a post-war boom into undertaking unwise expansions. The shipping industry widely miscalculated the demand for shipping ; cotton indulged in an expansion which an elementary knowledge of the facts might have prevented ; while the coal industry exploited the temporary post-war shortage in such a way as to hasten the very development of alternative sources of power which were to be its doom. Just as everyone in the war of 1914-18 thought of peace as a return to a brighter pre-war world, so everyone engaged in industry thought of the future of industry as being an extension of those developments which had been noticeable before the war. In that time of peace the Webbs had shown democracy in industry broadening slowly from precedent to precedent, and it was believed that after the war it would be in full flood. For some time the war of pamphlets turned on the question whether the new world of ordered plenty was to be introduced by persuasion or by a little well-placed violence. Some technicians of the creative strike believed in the mines for the miners, the railways for the railwaymen, and no doubt if pressed would have agreed that cows should belong to cowmen and ganders to geese. The rift in this simple lute of federal harmony came when the older Trade Unions awoke to the fact that their dominating position was being undermined by economic forces over which their political power gave them no control. Why run up the Jolly Roger of nationalization on an industrial ship which the economic tides had left high and dry. It was gradually realized that the impact of science on industrial structure and the flexibility which the rapid changes in demand imposed, required a much more complex organization than most nationalizers had then conceived. The clearer-sighted leaders in industry began, not to demand nationalization pure and simple, but appropriate constitutions for industry. The dream of nationalization passed into the hope of rationalization. In 1919 the Sankey Commission advocated for the coal industry " either nationalization or a method of unification by national purchase." In 1926 the Samuel Commission condemned nationalization as a " vast and hazardous experiment," and held that " the variety and freedom of private enterprise was more likely to conduce to the progressive development of this particular industry than control by the State." But if the bureaucratic reach-me-down of nationalization was found unsuitable for any of our major industries, the old antagonism to the principle of combination had to be modified. " The individualism of the British character (had) often led the manufacturers to retain personal control over a small and relatively inefficient works, rather than pool his brains and capital to the greatest advantage of the industry."[47] But during the 1914-18 war some industries had to be dealt with as a whole, while after the war the iron and steel industries, shipping, and agriculture sought the intervention of the State.[48] But the method of that intervention was determined by a series of almost casual emergencies, and influenced by a sound judgment that the forms of industrial organization must be many and various. A community which had avoided the straight-jacket of a rigid constitution for its political organization was not likely to impose crippling restraints upon its industrial organization. Nationalization might, as Mr. Tawney wrote, be simply a question of constitution-making, but constitutions were, his countrymen knew, the most kittle cattle in the world.

In 1928 the Liberal Industrial Report sought to demonstrate the " unreal character of the supposed antithesis between Socialism and

Individualism," and suggested that the abuses of private capitalism and unrestricted individualism could be reformed only on the lines already set.[49] In the first place there was "a necessary and important place for the public concern in the national economic system." Public concerns were "undertakings of great importance which require large amounts of capital yet fail to attract private enterprise on an adequate scale, either because of the necessity of limiting profits or for some other reason," or they were undertakings "where unavoidable conditions of monopoly would render unregulated private enterprise dangerous, or where the private shareholder had ceased to perform a useful function.[50] Public concerns consisted of (1) national undertakings operated by the Central Government—the Post Office, the Telegraphs, and the Telephones ; the dockyards and manufacturing establishments of the War Department ; the Office of Works ; the Royal Mint ; the Commissioners of Crown Lands ; the Stationery Office ; the State Management Districts under Licensing Act, 1921 ; the Roads under the Ministry of Transport ; (2) National Undertakings operated by officially appointed *ad hoc* bodies—the British Broadcasting Corporation, the Central Electricity Board and the Forestry Commission ; (3) local undertakings operated by the Local Authorities themselves—those public utility undertakings whose growth had been the inspiration of Fabian Socialism ; (4) the variety of local undertakings operated by officially appointed *ad hoc* authorities, e.g., the Port of London Authority, the Metropolitan Water Board, the London Passenger Transport Board ; (5) companies whose profits were regulated or restricted, e.g., building societies ; co-operative societies and parliamentary companies ; (6) numerous charitable undertakings not run for profit. Outside these public concerns was the whole world of large-scale business operated by joint stock companies. Of these some had passed out of the effective control of their shareholders, while others were still managed or effectively controlled by their proprietors. Some had attained something of monopoly position, while others were still subject to normal competitive conditions. " Where neither diffused ownership nor monopolistic tendencies were present it was only necessary for the State " to establish an environment in which normal competitive conditions " could flourish with the greatest efficiency and the least possible waste."[51] Where there was diffused ownership the abuse to be remedied was the inadequacy of the balance-sheet legally required which was " the cause of loss and deception for the investing public by placing a premium on inside information, gossip and breach of confidence."[52] " The honest financier spends his time in getting hold of true information to which he is not entitled, and the less honest in spreading false information for which, under cover of general darkness, he can obtain credence."[53] This last judgment was strikingly confirmed by the Macmillan Report of 1931, which reported that " in general the individual investor can hardly be supposed to have himself knowledge of much value either as to the profitable character or of the security of what he is offered." In 1931 the total market value of the £117 millions subscribed for capital issues, whether of shares or debentures, of 284 companies was £66 millions, a loss of over 47 per cent.[54] They proposed that better publicity should be given by requiring that information should be more accurate, that the responsibility of the auditors to see that the publicity provision of the revised Company Law was fully satisfied in the letter and in the spirit, and that " the Board of Directors should be subject to the criticism of a supervisory council consisting of members directly representing shareholders and in some cases employees."[55] Unless the State were to concern itself in the future much more subtly with the legal forms of competitive industry, the investor, like the unemployed before the establishment of labour exchanges, would remain " a stranger and afraid in a world he never made."

It was the opinion of the wiser economists that the working of self-interest was " generally beneficial, not because of some natural coincidence between the self-interest of each and the good of all, but because human institutions are arranged so as to compel self-interest to work in directions in which it will be beneficial."[56] But experience after 1918 showed that the existing human institutions were not so arranged that the industrial order must work for even a shadow of the general good. A feature of modern industrial progress due partly to the effect of scientific discoveries on the scale of the plant which it requires,.and partly to the growing complexity of the markets which it serves, is that it proceeds discontinuously in leaps and jumps.[57] It seemed that neither the search of individual investors for profit nor the powers of the most enlightened bankers could administer the stimulus to reorganization that was so obviously required.[58] In 1930 the Bankers' Industrial Development Company was established by the efforts of the Governor of the Bank. It had a capital of £6 millions, of which £1.5 millions was subscribed by the Bank of England and £4.5 millions by the Deposit Banks, Merchant Banks and finance houses. Its Board consisted of six members with the Governor as Chairman. Its purpose was " to receive and consider schemes for the reorganization and re-equipment of the basic industries of the country when brought forward from within the particular industry and if approved to procure the supply of the necessary financial support for carrying out the scheme."[59]   But it met with little success. It was unable to decide whether the provision of aid for one part of an industry might not do harm to the rest. The official Treasury view was that Government assistance for the reorganization of our basic industries was dangerous. While " Government money was available it is not natural to suppose that all the necessary sacrifices would be readily made." Rationalization is " a difficult and painful process involving the full recognition of losses, cutting down of creditors' claims, wiping out of whole classes of shareholders."[60]

In practice the Government was compelled by considerations of policy spasmodically to interfere with the organization of many of our basic industries. Whatever the limitations and problems of Government control it was unavoidable so long as the problems of the industries concerned were themselves produced by political activity in the rest of the world. The Government's action was necessarily distorted by the political pressure which each industry could bring to bear, and by the responsibility for the conditions of any industry which might be laid upon it as a result of Government action in the 1914-18 war and Government fears for another. Three industries may be briefly considered : Coal ; Iron and Steel ; Agriculture.

In the case of coal, the industry was not freed from the abnormal influence of temporary demands and subsidies until 1927.[61] " By reducing the length of the legal working day in 1919 the Government had attracted fresh labour into the industry ; by increasing the hours in a period of depression it enlarged the volume of the industry's unemployment. During the post-war boom it permitted coal to be sold at an exorbitant rate to the foreigner, with the result that the development of alternative sources of power was stimulated. In 1925 it adopted the opposite policy of subsidizing the industry so that the foreigner could be provided with coal cheaply at the expense of the taxpayer. In 1930 it proposed to achieve the same end at the expense of the domestic consumer."[62]

The Coal Mines Act of 1930 attempted both an immediate palliative for the partial suppression of competition, and a permanent cure for the evils of the industry by reorganization. For the first Parliament granted wide discretionary powers to a central elected council to arrange district schemes subject to the general supervision of the Board of Trade. For the second a permanent Coal Reorganization Commission was appointed by the Board of Trade, not directly responsible to any Government Department, for the purpose of promoting reorganization by amalgamations, arrived at, if possible by permission, and if not, by coercion. The plans of the Commissions met with strong opposition from the industry.

During the 1914-18 war extensions of the iron and steel industry were designed for the needs of war and not for the markets of the peace. In consequence we acquired many first-class works, but they were in the wrong place and they were not balanced for ordinary commercial business.[63] Investigation revealed that the heavy steel industry required to be gradually rebuilt on a national scale with plants larger than any yet built.[64] In 1932 the Import Duties Advisory Committee recommended the imposition of a temporary duty of 33⅓ on many classes of iron and steel and the Government extended the operation of the duty until October, 1934, on the understanding that the industry would proceed with schemes of rationalization. But the high tariff, by increasing the industries competitive in the home market, weakened the previous inducement to reorganization.[65]

The relation of the State to agriculture reveals in the most vivid way the pitfalls and the snares that must dog a Government once it takes, under whatever compulsion, to the economic road. In the first place agriculture is the occupation most directly threatened by the advancing industrial revolution in the world. Agriculture is the occupation of two-thirds of mankind and the application of science to its methods will involve the greatest displacement of labour in the history of the world. Secondly, because it is the occupation of the great majority of the world's workers it occupies in most political systems a preponderating influence in the councils of the State. Thirdly, in this country its position is peculiar and complex ; as we were the first industrial country in the world, agriculture occupies a position less politically powerful than in any other first-class power, and as we are strategically no longer an island, the wisdom of accepting its comparative subordination has been questioned. Agriculture is a fine example of the possible conflict between the interests of the national groups and the interests of the world considered as a whole.

In this country before 1914 the agricultural industry had lost its natural leaders. In the nineteenth century down to the depression of the 'nineties farm relief had been supplied by the land-owning class. But that depression wiped them out as an economic and political power and the actual control of British agricultural production passed almost entirely to the farmers themselves.[66] The system was one midway between the peasant system of the Continent and large-scale capitalist undertakings for plantation crops. Investigation suggested that it would be possible to organize the industry to feed half instead of one-third of our population.

The essential figure was that 28,000,000 acres would under any circumstances be under grass, and 12,000,000 acres under crops, but there was a margin of 6,000,000 which by subsidy or protection could be turned from grass to crops. But this simple analysis was complicated by the fact that the natural field for development of British agriculture—war apart—was in livestock, dairying, poultry, fruit, flowers and vegetables.[67] Even in the corn-growing area of East Anglia the sale of livestock and livestock produce amounted to 68 per cent. of the total.[68] If the economic advantage of the development of the livestock industry were sacrificed to the strategic need for crops, one-half of the food supply would still depend upon our ability to pay for it abroad and to protect the routes by which it must be carried.

In these circumstances it is not surprising that the agricultural policy of the Government after 1918 was most haphazard. There were, of course, many reasonable extensions of Government action to secure increased efficiency. Plant and animal diseases were controlled ; education and research provided ; special credit facilities provided which the preoccupation of the banks with foreign trade and investment before 1914 had failed to provide. But there were also confused and conflicting policies of protection and subsidy. In 1924 the sugar beet industry was begun. In ten years it received £39,500,000 and in 1934 employed 32,000.[69] In 1932 the Wheat Act provided a guaranteed price for a specified quantity of wheat grown in the United Kingdom. The amount paid in 1934 was £4.5 millions. In the same year £1.5 millions was paid to milk and £3 millions to beef.[70] The methods included " quantitative regulation, subsidies, levies, guaranteed prices, tariffs, and marketing schemes."[71] In 1933 the Marketing Act associated internal marketing arrangements with the regulation of imports by quotas. As a result of the adoption of a policy of Imperial Preference the percentage of her food supplies imported from Empire countries was increased from 38 per cent. to 50 per cent.[72] But while Empire self-sufficiency in most foodstuffs was possible, it would have deprived British manufacturing industries of large markets in foreign countries and would have prevented them from meeting their obligations on British investments.[73]

It is not surprising that to many we seemed to be wandering between two worlds. On the one hand the Government had had to provide a far more subtle legal framework for the working of competitive industry than the nineteenth century could have foreseen ; on the other the conflict between industrialism and nationalism had compelled a direct intervention of the State in regions Cobden hoped it would never know. The form of State intervention in industry had been determined by the particular emergencies and the political forces which in each prevailed. There was a mighty maze and nothing of a plan. It was of course, the argument of *laissez-faire* that this monstrous institutional complexity would in the long run exact a far heavier price than would the simple conflicts of competitive industry. With the State no longer umpire, but combatant and judge, where would justice be found?

However this may be we must observe that in its treatment of those social aspects of the industrial order which most would admit to belong to the sphere of Government the same conflict of principles and administrative complexity was to be found. Let us glance briefly at State action in relation (1) to the standard of living; (2) the provision of services which require collective action.

(1) At the end of the last century the enquiries of Booth (London, 1894) and Rowntree (York, 1899) revealed the startling probability that from 25 to 30 per cent. of the town population of the United Kingdom were living in poverty.[74] Of this poverty bad habits accounted for only 13 per cent., unfortunate circumstances for 19 per cent., and about 68 per cent. was due to the inadequacy and irregularity of the wages paid. Since then the increasing productivity of industry, the organization of the unskilled into Trade Unions, and the supervision of the unorganized by the State through Trade Boards had reduced the percentage of poverty to about 11 per cent. and of this poverty less than one in five was due to the insufficiency of the wages paid. Unemployment and not the insufficiency of wages was in the nineteen thirties the major cause of poverty.[75] In 1914 the real income per head had not shown for some years any tendency either to increase or to decline. The effect of the 1914-18 war was to increase the earnings of the unskilled as compared with the skilled and of the worker in sheltered industries as compared with those in unsheltered. It is difficult to estimate the real earnings of any class of worker, because the direction of his expenditure always changes. It was, however, estimated that wage earners as a whole had, in spite of the heavy increase in unemployment, secured substantially enhanced real earnings per head during the ten years after 1918.[76] At the same time expenditure on the social services had risen from £100 millions to £400 millions between the periods 1909-14 and 1932-1935. The ratio of expenditure on social services to wages it is estimated had risen from 3.4 per cent. in 1880 to 10.4 per cent. in 1913 and about 18 per cent. in 1930.[77]

But the action of the State in relation to the standard of living was uncertain and confused throughout. In the case of Workmen's Compensation it was decided that the employer should be held responsible for all accidents, whether they were due to his negligence or to acts of God.[78] This may have been justified by the administrative impossibility of discriminating between the accidents due to negligence and those due to unforeseeable circumstances. But the result was that the employer insured himself against liability, thus freeing himself from any incentive to initiate or to introduce safety measures, while the worker had no guarantee that he would get anything at all from an employer who had failed to insure.[79] The desire to distinguish Unemployment Insurance Benefit from Public Assistance caused family needs to have no place in the original benefits decided. The character of unemployment after 1918 compelled the introduction of family allowances first as a temporary expedient and then as an essential part of the system.[80] The National Health Insurance scheme made no provision for family needs, so that a man unemployed through inability to find work found his family needs taken into account, but were his unemployment due to sickness they would not.[81] The most notorious of these confusions was that the legally deterrent Poor Law was by pressure of circumstances compelled to provide a variety of preventative and curative services which overlapped with those provided for men and women who were not paupers.

The administrative chaos which can be produced by the pressure of unforeseen emergencies upon schemes born of confused principles was shown by the fate of the Unemployment Insurance scheme after 1918. Compulsory Unemployment Insurance could be justified by the fact that while a risk might be overwhelming and impossible to estimate by an individual worker or a particular industry, it might be measurable when considered from a collective standpoint.[82] While unemployment due to personal qualities and defects could not be foreseen, unemployment due to industrial fluctuations could. So the initial scheme of 1911 developed by a brilliant group of civil servants was limited to a particular group of industries—building, constructions of works, shipbuilding, engineering—which were thought suitable because, while they were liable to fluctuations they were not likely to decay. The scheme was compulsory to avoid the predominance of bad risks; it required a definite relation between contributions paid and benefits received in order automatically to exclude bad risks; it made the State a contributor so that it might provide stability and exercise the necessary controls. Its framers knew that fire insurance would fail if there were no protection against arson. But the extension of the scheme to the greater part of the field of industrial employment in 1920 led to the abandonment of nearly every principle which a sound insurance scheme must observe.

The original scheme had been intended to provide specific benefits to meet a measurable risk. The benefits provided were not supposed

214

to meet every need of those who drew them. The scheme assumed a normal working of the labour market. It could not meet the needs of those who were unemployed because a series of industrial and political revolutions had devastated our economic system. With the extension of the scheme to cover nearly the whole of industry it was found first that the benefits legally due in accordance with the contributions made would not save those who were unemployed through decay of their industries, from the Poor Law. But as soon as benefits were given beyond the amounts actuarially due the whole insurance character of the system was imperilled. Actually it became a system of Public Assistance for those who were considered to be available for work. It was a system of outdoor relief for the able-bodied poor. This was fair neither to the unemployed themselves nor to the community as a whole. What was required was that an insurance scheme should cover certain calculable risks of normal industrial fluctuations ; that those who were displaced from industry permanently because of the decay of the industries in which they had been employed should be trained for new occupations ; while those, if any, who were not capable of benefiting from the training offered should be regenerated by whatever health, educational or disciplinary measures were necessary. The adoption of the principle of " work or maintenance " involves the acceptance of compulsory allocation of jobs. But a free labour market can be organized if Labour Exchanges provide the conditions of a market, compulsory insurance gives protection against calculable risks, and if an authority for the able-bodied poor provides that maintenance and education of which the need by any individual or group cannot be foreseen because it is the result of revolutions in industry which no one can foretell.

(2) In the case of those social services which in the nineteenth century were clearly recognized to be within the scope of Government action there was added to the difficulty of conflicting principles the confusions of a legal and administrative system needlessly complicated. In the case of education the question of the age to which the State should provide that its future citizens must be educated was complicated by the mazes of the local educational administrative scheme. The Education Act of 1902, while it provided that in those towns which were County Boroughs the direction of whatever public education was provided should be under a single authority, divided the responsibility in the counties between the county council and the municipal boroughs and urban districts. The former it made responsible for secondary education in all their area, but elementary education it was to control only where the latter were not themselves the authority. As these elementary educational authorities were responsible for a large number

215

of post-primary schools whose work overlapped and conflicted with the post-primary and secondary education for which the county was responsible, the Director of Education of the county often had a task beyond the wit of man. He might have to adjust his system to the diverse elementary and post-primary schemes of thirteen different authorities.[83] The administrative organization which was determined by the balance of power, administrative, financial and sectarian, in 1902, was a handicap to educational reform. The fundamental reform proposed by the Hadow Report of 1926, that post-primary education, i.e., education after the age of eleven, should be systematically organized to meet the needs of adolescence was hampered not only by the inability of the electorate to realize that it should be their privilege to train those who must come after them, so that the school-leaving age was not raised to fifteen, but also by the confusion of educational authorities inherited from 1902. In Public Health, after a generation of talk, the confusion laid bare by the report of the Poor Law Commission of 1904-9 was removed in 1929. The counties and county boroughs of England and Wales took over the health services once provided by the Board of Guardians for the sick poor, and were in a position to provide skilled institutional treatment for all classes of the population. Only in London, however, were the possibilities of the new system fully realized. The transfer of the Poor Law Institutions to the London County Council made possible a clearly marked division between the field of local action concerned with the detection of disease and the local measures necessary for its prevention. Here again, as with education, the inspiration which the advance of knowledge provided was cribbed, cabined and confined by the administrative anomalies Parliament could not find time or temper to remove. Not until 1929 was a serious attempt made to deal with the fantastic inappropriateness of the smaller urban districts for their duties as a health authority.[84]

Finally, the organization of the police force provided an interesting example of that Bumbledom which breeds eternal in the English breast. " The local authorities upon whom it was originally necessary to force a police system have come to regard their government as a privilege which ought not to be taken away or modified."[85] A Department Committee on the Police Service in 1919-20 recommended that all non-county borough forces should be merged in the county. This might seem common sanity, for in a small police force, experience, specialization, and freedom from patronage were impossible. Inspector Frenchs could not be trained at Bridlington-in-the-Mud. Efficient policemen have to be not only stronger than lions but swifter than eagles. But such speed and strength come only from modern equipment and the power of concentration and dispersion which it gives. One day the force must patrol a distant racecourse, another control a busy fair, and all the time watch malefactors as they fly. For this it had been estimated in 1919 that 100,000 population was the minimum size of a borough which should claim a separate police force.

CHAPTER IX

GOVERNMENT AND PARTIES, 1918-39

The Constitution in the Post-War World—The New Franchise and the character of Post-War Elections—The nature of the Party System—The Labour Party—The Liberals—The Conservatives—The transformation of the Cabinet—The position of the Prime Minister—The Work of Parliament.

IN 1914 the English system of government, in spite of many parochial and insular peculiarities, still seemed to be a model for the world. In form it was not so complete a democracy as Scandinavia, Switzerland, France or the United States. Its machinery of administration and of justice was hampered by a long and tenacious past. But it had had a harmony of order with liberty which others in a world on the eve of revolutions in industrial· organization would be lucky to obtain. It had gone far to solve the problem of reconciling democracy with the technique of imperial administration which the clash of cultures in a shrinking world had brought. A believer in progress might see in the English system of government a state of political development which other less favoured States would one day reach.

We know now that whatever value for the world the English system of government may have it was not to be the glass of fashion and the mould of form for the twentieth century. The world may see a Prussian Napoleon, a Russian Augustus, a Japanese Louis XIV, but it will never see a Prussian Gladstone, a Russian Disraeli or a Japanese Victoria.

After 1918 the mark of the machine was already on every human activity. Government needed something of the speed and the precision of the factory. How to get this and secure a way of life worth living was not known. Many political and social forms cherished by the nineteenth century, including the minimizing of bureaucracy had to be abandoned. A Continental or even a world order may be possible in which national Governments would have only a parochial significance. Such a Federal world Government would depend at first on the spirit and the form of the national systems included in it. It was possible that the only way in which England could survive was to become part of a British Commonwealth of Nations. It was possible that the

218

English would lose their imperial heritage. With the breakdown of the international economic order of the nineteenth century new political forms, despotic and expanding emerged. In a dissolving world could the spirit of the Constitution, the technique, the style of our political parties aid and comfort and maybe save reason by their example ?

One change in the English political system since 1914 might be described as a transition from the spirit of the amateur to the spirit of the professional. Amateurism in the nineteenth century pervaded the whole of English life. Her industrial expansion was the expression of a vigorous amateurism, as had been the agricultural revolution which preceded it, and the scientific work which had made them possible. In the structure of her Government, in the framing of her machinery of administration, even in the provision of her courts of justice, the spirit of the amateur was everywhere to be found. Amateurism in business is disappearing. In politics the same process can be seen. We have now to do by deliberation and by plan what was once done by occasional genius or the general common sense. Our corporate life, once begot by idiosyncrasy on custom, has now to be sustained by complex planning. J. S. Mill's plea for liberty has been denied.

It was some time after 1918 before it was realized that it was not a brave but a new world passing strange in which our political life would have to make its way. It was not as in the early nineteenth century simply a question of releasing the natural man from the spell of privilege which bound him. We had to extend into the sphere of politics the system and the thought which science had already imposed upon business and the home. In Poor Law, public health, education, great administrative machines had had to be created. During the 1914-18 war the machinery of Government had been transformed. After 1918 it was clear that this reorganization would have to be extended into every detail of the State—to the Cabinet, to Parliament, and to the Crown itself. Whether or not there was a formal written Constitution, a Constitution there had to be. The rule of the wise men of the tribe would not be enough. Tradition had to be codified. There was an enormous field of technical administrative work to be developed. Now that religion had decayed, the simple rationalism of Bentham would be tried and tested in a world less stable and more violent than he ever dreamt of.

In anticipation of the problems of peace a Speaker's conference had been appointed in 1917 to revise the electoral system. The war-time unity of parties made possible a settlement of controversies which had embittered politics for generations. By the Representation of the Peoples Act, 1918, the franchise was extended to all adult males and to women who were at least thirty years old. A provision that no person might vote at an election for more than two constituences on different qualifications ended the major abuses of plural voting. The procedure of registration was greatly simplified by making the ordinary qualification six months' residence. So simple and automatic was the procedure of registration that fraud or the expenditure of party funds for the manipulation of the register was useless. All elections were to take place on one day. Returning Officers' expenses were to be paid by the Exchequer. Candidates were to be required to make a deposit of £150, to be forfeited if they did not poll more than one-eighth of the votes cast. The country was divided into single-member constituencies of approximately 50,000 voters each.

What effect had this simplification and extension of the suffrage? In discussing any representative system two faults must be avoided. We must be careful not to under-estimate the stability and the underlying rationality of the existing order. We must be careful also not to ignore underlying forces whose cumulative effects may suddenly produce a startling change. It is not the vagaries and occasional hysteria of the public mind on particular occasions that is important, but the basic changes in its habits and belief due, nor merely to the experience of particular individuals, but also to changes in the actual composition of the community. Births and deaths may have more effect on the strength of the parties than anything else. The following table gives some of the facts about the inter-war Elections :—

		Percentage of votes.			Number of seats.		
		Cons.	Lab.	Lib.	Cons.	Lab.	Lib.
1922	...	38	30	30	347	142	114
1923	...	38	30	30	258	191	159
1924	...	48	33	18	420	151	40
1929	...	38	36	25	260	287	59
1931	...	50	33	15	471	52	33
1935	...	50	40	7	387	154	17

The table shows the astonishing uncertainty of the relation of votes cast and seats won. This was a result of the English system of single members of constituencies. The existence of three parties contesting nearly every constituency meant the return of many members by only a minority of their electorates. There were as many as 313 such minority candidates in a single Parliament. At one time the disappearance of the Liberal Party would have affected half the membership of the House of Commons. There was a surprising incapacity on the part of the experts to foretell the result of any particular election. It was possible for a major party almost to be destroyed by a comparatively small shift of votes. The elector tended to vote against the leaders of the party which was out of favour in a particular crisis and to support a puppet of the popular cause. In 1918 it rejected Asquith and Simon and returned Bottomley and Pemberton Billing. In 1931 it rejected every leader of the Labour Opposition.

What was the effect of this new distribution of power? While it is impossible to interpret a single election, as the elements of contingency are so many, over nearly two decades it is possible to analyse certain tendencies. Before 1914 the Liberal Party was strongest in great industrial areas; in poor agricultural areas; and in those agricultural areas where there were smallholders with memories of the enclosure movement, e.g., in the Fenlands and in Norfolk and Suffolk. Discrimination in the past against Nonconformity had given Wales and Scotland to Liberalism. Conservatism was strongest in the rich agricultural counties: Surrey, Sussex, Hereford and the agricultural parts of Kent. The system of plural voting by which a man had only to maintain a legal lodging or pay £10 for lodgings to secure a vote, which the leisurely elections enabled him to exercise, secured to the Conservatives the business and warehouse districts of the boroughs. The Labour Party was of course strongest in the great industrial areas.

After 1918 the Labour Party naturally captured the great industrial areas: established an overwhelming superiority in the mining areas of Wales, Scotland and England; shook the Conservative hold in dockyard constituencies such as Southampton, Plymouth, Portsmouth and Sunderland. In 1929, of 330 seats of an industrial character only fifty were not Labour, while the spread of industry into suburbia had caused the fall of Acton and Romford. But it had not shaken the Conservative hold in the rich agricultural areas. In county districts it could not use its technique of door-to-door propaganda, nor had it the power of the great Unions. More fundamentally, while agriculturalists might be Liberal, opposed to parson and squire, the collectivist Trade Unionism was incomprehensible to them, and the beam of privilege in the eye of industry more obvious than the spark of justice.

In 1929 the Liberals still held Bedford, Cornwall, Devon and East Anglia, areas with a strong Nonconformist tradition, but only a fraction of Scotland and the Highlands. In the election of 1929 the figures suggest that in the boroughs the bulk of the new women electors had supported Labour and in the counties the Liberals. In 1935 Labour did well in the mining districts and in London, which between them provided one-third of the Labour representation. But it did badly in the Midlands (especially in Birmingham), Lancashire and in the distressed areas (except mining). While it advanced in the counties even more than in the towns, running in the West Country second to Liberalism, it made no serious impression on the Home Counties, coastal towns or University seats.

In the nineteenth century a political campaign was a leisurely affair conducted by an army of professional voters and a cloud of amateur witnesses. The function of the statesmen was to hold the balance between the forces of opinion and the result of the election. Elections were in the nature of an ordeal by battle to determine issues derived from public opinion interpreted by political leaders. The turnover was very small. Luck gave an edge to the pleasure of contending skill. A party was a federation of diverse local interests held in some political unity by a leader who embodied principles. However the ideal might be smirched by bribery the representative was considered to express the interests of his locality. So long as the different interests were geographically distinct a system of single-member constituencies would produce a workable House of Commons if they could agree to differ. Increasing unification made the country almost a single constituency. Instead of a struggle to secure support in different localities, elections became a struggle to secure the support of the country as a whole. Horizontal cleavages took the place of geographical variety. A small shift of votes could destroy a party. Paradoxically, a diversity of interests had compelled attention to principles, but the conflict of principles expressed by national parties threatened violence.

The bargaining of groups depends upon an underlying unity, but when that unity is thought to be threatened, people will vote to restore it if they can.

The two-party system in a democracy is an expression of diversity in unity; but when that unity is itself threatened the party system may break down. There was after 1918 a tendency for men of good will to draw up programmes upon which all members of the community might be supposed to agree. Intellectually and psychologically there was a centre party. The old party system reconciled a diversity of interests with a belief in argument. Parliament was the village pub or meeting house enlarged. Debate then could cope with the issues involved. Now the questions to be decided required the laboratory and the bureau of research. Debate was not enough. Decision had to be rooted in research.

In a democracy politics is one profession among many. Because of the peculiar conditions which may determine admission, and the oddities of fortune which decide success, those who succeed may have no quality of leadership. And so unstable is the world that the leader suitable in one decade may be useless in the next. In England the Cabinet had a heavy responsibility when it determined the date and the occasion of an election. Not only might it destroy itself, but it might do even worse—destroy the Opposition.

A professional organizer[1] described the new developments. There must be no question of regarding political opponents as persons to be pacified or even to be met half way. The spirit sought by a good committee was fatal to electoral success. " To regard the Opposition as merely mistaken in its ideas and not as deliberately dangerous, is wholly subversive of the will to win."[2]

Observance of a definite political strategy would give a chance of success. The party would not rely on its record but endeavour to create a new situation in which it could overwhelm the Opposition. The failure of Disraeli in 1878 to go to the country after the Congress of Berlin led to his defeat in 1880. In 1900 Chamberlain secured for the Conservative Party a new tenure of power by forcing the Khaki Election. The most successful campaigns were destructive offences, such as Mr. Lloyd George's campaign against the Peers in 1910 and the blasting by Mr. Snowden's broadcasting of his former colleagues in 1931. If possible a party would secure the initiative, present a programme of little detail, and repeat a clear and plain tale or lie. A constructive offensive was possible but difficult. It required careful preparation and constant watchfulness. The least hopeful was a defensive retrospective used by the Conservative Government in 1929.

The power of propaganda is the result of specialization in our lives. Things which are of direct interest provide no clue to those which indirectly will determine our future fate. The energies of men are involved in immediate tasks of thought or action, which give no clue to the nature of the whole of which they are a part. The propagandist produces a pseudo environment to secure action to his advantage. That is bad. It is worse that, if the propagandist did not make one for us, we should have no environment at all. Can anyone make himself a citizen of the twentieth-century world as he might have made himself a citizen of the eighteenth ? General education for most people stops at adolescence and is replaced by a technique of persuasion organized for profit. The advertisers are the sophists of the modern world. Without them people would have to educate themselves or accept the guidance of others. But those most competent to guide us in the modern world are busy seeking or creating even stranger worlds. Philosophers cannot be kings because they are preoccupied with a search for truths which will undermine all our traditional ways. The sophist advertiser or the unscrupulous dictator becomes our guide because so much ability is given to the service of science. The blind lead the blind in a world which new knowledge dazzles.

In England the political resources of the parties were many. They had some advantages in common : (1) the political education of war had taught that it could not be a preface to a pre-war peace but must be taken as the prologue to a strange new world ; (2) that the youth of this country had been less educated than that of any other first-class power and education could be started without the burden of a pernicious tradition ; (3) an absence of virulent internal problems which might cause fear to cast out thought ; (4) a deep though inarticulate understanding of the nature of industrial society. How else could the problem of Unemployment Insurance have been dealt with without disaster ? It may be said the community was drugged that it might suffer its wounds in silence ; but if so it knew that it was drugged and that the drugs might hasten the recovery. In other States, where the problem was not so clearly understood, not drugging but stunning would have been the remedy chosen. Here the worker was wise in his industrial environment as the peasant elsewhere is in his.

The parties also differed widely. There is a peculiar paradox about this. Each party feels that it could convert the whole community. Each party claims to represent the whole community. This is the essential advantage of the two-party system as compared with a system of groups. For though in theory a group system will reach unity by the arbitrament of reason between them, in practice reason will give place to barter. In a two-party system it is possible for a community to adapt itself by trial and error to a changing world. In so far as industrialism was incompatible with individualism ; in so far as planning was implicit in industrialism ; in so far as the application of science to industry suggested that it was worth while to call for an attack on the problem of scarcity which would require the sacrifice of freedom for longer than was required in war, the Labour Party was raising issues which would involve all the intellectual and moral resources of the nation. On the other side the Conservative Party was concerned to emphasize that whatever adjustment might be devised would have to take place in diverse national centres. Labour was for planning. Both Labour and Conservative, as against the Liberal, said that reason was not enough. While the Conservative as against Labour was concerned to show that any plan must be a national plan in an international world which was violent and unstable.

Until 1918 the Labour Party was a federation of Trade Union, Socialist Societies (like the Independent Labour Party and the Fabians), Local Trades Councils and Co-operative Society. In 1918 its basis of membership was widened to include individual men and women who subscribed to its constitution and programme. At the same time its basis became definitely Socialist. The Trade Unions that were its main strength had been converted by the war to a belief in the possibility of a Socialist society, and the ordinary man and woman was prepared to attempt the remaking of society. The party became a great political organization with Local Labour Parties in most constituencies and with a constitution and machinery carefully adapted to the new conditions of universal suffrage. The Labour Party Conference of 1918 adopted a comprehensive programme drawn up in 1917, mainly by Mr. Sidney Webb, called *Labour and the New Social Order*. In it the war was described as " the culmination and collapse of a distinctive industrial civilization, which the workers will not seek to reconstruct." It hoped that the individual system of private enterprise had received a deathblow. It would be the duty of Government now to secure to every member of the community all the requisites of healthy life and worthy citizenship. Unemployment was to be systematically and deliberately prevented. Economic wars, secret diplomacy, the formation of alliances, and the exploitation of subject people were to end. This programme served as a rallying-ground for all the idealism of the post-war world and secured the support necessary for some far-reaching reforms in the social services. But the party was divided between those who thought that Trade Union pressure would hasten the reform, and those who felt that constitutionalism must at all costs be preserved. In 1924 the Labour Party Conference excluded Communists from the party. In 1925 while the Trade Union Congress paid hearty attention to Pollitt and gave scant attention to Clynes and Thomas, the Labour Party Conference was dominated by the right. After the General Strike of 1926 the Labour Party Conference of 1927 showed a clear division between its executive's concern for the election and the left wing's concern for the millennium. The former won all along the line. In 1928 a fresh programme *Labour and The Nation* was adopted at Birmingham. This was clearly the Socialism of MacDonald and not the Socialism of Marx. The Labour Party was described as, not " the agent of this class or that, but as the political organ created to express the need and voice the aspiration of all who share the Labour of mankind." Its policy was one of peaceful transition " without disorder or confusion with the consent of the majority of the electors and by the use of the ordinary machinery of democratic government." The Labour Party had in fact become a party appealing to the whole nation and not to a particular class. The I.L.P. which in the past had supplied the intellectual yeast to leaven the Trade Union mass with Socialism, began to meet with opposition from the Trade Unions and the Parliamentary Party. In 1930 MacDonald severed his connection with the I.L.P. because of their policy of revolt. Mr. Snowden gave as his reason for resigning that " The I.L.P. as a separate body had served its purpose. . . . The Labour Party since it admitted individual membership and adopted a definite Socialist basis, adequately fulfilled all the purposes for which the I.L.P. originally existed."

The leaders of the Labour Party held that as it was pledged to introduce the Socialist State within the framework of democracy it must adjust itself to the conditions of democracy as it finds them. It must do all that it could to secure control of that superb instrument of Government, the Cabinet. After the collapse of 1931 the left wing of the Labour Party wanted to commit the Labour Party on assuming office, with or without power, to the promulgation of definite Socialist legislation. In 1934 the Socialist League, a newly-formed militant organization within the Labour Party, declared their objectives to be the same as the Labour Party's and their methods widely different. Neither history nor common sense, said Sir Stafford Cripps, gave any support to the theory of gradualism. They were anxious as far as they could to create the temper for action in office. At the Labour Party Conference in 1934 their common opposition to both Communism and dictatorship effected a reconciliation between Sir Stafford Cripps and the executive of the Labour Party. In 1933 the Trade Union Council issued a manifesto that if the British Working Class were to hesitate between majority and minority rule, and toy with the idea of dictatorship, Fascist or Communist, they would go to a servitude such as they had never suffered.

The organization of the Labour Party was tripartite. There was first the Annual Conference of the Party of some 900 delegates from the Trade Unions, affiliated Socialist Societies and Local Labour Parties. This Conference elected the national party executive, which was the controlling body. No member of the General Council of the Trade Union Congress was eligible for membership of this executive council, but twelve of the twenty-three members of the executive council represented Trade Unions. The Trade Union Congress was the second part of the organization. The third was a Parliamentary Party, consisting of all Labour Members of Parliament. A National Joint Council represented the General Council of the Trade Union Congress, the National Executive of the Labour Party, and the Executive of the Parliamentary Labour Party. This organization was intricate but effective. The Parliamentary Labour Party decided questions of imme-

226

diate tactics in the House. Out of office it elected an executive committee to deal with party business, and in office it elected a consultative committee to confer with the Ministers. A Labour Cabinet would consider this committee on all Parliamentary issues. On questions affecting basic party principles the National Joint Council had a decisive force. A bargain of the Labour Party with another in the constituencies would have required the sanction of the National Executive.

The control of the Annual Conference and the National Committee over the party organization was very close. It determined the party basis and organization. In 1929 at the Annual Conference the proposal that there should be a class of National Associates enrolled directly by headquarters was rejected, because it was feared that persons might join the party whose only interest was in its political prospect. To secure better discipline it was laid down that affiliated organizations must accept the programme, principles and policy of the party, agree to conform to the constitution and standing orders and submit its political rules to the National Executive. Headquarters were to control the selection of candidates and to see that they conducted their campaign in accordance with the declared policy of the executive.

According to Mr. Asquith, the disintegration of the Liberal Party began with the Coupon Election of 1918. The bulk of the old Liberal parliamentary machine deserted to the Coalition and in the new House there were little more than thirty members. The Liberal re-union of 1923-26 did not heal its wounds. For the control of the party was divided between the Liberal Central Office which was scantily, and the Lloyd George machine, which was richly endowed. In 1924 the Liberal group in the House elected Lloyd George as Chairman, and a Radical group who opposed him elected Runciman. In January, 1925, there was a Liberal convention to discuss a declaration of principles made by a committee appointed by Mr. Asquith. The convention approved a proposal to raise £1,000,000 for 600 candidates at the next election. In 1926 Lord Oxford's resignation left the Liberal Party derelict. The Shadow Cabinet which had been held in readiness to form a Liberal Government ceased to exist. The Liberal Party had inherited a faith in liberty of conscience, a tradition of resistance to arbitrary power, and a theory that economic relations required only a framework of political control. The Liberal Party could never identify itself with the Socialists for two reasons : first, many Liberals were rich men and captains of industry ; secondly, the Liberals feared not only the extension of the powers of Government, but also an extension of the power of any organized section of the community. A party whose tradition had been the protection of weak minorities and resistance to strong ones could not co-operate with the policy of the Trade Union Congress. But it feared most that freedom in matters of intellectual opinion could not survive state control of economic life.

Conservatism had been rescued from the suspected blandishments of Mr. Lloyd George in 1923. The average Conservative regarded himself, with Mr. Churchill, as part of a " solid central body of strong common sense and moderation for the maintenance of peace and tranquillity." After the General Strike of 1926 the political climate had radically changed. The Labour Party ceased to flirt with direct action and sought the hand of constitutional power. But it was not clear how Socialism could broaden slowly down from Fabian precedent to precedent. The Conservative and the Labour Parties had both to find political institutions for the preservation of English institutions in a world of violence and instability. Even under the uninspiring banner of " Safety First " the Conservative Party in 1929 secured the support of 8,000,000 voters. The Labour Party was returned mainly because the threat of the strike weapon had been removed. With the economic depression which began in 1929 and the renaissance of despotism which ensued, the principles of both parties had to be reconsidered. To the Labour Party it was clear that only the might and isolation of Russia could do without the capitalist system. An individual, but not a community, might be expected to die for the Liberal faith. Our relative weakness favoured the Conservative policy. The difficulty of all parties was increased by the fact that all Continental countries had been taught to admire the unity of English life, and the more urgently the parties protested their differences, the more were they suspected of Machiavellian dodges to keep the nineteenth-century swag. So from 1926 onwards informed opinion in America and on the Continent was observing how the country with the highest European standard of living, the largest possessions and the oldest system of Government or industrial organization would comport itself in a disturbed world. Granted that the Marxian theses were correct, and the duty of proletarians in all lands was to unite, would the British working class be so Christian as to give up their standard of living that others might live ? If Marxism were not true, would the British electorate be prepared to redraw the map of Europe, last drawn at Versailles in the belief that it would be framed and hung with the aid of American power ? To these questions no effective answer could be made by a country as vulnerable as England now was. A dim sense that the shape of things to come would not realise nineteenth-century dreams gave Mr. Baldwin his programme of " Safety First."

Even before the war of 1914-18 the Cabinet which Gladstone said had found " its final shape, attributes, function and permanent ordering " was changing under the pressure of business and the development of party organization. From the passing of the Reform Bill of 1832 the Cabinet had steadily absorbed the powers of the Crown and as steadily achieved a mastery of the legislature. The essential functions of the Cabinet system which Gladstone admired were that constitutionally it reconciled the legal claims of the Crown with the actual power of the parties, that politically it provided a technique for adjusting the character of the Government to the various changes in public opinion, and that administratively it secured the clear formulation of public policy and its development by legislative act and administrative device. The Cabinet exercised the prerogative powers of the Crown, controlled the legislature, and ran the administrative machine in such relation to public opinion that neither revolution nor repression were invoked. It provided at one and the same time a centre of initiative, a target of criticism, and a method by which government could be changed without shaking the fabric of the State. The complex and subtle understandings between those by whom it was run secured that towards any claims to important powers by the Crown it would present a united opposition able to prevent any development of personal power ; that in the House of Commons and the House of Lords it could state the need for, and the way to get competent administration ; and that to the electorate it was a guide to be followed and a servant to be kicked. It made possible at one and the same time a continuity of national policy, a diversity of party principles, and flexibility of administration in an age of change.

The Cabinet system was inevitably unstable. It had been born of revolution and by revolution it might die. It had developed as an administrative and political device which, after the revolution of 1689, stopped the claims of the Crown and the claims of Parliament being pressed to the arbitrament of war. Whatever the Kings or Queens of England might do someone was responsible to Parliament for their act. The chance that the Kings or Queens themselves might control the Parliament to which their Ministers were responsible was stopped by the development of parties and the extension of the suffrage. The struggle between the Crown and Parliament was ended by the Reform Act of 1832 and the Constitutional struggles of Victoria and her Ministers were only the dying echoes of a battle long ago fought and won. The extension of the suffrage and the growing functions of the State after 1832 raised far more difficult questions. Could the Cabinet system adjust public opinion, that amalgam of passing fancies and diverse and conflicting interests, to the planning and continuity needed by the new functions of the State ? The Cabinet was an excellent eighteenth-century device to reconcile the pretension of monarchy with the diverse interests of oligarchy ; it transmuted the former into a symbol of national unity and the latter into the organs by which the diversities within that unity might be urged. But with the extension of the suffrage the Cabinet had to reconcile the technique of research, the arts and science of administrative planning with the diverse interests and the many frenzies of a complex industrial society.

Even before 1914 the Prime Minister might find his duty to the nation as First Minister of the Crown in conflict with his duty to his party. There was a latent conflict between party loyalty and national duty. To say that a Prime Minister in disagreement with his party had only to resign, that another might succeed, ignored the difficulty that the party system was only an imperfect means to the government of the State. The real problem arose when it seemed to the Minister, who at the time knew all the facts, that the party system did not provide the necessities of State. The relation of the Cabinet to the party depended upon a complexity of traditions which were different in the different parties. The differences between the Conservatives and the Liberals were not very great, being both derived from the same oligarchic tradition. But there was implicit in the rising Labour Party a new conception of the relation of party to the Government which might require a change in the Cabinet system.

The Cabinet system before 1914 had some of the advantages of committee discussion and something of the precision and rapidity of an individual decision. It was the attempt of an oligarchy to combine the unity of purpose attributed to monarchy with the diversity of experience which democracy claims. Its success depended upon the complex social and political traditions which made a Shadow Cabinet fit to replace any Cabinet in power. A Philip drunk with power could hand over to a Philip long sobered by opposition.

We have seen that the old Cabinet had been transformed for the conduct of the war. After the war the politician, like the soldier, was eager to return to Blighty. Once more might the friendly game of ins and outs be played upon the party green. But there were two reasons, one transitory, the other permanent, to prevent this. First, the problems of peacemaking were as strenuous, though less bloody, than the problems of the war ; second, the brave new world of peace was to prove stranger than any had supposed. Peace was to demand victories no less renowned than war. Revolutions in science and in industry were to transform the scope and nature of the problems of the State.

There were three phases of the inter-war years ; in the first from 1918 to 1922, the Lloyd George Coalition responsible for the liquidation of the war developed all " the improvisations of an intermittent and incalculable dictatorship " ;[3] in the second from 1922 to 1929, the pre-war parties attempted to control the post-war world ; in the third after 1929, some idea of the new political order was brought home to all the parties by the destructive violence of the great depression and the resurrection of forms of Government which all good Liberals and sober Labourites had believed to be but " portions and parcels of the dreadful past."

No attempt was made to reform the Cabinet until the late autumn of 1919. For a year after the Armistice the Constitution was almost suspended. Could there be a Cabinet in England at all when the Prime Minister, Bonar Law, and the Foreign Secretary were delegates to the peace conference in Paris ? The King was anxious that there should be someone in England to take decisions, and Lloyd George toyed with the idea of two Cabinets, one of Home and the other for Imperial affairs. Bonar Law proposed that England might be ruled temporarily by a duumvirate. Finally, it was decided to continue the War Cabinet with Chamberlain as a member, though not as Chancellor of the Exchequer. The principal Ministers attended this Cabinet, whether they were nominally members of the War Cabinet or not.[4]

When in the late autumn of 1919 the Cabinet was reformed on the pre-war model it consisted of eleven Unionists, eight Liberals and one Labour member (Mr. Barnes, the Member for the Gorbals Division of Glasgow), and it included the Lord-Lieutenant of Ireland. A rapid disintegration of this Coalition set in. The Prime Minister's magician's robes of war became in peace a shirt of Nessus. In September, 1919, Curzon was complaining that the position of Secretary of State for Foreign Affairs, acting only as a substitute for the Prime Minister, was unsatisfactory and almost humiliating.[5] By 1921 the India Office was at war with the Foreign Office and the Foreign Office with the Prime Minister.[6] Lloyd George attacked the Turks while Curzon, his Foreign Secretary, was charged with the duty of making the best peace with them he could. The Prime Minister's private secretariat was negotiating independently of the Foreign Office.[7] Austen Chamberlain showed the need for co-operation between Unionist and Coalition Liberals and Lloyd George to rally the Constitutional and Conservative elements of the country in defence of the social and economic order. The Conservatives sensed that Lloyd George, having destroyed the Liberal Party, was preparing to destroy them.

On October 6th, 1922, Lord Salisbury, leader of the new Conservative

231

and Unionist movement, said that a " new method of Cabinet Govern-
ment had been introduced which was disastrous . . . an exaltation of
one-man rule in Government which had produced deplorable results."
On October 19th a Conservative Party meeting held at the Carlton
Club decided to fight the next election as an independent party.
Within three hours of this decision the Coalition Government of Lloyd
George had resigned. Bonar Law was elected leader of the Unionist
Party by a special meeting composed of 152 members of the House of
Lords, 220 members of the House of Commons and 67 parliamentary
candidates. He was asked by the King to form a Government.

Bonar Law resigned on May 20th, 1923, on grounds of ill-health.
The King sent for Baldwin, being advised that Lord Curzon was
unsuitable, and that the Conservative Party would not have Chamberlain
because of his support of Lloyd George.

The liquidation of the Georgian dictatorship did not mean a return
to the pre-war party world. In 1923 Baldwin decided that he could not
introduce Protection, the real remedy he believed for unemployment,
without the specific mandate of the electorate. A threat to Free Trade
united the Liberal Party. At a special conference of November 13th,
Asquith, Lloyd George and Sir Alfred Mond planned to co-ordinate
their forces. The Unionists had their special difficulties. Sir Allan
Smith, chairman of the Industrial Group in the House of Commons,
refused to support the Government. Lord Derby, a Lancashire mag-
nate, was given the delicate task of retaining for the Government the
allegiance of the Unionist Free Traders. At the 1923 election the
Conservatives were reduced from 347 to 255, Labour secured 191 and
the Liberals 158. A great responsibility fell to Baldwin and Asquith.
There was strong pressure on the former from within his own party
to resign immediately, so that the King might send for a Unionist
prepared, as Baldwin was not, to do a deal with the Liberals. Asquith
was approached by a leading banker with a message from the city
Conservatives that all the solid people in the country would support an
Asquith-Grey Cabinet if it were formed. Baldwin, after visiting
the King on December 10th and conferring with his Cabinet the next
day, decided not to resign but to meet Parliament. Asquith had then
to decide whether or not he would support the Conservative Government. On January 21st, 1924, an Amendment to the Address was
carried against the Government by 328 to 256 and the Labour Party,
as the next largest party, took office for the first time. Asquith's
constitutional propriety had made a peaceful revolution.

The Prime Minister, MacDonald, made it clear that as head of a
minority Government he would resign only on a direct vote of no

confidence, and not on a snap division on a matter of minor importance. His Cabinet contained the pick of the Trade Union officials and the teaching intellectuals of the Labour Party. Parliament adjourned for three months to give the Minister an opportunity to get used to their departments and to draft legislation.

On the surface there followed an era of good will. The Conservative Party, had failed to prevent a Labour Government by strategy, and tried now to kill it by kindness. The public had some hope that simple faith might succeed where Conservative cunning and Liberal skill had failed. The new Prime Minister, MacDonald, appealed to public sentiment.

But his Government had two serious weaknesses : there was no real agreement among its members about the nature of the task they had to do ; and it did not control a majority in the House of Commons. It was in office but not in power. It rapidly fell into arrears with public business, because it could only make a sparing use of the closure and the suspension of the 11 o'clock rule and these required the support of the Liberals. It was not prepared to give the Liberals the electoral reform for which they asked in the hope that a Central Party might be made. In April a Government Bill to prevent evictions where non-payment of rent was due to unemployment, was opposed both by Chamberlain and Asquith and allowed by the Government to be talked out. The House decided by 325 to 160 that a Capital Levy would be disastrous to employment. In May a Liberal proposal for Proportional Representation was left by the Government to a free vote of the House and defeated by 238 to 144. After that the Liberals were only biding their time to turn the Government out. But they were hampered in their own manœuvres by the division of authority and influence between Asquith and Lloyd George and the deep distrust which the latter then inspired. In July the Government suffered its eighth defeat when it opposed a Liberal amendment to the Unemployment Insurance Bill. It was compelled to accept 65 of the 76 amendments tabled by the Liberals to the Housing Bill. The Liberals decided to require the Government to delete the provision for a loan from the proposed Russian Treaty. This would have forced the Government to dissolve. The end came on a side issue. In October the Unionists moved a vote of censure on the Government's intervention in the Campbell case. The Liberals tabled an amendment for a Select Committee. Baldwin, seeing that the tactics of the Government were to defeat the vote of censure by Liberal votes and the amendment by Conservative votes, led his party to support the amendment and the Government, defeated, asked for a dissolution.

The Conservative Government formed after the Conservative victory in the election of 1924 enjoyed the advantage of a natural reaction after the high hopes raised by the Labour Party had cooled. It was lulled into a false sense of security by the ease with which it defeated the General Strike of 1926 and the apparent recuperation of the world from the economic losses inflicted by the war. Between 1926 and 1929 it made cautious advances towards Protection by introducing a few insignificant safeguarding duties. It gratified Conservative opinion by a rupture with Russia, the introduction of the eight-hour day in mines and by curtailing the power of the Trade Unions in 1927. It dare not strengthen the House of Lords nor dare it refuse the extension of the suffrage in 1928 to women on equal terms with men. Its main success, the defeat of the General Strike of 1926, was the cause of its own undoing. The defeat of the strike clearly revealed the supremacy of power enjoyed by a modern Government. The myth of the General Strike as an instrument of policy was destroyed. With the removal of the suspicion that the Labour Party contemplated direct action its programme of social and industrial reform made rapid progress at the expense of the Liberal Party. The country was moving in the direction of a planned State.

In 1929 the electorate decided that if there was little to be hoped from a Conservative Government there was even less to be feared from the Labour Party. Although the largest party, the Labour Government did not get a clear majority in the House. MacDonald, the Prime Minister, asked that the House should as far as possible act like a Council of State. Sir Herbert Samuel, for the Liberals, welcomed the appeal and suggested that members should be free to vote on the merits of all questions which were not such major issues that they must decide the fate of the Government.[8]

In everything of importance little progress was made. Thomas, the Lord Privy Seal, Mosley (Chancellor of the Duchy) and Lansbury (Commissioner of Works) were made responsible for the development of an unemployment policy. Their efforts may have been mountainous but the results were minute. A conference on electoral reform came to nothing. Lloyd George said that with a three-party system it was no longer the first duty of an Opposition to oppose and expressed the willingness of the Liberals to co-operate with the Government in fair conditions,[9] but he could not carry his party through the manœuvres he had in mind. The Government's majority was often as low as fifteen or nine. For the Budget of 1930 early and frequent resorts to the closure were met by repeated motions to report progress. No less than twenty parliamentary days were consumed in committee alone—three times as many as had been required for any of Churchill's Budgets.[10]

The party manœuvres of 1930 were overshadowed by the financial crisis of 1931. A Treasury memorandum declared that continued State borrowing on the present vast scale by the Unemployment Insurance Fund would quickly call in question the stability of the British financial system. A debate on February 11th led to the appointment of the May Committee. Its report demanded drastic economies in the public services if the Budget was to be balanced. An Economy Committee of the Cabinet consisting of five members with Snowden as chairman was appointed to study its report. On August 20th the Prime Minister laid its plan before the executive committee of the Parliamentary Labour Party, the General Council of the Trade Union Congress and the leaders of the Opposition then in London.[11] The attitude of the Trade Unions brought the difference in the Cabinet to a head. MacDonald, Snowden and Thomas were of the opinion that there should be the closest co-operation with the Bank of England. The latter declared that they could not secure the necessary loans unless there were cuts in unemployment benefit. The majority of the Cabinet could not agree. On August 23rd the King returned to London to interview the party leaders. It is said that late on Sunday evening, August 23rd, the Cabinet empowered the Prime Minister to tender to the King his own resignation, which they believed would automatically include the termination of their own.[12] It is also stated that the Cabinet believed that the King would send for Mr. Baldwin. But in the background another policy had prevailed. MacDonald had agreed to accept the Premiership of an emergency National Government. The dissentient members of the Cabinet professed astonishment that MacDonald was again Prime Minister. He had, they said, betrayed his party and acted contrary to the spirit of the constitution.

The Prime Minister of the new Government said that it was not a Coalition Government in the usual sense of the term but a Government of co-operation for one purpose only—to deal with the national emergency which then existed—and that that achieved the political parties would resume their separate lives. It was composed at first of four Labour members : MacDonald (Prime Minister), Snowden (Chancellor of the Exchequer), Thomas (Dominions) and Sankey (Lord Chancellor) ; four Conservatives : Baldwin (Lord President of Council), Neville Chamberlain (Health), Hoare (India) and Cunliffe-Lister (Board of Trade) ; two Liberals : Reading (Foreign Office) and Samuel (Home Secretary). The readiness of this Ministry of all the talents to accept office placed the Labour Party in an impossible position. To deny the crisis deceived no one. To assert that the crisis could have been met by rigorous measures to prevent the effect of an international financial panic on bourgeois *morale* at home might carry conviction with those who had mastered the dogmas of the class war. Tactically this assertion was open to the fatal retort that the most powerful members of the Cabinet were not convinced of the expediency of the proposed measures. The crisis was too severe for the Opposition to take office alone. No one believed that among the members of the Labour Cabinet who did not follow the Prime Minister there was the material for an alternative Government. On August 26th a joint conference of the Trade Union Congress, the National Executive Committee of the Labour Party and the Consultative Committee of the Parliamentary Labour Party passed a resolution that the new Government should be vigorously opposed. It accused the Government of determining to " attack the standard of living of the members in order to meet a situation caused by a policy pursued by private banking interests, in the control of which the public had no part." The Labour Party turned towards a policy of " Socialism in our time " to avoid another crisis with which it might again be incompetent to deal.

On September 21st the new Government departed from the gold standard which it had been created to defend. By the end of September it had decided that it would not, as originally intended, resign so soon as its economic schemes had been accepted by Parliament. It would ask the electorate for a mandate for whatever measures the future might require. It was returned at the election with the astonishing majority of nearly ten to one (554 to 61).

This brief and imperfect outline of as yet imperfectly known events has been necessary to place in some perspective the changes in the nature of the Cabinet system which were taking place. The change in the scope of functions which all governments have been compelled by science and by industry to undertake made the Cabinet give itself an organization proper for the work it has to do. The scale and pace of modern society have compelled the Cabinet, as they compelled many a private firm, to adopt an effective office routine. The new scale and speed caused the development of the Cabinet Secretariat and the complex committee organization of the modern Cabinet.

The essence of the old system before 1914 was as Asquith said in 1922, " corporate responsibility maintained not as a despot or even as a master by the Prime Minister, though individually he was the central and controlling figure. The essence of the whole thing was deep mutual confidence, and not only that, but of absolute secrecy." It was an inflexible though unwritten rule that no member should take any note or record of the proceedings except the Prime Minister for his letter to the King. "A Cabinet discussion" was considered by Lord Salisbury " not the occasion for the deliverance of a considered judgment, but an opportunity for the pursuit of practical conclusions." The freedom of private conversation would inspire a flow of suggestions. The whole spirit of the system was spoilt if one member were to *hansardise* another even in memory.

The old Cabinet system did not survive the 1914-18 war. Even before the war it had become more of a public than a committee meeting, and the orator already had undue attention. In 1917 Lloyd George appointed a small secretariat that the Cabinet might know what it was going to discuss, and after the discussion what had been decided. The war-time secretariat was continued after the peace. Its early development was hindered by the fact that in addition to the reasonable and proper Cabinet secretariat under the impeccable control of Sir Maurice Hankey, there was another secretariat attached to the person of Lloyd George, whose affiliations and powers no man quite understood. In 1922 the indispensable Cabinet secretariat was criticized severely in the House as tending to exalt the Prime Minister, encroaching on the province of the Foreign Office, destroying the informality of Cabinet discussion, and indirectly impeding Parliamentary control of the executive. Bonar Law stated in his election programme that it would be abolished.

The Cabinet secretariat became a vital part of the machinery of Government. The all-round pressure of work has compelled the Cabinet to attend to the order of its doings. The functions of the secretariat were in essence the very simplest. It had to prepare an agenda. It had to see that those concerned with the matters to be discussed were informed that a discussion was pending and supplied with the relevant material. It had to secure that those affected by Cabinet decisions were told what they were. It had to co-ordinate the working of the Cabinet as a whole with the committees through which it might work. It had to co-ordinate the work of the Cabinet with the activities of the particular departments. This simple expedient of business machinery to ease political action gave rise to problems of constitutional import. The essential change was that each Minister now knew what matters were coming up for discussion and could read the documents concerned. Most important questions were discussed by a committee of the Cabinet. There was only one Standing Committee : that on Home Affairs. It consisted of the Lord Chancellor (in the chair), two Cabinet Ministers, the Foreign Secretary, the Attorney-General and the Solicitor-General. It considered the proposed course of Government business for the session and the legal aspects of Bills in draft. It did not deal with policy and its work was only advisory. There were many *ad hoc* committees which were kept continually in existence such as those on Defence, the reform of the House of Lords, and the problem of Ireland. The effect of this committee system was that the Cabinet collectively was not overworked. On any matter on which there was difference of opinion or need for inquiry an *ad hoc* committee was appointed and its report accepted or rejected by the Cabinet as a whole. The long-drawn-out discussion once common on problems of Defence now took place in the Committee of Imperial Defence, whose recommendations were considered by a Defence Committee of the Cabinet and only then brought before the Cabinet as a whole. But while this committee organization reduced the work of the Cabinet as a whole it gave no leisure to important Ministers. The heads of minor offices could not man important committees. The important Ministers had to do the work of the important committees.

For any question to be discussed in Cabinet the Minister would ask the secretariat to put it on the agenda. Before this was done the department concerned must have had the problem examined by the Treasury, the Law Officers and any other departments directly concerned. The secretariat could refuse to circulate any memorandum until the Chancellor of the Exchequer had agreed. If he did not agree he produced a counter memoranda. No item appeared on the agenda unless notice of it and the papers concerned had been in circulation for five days. The agenda was compiled on Monday, circulated the same day, and the Prime Minister had, of course, the power to strike any item off or to add any item he desired.

The minutes of the Cabinet, did not refer to the opinions expressed by individual Ministers, but they might refer to the documents upon which they were based. They could be seen by any member of the Cabinet. But no Government might see the minutes of a previous Government without the consent of the present and the previous Prime Minister. There was a natural tendency for the existing secretariat to deprecate reference to past minutes, as such a policy might lead an outgoing Government to order its own minutes to be destroyed.

There were changes too, in the Cabinet as a political institution. The Cabinet in the nineteenth century was dependent upon the Monarchy, the legislature, and a party system, and was shaped by the means used by diverse interests and conflicting powers to resolve their differences by argument. Party programmes had been a tribute paid by diverse interests to the reason which might unite them. The development of industry and the extension of the franchise entirely changed the problems to be handled. Monarchy, legislature and parties were transformed. The Monarchy became a device to meet some emotional needs of the public mind. We know so little of the psychological forces involved in ceremonial, and we have so much reason to fear the power of symbols, that if we value our liberty—almost one might say if we value our sanity—we will not allow the ceremonial and the effective powers of the State to be combined. The monarchical idea if isolated in the ceremonial will not infect the organs of administration. The Monarchy will express and not create the unity it serves. Queen Victoria's personal power exacted an incredible expenditure of time and temper by her Ministers. It is a tribute to the decency of the nineteenth-century politics that only Disraeli abused his influence with her. During the reign of Edward VII most of the prerogatives in which he claimed a personal discretion—mercy, dissolution, dismissal and selection of Ministers, declaration of war and peace—were challenged and surrendered. There remained one critical issue through which the monarchical idea might once again infect the body politic. The legislature, though it may mediate between organized interests and opinions, and the central planning and executive machinery of the State, can no longer be the arbitrator between conflicting Governments and policies. The central problem of Government lies in determining the relation between the organized community—not to be expressed in any legislature even by the device of parties—and the central organ which is its guide and servant. Once it was a question of determining the relation between the legislature and the executive, when the legislature was the organ of an aristocracy and the executive a tool of a powerful Crown. Now the problem lies in the relation between the. Government and the parties as organs of the community. When a crisis breaks the normal harmony between parties and Governments there is a chance that monarchical power may revive. Among the merits of the Cabinet system before 1919 was its ability to combine the interests and energy of party with the play of reason and the sentiment of Nationality. It provided a smooth and simple technique for a change of Government. It secured Government by the few with the precision of one and the tolerance of many. It is a paradox of popular Government that the more the interests to be consulted, the smaller is the final organ of decision. The heptarchy could be governed by a Witagemote; a federal State by the Senate of the United States; but the United Kingdom requires a despotic Cabinet. The party system expressed both the unity and an admission that that unity is never quite complete. A party Government is like a king who has his fool in council. It is the Opposition which must see that power does not make the Government mad. The party system is suitable for a community which desires unity, which is capable of unity, but has still an open mind as to how that unity may be secured. It is an institutional expression of the experimental method in politics.

We have seen that the responsibility of the Government for policy requires complex legislation. This compelled the executive to transform the procedure of the House of Commons. But the time devoted to Government legislation did not exceed half the sitting time of the House. In 1930 the House sat for 160 days. Of these 32 were occupied by Supply, 21 by Ways and Means and all stages of the Finance Bill, 67 by Second Readings, and Motions, and 40 by all stages of other Bills beyond their second stage. It was a sound Parliamentary tradition that the Opposition should have more of the time of the House than their opponents. A Government in office does not want its own supporters to raise difficulties. There is in fact a conflict between the demands on Parliament as legislative and executive machine and the demand that it should be an effective organ of publicity. The House of Commons failed to focus public attention on important issues. The use of questions was not properly developed. They were used to make debating points rather than to secure information. It was well known that to get a thing done it was best to write to a Minister. To make a row a question could be used. As an effective weapon of party warfare the question was used to drive the Minister by successive questions to divulge more and more. Exciting as this cross-examination might be, its value was largely lost because there was no opportunity for summing up. The character of debates themselves had changed. Before 1914 there were three-day debates and the leaders closed the debate by two speeches of one hour each, and a Government worsted in debate suffered serious injury. Now the leaders spoke early, that their views might get into the Press. Most Members made no attempt to answer those who had spoken before. There was a growing disposition on the part of Members to make their contribution and a growing indisposition of others to listen to them. The opponents of the Government had no machinery for pursuing the subjects discussed in practical detail. Save for debates on a vote of censure not 10 per cent. attended those on employment and trade. Noncontentious legislation was obstructed in order that there should be less time for the passage of contentious measures. Time was not found for the reorganization of executive departments, even though it raised no party issues. To have mastered the rules of the House had become in itself a claim to political distinction.

CHAPTER X

MACHINERY OF ADMINISTRATION, 1918-39

Some causes of Administrative Confusion—The Haldane Report on Machinery of Government—Its Principles examined—Their development traced : In Health—At the Treasury in the development of Treasury Control—In the Economic functions of the State—In research and the problems thrust by Science on Government—The Ministry of Defence—The special case of Justice—The Structure and technique of the Civil Service—In general—In some selected departments—The judicial functions of Administrators—The Expert and Government.

BEFORE 1914 the administrative machinery of this country was becoming too tangled to provide the service our national and social problems required. The distribution of available funds was made more difficult than necessary by the efforts of each department to defeat the parsimonious Treasury view. The discussion of the Estimates by the Chancellor of the Exchequer and the departments concerned was a scuffle of dogs for the largest bite. A series of departmental disputes was a symptom of the faulty distribution of powers and responsibilities. There was for example great confusion as to the responsibility of the Local Government Board, the Home Office and the Board of Trade in relation to local government in general and for the care of children in particular. There were prolonged disputes as to whether the Local Government Board should allow the Home Office to inspect laundries in workhouses, or the Insurance Commissions to inspect the sanatoria provided by the local authorities ; whether the Local Government Board, as the authority responsible for local finance, might veto the educational institutions required by the Board of Education.

This confusion was worse confounded by the exigencies of the 1914-18 war. Ten new Ministries and over 160 boards and commissions had been created. Border-line questions of responsibility were settled in an arbitrary fashion ; Treasury supervision was relegated to the background. With the return of peace the financial responsibility of each department had once more to be clearly defined. On what principles were the duties of departments to be allocated ? When the Great War Ministries of Munitions, Food, and Shipping should have withered in peace, what departments were to deal with the inevitable conflicts, between industrial leaders, anxious to beat swords into ploughshares at the maximum speed and for the maximum profit, and the new labour from the battlefields seeking homes for heroes ? The enormous development of State control over the whole field of national industry had destroyed the pre-war concentration of the economic functions of the State in the Board of Trade. How were those functions to be performed in the future ? Were there to be Government departments concerned each with some problem common to all industries—research, the conditions of labour, and the stimulus of production—or were there to be departments each concerned with all the problems of separate industries—shipping, mines, textiles, engineering ? What were to be the relations between the rising Air Ministry and its earthbound and waterlogged seniors, the War Office and Admiralty ? And there were minor problems without number. Who was to be responsible for the training of disabled men—a Ministry of Labour, the Board of Education, or the Ministry of Agriculture ? Was there to be the separate Ministry of Pensions to which the War Office and the Admiralty were opposed ? In these circumstances the Haldane Report on Machinery of Government, 1918[1] made the most thorough examination since Bentham of the problem of the proper distribution of the functions of the executive. It attempted to formulate the principles that should govern the distribution of the work of the departments of State whatever might be the policy of the party in power. It was concerned to solve a problem in administrative science and not to determine a political programme. The fundamental question which its researches led it to face had been raised by Aristotle when he asked " should officers be divided according to the subjects with which they deal or according to the persons with whom they deal . . . should one person see to good order in general or one look after the boys and another after the women, and so on ? "[2] The Haldane Commission was of the opinion that there should be a department or departments for good order in general and not separate departments for the boys and women and so on. Of the two principles on which the functions of the State could be allocated to departments : (1) " distribution according to the persons or classes to be dealt with " or (2) " distribution according to the services to be performed " the Haldane Report preferred the latter. The first would involve having separate departments to look after the interests of particular classes of persons—paupers, children, insured persons, the unemployed, and in the case of industry perhaps separate departments to deal with each particular industry in every aspect of its relation to the State—labour conditions, safety and health regulations vocational or technical education, bounties or taxation. On the second principle there would be separate Ministries dealing with Finance,

Defence, External Affairs, Research, Production, Employment, Supplies, Education, Health and Justice. This, the report held, was less likely to lead to confusion and overlapping and most likely to secure the widest knowledge and its most useful application.

While avoiding the Lilliputian organization which would result from having separate departments of State to deal with every class of persons who could claim a separate interest in its work, the report did not wish to create the pedantries of Laputa. Classification according to services might be better than classification according to the persons concerned, but provision must be made for co-operation in all marginal cases. Work which is the primary concern of one department must be the secondary concern of others. Every department must study its own problems of staffing, though the general problem of staffing is the business of the Treasury. Every department has a responsibility for its own financial order, though finance, too, is the main concern of the Treasury. For legal problems and the development of scientific research the same principle would apply. Specialization is sterile unless mated with co-operation. The health and safety of industrial workers may be the primary concern of a Ministry of Employment, but it requires concerted action between the Ministries of Employment, Justice, Health and Education. Any attempt to deal with industrial fluctuations involves the co-operation of every department of the State. The Defence departments may produce some of their own weapons of war but they will get others from a Ministry of Supply working to the plans of a Ministry of Research.

The Haldane Report asked that the chaotic distribution of the work of departments, the result of the compromises involved in Government by discussion, should be replaced by the rational order technical efficiency required. The real difficulty lay in weighing the need to compromise with political forces against the claims of technical efficiency. An important condition of the economy and efficiency of Government departments is that their functions should have popular support. It is almost inevitable in a system of Representative Government that the development of its services should be in response to casual emergencies. If the State is to extend its range of action single spies must precede the departmental battalions.

The principles advocated by the Haldane Report were after 1918, followed to the extent of the creation of the Ministry of Health, an improvement in the organization of the Treasury and its method of co-operating with other departments, and a great advance in the provision made for investigation and thought as a preliminary to action. But the rapid changes in the economic and social structure of the country imposed on successive Governments the necessity of meeting casual emergencies by unco-ordinated expedients. The general principle of the report, that the work of Government departments should be distributed according to the nature of the service with which they are concerned, did not go unchallenged by departmental experts.

In 1926 a committee on the amalgamation of services common to the Army and Navy[3] reported that there was " a noticeable tendency of administrative theory of the present day . . . to suppose that a reorganization of the departments of Government, by which one department shall undertake all work of a particular nature for the whole Government service, will make for economy. The view we have taken on this point is that each case must be considered on its merits and not merely on *a priori* theory." The committee was of the opinion that the establishment of a general pool of common stores to meet the needs of the three fighting services was impracticable owing to the differences in the needs of the three services and in their organization and geographical distribution. A partial amalgamation of the work branches with the Office of Works would lead to complications which would tend to increase the administrative difficulties of the fighting services ; while the whole could not be handed over because part of it was so highly technical in character. The proposal to amalgamate the work of the Stationery Office the largest printing establishment of the Government, with the Office of Works, the largest building establishment, has received no official approval. The Treasury indeed professed " fully to recognize the importance of avoiding duplication in administration between departments " and constantly to seek " with the co-operation of the departments to avoid such duplication." But in 1920, when they examined with the departments concerned the question of re-allocating the functions of the Home Office, the Ministry of Health, the Board of Trade, and the Ministry of Labour, they decided on practical grounds that the situation should remain unchanged.[4]

The nature of the problems involved can only here be briefly considered. It will be convenient to take the special cases of (1) the Ministry of Health ; (2) the Treasury ; (3) the economic functions of the State ; (4) the organization of research ; (5) the Ministry of Defence ; (6) the Foreign Office, and (7) the Ministry of Justice. Of these the Ministry of Health is of special importance, because it involves the question of the proper relation between the central and local authorities ; the Treasury shows the fruitful application of the principles the Haldane Report had analysed ; the economic functions of the departments show the dependence of administrative logic on political persuasion ; the organization of research is the most vital problem of the modern world ; the Foreign Office shows that privilege will soon have nowhere to lay its head ; the Ministry of Defence raises problems new in English history ; and the hope of a Ministry of Justice will be always with us.

Ministry of Health. The complex history of this department has already been described. It was the working of the Poor Law and the medical services in this country which the Haldane Report had particularly in mind when it pressed for a rationalization of our administrative machinery. The provision by the State of one set of essential services for paupers and of another set for those who were not, had led not only to an inefficient duplication in the health and education administration of the State, but was in principle not defensible. There ought not to be one administrative law for the rich and another for the poor. If certain health services are essential to the community they ought not to be given in different qualities to different income groups. People with moderate or large means may be allowed the superficial comforts to which they are used, but it would be monstrous to give the poor an inferior scientific treatment. The wards for rich and poor may be differently furnished, but the surgeons' knives should be clean and sharp for all.

The creation of the Ministry of Health secured that the responsibility for the scattered health services should be concentrated in one department. The work of the department remained extremely complicated, because it was still responsible for the supervision of the administration by local authorities of the Poor Law. Until 1929 that Poor Law was administered by the specially-elected Guardians of the Poor. The Act of 1929 provided for the abolition of the Guardians of the Poor and the transfer of their functions to the Councils of Counties and of County Boroughs. The deterrent poor law was to be replaced by a system of services designed to prevent pauperism altogether. The Ministry of Health remained the department primarily responsible both for the structure and for the finance of local government. It was a Ministry of the Interior with a sanitary bias.[5]

The Treasury. The Government of any highly-organized community must have a department or departments responsible for : (1) the control of banking and currency and the public debt ; (2) the imposition of taxation, the collection of revenue and the provision of the day-to-day expenses of the Government ; (3) in addition to these purely financial duties it has to determine how much the various departments of State may spend. It is possible in theory to separate the three functions of securing financial order, collecting revenue and deciding how much to spend. In an economic Utopia, where production and distribution

245

moved to their appointed ends guided by the foresight of a milliard *entrepreneurs*, the function of the State in securing financial order might be reduced to noting phenomena important for the determination of the trade cycle, and broadcasting financial statistics. The expenditure of the State would be balanced by its receipts for services rendered, or income from State property, and the collection of revenue by compulsion would be unnecessary ; or perhaps the expenditure of departments might exceed their receipts by amounts so small that they could be met from the proceeds of a special broadcast appeal.

This financial fantasy reveals by contrast the essential problem of Treasury administration in England. The responsibility for determining expenditure and the raising of revenue is concentrated in the same department. The Minister responsible for raising revenue has a predominant voice in deciding the amount and in some degree the character of expenditure. As the expenditure of the State becomes an increasing proportion of the total national income, the dependence of the determination of financial policy on the scale of expenditure and the raising of revenue increases. In a completely Communist State they would be diverse aspects of a single problem. The financial order would be the resources of the State and its resources would be its expenditure. In a very rich *laissez-faire* community, such as the United States before 1914, the collection of revenue was a mere executive stage in the carrying out of a policy determined independently of financial control. While the *laissez-faire* State has merely to send a bucket to the well which man and Providence have filled, the interventionist State has to maintain reservoirs and control irrigation.

The Haldane Committee found that there was a tradition before 1914 that all departments have a natural disposition to be extravagant and that the Treasury was irreconcilably opposed to all increases of expenditure whether meritorious or not. To improve their relations it proposed : (1) that the obligation of the department to state a reasoned case for increased expenditure should place upon the Treasury a corresponding obligation not to assume an attitude merely negative ; (2) that more frequent inquiries should be made by the Treasury into the general administration of departments ; (3) that in each department there should be an establishments officer concerned with problems of staff, and in the Treasury itself an Establishment Branch.

In 1919 to meet the problems of staffing and reorganization in the Civil Service created by the 1914-18 war, a separate Establishments Branch was created in the Treasury and separate establishment officers in each department. These establishment officers were appointed by the head of the department in consultation with the Treasury, and they became the eyes and ears of the head of their department in all problems of staffing.[6] They were expected to know the practice of other departments in staffing problems and to know the general trend of staffing policy throughout the Service. A committee of establishment officers was set up and frequent informal discussions were held by the permanent heads of all departments. Before 1914 the Treasury only knew of increases of staff through proposed increases in the Estimates; they only heard of decreases of staff or possible reorganization if the departments voluntarily disclosed them. In 1930 it was said that " the officers of the Establishment Department of the Treasury are in and out of the departments the whole time. They are not at arm's length but they are in intimate touch. . . . If a department is shortening work . . . there will be no endeavour on the part of the department to conceal it. . . . The Treasury has powers under Order in Council to order an examination of the staffing of departments, but it does not need to use them."[7] The Treasury had taken the departments into council. It told them the amount that was in the till and persuaded them to the necessary sacrifices.[8] The Treasury and the departments in commission determined the allocation of available revenue. The Treasury was continuously engaged in co-ordinating and supplementing the efforts of departments to do their work in the most economical way. A particular section of the Treasury had people skilled in the use of every conceivable kind of labour-saving device, who went round the departments to see if they could not equal and if possible surpass the most advanced business organizations.[9] " The process," wrote the May Committee, " is not spectacular, but it is continuous and effective . . . such economies as are from time to time possible will be secured as opportunities arise and will not be accelerated by any recommendations which we could make."[10]

The Committee on National Expenditure, 1918, recommended that the Public Accounts should be cast in the form of Income and Expenditure Accounts in place of the mere cash accounts which gave no clear account of the real position. The new system was introduced experimentally into the War Office, but was rejected by the Public Accounts Committee of 1925 because it required an administrative decentralization to which the Army Council were unable to agree. But the Trading Accounts of departments whose work was of the nature of a commercial undertaking were kept on an Income and Expenditure basis, while in others the practice of making special financial studies provided the administrative officer with as much information as possible about the financial implications of his work.[11]

(3) *Economic functions of the State.* The Haldane Report wanted

the economic functions of the State organized around three Ministries—one concerned with conditions of employment, another engaged in the stimulation of private enterprise, and a third operating such enterprises as time had ripened or politicians taken for nationalization. But after 1918 the machinery of the State in its dealings with our economic life was adapted by temporary expedients to meet a series of emergencies. An astonishing variety of unco-ordinated devices of investigation, advice and control was developed. Politicians in travail produced a litter of commissions ; and boards came not single spies but in battalions. The tendency before 1914 to concentrate the economic functions of the State in the Board of Trade had been interrupted by the war. Afterwards in the confusion of an economic retreat distressed industries each sought and found its own nurse and shelter in the ample bosom of the State. The Board of Trade dealt with coal ; the Ministry of Agriculture attempted whatever miracles could be performed with loaves and fishes ; Transport had its own Ministry ; and the reconstruction of our basic industries was attempted by a Tariff Commission. An Economic General Staff to determine general economic policy remained a Utopian dream.

The underlying causes of this confusion lay partly in the weaknesses of our parliamentary procedure. A majority, however determined, could not pass with the ordinary procedure half the measures necessary to bring the law up to date.[12] More important was the mental uncertainty about the policy to be pursued. The Labour Party did not really believe that the evils that men do were the result of private property ; the Liberal Party did not really think that Cobden had new worlds to conquer ; and the Conservative Party did not know what order it should patriotically defend. The Cobdens of the nineteenth century could assume a society; the Cobdens of the twentieth century had little faith that the loom was mightier than the sword.

In such conditions administrative empiricism was inevitable. And wisely was empiricism adhered to when far-reaching reorganization was suggested again and again. The problem of unemployment was compared to the problem of war. " I do suggest," said Sir Oswald Mosley, " that to grapple with this problem it is necessary to have a revolution in the machinery of government. After all it was done in the war ; there were revolutions in the machinery of government one after another, until the machine was devised and created by which the job could be done."[13] But appeals to the experience of war are often a symptom of the weakness which follows that disease. " The job to be done " in war was the organization of the nation for victory in the field at whatever cost to the living or those yet to be born. It was a limited objective to be gained or lost within a few years. The cure of unemployment is entirely different. It is not a question of finding the means at whatever cost to secure a definite end but of discovering the conditions necessary to the co-operation of men in society. For a time everyone was under the delusion that the efforts of war could be sustained in peace, though directed to ends which were rational and general, instead of to one end, instinctive and passionate—self-preservation and victory.

As the full complexity of the post-war problem was revealed old departments were reorganized, new departments created, and innumerable experiments made in the public control of economic activities.

The Ministry of Labour was created in 1916 and had been responsible for the organization of the labour market through its administration of the Labour Exchanges, the promotion of conciliation and arbitration under the Conciliation Act of 1906 and the Industrial Courts Act, 1919, and since 1917 the administration of the Trade Boards system. But the special wage problems of agriculture and coal-mining were handled by special departments. In 1924 the Ministry of Agriculture and Fisheries was made responsible for a system of agricultural wages committees in each county or group of counties analogous to Trade Boards. In 1912 the Coal Mines (Minimum Wage) Act provided that minimum rates should be fixed in each district by similar boards.

In 1919 the scattered powers of the State relating to inland transport were concentrated in the Ministry of Transport. The control of civil aviation remained with the Air Ministry. Coastwise shipping, navigation and pilotage remained with the Board of Trade. The proper functions of a Ministry of Transport are difficult to determine. Its powers might be distributed : roads to the Home Office ; rail transport and bridges to the Board of Trade; alternatively, it might control every aspect of communication by sea, air, road and rail, and perhaps even the Post Office. It is a good example of the technical, economic and political forces which determine the distribution of the work of Government Departments. In 1914-18 the railways were run under the Board of Trade by a committee consisting of the General Managers of the dozen leading companies.[14] After 1918 they were not nationalized. The Railway Act of 1921 laid down the outlines of the amalgamations desirable, and set up an Amalgamations Tribunal to control their formation. The rapid development of road transport led in 1920 to the Road Act and then to the Road Traffic Act of 1930. By the latter twelve bodies of regional commissioners (three in each area) were established, with wide discretionary powers to determine the conditions of competition in the road transport industry ; the Minister of Transport was empowered to expend money in " disseminating know-- ledge and otherwise informing the minds of the people " ; the Act marked an important stage in the development of State action from force to persuasion by empowering the Minister of Transport to publish a code in a language which all could understand, and of which a breach would not in itself constitute an offence. But the vital problems remained. The Ministry of Transport inevitably became responsible for the main roads for whose maintenance the revenue of local authorities could not be fairly charged. A *thoroughfare* cannot be a local charge. In becoming responsible for roads the Ministry of Transport came into close co- operation with the Ministry of Health as the main town-planning authority.

Whatever the need for State regulation of particular industries, direct Ministerial responsibility for their management by a State department was felt to be unwise. It would mean a plague of Ministers on an already overcrowded front bench and their preoccupation with executive detail rather than with principles of statesmanship.[15] Either the inherent flexibility of industrial organization would provide problems too numerous for political control or political exigencies would destroy the vitality of the industrial order. They would make a plan and call it wealth. There were therefore many experiments in the forms of public concerns able competently to conduct particular services in the public interest.[16] In 1919 the relevant powers of the Board of Agriculture and Fisheries, the Board of Agriculture for Scotland and the Department of Agriculture and Technical Instruction for Ireland were transferred to the Forestry Commissioners. In 1919, also, five Electricity Commissioners appointed by the Board of Trade (after 1920 by the Ministry of Transport) were made responsible for the conduct of the whole of the policy dealing with the electrical industry in the country. Their duties were to co-ordinate ; they were not given complete executive control of the industry. In 1927 the Central Electricity Board was established consisting of a chairman and seven members. The Board was composed of men of wide experience in finance and business organization, rather than representatives of particular interests. It was appointed by the Ministry of Transport after con- sultation with a large number of associations and individuals representing local government, electricity companies, industry, transport, agriculture and labour. Its commercial discretion was to be unfettered ; it was not to be a Government Department in any sense of the word. It was to prepare a scheme and submit it to the Electricity Commissioners who, acting in a semi-judicial capacity, would give the interested parties an opportunity of being heard and confirm the scheme with or without modifications.[17]   In 1926 it was decided by a committee of inquiry[18] that for the control of the unknown powers of radio the most appropriate organization would be a public corporation. " Such an authority would enjoy a freedom and flexibility which a Minister of State himself would scarcely exercise in arranging for performances and programmes and in studying the variable demands of public taste and necessity."[19] The actual commissioners were not to be persons representative of various interests, such as music, science, drama, education and industry, but " persons of judgment and independence, free of commitments " and able to " inspire confidence by having no other interests to promote than that of the public service."[20]   While the State, through Parliament, was to retain the ultimate control, the Postmaster-General being its spokesman on broad questions of policy, the commission was not to be the subject of " the continuing Ministerial guidance and direction which apply to Government offices."[21]

Because it seemed that the long era of expansion of the British coal industry was at an end, and that its 1,500 independent concerns producing coal caused a widespread and continuous dissipation of effort at a time when there was need for concentration of effort against a common peril, the Coal Mines Act of 1930 established the Coal Mines Reorganization Commission.   It was intended to secure the concentration of production in selected pits and to assist majorities in particular areas who had been hampered by minorities in carrying out a reorganization scheme. The chairman, Sir Ernest Gowers, was appointed for seven years.   He had been Chairman of the Board of Inland Revenue.[22]

In 1931 the abandonment of Free Trade led to the appointment of the Import Duties Advisory Committee of three members : Sir George May, the chairman (£5,000 a year) ; Sir S. J. Chapman (late Economic Adviser to His Majesty's Government) and Sir George Allen Powell.

Finally it may be noted that the special problems of the agricultural industry were attacked with a variety of administrative experiments. The State attempted entirely to reconstruct the industry in some of its most important functions and completely to revise our economic relations with foreign countries.[23]   In 1931 the Agricultural Marketing Act was passed as an enabling measure to facilitate the organization and distribution of any given commodity by a majority of its producers, a dissentient minority notwithstanding.   The Act of 1933 was designed to raise the prices of agricultural products by the quantitative limitation of imports and by the control of domestic agricultural production.   It established a twin dictatorship by the President of the Board of Trade and the Minister of Agriculture, which went far to introduce a rigid system of State control over one of the largest of our basic industries.[24]

The first part of the Act enabled the Board of Trade to restrict the imports of any agricultural products subject to a marketing scheme if the Board, after consultation with the Minister of Agriculture, was satisfied that such a scheme could not be brought into effective operation without the limitations of imports. The second part of the Act provided for development schemes to be administered by boards composed of three members appointed by the Minister and a number of other persons elected by the constituent boards.

(4) *The organization of research.* The Haldane Report expressed the opinion " that in the sphere of central government the duty of investigation and thought as a preliminary to action might be more definitely recognized." Such thinking, it said, could not be carried out in the spare time of an efficient administrator. It urged (1) that in all departments better provision should be made for enquiry, research and reflection before policy was defined and put into operation ; (2) that for some purposes a special department was necessary to supervise and carry out the necessary enquiry and research ; (3) that special attention should be paid to the methods of recruiting the staff to be employed in such work ; and (4) that in all departments the higher officials in charge of administration should have more time to devote to that portion of their duties.

Most Government departments had developed an intelligence branch concerned partly with the investigation of specific problems related to current policy and partly with inquiries that had established a claim to disinterested research. Departments are able to collect information inaccessible to the private individual through the exercise of powers given to them by Parliament. But the powers had been determined by the exigencies of the particular political or administrative crisis in which they were required. Their powers of investigation were secreted in the interstices of political and constitutional procedures. The Government's " very knowledge of the nation it rules is only the by-product of its specialized administrative activities."[25] The attempt to cure the sickness of an acquisitive society had involved all Government departments in a confusion of publicity and measurement. The strange principle " that Government is to seek only such information and is only to record such statistics as are incidental to its current information " had made our research organizations a myopic and squinting Argus. Outside the research work of particular departments the development of special departments for investigation and research had taken place in almost every instance in response to the pressure of a practical need and not in pursuance of a reasoned policy."[26]

The British system of statistics in the thirties was in a state of chaos. There were four Government departments responsible for industrial

￭tatistics—the Registrar-General, the Board of Trade, the Inland Revenue Department and the Ministry of Labour ;[27] five different departments separately undertook the work of classifying employers of labour according to their trade : the Board of Trade, Ministry of Labour, Census Office, Inland Revenue, Home Office.[28] The Board of Trade and the Inland Revenue Department compiled and published estimates of the value of income from overseas investments, each disavowing the work of the other.[29] The statistical and research work of the Ministry of Agriculture was divided among seven departments, with the result that in the mind of the farming community " the Ministry was associated with the idea of nagging inspection, not with the idea of disinterested advice." The need for co-ordination had been recognized. An inter-departmental committee co-ordinated the classification of industrial and labour statistics. Information about earnings was related to the census of production. A permanent committee on official statistics,[30] was set up to keep the whole field under review. A new cost of living index replaced the one founded on a special survey, undertaken more than twenty-five years before of less than 2,000 budgets.[31] The creation of a central statistical department was believed to be impossible because statistics were collected by departments to use in their work.[32]

It has been wisely said that " before the modern world can feel confidence in trusting its fortunes either to planning or to *laissez-faire*, or to some mixture of both, the apparatus and technique of investigation into social and economic problems will need to be vastly improved and strengthened."[33] The provision of such improved technique raises problems which go to the root of government. It is easy to say that responsibility for policy must be separated from responsibility for routine administration.[34] A policy involves the co-ordination of the work of many departments. The research and planning for the former may involve serious modifications of the work of particular departments. How is an adjustment to be made between the time given in particular departments to specific investigations on matters of immediate administrative and political urgency and the time given to the investigations appropriate to general policy ? When there are conflicting policies within a Cabinet the research facilities of each department will be used by each Minister for his own ends. Serious co-ordination can only come from a Minister of a Committee of Ministers in a position to override the obstruction of particular departments. The comparative failure of the Economic Advisory Council was partly due to this very difficulty,

The Economic Advisory Council was established in 1930. It was to provide a continuous study of economic problems over a wide field.

253

It was placed directly under the Cabinet with the deputy secretary to the Cabinet as its secretary. Its inquiries were to be with the sanction of the Prime Minister and the results were to be communicated to the Cabinet. It was composed of three elements : an advisory council of business men, Trade Unionists, economists and technical experts and others ; the Prime Minister as chairman and such other Ministers whose departments might be particularly concerned ; and a small full-time staff of expert economists. It was not a success because neither the problems it was to study nor the resources of investigation which it might use were defined.[35] It could not co-ordinate the economic activities of other departments without itself exercising executive powers which would have made it practically a department of the Prime Minister.[36] It remained " an appendage hooked on rather than an internal digestive organ."[37] If its powers were ill-defined its membership was ill-assorted. A miscellaneous collection of economists, Trade Union leaders and business men, invited to speculate at large on problems of policy, could only succeed in darkening each other's light. In matters calling for immediate action the practical men sought support in theories they did not understand ; the speculative thinkers relied on experience they were ill-fitted to judge. A combination of the theory of practical men and the policy of academic men produced pontifical obscurity. In practice the Advisory Council was only effective when it functioned through small committees which considered measures submitted to them by the Prime Minister and received from him and the Chancellor of the Exchequer power to override departmental obstruction.

Economics was not the only science with which Governments were anxiously concerned. Increasingly in the present century they have had to find a policy and devise administrative machinery which would use the physical and biological sciences in the service of government. We can only outline the bare bone of the problems of policy that have arisen. It is dangerous to organize pure research. "The less the scientific worker is concerned to produce some specific result and the more he is animated by the spirit of disinterested scientific curiosity the more likely he is to hit upon fruitful discoveries."[38] Pure scientists, like great poets, are the gifts of nature. The wind of the spirit bloweth where it listeth and no meteorological office can forecast or control its vagaries. But if we cannot raise the wind we can erect the windmills. A Government must decide how far the material embodiment of the spirit of science is to be encouraged.

In the first place experience has shown that there are certain types of research essential to the progress of pure science itself and of direct importance to industry which cannot be left to private initiative : e.g. the determination of physical constants and the standardizing of instruments. In 1901 the National Physical Laboratory was founded as a public institution for standardizing and verifying instruments and for testing materials and for determining physical constants. Until 1918, except for a small State grant, the Royal Society bore the whole financial responsibility. The Laboratory was then taken over by the Department of Scientific and Industrial Research and a policy determined. The Laboratory can pursue fundamental research work on its own initiative and its own discretion. It can do work for outside persons and firms as well as for the Government on payment of a fee. But such special investigations are only undertaken if they cannot be done elsewhere and when the results are likely to be of general interest and on condition that they are available for the confidential information of the Government.[39]

Secondly, there are certain services so fundamental that the State must concern itself with their efficiency. The Department of Scientific and Industrial Research assumes direct responsibility for industrial research in food, fuel, building and clean water supply. Sometimes the solution of a specific problem—such as the best way of detecting the presence of a submarine—may be of urgent interest to the State. Sometimes a group of industries may be induced to co-operate in the solution of some common problem, e.g., the stress of bridges, or the best locomotive design. Sometimes a new industrial process may be established by well-planned research, e.g., the economical extraction of oil from coal. The State has here to attempt the delicate task of guiding and supplementing the demand of private industry and the provision made by private endowment for particular forms of research. It has to secure such a union between pure research and business acumen as shall be fruitful of material advantages to the community. It has to overcome the suspicion and hostility that many industrialists show to the potentialities of scientific investigation. The ordinary citizen of the nineteenth century could not see that education paid, and a twentieth-century industrialist may not always see that research brings dividends. How can they make convincing calculations for their shareholders for the development of a province on the edge of the unknown. " Research being a venture into the unknown success is not certain . . . except in such a case as the cure of disease it is rarely possible to estimate the economic return even if success is attained."[40] The time-lag between a new discovery in the laboratory and its commercial development is too long for the technique of business forecasting or the investors' courage to span. It was two generations before

Faraday's electro-magnetic experiments were of interest to a Chancellor of the Exchequer. Many of the most valuable conclusions to be drawn from the Rothampstead experiments did not emerge until the trial plants had been continued under the same treatment for twenty or thirty years. It took a million pounds and twenty years to place artificial indigo on the market after it had been synthesized in the laboratory.[41]

In what cases Government intervention is justified is as subtle a problem to decide as the analogous problem of the duty of the State to provide the necessary conditions of freedom, e.g., in making education compulsory. Unless there is a certain framework of scientific knowledge and research in existence it is impossible for the industrialists or consumers concerned to know the significance of what is happening around them.

The third problem is to encourage and assist the movement for industrial research without encroaching on activities best carried out by industry itself.[42] Industrial research can be as integral a part of production and distribution as advertisement or insurance, and its progress is best promoted by measures which enlist the active co-operation of industrialists themselves. Before 1914 the Development Commission had found that there were two methods by which the State could assist research : by a series of grants for specific objects ; by the provision of a permanent revenue to certain institutions. The first had the advantage that the commitments of the State could be limited. But it was not always possible to determine the expenditure and indicate the nature of the research proposed in advance. In the case of agriculture there was no organized body to whom the grant might be made. The study of animal diseases had not received the philanthropic support which had been given to human sickness and there were in existence no organized body of veterinary surgeons or research workers. The essential nature of the problems of agricultural research precluded intermittent grants for distinct and clearly defined ends. " The distinguishing character of agricultural research is that a continuous policy is essential ; the investigator is often in possession of a method rather than a particular scheme of work which will succeed or fail within a given time." After 1918 the Department of Scientific and Industrial Research, instead of forming a central institution to which industries could turn for the purpose of having their research problems carried out, adopted a scheme of research associations. These—which are without parallel in any other country—are organizations set up by the industry for the industry. They appoint their own staffs and decide their own policy but they receive a grant in aid if they satisfy the department that they are duly prosecuting research. The department keeps in touch with the work of all research associations. A clearing-house has been established, so that if a discovery emerges in one association of no direct interest to itself it is passed on to where its importance may be vital.

Underlying all schemes of Government co-operation with industry are vital questions of economic policy. "Accuracy and caution are part of the essence of scientific research and nothing is more destructive to its true spirit than the immediate demand for something definite to win applause or satisfy impatience."[43] It is necessary to take due precautions " against transferring to the State the burden of ordinary industrial research which have become one of the essential costs of production."[44] But it is when we come to the so-called development schemes where a policy of doles may be covered by a veneer of research that the danger is found. Doubtless private enterprise has done those things which it ought not to have done and left undone those things which it should have done. But a blind State may lead those with short sight down a steep place. Before 1914 the Development Commission had to explain that decaying harbours and local industries had no claim to support against the competition of efficient rivals. After 1918 they were saying that in the absence of credit facilities which would give to village artisans power and machine aids " it would hardly be contrary to economic science . . . to make the attempt to supply them."[45] In 1930-31 they were saying that " the spread of well-designed and well-constructed machinery has at the present time discounted the qualities or the old-fashioned craftsmen ; but as competition increases our world markets may depend upon our using their skill."[46] How far should this preservation of what once was useful but now is valueless, but may have value in the future, be carried ? Should the State garrison economic deserts because they may one day blossom like the rose ?

The development of the administrative machinery for the supervision of research has been slow and cautious. The Development Commission was appointed first in 1911. It was at once involved in administrative toils. It had only powers to recommend ; it had no executive powers and no knowledge of proposals made for grants except through the Treasury, with whom the final decision rested. While no scheme could be financed without its approval, no scheme could be carried out without the co-operation of the Government Department concerned. The Commission was hampered by the complications of the administrative machinery of the United Kingdom. Where a problem required a plan for the whole United Kingdom, negotiations might be necessary with two authorities in England and Wales, one in Scotland, and one or two in Ireland. There were acute difficulties when any plan involved the co-operation of central and local authorities. In the case of canal development, fishing harbours and the prevention of coast erosion there might be no executive body to whom a grant could be made. In the case of agriculture and rural industries, forests and afforestation, the number of men really qualified to conduct research was very small. Before 1914 the organization of a research top to our educational system was considered by the Board of Education. At that time only 1,500 research workers were employed in British industry. In 1915 a special committee of the Privy Council and in 1916 a special department under it, was provided for enlarging and organizing the work of scientific research. The political and financial responsibility lies with the committee of the council, presided over by the Lord President, but the actual work is done by an advisory council of persons appointed for their scientific, or scientific and industrial, qualifications by the Lord President after consultation with the President of the Royal Society. The secretary of the advisory council is the permanent head of the department—the Department of Scientific and Industrial Research. The advisory council or scientific experts working harmoniously under a lay chairman plan a policy of scientific research within the financial limits laid down by the department and suggest to the department the best means of carrying out the accepted policy.[47] Following the recommendation of a Cabinet committee on the co-ordination of research work, an inter-departmental conference was set up in May, 1922, to consider border-line cases between the Development Commission, the Department of Scientific and Industrial Research, and Medical Research Council. The discussions of the conference drove home the lesson that a national policy in research, complex as it must be and directed by diverse and suitably-designed organs, must be conceived and implemented as a unity.[48] In 1911 the National Health Insurance Act established a committee to administer a fund for medical research. The amount was about £53,000, the equivalent of a penny for every insured person. In 1913 a Medical Research Committee began to frame a policy and plan a programme of work. By the Ministry of Health Act, 1919, administrative control was transferred to a committee of the Privy Council. In 1920 a Medical Research Council succeeded to the Medical Research Committee and took its place by the side of the Department of Scientific and Industrial Research.[49] In 1931 a committee of the Privy Council for the organization and development of agricultural research was also established. Its relations on the one side with the Medical Research Council and the Department of

258

Scientific and Industrial Research and on the other with Ministry of Agriculture and the Development Commission make its administrative work both complicated and difficult.[50]

It might appear at first sight as difficult to make philosophers kings as to combine activities so distinct as administration and scientific research. The methods of research are "anarchical and ought to be continuously destructive of accepted opinion,"while it is the function of government everywhere to prevent anarchy. But their seeming antipathy veils a deeper harmony. The anarchy of science is rooted in a profound order, and the order of government must rest ultimately not on force but upon persuasion. "The method of science seeks to conquer doubt by cultivating it and encouraging it to grow until it finds its natural limits and can go no further."[51] It must be ready always to abandon a conclusion, but when such abandonment is based on evidence the logical consistency of the whole system is thereby strengthened.[52] If the certainties of science are based upon the scepticism of research, the order which governments seek depends upon the skill with which they can adjust their organs to a changing world. The development of science now imposes a rate of change faster than the most skilful and autocratic rulers have ever achieved. It is breaking the crust of custom on which rulers have hitherto relied. Only as allies can science and government secure the knowledge and the peace which are their complementary aims.

Governments must take account of all those changes in scientific knowledge which might threaten its superiority in physical force : policemen must have motor cars ; Scotland Yard its poison experts ; Customs officials their X-ray apparatus. The State, as our detective fiction should remind us, can only hold its own if it pays the tribute which force must always pay to knowledge. The advance of science has also compelled Governments to consider far more closely their duty to provide those goods and services which, however necessary have not been produced by private enterprise. That some pure research should be endowed would seem to be as obvious as that some teachers should be endowed. But it is difficult to determine how far the State should subsidize technical experiments and research. Perhaps the economic system is self-regulating ; perhaps we are led by an invisible hand ; perhaps it is unwise to flee the goods we have for others that we know not of except under the spur of profit and guided by the reins of effective demand. But the evidence would seem to be overwhelming that there are more things on earth that men could have and would desire, than are to be won without the assistance of the State. What would be to the benefit of all may not be to the profit of any one. It does not, for example, pay anyone to make a concerted attack on dirt,[53] or to discover the essential principles of dietetics. The inter-dependence of the methods and results of scientific research make it impossible for private enterprise to estimate the cost of every service it might desire to provide. Bovril may put beef into men, for the cost of breeding beef is known. Vitamins may put life into men, but the cost of their discovery is not. For any application of science to human need depends upon a combination of basic research such as animal breeding or the science of the soil or mineralogy, with *ad hoc* research on urgent problems such as the life history of a destructive insect, and the development and application of their results, and all this in a scientific background provided by the fundamental scientific concepts of the age.[54] The community should support laboratories as it once supported Cathedrals. The State could remove hindrances to freedom by guaranteeing in peace some of the experiments it directly makes under the stimulus of war. Were war abolished the State would have funds for audacious experimental research which would have the further advantage of providing a psychological equivalent for war. Even this side of Utopia some provision for research could be made by diverting some of the funds now spent on self-evident quackery. A special tax on worthless medicines would help the Cancer Fund.

Defence. The Haldane Report assumed that the three great departments of defence—War, Admiralty and Air—would in the future, as in the past, be independent Ministries. General supervision would be normally effected by the Committee of Imperial Defence under the Prime Minister. This Committee of Imperial Defence was a purely advisory and consultative body which inquired into and made recommendations on problems brought before it by the separate department concerned. The Prime Minister was alone responsible for anything in the nature of a consistent policy. In 1923 it was proposed that responsibility for the initiation of policy should rest with the Chairman of the Committee of Imperial Defence, with the assistance of the three Chiefs of Staff of the War Office, Admiralty and Air Ministry. The Committee of Imperial Defence was to consist of the Prime Minister as president, a chairman, the Secretary of State for War, the Secretary of State for Air, the First Lord of the Admiralty, the Chancellor of the Exchequer, the Secretaries of State for Foreign Affairs, for the Colonies and for India, the three Chiefs of Staff and the Permanent Secretary to the Treasury. In the absence of the Prime Minister the chairman was to preside, to report recommendations to the Cabinet and to intepret in matters of detail the decision of the Cabinet to the departments. Assisted by the three Chiefs of Staff, he was to keep the defence situation as a whole constantly under review. The three Chiefs of Staff were to be individually and collectively responsible for advising on defence policy as a whole and to constitute a "super chief of war staff in committee."[55]   After 1927 these recommendations were followed.   Instead of the initiative resting entirely with the Prime Minister, the three Chiefs of Staff, a "super-chief of war staff in committee," had a direct responsibility for advising the chairman (invariably the Prime Minister) of the Committee of Imperial Defence on the initiation of policy.   They furnished the Committee of Imperial Defence every year with a survey of the whole problem of defence based on a separate survey of the international situation provided by the Foreign Office.   They constituted a sub-committee of the Committee of Imperial Defence over which the Prime Minister presided; their report swept the whole field of imperial defence in its minor as well as its major aspects.   Their report was discussed by the Committee of Imperial Defence and sent to the Cabinet.   The Secretary to the Committee of Imperial Defence was also secretary to the Cabinet.   There were four assistant secretaries, one each for the Air, Navy, Army and Indian Army.   Separate Ministerial committees were concerned with special problems such as the defence of India or of the Middle East.   Over fifty sub-committees dealt with such problems as disarmament, censorship, imperial communication, oil, fuel, insurance in time of war, air-raid prevention, etc., etc., and a co-ordinating committee keeps the war book up to date.   Co-ordination between the services was improved out of all knowledge;[56] the system preserved the responsibility of the Cabinet, provided for the continuous investigation of every kind of problem of defence whether of policy or of detail, and could swiftly pass from a state of peace to a state of war.

There were also many criticisms.   It was said that the Chiefs of Staffs sub-committee had "done very little to explore and still less to settle" the larger problems of defence policy.   Unanimity had been too often reached by tacit agreement to exclude vital differences of opinion; there was no provision for the examination of defence requirements untrammelled by departmental compromises.[57]   It was felt by some that the advance of science was tending to make the three services into three branches of one defence force and that it was an anachronism that they should scramble for their estimates; without careful co-ordination the three services might find themselves preparing each to meet a different danger : the Navy a threat in the Pacific; the Army a threat to the Indian frontier; the Air Force a threat in Europe, without any decision being come to as to which of the possibilities was probable. For these reasons and because it was impossible for the Prime Minister with all his other duties really to supervise both the Committee of

Imperial Defence and the Chiefs of Staffs sub-committee, or to state their problems to the Cabinet, or to hold the balance between the conflicting financial claims of the three services, there were advocates of a Ministry of Defence. This proposal was at that time doubly damned. " No substantial reduction of cost would follow from its creation ";[58] " there would be serious risk that the efficiency of the service might be impaired by the alteration of the system involved."[59]   Lord Haldane had said, a Minister of Defence, " if established with anything like adequate power of control . . . would be bound to interfere in administration . . . by reason of (his) direct responsibility to Parliament. " He would be looked to as responsible not only for efficiency but for economy.   " He would therefore require a considerable staff, whose duties would overlap and duplicate those of existing departmental staffs."   A Minister of Defence " would . . . be in considerable danger of proving himself to be either too great or too little.   If he were effective for the job he would be the rival of the Prime Minister.   But in fact the problems of organization for modern defence require powers of influence only to be exercised by the Prime Minister."[60]   The conduct of a war is only to be carried out by a small body of Ministers having no other duties to perform.   As this organization was not feasible in peace its place was taken not by a Minister of Defence, but by a Council of Imperial Defence, which could form a nucleus for war.[61]

With the transformation of the European scene by the rise of the Nazi dictatorship the organization of defence was examined by a sub-committee of the Committee of Imperial Defence composed of the Secretary to the Committee of Imperial Defence, the Permanent Secretary to the Treasury, the Permanent Under-Secretary of State for Foreign Affairs and the Chiefs of Staffs.   Their conclusions were submitted to a Defence Policy and Requirements Committee presided over by the Prime Minister, who invited Lord Weir to become a member.   This Defence Policy and Requirements Committee served both as a general purposes committee of the Committee of Imperial Defence and as a committee of liaison between the Committee of Imperial Defence and the Cabinet.[62]   In 1936 a Minister for Co-ordination of Defence was appointed with the duty of generally supervising the Committee of Imperial Defence and the co-ordination of whatever executive action its defence plans might require and in particular the education of the reconditioning plans already determined upon.   The new Minister was the deputy-chairman of the Committee of Imperial Defence and of the Defence Policy and Requirements Committee, and, in the Prime Minister's absence, chairman of the Committee of Imperial Defence.   He had the right personally to consult with the Chiefs of Staffs together, including the right to convene under his chairmanship the Chiefs of Staffs Committee whenever he or they think it desirable.[63] Mr. Churchill said that the new Minister " had an office so absurdly constructed that the very conditions of his commission revealed a confusion of mind in those who had defined it." His responsibilities were so " strangely, so inharmoniously and so perversely grouped," he was endowed with powers " so cribbed and restricted that no one, not even Napoleon himself, would be able to discharge them with satisfaction." They included " the co-ordination of high strategic thought on land, sea and air including food supply in time of war ; the securing of the punctual execution of the existing very large programme ; the planning and organization of British industry so that it would be ready for war expansion."[64]

The root of these difficulties over so fundamental a problem lay in the fact that the Committee of Imperial Defence was adapted to meet a situation where sea power came first, and where the two other services were in some measure merely its adjuncts, and to meet the necessities of the self-governing dominions, which were united to us only by unwritten and elastic obligations. The Committee of Imperial Defence was an organization that had nothing quite resembling it in any other country.

The Foreign Office. Investigation had shown that of the 249 men who served in the higher ranks of the foreign or the diplomatic services between 1851 and 1929, only nine had been to schools other than public schools, or one of the recognized naval and military colleges. There was therefore a wan hope after 1918 that if many battles won on the playing fields of Eton had been unnecessarily provoked by the esoteric doctrines taught in her school rooms the democratization of the service might in future strengthen the forces making for peace. In 1919 the requirements that a candidate for the Foreign Office or the diplomatic service must, before he could sit for the examination, have received a nomination from the Secretary of State, and be possessed of some £400 a year, were abolished. The two services were at the same time amalgamated.

The peculiarity about the nineteenth-century Foreign Office had been the absence of any rational division of labour. Its old men had little time for vision and its young men more than enough time to dream. In 1905 a committee of investigation was appointed to discover the way business might be done. In consequence a General Registry was created and Foreign Office clerks began to produce their own detailed suggestions on problems to be decided by their superiors. The Office became a body with a highly influential opinion of its own with which the

Secretary of State must reckon.

With the growth of the complexity of international affairs the Foreign Office provided a complex example of the distribution of departmental business. Most of its work had to be divided geographically. But there were some departments—Treaty, News, Consular and Library—which dealt with blocks of subjects in all countries. A few had to be controlled by the department most nearly concerned with a given area. The American Department dealt with Disarmament; the Department concerned with Central Europe with the execution of the Peace Treaties; the Eastern Department with the Foreign Relation of Palestine; the Far Eastern Department with the traffic in dangerous drugs; the Northern Department with Bolshevism; the Western Department with the League of Nations.[65]

Ministry of Justice. In 1918 the Committee on Machinery of Government, inspired by Lord Haldane, was of the opinion that there was a strong case for the appointment of a Minister of Justice. It was impressed " by the representations made by men of great experience, such as the President of the Incorporated Law Society, as to the difficulty of getting the attention of the Government to legal reform, and as to the want of contact between those who are responsible for the administration of the work of the Commercial Courts and the mercantile community, and by the evidence adduced that the latter are in consequence and progressively withdrawing their disputes from the jurisdiction of these courts." They were no less impressed " with the total inadequacy of the organization which controls the general administration of the very large staffs, with the voluminous business, required to give effect to the decrees of the Courts of Justice throughout the country." They were of the opinion that " one of the chief reasons for this inadequacy " was " the magnitude and variety of the duties with which the Lord Chancellor is charged, without really being allowed either the time or the machinery requisite for their performance."[66] We cannot here explore the dusty chambers of " old father antique,, the law." The exigencies of the 1914-18 war had brought many of our legal experts into consultation and collaboration with those of Allied powers, with some wholesome shocks to their insular pride. A Ministry of Justice was wanted primarily because there was no general machinery to improve the law of England. It was also wanted that there might be some authoritative body, other than those professional organizations in which the best minds were given to the labours of heavy and lucrative practice, for the development of research and training in the law. It is a paradox that among the people who are the most law-abiding in the world there should be the least general knowledge of the nature and principles of law. It is about the only subject of which an English-man thinks it folly to be wise. "For the most part the public take but little interest in the machinery of the law, which is in itself difficult to understand and makes but small appeal to the popular imagination." It is as true now as it was in 1872, when Fawcett said that "there is no country in the world whose legal system is so complicated as ours and where the process of obtaining justice is so dear and so slow."[67] It was said that "every practising lawyer is aware that the public are rapidly losing faith in the present judicial system as a means of settling disputes."[68]

What then are the objections to a Ministry of Justice in this country? The need for such a Ministry is deemed to be self-evident in every Continental country.[69] "Nor has Great Britain ever ventured to argue otherwise in taking over responsibility for a country which has previously had one, in however imperfect a form."[70] It is feared perhaps that the pressure upon a Minister of Justice in the House of Commons for patronage would be unbearable.[71] "What keeps the English lack of system going, apart from vested interests, is a Whig feeling (still powerful in our mental make-up) about the danger of efficient public controls."[72] It is argued that the position of the Lord Chancellor as a member of the executive government and head of the judiciary provides a link between two sets of institutions which should not be severed. "It is difficult to believe that there is no necessity for the existence of such a personality, imbued on the one hand with legal ideas and habits of thought and aware on the other of the problems which engage the attention of the executive Government."[73] Only a man equipped with the prestige or the authority or the personality of the ambitious and successful barrister can be a successful head of the profession and competent to push forward legal reform.[74] But it may be replied that the danger of patronage may be avoided by continuing our present system of keeping pro-motions as rare as possible.[75] At present the amount of promotion from one grade of judge to another is so small as to be negligible.[76] The Bench could be recruited by a committee of the judges themselves from men of some age at the bar.[77] Under our present system the Lord Chancellor or the Lord Chief Justice and the Master of the Rolls are appointed by the Prime Minister usually from his political followers—the Law Officers (or ex-Law Officers) of his party's present (or last) Government. The seven Law Lords similarly are appointed by the Prime Minister usually from among barristers who have rendered political services in politics, but held no previous judicial post; and the President of the Probate, Divorce and Admiralty Division and the five Lord Justices are also appointments in the hands of the Prime

Minister.[78] The possibility of political misappointments remains. To those who fear efficient public controls it may be pointed out that only the creation of the departments responsible for education and for health overcame the deficiencies of those services, and did so without impairing the self-guidance of the professions concerned.[79] The peculiar merits of the Lord Chancellor's combination of experience of the world with the learning of the law might be retained by making him the Minister of Justice.

The Civil Service, like the Constitutional Monarchy, Parliament or the Cabinet is *sui generis*. We cannot say that the politician is concerned with principles while the Civil Service is concerned with details. We cannot say that the politician is concerned with opinion and the civil servant with research; that the civil servant is concerned with the permanent aspects of policy and the politician with innovation. We can only say that the civil servant is concerned with that part of the work of Government which is not done by Parliament and the Ministry. The civil servant has not got to consider while the politician must the opinion of the electorate. The civil servant is the kind of expert which the party system requires.

The Civil Service has to work under the special conditions of representative government. It is this which distinguishes it from bodies engaged in scientific research or the staffs of private businesses. The most important problems of the modern Civil Service arise from the fact that many of the problems formerly dealt with by private enterprise, or academic research, must now be regulated under the very special conditions of parliamentary control.

Everything that the civil servant does is an exercise of the power of the State. As an agent of the Government, entitled in the last resort to use force for the enforcement of its commands, he has a duty of fairness greater than anyone engaged in private enterprise. His business is not business as usual but an act of State. He must attain an equality in the application of the law to all whom it may concern, or he will undermine the very principle upon which his power is based—that the State is the organ of the common will.

In private enterprise it may not pay to discriminate between customers —charging one price to a man in furs and another to a man in rags— but equal treatment is not a duty. It may be unwise but it is not wrong to make the good customer pay indirectly for the debts of the bad. The competitive system assumes that there is a trial of wits between all buyers and all sellers; justice only comes in when the State prevents certain frauds, and enforces agreements made in a certain way. When the buyer or seller does more than the law commands it is to please his conscience or because he feels that honesty pays. In business no omission or commission is a sin save when a legal penalty or possible loss of business is involved. The State must collect the last local licence, even though it would cost less to let it go unpaid, not merely because to do so would encourage non-payment, but also because the State has a duty to apply the law equally to all.

This duty of fairness is owed by the officials of any State. But where there is a representative system the performance of this duty is safeguarded in certain very special ways. Criticism of the administration becomes a part of the tactics of party warfare, and any individual case may be made the test of a principle and determine the fate of a Government. In private enterprise the rising curve of sales is the proof of efficiency; in the public service it is the fairness of any individual case. The civil servant has to work in a particular way. He must be " able at short notice to put the Minister in a position of justifying anything that he has done down to quite small details."[80] Public departments must be organized so that there is a consilience between decisions made for different places and at different times. Not only must there be such consilience but its existence must be provable to unfriendly critics. This necessitates an administrative machine of a complexity unknown to private enterprise. In private enterprise a policy can and must depend to a large extent upon the men at the head of a particular department; but in a Government office there has to be complex organization in which each grade of officials has a defined authority delegated to them. This complexity affects every detail of the civil servant's work. He must show in meticulous detail that public money has been spent only for the purpose for which it was given. With no automatic test of profit, every proposal for fresh expenditure or change in the direction and scale of Government activity has to be made convincing in advance. The civil servant has to work by written memoranda and in accordance with general regulations decided at the appropriate level in the hierarchy. Red tape is a symbol of the citizens' equality before the law.

A Government department has to determine policy and to apply policy already decided. It has to assist the Minister to determine what legislation shall be passed and to see that legislation which has been passed is applied. It is its function to make the best use of permitted means to ends commanded or allowed. While applying the powers it has it must gather the experience needed to adjust them to new conditions. " It is not only necessary that the legislature should make provision in the laws for their due execution; it is also desirable that the executive agency should work towards new legislation on the same topics. For the execution of laws deals with the particulars by an induction from which the results to be aimed at in legislation are to be ascertained ; and the generalization from those particulars can only be well effected when the lowest in the chain of functionaries is made subsidiary to the operations of the highest in a suggestive as well as in an executive capacity—that is, when the experience of the functionary who puts his last hand to the execution of any particular class of enactments, is made available for the guidance of the legislature."[81]

It is under these very special conditions that the politician and the civil servant have to work together. Their relations have been determined by long experience and countless subtle precedents which have become part of the spirit of the constitution. Their relations have become a vital part of the conventions of the constitution. But continuity with the past is defensible only so long as it produces a tradition capable of being adapted to whatever changes the future may hold. No hard and fast rules can be laid down for the guidance of the two parties to this vital partnership.

Any attempt to describe this most important part of our working constitution is limited by certain obvious difficulties. The civil servant it has been said must take the triple vow of poverty, anonymity and obedience.[82] Their biographies are scanty, anecdotal and discreet. Those who possess too much or too little character to remain in the service are restrained in their revelations by the Official Secrets Acts. In the biographies of statesmen the few references to their permanent and silent collaborators are as complimentary but uninformative as tombstones. Even in evidence before Royal Commissions and departmental inquiries the greatest reserve is shown by politicians and civil servants on the subject of their official relations. The work of a department like the Foreign Office can only be understood by studying the marginalia on dispatches, private correspondence of Cabinet Ministers and M.P.s and ambassadors in London.[83] And doubtless it is in the public interest that the relations between politicians and civil servants should be a marriage of true minds with no impediment of publicity to its consummation.

The war conditions of 1914-18 broke down some of the traditional reticence of statesmen. We have Dr. Addison's opinion that the Admiralty had a habit of " going its own way regardless of other people, and that some of the officials at the Local Government Board were just a little slippy.[84] We know that Mr. Lloyd George was more than thankful when the Admiralty could not see their way to lend him any of their staff for his new Ministry of Munitions.[85] He has also described " the amazing and incomprehensible difficulties encountered in inducing the Admiralty even to try the convoy system."[86]   But in all these cases we must be careful to distinguish between the limitations of individual civil servants, the limitations of the organization and traditions of particular departments, the general limitations of the expert and his special limitations in an emergency.

It has been said that the civil servant has the duty " to set the wider and more enduring considerations against the exigencies of the moment which may be the concern of his perhaps fleeting political partner."[87] Or more bluntly : " In this democratic age it is absolutely essential that you should have at the head of a department a man who will express his opinion absolutely fearlessly . . . whether or not the Minister accepts his advice. It is vital to the interests of the country that successive waves of political opinion in a department should be confronted by this wall of experienced opinion."[88]   It was once the duty of the Minister to tell the civil servant what the public would not stand ; it is now the duty of the civil servant to tell the Minister what the facts will not allow.

But the distinctions between the sphere of the civil servant concerned with enduring and the sphere of the Minister concerned with ephemeral things is both superficial and misleading. It may be true that some politician after the orgy of lying into which the technique of a modern election may have seduced him will require the sobering influence of departmental detail to restore his sense of reality. But the number of politicians of ministerial quality who are deceived by their own election speeches must be very small. If it is the function of the civil servant to sober the Minister it is equally the function of the Minister to inspire the expert. However brief may be his term of office he must try to reveal to his technical experts the wider and enduring problems underlying their specialized knowledge. Constitutional conventions and a strong tradition of mutual respect has produced a working system of co-operation. But any sudden change in the nature and scope of political activity might show that the principles of their co-operations are only imperfectly understood. The factors are many and various.

First, the bulk of official activity is concerned with the application of principles and the running of machinery previously established. In normal times no government attempts to establish a new machinery of government. Most of the activities therefore of departments will be routine and non-political. Unless some change in social conditions or opinion produces unexpected difficulties the Minister must necessarily be guided by his experts on any detail of this traditional policy. But the relation between the application of policy already approved by Parliament and the determination of fresh policy is complex and subtle. " The application to particular cases of general principles laid down in statutes or the administration of financial provisions made by Parliament will involve also the preparation or study of proposals for the alteration of existing law in the light of changed circumstances or new policies or experience."[89] Morant at the Board of Education, by skilfully revealing the weaknesses of the system he had to administer, secured the passing of the Education Act, 1902.

The work of Morant at the Board of Education and of Llewellyn Smith at the Board of Trade showed that with the new responsibilities undertaken by the State, the permanent head of a Government department must himself be a statesman in everything except the ability to lead a party. " My own conception of the permanent head of a large Government department is that he is not (except by accident) a specialist in anything, but rather the general adviser of the Minister, the general manager and controller under the Minister, with the ultimate responsibility to the Minister for all the activities of the department . . . including those directed to secure economy in policy and management. The Permanent Secretary is a general manager rather than an expert. His duty is to shopwalk the department and to see that the Minister gets the best technical advice."[90]

After 1918 the permanent head and his immediate assistants had three complex tasks : they had to see that the department in the exercise of the powers given by Parliament neither broke the law nor provoked criticism which the government of the day could not answer in Parliament ; they had to interpret to the Minister the policy which the experience of the department might suggest. In every department there was a tradition which only the strongest Minister could override. The Permanent Secretary himself could do little more than help the Minister to whatever knowledge corporate or individual the department had. Thirdly, they organized the resources of the department to assist the Minister in whatever policy he decided to adopt. " The popular fiction that the civil servants are anxious to foist their own policy upon Ministers is not true . . . The Civil Service like their Minister to do well ; they feel personally humiliated if he makes blunders ; they take enormous pains to give him all the facts and to warn him against pitfalls. If they think the policy he contemplates is wrong they will tell him why, but always on the basis that it is for him to settle the matter. And if the Minister, as is sometimes the case, has neither the courage nor the brains to evolve a policy of his own, they will do their best to find him one ; for after all it is better that a department should be run by its civil servants than that it should not be run at all."[91] The part played by the civil servant in the determination of policy varied with the nature of the problem to be decided. Proposals for legislation, for example, fall into three main classes : the more important Bills which the Government have announced that it is their policy to carry into law and on which they stake their political existence ; the principal departmental Bills which reflect Government policy which are not concerned with major issues ; Bills of a non-controversial type which reflect departmental policy on particular points and which it is thought will prove useful additions to the statute book. In the case of the first class the broad outlines of the Bill are usually settled by the Ministers themselves with such assistance as they may require from the various departments ; the other two are mainly the work of the individual departments.[92]

A Minister at the head of a large department found not only a departmental tradition but within that tradition conflicting schools and policies. His real problem was to lay bare the unconscious presuppositions upon which his civil servants worked. In a large department the Permanent Secretary himself had to interpret the various technical policies within the department. The Permanent Secretary in relation to the technical experts was in the same position as the Minister to himself. Both were amateurs dependent on various technical advisers. In some cases the political head of a department was himself an expert on policy. A Permanent Secretary of the Foreign Office could present his Minister with a memorandum giving objections to a policy proposed. On a general policy he would have only that advantage over the Minister, normally possessed by a mind trained to consider problems over a mind skilled to sway opinion. In most cases the policy adopted would depend upon the interpretation of a variety of expert opinions. The Ministry of Agriculture had many economic and statistical experts ; but neither the Permanent Secretary nor the Minister could always secure from their crowd of experts the guidance wanted for a consistent policy.

Where the department realized that the Minister was committed to a policy for which there was nothing to be said, their duty was simple—who cannot lead the blind must in mercy soften their fall. The real difficulty occurred when a difference between the leading civil servants in a department and the Minister was thought by the latter to be due to the former misunderstanding their own technical experts. Strong Ministers were not " forbidden by any rule of honour or etiquette from sending for any person either inside or outside his office, whatever his rank, to seek enlightenment on any subject affecting his administration. If a Minister learns that any subordinate in his department possesses exceptional knowledge or special aptitude on any question he should establish direct contact with him. The political head of a department has not merely the right, but the duty to send for anyone who will

271

help him to discharge his trust to the public."[93]

When an entirely new policy was being started, e.g., Old Age Pensions, National Health Insurance or Unemployment Insurance, all the outstanding men in the Civil Service were brought in.[94] Not only would a Minister responsible for a difficult Bill call upon the whole resources of the Civil Service; a Cabinet faced with a vital problem of policy could demand the opinion of civil servants even if it were contrary to the political head of the department from which they came. " If an official disagrees with the head of his department it is usually his duty not to resign, but to state fully to the head of his department and, should any proper occasion arise, to other members of the Ministry, what are the nature of his views."[95] A first Lord of the Admiralty could not expect his civil servants to support him against other Ministers when the position was so serious that a joint consultation had been called. How far a consilience of expert opinion scattered in a variety of departments was revealed depended upon the steps which the Cabinet took for investigation and thought.

A simple form of the problem of the relation between the permanent or administrative head of a Government department and its technical experts was the question whether or not such experts—medical, engineering, economic, biological, etc., had the right of direct access to the Minister. Could the Medical Officer of Health directly challenge the presentation of departmental opinion made by the Permanent Secretary to the Minister? Sir Warren Fisher stated that no Permanent Secretary would refuse to permit his technical experts to communicate with the Minister should they wish. Systematic co-operation existed between experts in different fields employed in separate departments. In finance it was obligatory for Establishment Officers to keep in close touch with one another and for accounting officers to communicate directly with the Treasury. The influence of the Whitley system and the urgent need for economy after 1918 imposed on the heads of departments a practice of consultation almost unknown before. Frequent consultations were held on staffing and administrative organization. In the nineteenth century permanent heads of departments had not pooled their ideas on these things. The purchase of a typewriter or the employment of a typist was then a domestic detail of the department using them. Before the establishment of the Cabinet Secretariat there was no method by which departments were informed as a matter of course of the Cabinet decisions which concerned them. The responsibility for advising the Cabinet on matters of Defence was made the joint and several responsibility of the three Chiefs of Staff to the War Office, Admiralty and Air Ministry. If the Treasury had its eyes and ears in every department so, too, could the statistical and research departments. But the older departments clung to a tradition of non-co-operation. The Admiralty was perhaps the greatest offender. The legal departments, save in the technical matter of drafting, failed to use the experience of those who might have helped them.

The conditions which we have described as common to all Civil Service work—the duty of fairness and the need of producing a detailed defence of any action which may be challenged—had to be satisfied under a great variety of conditions in the different departments. But in the organization of all Government departments there were certain common features.

All departments had a registry. It was the function of a registry to record all movements of documents in and out of a department and to be a storehouse of precedents. In 1930 the Board of Education dealt with 1,350,000 letters, the Ministry of Agriculture with 1,300,000, the Ministry of Labour with 825,000 and the Ministry of Health with 750,000.[96] From the standpoint of the registry the efficiency of a department could easily be judged. One department " selected a high official, placed him in personal charge of the registry, instructed him to observe from that point of vantage what was going on and armed him with power to interfere and get things put right. He was not concerned with what the decision might be, but he was concerned to see that there was a decision taken at the proper time and properly arrived at."[97]

The registration of all correspondence at a single point enabled the official to study the life history of any question. The file was both an instrument of co-ordination and a record of official action. It had certain obvious drawbacks. Only one section could use a file at a time. One of the minor arts of the civil servant was the retention for his own use of files sought by others. A divided file has brought confusion and trouble.

Every department had an Establishments Branch concerned, in consultation with the Establishments Branch of the Treasury, with all problems of staffing. Establishments Officers had to know not only the detailed conditions in their own department but also to be familiar with general conditions throughout the Service. They had to make a proper use of the available staff and make it content and efficient. In all departments there was an Accounting Branch concerned with whatever financial control the Treasury imposed on the particular work which the department had to perform. In the larger departments like the War Office and the Admiralty, the Accounting Branch was almost a Treasury within a department. An Accounting Branch had to see that the letter and spirit of the authority to spend, given by Parliament, was observed. All departments needed advice on the scope of their powers and duties and to conduct legal business, e.g., cases in the courts and the drafting of bills and rules and orders. Some departments had their own solicitors' department; others their own legal advisers and the Treasury Solicitor for their litigious work, while in others all legal business was transacted by the Treasury Solicitor. Departments drafted their own rules and orders but the final instructions for a Bill were sent by the department concerned to Parliamentary Counsel. Large departments had a special branch concerned with publicity and answers to parliamentary questions.

The earlier classification of the work of the civil servant into routine and policy had developed into administrative, executive and clerical, with complex variations of " other executive," " other clerical " and a growing number of professional and technical workers. Administrative work was defined as that which was concerned with policy or the formation of policy; executive, that which was concerned with giving effect to policy that had been determined—the application of a code of law or administration to obtain results. While clerical work dealt with particular cases in accordance with well-defined regulations, instructions or general practice.

The work of the administrator varied widely from department to department. In each department a different form of ability of a high order might be required. The Treasury official had to master complex problems in currency or finance. The Foreign Office required a social, if not a spiritual, gift of tongues. The Colonial Office was a governing department. While it performed the functions common to other departments in this country, it was also charged in regard to all Crown Colonies with many of the duties which would in other cases have been dealt with by separate departments, e.g., the construction of a public building, police, education and the raising of loans. In some fifty communities it had to answer all the political and administrative questions which might arise. It had to appoint overseas staffs able to preserve what was best in the traditional native cultures. It had to produce reports which could be published as State Papers in distant communities; it was concerned with the impact of science on the structure of backward communities. The Admiralty was not only the architect of the house in which Jack floats, but his butcher, baker and candlestick-maker as well. The Home Office was not only responsible for internal order but also for all business not assigned to some other department. It secured through its inspectors the efficiency of the local police, supervised reformatory and industrial schools and sent representatives to international conferences on industrial relations, opium, and the traffic in women and children. The Board of Trade studied the course of trade but was also responsible for the administration of a variety of statutes relating to patents, industrial and commercial standards and the mercantile marine. The Ministry of Health supervised the medical profession in its relation to the general public where health insurance was concerned, and was responsible for the structure and efficiency of local government as a whole. At the Ministry of Health and the Board of Education it was an important part of the duties of an administrator to maintain good relations with the representatives of a variety of local authorities, and to see that they kept to the standards of local administration Parliament had prescribed. In the Ministry of Agriculture and Fisheries the administrator had the almost impossible task of harmonizing the science of animal and plant breeding with the intuitions of economists, and the conflicting prejudices and experience of landlord, tenant and consumer.[98]

Administrators were classified in three groups : (1) the Permanent Under-Secretary of State with a Deputy Secretary, found in the larger departments and the Principal Assistant Secretary ; (2) the Assistant Secretaries ; (3) the Principals and Assistant Principals.

The first group was a Civil Service general staff. It dealt with general policy, with administrative decisions in which Parliament was directly interested or with specialized functions covering the whole range of a department's work. The Permanent Secretary was a general manager rather than an expert. Of some twenty posts of this status (carrying over £3,000 a year) fourteen were held in 1930 by men promoted from other departments. Since 1918 the increased complexity of the Government problems and the influence of Whitleyism has secured a habit of continuous and informal co-operation between the Permanent Heads of the Departments under the Permanent Secretary to the Treasury, the official head of the Civil Service.

The division of duties between the Permanent Secretary and the Deputy Secretary was determined by the nature of the work which the department does. In some cases policy was the concern of the Permanent Secretary while the general control and direction of the running of the department was assigned to the deputy ; in others policy and general supervision were divided between them on a functional basis. The Principal Assistant Secretaries directly supervised finance and establishment and took final responsibility for administrative work which could be settled without the personal consideration of the Permanent Head or the Minister. An Assistant Secretary was the head of a unit known as a Branch, which was organized on either a functional or a territorial basis. In the Home Office, Assistant

Secretaries were the head of seven branches—industrial, aliens, criminal, children, miscellaneous (the King's pleasure, vivisection and dangerous explosives), police, Ireland (Northern Ireland and the Channel Islands and the Isle of Man).[99] In the Colonial Office the division of the work was territorial. The Board of Education had a functional and a territorial organization, so that local Directors of Education could confer with officials who knew the general situation in a particular area. The work of a branch was divided into sections directed by a Principal. In the Board of Trade a Principal had charge of the administration of the Merchant Shipping Acts. In the Board of Education a Principal was the opposite number of the Director of Education. The Assistant Principals were -the understudies and assistants to the Principals. They were a cadet corps from which the higher administrative posts could be filled.

The tendency was to do more and more of the work in the higher ranges by discussion and less and less by writing letters or putting minutes on official files. In the nineteenth century the Minister had been responsible for a fantastic accumulation of detailed work. A mass of unimportant work had hastened the death of Lord Clarendon, who had to initial a heap of trash.[100] The clerks in the Foreign Office were mere copyists. Waddington of the Home Office thought that minuting was the exclusive function of the Under-Secretary.[101] In the Colonial Office clerks had been early encouraged to make their own memoranda. By 1872 minuting and drafting were not restricted to one class of clerks.[102] In the Board of Trade by 1888 even a junior clerk was encouraged to put his ideas on paper. It was established in all departments that the juniors should settle what they could and send up to their superiors what they could not.

The Administrator had to decide the policy to be followed ;[103] an executive officer carried out the policy decided. His work involved the interpretation and application of law and regulations to cases which required decision. He might have to apply a very difficult and complex code of law to the circumstances of individual cases. The Executive class developed when men were needed to apply the complex codes of law which developed after 1870. There was an executive class only in those departments which needed a special class of officers to carry out policy rather than to advise and devise. There were no executives in the Home Office, though it would be fantastic to say that there was no executive work for them to do.[104] Executive officers were used mainly for the Accounts, Finance and Supply branches of Government departments. A few large and important classes were known as Other Executives e.g., the outdoor staff of the Customs and Excise Department, the tax inspectorate, the staff of the Estate Duty Office of the

Inland Revenue and the Employment Officers of the Ministry of Labour.

A clerical officer was required to know but he was not required to exercise discretion.[105] He prepared the material on which the administrative or executive officers would form a judgment. He drafted simple letters and kept records. They staffed the registries. In the Board of Education a clerical officer collected and kept the precedents on secondary education; a higher clerical officer drafted replies to petitions and congratulatory messages received by the King; another sanctioned the disposals of human remains. In fact the average citizen would receive his government letters from a clerical or junior executive officer, using a draft his Principal had prepared.

Two other classes of officers played a vital part in the work of Government departments—the Inspectors and the professional and scientific staff. There were in the thirties more than 2,000 inspectors employed in twenty-eight different departments. They had to inspect and report, but they had no responsibility, for the execution of any decision. And that mainly distinguished them from other civil servants. Their duties covered a wide field, e.g., the inspection of schools, reformatories, factories and workshops, mines, quarries and Poor Law Institutions. The great majority of them had technical and professional qualifications similar to the professional and technical staff. But the latter shared in the formation of policy and its execution. The problems raised by the importance of science for the work of the State have been discussed. The professional and scientific groups were complex and varied. They all had some professional qualification given by an outside body, e.g., the qualification possessed by a barrister, doctor, solicitor, architect, valuer, surveyor, etc. Half the legal officers (about 550) were employed in the legal branches or solicitors' departments of Government departments; the others in legal or quasi legal departments such as the Supreme Court of Judicature, the County Courts department and the Land Registry. The medical officers were employed in the Ministry of Pensions (200), the Ministry of Health (114) and the Prison Commission (52). The Office of Works employed over 400 architects and surveyors and over 200 others were shared between the Defence Departments, the Ministry of Agriculture and Fisheries and the Department of Agriculture for Scotland. Over 1,200 engineers, civil, mechanical and electrical, were employed by the Defence Departments, the Office of Works, the Post Office, the Ministry of Transport and the Mercantile Marine Department of the Board of Trade. The Department of Scientific and Industrial Research employed over 350 chemists, scientific and industrial research workers; the Department of the Government Chemist another 79, and over 300 were employed in the research departments of the Defence Departments.

It was obvious even before 1939 that both politicians and civil servants would be drawn from a more violent and less stable world. For the politician the technique of the manipulation of opinion was becoming every day more important. The mass stamping of the gutter Press had replaced the oratorical duel and had itself been superseded by the hypnosis of the stage-managed plebiscite. The maintenance of political power required abilities and means in startling conflict with the abilities and means required to solve the real problems of the State. One is reminded how the deification of the emperor and the spread of Eastern mythology coincided with the development of the bureaucracy and the subtleties of Roman law in the later Roman Empire.

What were the prospects for co-operation between the expert and the politician ? Both the civil servant and the politician had a problem of weighing evidence every day more complex than the day before. But this should not be exaggerated. With the advance of scientific know-ledge the nature of the evidence they would have to consider would be greater in bulk but more manageable in form. Quantitatively there might be an increase, but qualitatively there might be greater simplicity. In the formative days of our political and administrative traditions the worlds of the professions and the sciences were even more chaotic than those of Government itself. The only order anywhere to be found was in the routine of custom, the inexplicable order of trade and commerce, and the general unseen order providence was supposed to maintain. Now many of our problems, though yet unsolved, are in matters of a measurable and demonstrable kind. To deal with them need not rouse the black passions of a threatened creed. The nature of the trade cycle may occasion heated argument and lead some to take up intellectual arms against their spiritual fathers, but it has not the dividing power of a disputed theory of eternal salvation. Even an economist may call his economic brother a fool without feeling in danger of hell fire. But agreement to discuss and the toleration of differences in theory does not remove the fact that the material consequences of the application of the wrong theory may be more serious than before. Economic experts at the Treaty of Versailles did not feel in danger of hell fire, but their errors played the devil with our affairs. If the penalty for spiritual error was once supposed to be physically painful, intellectual error threatened material devastation. The real problem of government is that such disasters are felt by those who suffer to be due to men like themselves who can be held accountable. It was not a question of offering propitiatory sacrifices to unknown gods, but of deposing and even punishing household gods of insufficient skill. The time and the technique required by those who could really help might not correspond with the pace and action of those who could get them power to act. There was a widening gap between the arts of persuasion and the technique of research, between the power of leaders and their vision. In Plato's language, reason, courage and the instincts were never more widely divorced. The danger was that unless those who were able to deal with problems could secure the co-operation required, others might rule who would secure co-operation by fear.

CHAPTER XI

REGROUPING AND ADVANCE

IN the previous chapters we have outlined the development of a political system in conditions which will not occur again. The power of Britain which, in the nineteenth century, rose more swiftly and was sought less deliberately than that of any previous world power has in this century waned with almost equal speed. The causes of her temporary supremacy are in retrospect clear enough. There was the early political unity made possible by the sea which served her :—

> " . . . in the office of a wall,
>   or as a moat defensive to a house."

There was the latent resource of iron and coal lying in convenient and fruitful juxtaposition. There was, after the discovery of the New World, her central position at the cross roads of the commerce of the world. She had, too, her reasonable share of the general European intelligence. These in their varying proportions will be a theme for schoolboys so long as English is understood and there remains any interest in the mutability of human affairs.

In this century we have lost the natural advantages which formerly assisted our natural growth. We lack the raw materials for many of the newer industries—oil, pulp, and bauxite ; we lack the advantage of cheap fuels—natural gas as well as cheap coal ; and we have no access to great resources of cheap hydro-electric power.[1] Politically, too, in the 19th century the economic nationalism of which the German Empire was pioneer " negatived the British conception of the world as potentially a great commercial republic advancing towards a maximum world division of labour."[2] The same policy was followed by the United States and has been taken up by the new secular religion of Soviet Communism. It is not therefore surprising that from being the first of the few we should have become the first of the relatively weak. This change in our relative status will involve profound psychological and political adjustments in the life of our people. We have like Gulliver passed from the problems of the Man Mountain in Lilliput to the trials of a *splacknuck* in a world of Brobdingnagian giants.

It is now obvious that western civilization is threatened in the most deadly way. It is not merely threatened by the particular threat of militant Soviet Communism but by the deeper trouble that the inter-dependence of men and the conflict of group loyalties, which are the outcome of human control of the invisible texture of matter, are creating administrative problems which we may be unable to solve. We can see into the heart of matter but we are as far as ever from knowing our own hearts or what they shall some day suffer.

In this grim perspective of accelerating and terrifying change the adaptability so far of the English political system has some interest for the world. It has been said by an American student that a good book on Government should give the low down on the high spots. This is a pleasant phrase from the innovating West. It has the most diverse associations—it could refer to the dirt on the heels of the *roi soleil* as he paraded the noisome corridors of eighteenth century Versailles or to the reflection of Orion seen by Thomas Hardy in a pool of rain. But for the student of political change a low down on the high spots will mean a search for the deeper causes of the passing show. So long as the British people retain their political freedom the development of their political institutions can be more thoroughly documented than any others in the world. And this for two obvious reasons : (1) the general character of western civilization in the last two hundred years in which the methods of the natural sciences were applied as far as it was possible to the activities of men—the analytical skill of economists, the mathematical skill of statisticians, and a freedom in discussion to follow the argument wherever it led, have made it possible for western man to know more about the nature of his government than any people has known before ; (2) in this country the smallness of the area and the continuity of political change have made the record more intelligible than in any other part of western society. If any of the totalitarian systems were to succeed in their drive for world power their origins would rapidly become as clouded with legend as the early history of the Roman Empire or the Christian Church. Real freedom of debate does not only secure that the gates of the future remain open but also that the experience of the past is never really lost.

The relation between the state and individuals, between the govern-ment and the people, has always been under the critical eye of a diversity of talents. In England the politician, the administrator and the phil-osopher have perhaps worked more closely together than elsewhere. But we too have had our critics of the bases of our common life, and today

Herbert Read continues the work of Godwin, T. S. Eliot that of Matthew Arnold. But the Englishman has never forgotten that politics is a craft before it is an art—that its ideas must be workable and not merely beautiful. He has looked to his poets to restate the case for tradition whenever its viability has been in doubt. The problems of the craft have been to understand the full implications of the economic order by which we get our daily bread and all the necessary conditions of a civilized life. This is intrinsically difficult and it has recently become a problem to be solved on pain of death for any civilization we have known. It is here that we touch the darkness at the heart of our current problems. From Plato to Marx it could be said that the idea of a natural order had taken some of the tension out of politics

> " For government, though high, and low and lower,
> Put into parts, doth keep in one concent,
> Congreeing in a full and natural close,
>   Like music."

But with the passing of religion as an effective determinant of the social and political action of western man the terrible demand for human justice has been raised. We are now our brothers' keepers. A sense of guilt has replaced the dogma of the fall and our new scientific kings may feel they have a duty to kill all free men because, they argue, the latter know not what they do, postponing an inevitable millennium.

" The slow issue of general ideas into practical consequences," wrote Whitehead, " is not wholly due to inefficiency of human character. . . . It may be impossible to conceive a reorganization of society adequate for the removal of some admitted evil without destroying the social organization and the civilization which depends on it."[3] The Government's *Economic Survey of* 1947 was described by a writer in the *Times Literary Supplement* as " the first attempt that a British government, or perhaps any government, has made to exhibit the nation's economic needs and resources as a whole, and as a material which must be moulded into a coherent plan." He continued "We have become the subject of a great and crucial experiment in national psychology. Can Britain organize for peace as efficiently as she did for war, and remain a free country."[4] On this crucial issue, of the relation between freedom and the powers which the growing mastery of matter compels all governments to take, the future of our political system will turn. It had a comparatively simple beginning in the stream-lining of our rather gothic administrative forms under the exigencies of 20th century wars.

The " infinite flexibility " of the Committee of Imperial Defence enabled a democracy roused by the blast of war to give a very good imitation of the " action of the tiger." It had been formed after the Esher Committee had shewn that we had entered the South African War without " adequate means " of obtaining a " reasoned opinion on which to base a war policy." It was so planned that it had every freedom to enquire and every power to persuade. In it the free association of amateur and expert which is the heart of the British Cabinet system in domestic affairs, was given an efficient and protean form needed to preserve our civilized order in a violent and nasty world. The Prime Minister who was always its chairman could attach any necessary persons to the permanent nucleus of some half a dozen ministers and heads of the fighting services. Experts on naval warfare and experts on military affairs were associated in the formulation of a defence policy with the political and expert members of the economic and political departments which would be most closely involved, the Foreign Office, the Treasury, the India Office and the Colonial Office. A secretariat was as necessary to such a varying and complex body as his " continuity " staff is to a film director. It was needed to keep a record of all the problems discussed and the decisions made, to assemble facts about every aspect of defence and to prepare such memoranda or other documents as the Cabinet might require. It has been possible to trace from its well kept records the origins and development of every problem that came within the scope of the Committee of Imperial Defence. By one of those fortunate subtleties which are so clearly visible in retrospect and so often missed in prospect the fact that the Committee had no power to command but only a duty to recommend was to prove the basis of the widest authority. Because it could do no more than advise it was allowed to extend the range and depth of its investigations until it could proffer advice more cogent than any command. It has operated mainly through a network of committees, of which there were between July, 1909, and August, 1914, some thirty, in which specific problems had been studied by over 130 people excluding the experts who might have been summoned to give evidence before them. These committees had been serviced by the Secretariat.[5]

This mechanism of investigation, persuasion and preparation which made the blue prints of defence for 1914 was absorbed into the War Cabinet system of the first world war. In 1914 the War Council, and in 1915 the Dardanelles and War Committee were attempts to re-enforce the system of peacetime Cabinet government with the mechanisms of the Committee of Imperial Defence. The secretariat and all its techniques of procedure and ordered record were taken over. When in December, 1916, Lloyd George created a War Cabinet of four to six members with the supreme power of decision it too used the techniques of the Committee of Imperial Defence. The official historians of World War II see a continuity in the essentials of the War Cabinet of Lloyd George in 1916, and those of Chamberlain in 1939 and Churchill in 1940.[6] In all three the power to know, to plan and to decide were fused. The knowledge and power of the centre were sustained by a systematic delegation of the power to enquire and to do. The more subtle the mind and the clearer the will of Leviathan in war the more numerous and varied grew its limbs. While final decisions were made in the War Cabinet, operational functions were delegated to departments, and the necessary integrating of related functions was obtained through a system of Cabinet committees. It was shown that the apoplexy at the centre and the anaemia at the extremities which normally afflict Leviathan could be checked by a committee diet. The Secretariat was vital to the system. The problem of liaison between the War Cabinet, its committees and the executive departments was extensive and intricate. The record of all decisions had to be exact. Those responsible for action must be told what it had been decided they must do and a check had to be kept that each " bloody instruction " had been carried out. In doing these things the Secretariat though it had no executive powers became " a specialist in sign posting and clearing the traffic of government business."[7]

In November, 1919, the Committee of Imperial Defence resumed its separate peacetime personality. A new peacetime Cabinet rose phoenix-like from the dying flames of war. The Cabinet had now its own secretariat which continued parallel with the Secretariat of the Committee of Imperial Defence and both of them were under the same head.

" Reason in itself confounded
saw division grow together."

As we have seen in Chapter X the too simple ordering of governmental machinery suggested by the Haldane report of 1918, made when there seemed to be a promise of endless Fabian ages, did not survive the growth of the scope of government between the wars. But after 1918 the essence of our Cabinet system, the two-hourly symposium of political brothers in power on not more than two days a week, was preserved by using a network of committees, of which there were about twenty in any one year.[8] Most of them were for a particular and limited subject and were wound up after they had made their report or otherwise done what they had been set up to do, but there were others which were standing committees destined in time to become vital parts of the permanent though hidden mechanisms of our working constitution.

In the same period the Committee of Imperial Defence adapted itself to a dangerous and unstable world. It grew in size until there were some twenty permanent ministers and experts and in 1938 some 900 people, manning its fifty and more committees.[9] Its work included strategy and planning, organization for war, man-power, supply, experiment and research. It was strengthened in 1923 by the setting up of a Chiefs of Staff Committee to be a " super-chief of a war staff in commission." A Ministry of Defence and a Minister to act as the deputy of the Prime Minister as chairman of the Committee of Imperial Defence, which the Salisbury Committee had recommended, were not provided. And there was to be no deputy to the Prime Minister until 1936, when a shadowy and short-lived Minister of Co-ordination of Defence was appointed. But there was an extremely powerful and flexible organization able to advise and warn the government of the day. From 1923 to 1939 the Chiefs of Staff Committee surveyed a darkening scene. No real defence plans could be made so long as a Cabinet rule—adopted in August, 1919, and re-affirmed in 1928—that no great war was to be expected for a period of ten years was in force. In 1932 moved by the Japanese aggression in Manchuria and Shanghai the Chiefs of Staff roundly denounced this rule and it was rescinded by the Cabinet. The Chiefs of Staff were the most important part of a Defence Requirements Committee which was appointed by the Cabinet to " prepare a programme for meeting our worst deficiencies." In July, 1935, an even stronger body, the Defence Policy and Requirements Committee, was set up to " keep the defensive situation as a whole constantly in review so as to ensure that our defensive arrangements and our foreign policy were in line." In January, 1933, Hitler came to power and from 1934 on the Chiefs of Staff were no longer hampered by having to consider one hypothetical enemy at sea, another on land and a third in the air, because Germany and Japan were known for the actual threat they were. Before 1935 the Committee of Imperial Defence had almost leisurely considered the shape of possible wars ; after 1935 it was rapidly immersed in the precise details of a certain threat.[10] June 1935 saw a new Air Defence Research Committee at work, of which the government's most drastic critic Mr. Churchill was a secret member.[11] The pressure of informed opinion was percolating to the centres of power. One of the ablest officials of the Foreign Office, Ralph Wigram, had communicated to Mr. Churchill his sense that war could no longer be prevented.[12] In 1936 it was known that the German war budget must be at least £1,000 million a year.[13]

The Committee of Imperial Defence prepared a War Book for 1939 as they had prepared one for 1914. It was sound and precise as far as it could go. There was even advice on the form of central control which would be needed and the machinery of a War Cabinet was designed. The legislation which the government would need was drafted in every detail which could be foreseen. As far back as 1924 a study had been started of the emergency powers which might be required. A draft Defence Bill and a draft code of Defence legislation were approved by July 1937, and subjects which would need special legislation had been reviewed.[14]

The Committee of Imperial Defence had not limited itself to adapting the experience of 1914-18 to what could be foreseen in 1930 of the opening moves of war. In 1914-1918, and even more in the disorders which had followed, many civil servants and a few politicians had seen deep into the real roots of strength in war and prosperity in peace. But in 1914 the British Government had no conception of the nature and scope of modern war. It had inherited a sound financial practice from the worlds of Pitt and Gladstone.[15] It had, too, a deep and firm tradition of administrative competence not merely in what must be done but also in the technical skills with which to do it. But this was not enough. An administrative machine must not be over-strained. Financial purity is not the whole of economic power. The engine of income tax, however finely tuned, could not drive the juggernaut of war. It was clear that the scarcities which in modern war are the result of the flow of men and matter to the front of battle would, if they were not controlled, cause a collapse of social order. In 1914 there was no clear idea of a war economy as a structure within which military and civilian requirements must be kept in proper balance. As with most economic truths the elements were clear and even platitudinous. If every male went to the front there would be none to feed and clothe them while they fought. This is obvious enough and yet Russia mobilized so many men that she could not till her fields to feed them, and the Germans so stripped their farms for war that they could not feed themselves when the war was over. Nearly every schoolboy can be brought to see that an increasing supply of money and a diminishing supply of goods will lead to a decline in the value of the former. It was the subtle and far reaching implications of these simple truths which could not then be seen. And it was only very slowly that a technique for handling them could be empirically devised. The political economy of war came into existence as a fact between 1914 and 1918 before it was analytically understood. The hundreds of improvisations needed to meet a shortage of food, of sandbags or of shells, and the underlying scarcities of men and ships were found to fall into a pattern which expressed the subtlest logic of the economic art.[16] Even economics was not enough. The control of scarcities, the adjustment of the proportions among things in peace to their proportions in war, the finding of a fit and proper balance between guns and butter would tax the spirit of a people. We had to estimate the national income, the total sum of home produced and imported resources from which we could draw our power to make war, and we had also to find out how much of this total could be used in war. Such sums could not be done without calling spirits from the deepest levels of the nation's life. To use man-power in the best way is not merely a technical problem in the economy of war ; it is also a problem of national consent. In nearly every man a very human desire for 'business as usual' strove with a patriot's wish to do his bit. The real problem was to decide what bits should be done and by which men and by which women. We had to persuade the men in uniform and the men who might wish to put it on, that they also served who only dug or spun. Not until 1917 was it found how a balance could be struck between industrial and military power in accordance with the major policies adopted by the Cabinet. In 1917 the Ministry of National Service had got a reasonable schedule of protected occupations.[17] The weapons of war would not be jammed from lack of stuff to grease them. A balance had been struck between the fighting man and those who armed and fed him. The butcher, the baker, the miner and the builder, were rare enough to allow comparison with the British grenadier. It could be said :—

" young boys and girls are level now with men."

It was, however, never really settled how the jobs othen than fighting should themselves be shared. It was agreed that labour must not be wasted in strikes and lock-outs ; that it must not be permitted to shift at will from job to job ; and that skilled labour must be diluted. The freedom of the market for labour was limited ; but it was not abolished. The hierarchy and the discipline of battle were not applied to the infinite variety of the process of production. Labour was told that it could not shift about at will. No government dared tell it that it would be moved about in accordance with the nation's need.[18]

The problems of man-power go to the very roots of democratic life and can be seen to do so. The need to understand and control the inflation threatened by a war-created scarcity of goods and services and a war-created abundance of money was not so obvious but every bit as vital. Failure in this spreads corruption through the state. The comparatively mild inflation between 1914 and 1918 " created conditions under which profiteering became an involuntary and inevitable state of grace, or disgrace." Honours could not there be easy. " It branded upon a decent, patriotic people new and raw marks of inequality, vulgarity and callousness."[19]   The luck of the game with death at the front was accepted and understood by the players but the favours of inflation undermined or flouted the very sense of justice which the war was being fought to defend.   The poison of inflation was to do almost as much harm in the years after the war to the life of Europe as the loss of her many million dead.

The experience of post-war inflation caused a more critical study of the process of economic change.   It became every day more obvious that the specialization implicit in the division of labour required by modern technologies would be dangerous to civilized life unless economic analysis and administrative techniques were able to deal with the human problems it creates.   The causes of the great depression were sought as urgently as the causes of the war itself.   And we do not know how far Hitler was the penalty we suffered for a failure of economic skill.   In 1929 a memorandum on *The Course of Prices in a Great War* prepared for the man-power sub-committee of the Committee of Imperial Defence started investigations into the chief focal points of economic planning.   It surveyed the measures that government might take to reduce the pressure of increasing purchasing power upon a decreasing supply of goods which war involves.   It contained both a modern doctrine of war finance and far-reaching proposals for economic control—drastic taxation, a borrowing policy purged as far as possible from all inflationary expedients, control of prices, control of profits, control of wages, control of imports and consumer rationing.   It was pervaded by a conviction that excessive inflation of the money unit would open the way to great calamities.   Bomb or bullet might kill or mutilate their thousands but the withering of a currency would corrupt and waste the body politic itself.   The document assumed that in a war the price mechanism of a free market would not be able to allocate resources, determine the order in which necessities were made, or distribute the final product among buyers.   The Committee of Imperial Defence was therefore invited to begin far-reaching studies of economic policy.   But although a food-rationing scheme was carefully prepared and a beginning made with man-power policy, the major problems of a defence economy were only fully investigated after the war had revealed the full scope of its menace.[20]

The Committee of Imperial Defence had considered before 1939 the form of government appropriate for a small, medium or a great war. There was never any doubt that the model which had been approved for a great war would be needed in a Hitler war. On 1st September, 1939, Mr. Chamberlain told the Cabinet that he would set up a War Cabinet on the 1916 model and he did so on the first day of the war. The Cabinet resigned, the Committee of Imperial Defence died, its spirit entering the new body of the War Cabinet which at once held its first meeting.[21]

We do not yet know whether in the atomic age the life of civilized man will be long enough to write the history of the war which now began. Some thirty volumes are promised on the British civilian effort alone. They will tell the means by which a deadly peril was escaped and a supreme administrative task achieved. About two things there can be little doubt : that the Battle of Britain was one of the decisive battles of the world ; and that the British administrative skills kept the war going until the United States could deploy her strength in aid of Russia and the West. Had the Battle of Britain been lost not even his extreme incompetence could have lost Hitler the mastery of the world. In not so many years the German fleets would have altered the skyline of New York and German panzas would have debouched from the valleys which had been the romantic routes of covered wagons. Two other things are obvious enough : the simplicity of British unity which appeared when she stood alone, a simplicity which is not at all surprising, for as Santayana has rightly said " courage is the commonest of the virtues " and here were conditions particularly favourable for the exercise of common virtues ; secondly the extreme subtlety of the administrative machine which took the strain. What happened was so very simple that we must be careful not to take it as any evidence of what can be done in the complexities of peace. The speed of a man who is paced by an angry bear is no proof of his ability to catch a bus. For a time the distinction between government and people on which the life of a democracy normally depends vanished and a real totalitarian state appeared. It was comparatively simple with modern technological resources for a beleaguered island to achieve the unity of a beleaguered fortress. But it could not have been maintained if certain political and administrative skills had not been at hand when the need arose. The spirit of a people can be aroused at any time by a threat to what it may hold most dear and in 1940 all our past did come into our minds with most excellent effect upon our nerves. But the spirit would have been useless save to prolong a slaughter had there not been a tradition of real self government which could be used. The topmost towers of Ilium were not burnt because most of the Trojan horses were safe in her own stables. The backroom boys were on top and on their toes. It was not a case of not knowing we were beaten, for we now know that the instinctive do or die of 1940 was grounded in sound conditions of strategy. The Chiefs of Staff Committee knew that the German army could not cross the North Sea so long as the air defences on which the Committee of Imperial Defence had so long been concentrating were unbeaten. There was an element of luck as in all human affairs, but the luck could hold because we had a good hand, and that we did so was not a matter of luck at all.

The War Book of the C.I.D. could not provide for the conduct of the whole war. It could and did prevent a checkmate in the opening moves. A War Cabinet was formed. Mr. Chamberlain was unable as he had hoped to persuade either the Labour Party or the Liberals to share in a national coalition. His need to include Mr. Churchill as First Lord of the Admiralty involved the inclusion of the two other service ministers and the Minister for Co-ordination of Defence, so that he had a Cabinet of nine, of whom five had heavy departmental duties. The Dominion Secretary, the Home Secretary and the Minister of Home Security had in practice to be present at most meetings, and with the Permanent Secretary of the Treasury and one or other of the Chiefs of Staff there were fifteen in all. They met once or even twice every day in the autumn of 1939, but in the winter of 1939-40 Sunday meetings were discontinued and Saturday meetings were held only for very urgent business and were manned on a rota system. Some 60 War Cabinet committees were set up of which about two-thirds were inter-departmental non-ministerial bodies.[22]

The civilian machinery was not so well organized at first as that of the services. The service ministers were all members of the war Cabinet. The military committees had a firm basis of experience. The Chiefs of Staff Committee and its sub-committees were already in existence. The majority of the civil departments was represented in the War Cabinet. The War Cabinet had to set up committees with substantial authority to focus on the facts of war : a Civil Defence Committee, a Home Committee, and a ministerial priorities committee. A sub-committee of the latter, the Food Policy Committee soon became an independent committee of the War Cabinet.[23]

Underlying every pattern of committees was the basic problem of the economy—of the stomach, the nerves, and the sinews of the war. In October, 1939, the Prime Minister and the Chancellor of the Exchequer appointed an interdepartmental committee in order to keep under review and to co-ordinate the functioning of the departments in relation to the economic effort of the country as a whole and to make any

necessary arrangements for Anglo-French co-operation. There was at
first only a committee of officials presided over by Sir Josiah Stamp but
two days later a Ministerial Committee on economic policy was installed
over the official committee. This was the first example of the double
decker, the ministerial-official, committee system which was to be so
widespread.[24]

It was not easy to draw clear lines of jurisdiction between these
nascent committees. The Home Policy committee did not become the
effective power over all domestic affairs. But the Economic Policy
Committee was compelled by the inner logic of the scarcities of war to
take great powers. At first it developed the pre-war method of economic
co-ordination in which the Treasury was the queen. The Chancellor
of the Exchequer was in the War Cabinet. The Permanent Secretary
of the Treasury was chairman of the official economic policy and food
policy sub-committees. In this first phase of the war our efforts were
still assessed more in financial than in physical terms. A symptom
of this was that the vital factor of shipping escaped all the committees
and found a temporary harbour with the Lord Privy Seal.[25] Before
May, 1940, too, the survey of man-power had hardly begun.[26]

While the two patterns of military and civilian committees were
shaping like the roots of a growing plant it was felt that a ministerial
committee was needed to save the time of the War Cabinet by making a
first study of the complicated reports of the Chiefs of Staff and being a
clearing house for strategical ideas. So in October, 1939, a ministerial
committee on military co-ordination with the homely title of the
M.C.C. was set up and served by the Minister for Co-ordination of
Defence, the service ministers and the Chiefs of Staff. It did not oust
the War Cabinet, which was the real co-ordinator of policies for war, and
when in April, 1941, the Minister for Co-ordination of Defence tactfully withdrew and Mr. Churchill the First Lord of the Admiralty
was chairman in his place, even he asked the Prime Minister to take the
chair when really important matters had to be discussed.[27]

The weakness of this early set up has been briefly summarized by
Mr. Churchill. The War Cabinet was, he said, " an earnest and work-
manlike body " but it was hampered by the fact that the Ministers
seldom sat together alone without secretaries or military experts.
In September, 1939, he asked the Prime Minister whether it would not
be possible to have informal meetings of Ministers who could discuss
among themselves the large issues of policy. The Chiefs of Staff were
then working as a separate and largely independent body without clear
direction from the Prime Minister. The leaders of the three services had
not yet got a conception of the war as a whole.[28]

In April, 1940, the war was vastly simplified. There was no longer world enough and time for our vegetable power to grow vaster than empire and more slow. The sprawling pattern of committees had to be shaped into a single organ fit to take and give the full shock of war. The essentials were three : the powers of a Prime Minister used by a leader of genius ; the Chiefs of Staff Committee as his finely tempered tool ; a network of committees assimilating every skill of thought or action which might serve the cause. On the 10th May, it being clear that Mr. Chamberlain no longer had the confidence of the House of Commons and Lord Halifax admitting that a Peer could not discharge the duties of Prime Minister in war because he would have no power to guide the assembly upon whose confidence the life of every government depends, Mr. Churchill was asked by the King to form a national coalition.[29] Freed by eleven years in the political wilderness from ordinary party ties he could summon whom he pleased. " Once the main arrangements had been settled with the leaders of the other parties, the attitude of those he sent for " was, he tells us, " like soldiers in action, who go to the places assigned to them without question."[30] There were even now certain limitations. Mr. Chamberlain could not be leader of the House of Commons because the Labour Party made it clear that they would not have liked him; Mr. Bevin had to consult the Transport and General Workers Union of which he was the Secretary before he could take the post of Minister of Labour ; the Liberals who thought that their leader Sinclair should be Secretary of State for Air and in the War Cabinet (which was impossible without abandoning the principle of a small Cabinet) had to be placated by a promise that he would be present whenever any matter affecting fundamental issues or party functions were involved ; a churchillian affection for Lord Beaverbrook made him Minister of Aircraft Production; Halifax, Simon and Hoare were accepted in spite of their pre-war record because if Churchill was prepared to forget the past, no member of the Labour Party was in a position to refuse.[31] But all these points were political *trivia*, of interest only to the constitutional historian, who may find a pleasure in seeing thin wisps of party practice clinging to a constitution stripped for war. The vital change was that the Prime Minister assumed the general direction of the war subject to the War Cabinet and the House of Commons ; that he would do so by supervising and directing the Chiefs of Staff Committee as Minister of Defence, a title which the King approved and which involved no legal or constitutional change. As Prime Minister he could do whatever he desired as Minister of Defence, and in the Chiefs of Staff Committee and the service committees of the C.I.D. he had in fact the equivalent of a finely articulated Ministry of Defence. The Chiefs of Staff Committee now took its due and proper place in daily contact with the executive head of the government and in accord with him had full control over the conduct of the war and the armed forces. In total war it is quite impossible to draw a precise line between the forces in contact with the enemy and the forces which keep them there, between the sinews and the fist, the factories and the front, and the union in the same person of the civilian and military powers of a Prime Minister and a Minister of Defence was a fine example of the subtle working of the British Constitution. There were no changes in machinery and no officials were dismissed. For a time the War Cabinet and the Chiefs of Staff still met every day. But in spirit everything was changed. There was now an organization subtle, swift and full of power. Mr. Churchill had always felt that a Cabinet of five men with nothing to do but run a war would not give the necessary drive. Such an Olympian five would not be able to cope with the heads of the departments service or civilian which were vitally involved in what had to be done. No body not itself directly responsible for day to day events could bluntly challenge responsible ministers who were responsible and armed with all the relevant facts and figures. Churchill's own experience had set him against having unharnessed ministers around him. When he was First Lord of the Admiralty under Chamberlain he had had a definite job which he had vastly preferred to the " exalted brooding over the work done by others " which he said falls to a Minister however influential who has no department.[32] A naked athlete can never move in comfort among armed men.

The Churchill War Cabinet had at first only five members of whom only one, the Foreign Secretary, had a department. But the Chancellor of the Exchequer and the leader of the Liberal Party had often to be present. The number of constant attenders steadily grew but the five were the only ones who had " the right to have their heads cut off on Tower Hill if we did not win." They alone were responsible for the policy pursued. Mr. Churchill set up a Defence Committee (Operations) and a Defence Committee (Supply) and both of them were bodies of infinite flexibility. The new machinery enabled him to give an integral direction to almost every aspect of the war. The decisions coming from the top were strictly, faithfully and punctually obeyed. At the top itself he found as the accepted leader that there were " great simplifications." He had only to be sure of what it was best to do, or at least to have made up his mind about it. " The method was accepted because everybody realized how near were death and ruin."[33]

As Prime Minister and Minister of Defence Mr. Churchill sent out a daily flow of minutes and directives to the departments and Chiefs of Staff Committee. These were taken by General Ismay (deputy secretary to the War Cabinet) who was his representative on the Chiefs of Staff Committee. By the afternoon of the same day a whole series of such orders had been agreed. If there was any difference of view on larger questions a meeting of the War Cabinet Defence Committee was called which comprised at the outset Chamberlain, Attlee and the three service ministers with the Chiefs of Staff in attendance. The daily meetings of the War Cabinet and the Chiefs of Staff were soon discontinued. But every Monday there was a Cabinet " parade " at which the War Cabinet, the Service Ministers and others most directly concerned had the war explained by the Chiefs of Staff and the current foreign affairs by the Secretary of State for Foreign Affairs. On the other days of the week the War Cabinet sat alone.[34]

This system of the control of operations by the three Chiefs of Staff under a Minister of Defence, who had too the full powers latent and actual of the office of Prime Minister, gave a standard of team work, mutual understanding and ready compromise which had never been seen before. There were of course political faults and strata below the granite harmony of a Cabinet in arms. When Mr. Chamberlain had to resign his leadership of the Conservative Party because he was a dying man, Churchill accepted the leadership as his successor. The Conservatives had a very large majority over all other parties. Churchill considered that his position would have been impossible had he had to secure the agreement not only of the leaders of the two minority parties but of the Conservatives as well.[35] The real political power would have been with the leader of the majority party while the executive responsibility would have been with Churchill. Ultimate responsibility can only be borne where the final authority also rests. As the leader of the majority party Mr. Churchill knew that he could in the last resort carry parliament against the minorities with which he had to deal.

For the service side of war there was from the beginning the effective machinery of the Chiefs of Staff and their sub-committees. It was necessary, too, that a machine of equal power should be found for the problems of scarcity, the political economies, which war involves. Strategy and scarcity, the warp and woof of war, had to be interwoven. In 1939 there was no machinery with the power to collect the economic information required. In November, 1939, a central Economic Service was begun by appointing one or two economic experts to assist Lord Stamp. From this modest beginning there grew the Economic Section of the War Cabinet and the Central Statistical Office.[36] After May, 1940, the Government came to think more in terms of how best to use the scarce goods and man-power which they had, in essence an economic problem, and less in terms of the financial shadows which they cast. The Chancellor of the Exchequer was neither the Chairman of the Economic Policy Committee nor had he a seat in Churchill's War Cabinet. Arthur Greenwood, the Minister without Portfolio, was chairman of the Economic Policy Committee and of a Production Council. Mr. Attlee, the Lord Privy Seal, was chairman both of the Home Policy Committee and the Food Policy Committee. The Minister of Labour and National Service, Mr. Bevin, was in the War Cabinet. The Lord President of the Council became more and more the head of an office pre-eminent in the control of the nation's economic energies. The simplicity in principle and the efficiency in detail of the war machine was made by the naked simplicity of the stakes of war. When the direct threat of death and ruin passed away it was felt that some idea of how to live the life which had been saved would help the fight itself. There developed as the historians of the British War Economy have said " an implied contract between government and people ; the people refused none of the sacrifices that the government demanded from them for the winning of the war; in return they expected that the government should show imagination and seriousness in preparing for the restoration and improvement of the nation's well-being when the war had been won."[37] The preparation for peace in war is almost as difficult as the preparation for war in peace. Those who wish to take thought for to-morrow may be told that it would be a waste of time when to-morrow must still be won by victory in the field. It is a measure of the sober realism of a democracy in arms that the problems of peace were never ignored. Even in 1940 a War Aims Committee of the Cabinet sought a declaration of war aims which might be an aid to victory—sought but did not find one ; at least in that summer nothing precise enough to publish could be drafted. But by the end of 1940 a Minister without Portfolio was appointed to " plan in advance," as the Prime Minister said, "a number of practical steps which it is indispensable to take if our society is to move forward." While it was necessary to win there was a further duty not to die from shock. The new Minister's functions were at first merely to co-ordinate and his staff was small. But in 1941 and 1942 his work was assisted by War Cabinet Committees both at ministerial and official level examining the main problems of post-war planning. In November, 1943, Lord Woolton was appointed Minister of Reconstruction and his small staff found that departments were now able to give some help.[38]

Some of the problems were urgent and obvious enough. Unless the transition from war to peace was carefully made, fatal damage might be done to the quality of life we had dared to defend. The mistakes of the previous war had been serious. They were reviewed in a careful report by an official committee in 1942. The demobilization of 1918 had been a failure. It had taught us that whatever might be the economic case for demobilization by economic categories civilian armies would resist it to the verge of mutiny. As early as 1941 the government had adopted a scheme which was based on age and length of service. It was necessary to provide for an orderly disposal of surplus stocks which would exclude profiteering and serve the interests of consumers without disturbing current production. Inflation must be restrained and productive resources transferred to the most necessary tasks. These and many others were the urgent practical measures for securing an orderly unravelling of the tight-knit garment of the war; beyond this lay the wider questions of the way of life it would be possible to choose. In 1941 the Economic Section of the War Cabinet offices had produced a paper on the maintenance of full employment after the war; in 1943 full employment and related subjects were intensively studied by a small committee of officials, and in 1944 a statement of government policy was made on Employment Policy.[39] Some knowledge of the real cost of the war to this country had by this time been widely diffused among critical minds and there was in 1944 a warning from the Treasury that the time and energy and thought we were giving to the Brave New World was widely disproportionate to what was being given to the Cruel Real World.[40] Unless the heavy deficit in the balance of payments could be wiped out " the whole fabric of reconstruction " was " in danger " and we ran the " risk of a failure to maintain essential imports and of a major inflation."[41]

During the war freedom and organization had been two aspects of a single scheme. What was freely offered had been freely taken. As the partnership in every science, in administrative techniques, and in political wisdom with the U.S.A. drew to its close we tried to convey to the Americans in 1944 what real strains had been endured. For more than five years nearly every man, and woman under 50 without young children, had been subject to direction of work, often far from home. The hours of work had averaged 53 for men and 50 overall. In addition every citizen without special excuse for exemption had done 48 hours a month duty in the Home Guard or Civil Defence. The queue had become a part of normal life. The severest taxation in the world had been coupled with a continuous pressure to save.[42] It was only too true. Things had been done by the British state which before the war were believed to be impossible. The compulsory mobilization of women would have astonished Sparta herself. The compulsory insurance scheme for all property had been rejected by the experts until a personal experience of the Prime Minister of the sufferings of little men had got it done.[43] The rationing scheme had been a supreme example of what might be done when the skill of experts has the backing of a united people. But all that had been endured was now a part of history. People had perhaps never in fact been happier or healthier in their lives. But adventure recollected in tranquillity is a joy for individuals and not for communities. The world was not bound to give us back what we had freely offered up. Any bread we had cast upon the waters would not return as cheap food.

In fact the British military effort since 1940 had been out of all proportion to her economic strength. It had, Lord Keynes wrote in the U.S.A., involved a " financial imprudence without parallel in history." But that financial imprudence was perhaps " a facet of that single-minded devotion without which the war would have been lost."[44] We had in fact already jeopardized our economic survival as a nation. On the strength of lend-lease we had sacrificed the export trade upon which, when peace returned, we would depend for daily work and daily bread. The recovery of the export trade would in the future be a matter of life and death for a nation of 47 millions crowded into an area one third the size of Texas. By August, 1945, it was clear that the prospective deficiency was so great that unless substantial new aid were secured from the U.S.A. to compensate for the ending of lend-lease the nation would be " virtually bankrupt and the economic basis for the hopes of the public non-existent."[45]

And here for a moment, before glancing at the new political structure in which Britain, the one-time centre of the strong and subtle free trade world, must struggle to survive, we must give some hint of the dark problems associated with the name of Keynes.

After Churchill, who was the supreme man of action, Lord Keynes was the most significant figure of the inter-war years. If Churchill had the strategic eye and a sense of the past it was Keynes who sensed most acutely the changing economic climate of the world. It was significant that the most formidable critic of the men of 1918 and after, should have been the greatest innovator in the science of economics on which in the last resort their wealth and ease depended, and that he should have been one of the most subtle interpreters of those climates of opinion on which civilizations depend equally with the technologies which give them power. In the modern world Keynes had written in 1922[46] there were " two opinions " not as in former ages " the true and the false " but " the outside and the inside." There was " the opinion of the public voiced by politicians and newspapers ; and the opinion of the politicians, journalists and civil servants expressed in limited circles." This paragon of Cambridge dons and Bloomsbury coteries sensed in all its subtlety the political problem of a period in which, whatever working order tradition might have established for the world of farm and craft, it would irrevocably be shattered by the thronging complexities the mastery of matter must bring. Because he was an expert on probability as well as an economist he was able to understand the full implications of the penetration of mathematical analysis into every fibre of the material pattern of the world. He had written a famous essay on *The End of Laissez Faire*; he had explored the intricate analytical and statistical problems to be solved if the division of labour which science brings was not to become the basis of a new slavery with a Marxist myth. Speaking to an intimate group of friends he had shown that the naive utilitarianism which had done service in the era of nascent British industrial leadership was in principle not to be distinguished from the communist creed. This awareness of the distinction between popular appearance and technical reality was given subtlety by the distinction which he noted within the popular opinion itself. There were in fact two outside opinions : that which is expressed in the newspapers and that which ordinary men suspect to be true. There was a world of difference between the dogmatism and definiteness of the press and the living indefinite belief of ordinary men. In fact, Keynes held, " inside opinion gradually percolates to wider and wider circles ; they are susceptible to time, to argument, common sense or self-interest." On the relation between these three opinions, expert, propaganda, and common sense awake to the perils of a dissolving age, the quality of government in any state and the survival of western civilization itself must depend. Their interplay is exampled in the government of the British people since the surrender of Japan.

On whatever opinion government may be based in it can only act with the help of the informed opinion of limited circles. It was to improve such opinion that the Haldane report in 1918 asked for investigation and thought as a preliminary to action. This inner opinion is formed in a modern government by a complex interplay between political leaders and their expert advisers. On its quality the life of the government depends. There is a note on its formation in 1836 by Sir Henry Taylor who wrote " what is wanted is that the crude knowledge collected in the execution of the laws should pass upward from grade to grade of the civil functionaries interested in their administration more and more digested and generalized in the progress ; and lastly should reach the legislature in the shape of a material project of law whereby what was superfluous in the legislation might be abrogated ; what was insufficient enlarged ; what was doubtful determined ; what was wanted added." The words suggest the competence, the complacency and the common sense of a simpler world.

The experience of 1939-45 did stream-line the central machinery for investigation, thought and action. The Cabinet system developed an intricate but well-planned committee system, organized in two layers— the ministerial and the official—and served by the Offices of the Cabinet, the mature form of the Secretariat of World War I. The inner history of the Cabinet system since 1945 is for the political historian of the future. It was the supreme political organ and because, whatever our economic health, our political life was most vigorous, the structure and working of the Cabinet was still one of the hidden places of the constitution. Some of its characteristics are clear enough. The creation of eleven new departments for the necessities of war and post-war reconstruction, of which five were temporary (Production, Information, Shipping, Aircraft Production and Home Security) and six survived (Fuel and Power, Supply, Food, National Insurance, Civil Aviation, Town and Country Planning) ended the hope of an apostolic Fabian twelve so fancied in 1918. The membership of the Cabinet was a matter for the Prime Minister as it had been before the war, but the pieces he had to place were more numerous and the forces involved, personal, political and technical, were more intricate. When in 1945 the Labour Party withdrew from the war-time Coalition, Mr. Churchill formed a caretaker government of 16. The new government formed by Mr. Attlee in 1945, after the election had returned the Labour Party to power, had 20 members. The creation of a Ministry of Defence and the passing of the need for a Secretary of State for India or Burma made it possible to reduce the Cabinet to 17 in 1949. There were 15 ministers of Cabinet rank who were not in the Cabinet. They could be members of the Cabinet committees dealing with the matters which concerned them. They could be invited to attend meetings of the Cabinet when they could be useful. The Cabinet was so flexible an instrument and its problems were so variable that it is almost impossible to describe its subtle short term changes. But there were certain long term tendencies which determined what it had to be and to do. There has always been an inner Cabinet in the sense that the Prime Minister has usually some more sympathetic or more powerful colleagues. The character of the Labour Party and the temperament of its leader are sufficient to account for the rather definite inner Cabinet which was perceived after 1945, of Bevin, Morrison, Sir Stafford Cripps and Bevan. More important were the long term forces making for : (1) the increasing importance of the office of Prime Minister : (2) the establishment of a Ministry of Defence : (3) the integration of the economic machinery of the State and (4) the relation of government to scientific research : (5) the working of the system through a pattern of committees.[47]

The power of a Prime Minister will depend on the power of the office which he holds, the nature of his party and his own personality. Even before 1939 it was known that the change from being a Cabinet Minister to being the Prime Minister was not merely a change of place but a change of climate. A Prime Minister, it was said by an expert on the species, has entered the stratosphere and may become telescopically distant from his colleagues while at the same time to the public he is drawn microscopically near, an insect whose every movement is recorded.[48] Since 1939 we have had examples of the extreme variations personality and political conditions may cause. Mr. Churchill describing the dread simplicities of war said that " in any sphere of action there can be no comparison between the position of number one and number two, three, or four. The duties and problems of all persons other than number one are quite different and in many ways more difficult. It is always a misfortune when number two or three has to initiate a dominant plan or policy. He has to consider not only the merits of the policy, but the mind of his chief ; not only what to advise, but what it is proper for him in his station to advise ; not only what to do, but how to get it agreed, and how to get it done."[49] At the other extreme Mr. Attlee faced with the fog of peace in which those behind cry forward and those in front, if they can see at all, cry back, assumed the invisible cloak of modesty. But even he " mantled in light's velocity " had to dive into our hearts with humble and familiar courtesy " winning poor craftsmen with the craft of words." It was an excellent convention of the constitution that the ethereal medium was fairly rationed. The B.B.C. became the Speaker of the Air. The Prime Minister's broadcasts were few and far between but there was there a latent power which might save or lose a world. He could not escape a steady accumulation of power in the office which he held. Not only did he with the king's consent appoint to the ministerial posts, he had also to be consulted on the most important official posts as well. In the great issues of policy he had at the very least to arbitrate between the mighty opposites of departmental drives. He had become responsible for the pattern of committees through which the tough and technical administrative facts of policies in being were at the ministerial and the officials' levels meticulously examined or prepared. We know that in the National Government of 1931, though Macdonald's power was withering from the time he had been severed from his party and though his personal abilities were in swift decline, so long as he held office Baldwin with whom political power really lay could only act through him.[50] We know that Mr. Chamberlain without any understanding of the European world was able to carry out a foreign policy apart from and opposed to his own Secretary of State for Foreign Affairs and the collective wisdom of the Foreign Office itself.[51] We know too that in the last war Mr. Churchill was able to do as Prime Minister whatever he might wish as Minister of Defence so that there was no need for that office to have any formal powers. But he would not have felt his power secure had he not been the leader of a party with a clear majority in the House itself.

Some of the Prime Minister's tasks were simplified a little. The Cabinet Office was virtually a department of the Prime Minister and could tell him what he might wish to know about the position of his country in so far as such knowledge could be found anywhere within the governmental machine. Its secretaries advised him about the committee structure through which the Cabinet did its work. The Ministers of the Crown Act, 1937, by providing that certain Ministers whose salaries were low might have £5,000 a year, if and so long as they were members of the Cabinet, removed a financial dimension from the jigsaw puzzle of personalities and powers which as a cabinet maker the Prime Minister has to solve. The Ministers of the Crown (Transfer of Functions Act), January, 1946, allowed functions to be transferred from one Minister to another by Order in Council subject to a negative resolution but laid it down that a department of state could not be dissolved without the House of Commons giving an affirmative resolution to such an order. This simplified the task of setting the political and administrative field in the game which the Prime Minister must play. There were changes in the Cabinet which merely completed or adapted to peace conditions changes which were made during the war. Many of the new departments simply carried further a machinery of the welfare state which was implicit in the *Wealth of Nations* and which had been built up step by step by a line of forceful administrators from the philosophical radicals of the 1830's to the reports and plans of Beveridge, Scott, and Uthwatt. In a few cases the grouping of the powers of departments according to the particular services which they do for the community had been followed, e.g., Transport, Health, Labour and Supply. And in detail too, a number of powers were transferred from one department to another on this principle, e.g., the factory inspectorate from the Home Office to the Ministry of Labour ; the addition of National Service to the Ministry of Labour ; the surrender by the Board of Trade of Merchant Shipping to the Ministry of Transport. But the Colonial Office and the Scottish Office remained territorial in their basis. Responsibility for Housing remained divided between Health, Works, and others. Responsibility for local government was not clearly integrated either with the economic or with the constitutional forces involved.

The need for a Ministry of Defence was made clear by the war. As we have seen, the direction of the war after May, 1940, was in the hands of the Prime Minister and the Chiefs of Staff. The members of the War Cabinet were collectively and individually responsible for the whole policy of the country and they were the ones who would have been held accountable for any disasters. But each member had responsibility for a particular sphere of superintendence. Mr. Attlee, the leader of the Labour Party, was deputy Prime Minister and Dominion Secretary; the Lord President of the Council presided over what in certain aspects was almost a parallel Cabinet concerned with Home Affairs. Mr. Churchill himself because he was Prime Minister was able to deal easily and smoothly with the three service departments without prejudice to the constitutional responsibilities of the Secretary of State for War, the Secretary of State for Air or the First Lord of the Admiralty. But this brilliant improvisation does not alter the fact that in 1939 we had been dangerously unprepared for war. And while the postponement of rearmament until it was too late, except by war, to stop the German bid for world power, was the result of the economic conditions of the thirties, the political blindness of some and the illiterate delusions of others, there had also been administrative weaknesses which could be remedied. The machinery of the Committee of Imperial Defence had no one who was responsible for formulating a unified defence policy for the three services. The separate aspects of our defence on land, sea and in the air were examined one by one. And when in 1936 an ephemeral and shadowy Minister for Co-ordination of Defence was appointed he was given no power to take executive action. He had no power or responsibility to divide the very limited supplies among the almost unlimited demands. As it would be unwise to expect that other Churchills would appear in every future war the Government gave some thought to getting a unified defence policy in time of peace. It might be desirable to put the three services under a single minister of the Crown at some future date when the shape of coming wars is more hideously known but " it could not and should not " be done in 1946. Common sense and captured German documents confirm that a Combined General Staff means a cleavage between planning and execution which is dangerous. It has been a cardinal principle of the British Joint Staff system that " the men responsible in the service departments for carrying out the approved policy are

brought together in the central machine to formulate it." Experience
has taught that tools for a job must be made with the advice of those
who have to use them. So no drastic change was made in the main
structure of our machinery for making a defence policy. But some
changes were needed to consolidate the advances already made. A
Minister was wanted with both the time and the authority to formulate
and apply a unified defence policy for the three services. The Ministry
of Defence Act, 1946, provided that the Minister for Defence should be
" in charge of the formulation and general application of unified policy
relating to the armed forces of the Crown as a whole and their requirements." He was to make the three things one.

The Prime Minister must of course retain the supreme responsibility
for defence. But the Minister of Defence relieved him of the details
which are concerned with the co-ordination of the three services
and their supply. The organization of national defence in its broader
aspect must be the final responsibility of the Cabinet. There is a Defence
Committee responsible for the review of current strategy and for
the preparation of plans for a transition from peace to war. The Prime
Minister is chairman of this flexible committee with its network of
sub-committees but the Minister of Defence will deputize for him.
The new Minister is also chairman of a standing committee responsible
for defence and for the apportionment of all resources including the
development of research and the correlation of production programmes.
The Chiefs of Staff continue to present their advice directly to the
Defence Committee or to the Cabinet. There is a home defence committee which is responsible for the home security services, which will
not be the concern of the Minister of Defence.[52]

We have mentioned in chapter X the tangles and confusions of the
British system of statistics before 1939. Although it had led the world
in the nineteenth century it had weaknesses on the demographic
and economic side which did not exist in other countries. Neither the
government nor the people had seen that a free people may have to
find out where they are. When Churchill went to the Admiralty in 1939
he found that there was no general Governmental Statistical Organization.[53] Every department told its tale in its own statistical dialect.
Mr. Attlee has said that when he joined the War Cabinet there was no
proper statistical survey which would show how our munitions and
labour and everything were going.[54] Mr. Churchill improvised his own
statistical machine. A small group of statisticians and economists was
installed at the Admiralty with instructions that they were to attend
only to realities and to produce tables and diagrams based on a ruthless
analysis of every departmental paper on which they could lay their

hands. The needs of scientific war, which called for a quantitative study of everything except the will to win, and the more elusive claims of peace called into existence improved machinery for collecting information and bodies responsible for systematic surveys. The new Statistical Survey which was begun in 1947 summarized the human rather than the financial resources which we have. The curtain of money was not to be allowed to hide the economic facts of life. The government was prepared to give the information which was vital to the health of the state even though it might mean giving the Opposition ammunition for the party fight.

It was already clear that no easy hopes or lies would bring back the power and comfort we had once enjoyed. The foundations of our national life would not be restored unless we concentrated on the improvement of our production and the increase of our exports. Unless production was increased our standard of living and the stability of our industrial system were in peril. In the war we had deliberately distorted and unbalanced our economic system and since the war we had rapidly expanded our welfare services. But if the elements of social justice which were common elements of the Christian, the utilitarian, and the socialist creeds were to be secured—care of children, employment or maintenance, and public responsibility for the control of disease and dirt—our productive system would have to find a 20th century level. Social security, Mr. Morrison said in 1945, could only be built on industrial efficiency. But a proper use of the nation's resources could only be made by foresight and conscious contrivances. It was necessary, he said in 1946, to find the facts, assess their significance, make a choice and carry out what had been decided. For every stage official machinery was needed and for every stage a wide publicity.[55] This was easier said than done.

Before 1939 we have seen that the Economic Advisory Council had not done very much. It had not been able to work in with the departments which were essential to its success. Its ministerial responsibility had been too diffuse. For the serious problem of unemployment an entirely new body had been used, a panel of senior civil servants under the supervision of the Permanent Under Secretary of State of the Home Office which reported to the Cabinet through the Lord Privy Seal. In 1939 Lord Stamp became adviser on " economic co-operation " presiding over an interdepartmental committee on Economic Policy. And when towards the close of 1940 the Stamp survey was ended, the staff of economists and statisticians, " the Central Economic Information Service " within the War Cabinet, parted with their statisticians, who then became the Central Statistical Office while the economists became the

Economic Section of the War Cabinet, working under the Lord President of the Council as Chairman of the Lord President's Committee. In February, 1941, Churchill entrusted the Lord President with a special responsibility for the economic side of the Home Front and laid it down that the Economic Staff should work under his general direction. Care was taken to ensure that these experts should be the allies and not the rivals of those concerned with executive responsibility. They were to contribute to that inside opinion of men of good will which was fed and shaped by the continuous discussions of men whose only object was the better deed. It was not a wire to be pulled but a valuable thread in the grand design to win the war. In 1946, Mr. Morrison could say that the machinery of economic co-ordination and administration had much improved in recent years. The Economic Section of the Cabinet was neither an executive nor administrative body and for that reason was a most valuable part of the machinery of government. A place had been made for the persuasion of facts even in the seat of power. There was also the Central Statistical Office and the Cabinet Secretariat.

These central sections discharged certain common service functions. They could co-ordinate, advise, look ahead and put economic administrative and statistical knowledge at the disposal of the separate departments of the State. This was he thought better than an Economic General Staff which if it were to make a plan and see it through would in fact have to be a duplication of the machinery of government itself, generating endless friction with the existing departments. The task was to get co-operation between the economic section, the central statistical office, and the Cabinet secretariat, on the one hand, and the officers, the experts in the departments which were properly concerned on the other. This official organization was the equivalent of an economic Chiefs of Staff. Over it were the ministerial committees which decided policy when the reports of the economic planners had shown what might be done. The ministerial committees told the officials what enquiries should be made and what reports they were to make.[56]

In March, 1947, the machinery was modified by the appointment of a Chief Planning Officer responsible for the supervision of an interdepartmental planning staff and for the development of a long term plan for the country's man-power and resources. He was to keep in touch with all departments whose co-operation would be necessary. He was to work under the Lord President of the Council and to have access to all Ministers directly concerned with questions of production. In September, 1947, Sir Stafford Cripps became Minister of Economic Affairs and it was announced from Downing Street that his appointment would unite economic policies hitherto divided. The Lord President of the Council had been responsible for co-ordinating domestic policy while another committee had handled overseas policy. Now a new committee with the Prime Minister as Chairman would be responsible for both internal and economic policies—while Sir Stafford Cripps as Minister for Economic Affairs would preside over a committee of the departmental ministers most directly concerned. He was to have the assistance of a small personal staff, the Central Economic Planning Staff, an Economic Information unit and the economic section of the Cabinet secretariat. In November, 1947, Sir Stafford Cripps became Chancellor of the Exchequer as well as Minister for Economic Affairs a new office of Economic Secretary was added to the Treasury.

There is some analogy between this joint planning staff in economic affairs and the planning staff responsible for strategy in war. Those who have to do, have been associated with those who suggest what can be done. The thinkers and the doers have been integrated with the Cabinet without whose power nothing can be done at all. There is the Prime Minister who will speak for and to the Cabinet; there is the Minister responsible for the policy and the departmental committees from which it flows; there is the Central Planning Officer who will preside over the official committees which are required. The co-operation of the public was sought at the same time. The National Production Advisory Council for Industry and the Engineering Advisory Council were to be consulted in the forming and the execution of the plans. So was there shaped a central economic organization in which the departments directly dealing with economic problems had their place; which could make use of statistical and economic studies prepared by a specially selected technical staff itself in touch with professional opinion outside. Contacts with organized industry and trade were to be close and special steps were taken to let the public know what it was all about.

It was stated at the time the new Minister for Economic affairs was appointed that the Lord President of the Council would be responsible for the co-ordination of matters other than economic. The office of the Lord President of the Council is one of the most interesting in our present working constitution. To appoint a Committee of the Privy Council was in the past a way of opening up new fields of public policy. As the power of the Prime Minister has grown he has been glad to have a sturdy political colleague who would look after the party and parliamentary as distinct from the economic and strategical aspects of governmental affairs. Before 1939 the Lord President of the Council was often leader of the House, and he had no doubt presided over the Home Affairs Committee of the Cabinet which was responsible for determining the volume and the order of the government's major legislation. During the war a Home Security (or a Civil Defence) Committee, a Home Affairs (or Home Policy) Committee which dealt with " all domestic affairs " and a Ministerial Priority Committee to supervise the allocation of productive resources, were set up.[57] It is an interesting example of the subtle empiricisms of the British governmental system that it should be the Lord President of the Council, whose functions are so deeply party, who became the Minister mainly responsible for the government's relations with the natural sciences and the place of science in the development of industry. We described in chapter X the emergence of the Department of Scientific and Industrial Research in 1916 from a committee of the Privy Council in 1915, the Medical Research Council of 1920 in place of the medical research committee of 1914 which had administered the research funds accumulated out of the working of the National Insurance Act of 1911, and the Agricultural Research Council of 1930. These three councils became the hub of the government's direct research activities. In 1947 the government yearly employed nearly 20 per cent. of the scientists in the country and of these D.S.I.R., the M.R.C. and the A.R.C. had less than half. Although during the war science had been represented in the Cabinet by Lord Cherwell, a personal friend of the Prime Minister, as Paymaster General, the essentials of the system were not changed. Ministers after the war were directly responsible for their own departmental scientific organizations but the general oversight of the whole governmental scientific work was the responsibility of the Lord President of the Council. An Advisory Council on scientific policy and a Defence Policy Research Committee both with the same president, and with staffs working in close co-operation reports the first through the Lord President of the Council and the other through the Chiefs of Staff and the Minister of Defence. The University Grants Committee answers administratively to the Chancellor of the Exchequer and is represented on the advisory Council. There is also an advisory committee on atomic energy under Sir John Anderson which is separate and directly responsible to the Prime Minister.[58]

The pattern of committees is always being changed. There are certain conditions which are essential to the unity and drive we need and one of those is flexibility. Over the thirty years between 1918 and 1948 the committee system has become of increasing constitutional importance. It is a way of getting ministers and departments responsible for different parts of the same subject to work together which is more supple and effective than a system of super-ministers in charge of global subjects. The latter would suffer from the weakness described by

Churchill in the case of defence, that it is easier to brood over the work done by others than to control the work of the departments for which others would in fact be responsible. Supervising ministers are inconsistent both with the parliamentary responsibilities of departmental ministers and with departmental control. To have any real power the supervising minister would need a staff of his own and such a staff would generate friction wherever it went. The actual pattern of committees is a matter for the Prime Minister of the day " who can alone justly measure both the problems and the personalities involved." For obvious constitutional reasons the pattern is never actually described. " The Cabinet as a whole " Mr. Morrison has said " must be responsible for everything that happens . . . . How the Cabinet does its business, and to what extent it delegates certain things to Cabinet committees is . . . the Cabinet's business because it accepts responsibility." Decisions on policy, he added, " according to the nature of the decisions and their importance, the degree of their significance and also the degree to which they may cause trouble and controversy in the House or the country, are settled at the appropriate level." The number of committees used to carry out a series of functions is a matter of convenience and administration. The government does not give the membership or the Chairmen of committees if it can be avoided and usually does not say what committees exist. A published chart of the committee structure of the Cabinet would be as harmful as a verbatim report of Cabinet discussions. The committee structure is a function of personal, party, and technical factors, and the government is right to protect itself against irresponsible criticisms of the process of policy-making. It has no duty to expose the soft belly of its unity to the thrust of the opposition. Politics is the art of the possible and the unity of the Cabinet on which sane government depends is only possible if it can resolve its divisions in secret.[59]

We can however infer the nature of the general pattern of the committee system from details which have been given and from the things which we know that it must try to do. There are : (1) the important committees dealing with Defence, Economic policy, and External Affairs ; (2) the domestic committees which are responsible for Home Affairs and which study the programme to be carried out and survey the policies to be pursued. Such matters as the timing of the Parliament Bill of 1948 in relation to the Iron and Steel Bill or the actual order of the major governmental bills is obviously a committee affair. The essential feature is a dependable elasticity. The Prime Minister must have full scope to plan the best executive machinery his problems require and his resources allow. We know too (3) that the pattern of ministerial committees is lined by an appropriate set of official committees, e.g., the case of the Stamp committee at the beginning of the war and the Food policy committee. The officials who at international conferences prepare the way for ministerial conferences are paralleled at every level of the policy-making process. One example of the elasticity enjoyed is illustrated by the instruction of Mr. Churchill as Prime Minister to Sir Edward Bridges, the Secretary to the Cabinet, on 10/VII/40 to set up a small standing ministerial committee to consist of the Secretaries of State for War (Eden), India (Amery) and Colonies (Lloyd) to consult together upon the conduct of the war in the middle East and to advise him as Minister of Defence upon the recommendations he should make to the Cabinet.[60]

The working of the committee system depends upon the willingness of the members to accept a doctrine of collective committee responsibility in addition to the basic constitutional doctrine of the collective responsibility of the Cabinet as a whole. The aim of the system is to make certain that nothing will come before the Cabinet which has not been made as ready for decision as the resources of the government will allow. The Cabinet should be an organ of decision and not a committee of investigation. The system would not work if it were not serviced by a competent staff. This is provided by the Cabinet secretariat which may be said to " service " the Cabinet committee at both the ministerial and the official level. There is the staff which serves the Defence Committee, the Economic section of the Cabinet, the Central Statistical Offices and a scientific section which is in process of creation. They include men who are seconded for a period from departments and outside experts who may be brought in. The Permanent Secretary of the Cabinet Office is also Secretary to the Cabinet and he will advise the Prime Minister on the structure and running of the Cabinet committee system. There has also been for some years a small section of two or three people examining together with a group of high officials the problem of government machinery, and there is a ministerial committee associated with them. Another small committee of high officials, permanent secretaries, and with the Head of the Treasury as Chairman has been studying the problem of efficiency. Within the Treasury itself there is the Organization and Methods division which is responsible for the adaptation of the structure of the departments to the work which they have to do. The work which it could do will be better understood if we glance for a short time at the membership and character of the Civil Service itself.

In its essential structure the Civil Service has not been vitally changed since 1939. But during the war the permanent staff was supplemented by a miscellaneous collection of academic skills, business experiences and a variety of temperaments. In April, 1939, the Administrative grade consisted of just over 2,000 (of whom 2,068 were men and 52 women) and in July, 1945, it had risen to nearly 5,000 (of whom 3,860 were men and 928 women). In the same period the Executive class was more than doubled from 20,000 (18,276 men and 1,031 women), to over 50,000 (38,844 men and 12,224 women), the clericals doubled from 100,000 (77,540 men and 35,313 women) to 250,000 (90,553 men and 161,772 women) while the professional and scientific grades increased from 11,000 to 30,000.[61] This overall figure covers the very special problems faced by entirely new ministries, such as Aircraft Production, which if they were to exercise the detailed control over the trade and industries for which they were responsible in war had to expand their staffs with great rapidity. The dilution of skilled administrative labour was secured by adding big drafts of academic persons and business men who had had experience of the industries to be controlled. " This partnership of civil servant, don and business man " was we are assured one of the most interesting and fruitful of the war. The detailed tales have yet to be told. But some general facts about the administrative problem of the modern state have already been confirmed.

After 1945 as after 1918 certain criticisms were made about the professional civil servant partly because in war he was working under conditions in which the normal Treasury and Parliamentary control was greatly reduced and partly because the academic and the business minds could in war observe from within this unfamiliar world. After 1918 Sir William Beveridge had surveyed the popular criticism of the civil servant : that he frittered time and energy in interdepartmental squabbles or tugs-of-war ; that he lacked initiative and willingness to take responsibility and had not acquired the common touch. He had retorted then that where there was a tug-of-war it was because the civil servant was putting his back into precisely those duties which Parliament had conferred on the department in which he served and that in practice his whole training was in consultation and co-operation in accordance with the instructions his political masters put out. As a servant he had in principle no power to decide anything. For his initiative a political head must be responsible and would only be willing to be so if the public were to take a less humorous and the Opposition a less acrimonious view of departmental mistakes. The lack of a common touch could be made good by the use of advisory councils, further education and as much variety in his work as the exigencies of the service would allow. Similar criticisms were made in 1944 by the

committee on the training of civil servants.[62] It referred to overdevotion
to precedent, remoteness from the rest of the community, lack of
initiative, unwillingness to take responsibility and ineffective organization and misuse of man-power. In all this there was clearly a desire
to have both the bread of freedom and the cake of guidance. Most
of the criticisms were based either on a misunderstanding of the
position of a servant or a failure to allow for the climate of a war. The
qualities of the Admiral Crichton appropriate on a desert island would
be insufferable in a drawing room and earn two lovely black eyes in the
local pub. Many academic persons were surprised that the civil servant
did not show that wide and sympathetic interest in the social sciences
with which the academic person will decorate his lectures or annotate
his books. There were others who found that the professional civil
servant was lacking in that power of cut and thrust which is the condition
of survival in the market world. The civil servant had neither the vision
of the scholar nor the trader's bounce.

The scope of government activity in war did throw a flood of light
on the very real problems of the bureaucratic man. We may glance
very briefly at three of them : the nature of the administrative art ; the
supply of competent practitioners; and the kind of machinery in which
it can best be exercised. First the nature of the administrative art.
The work of the administrator is difficult to describe. It may require
the greatest powers of the mind and yet be only interesting in its results.
And the results are usually collective. The administrator never has the
solitary triumph of the artist ; he is a Hamlet who must set right whatever rottenness may be referred to him in consultation with Polonius,
Horatio and the Ghost. He must never put an " antic disposition " on.
A good administrator has some of the qualities of the American tycoon.
He must know " where everything is ; why it is where it is and whether
it should be left there."[63] His task in the Civil Service is complicated
by the need to adapt himself not only to all the relevant facts of men
and matter but also to the political traditions and party persuasions
which he has to serve. It is impossible for him to stream-line the
machine he drives. As well transform Burke's mighty oaks into well
spaced telegraph poles. The experience of war threw a flood of light
for the general public on the real problems which the civil servant has
to solve. It is true that in peace the pace would not be so hot but the
course at any time is not unlike. Sir Oliver Franks has described[64]
a few of the essentials of the administrative art : (1) it involves the
ability to transact business by word of mouth, either in conversation
with individuals of ability and power from other spheres, or by tough
and technical discussion in committee. And most meetings " whether

311

of two individuals or of a group, were severely, even bluntly practical in character, and involved consequent action to give effect to the decision made." (2) there was a stream of correspondence and a flood of papers to be negotiated and such paper work was needed either to communicate at a distance, e.g. cables on essential policy between London and Washington in the war, or the cables relating to O.E.E.C., or to make a formal record of agreements reached in a wording which would establish clearly who was to act next and to meet possible criticism; for as Bacon wrote " Letters are good, when a man would draw an answer by letter back again; or when it may serve, for a man's justification, afterwards to produce his own letter; or where it may be danger to be interrupted or heard by pieces." Finally writing was used to clarify thought on any matters of importance where a situation had to be analysed and proposals for action put forward in the light of the analysis. The administrative civil servant needed, concluded Sir O. Franks (3) " much more than analytical power and ability to make proposals based on an analysis of the situation. He had to take a line, expound it, persuade and convince. He had to have a keen sense of what was practical and of timing." The point which impressed him most " was the reality and extent of delegation . . . . the presupposition seemed to be that one was competent to do the work and would know when something too important, too awkward, or too ramifying to be settled at one's own level turned up. Very few rules were laid down in advance which limited the authority or freedom of action of the junior grades. And if senior officials were quick to help when asked, they were also slow to intervene, unasked." Sir O. Franks confirmed what one had supposed about the relation between the Minister and his department. " How limited in number, in a large department . . . . were the topics on which a minister could keep himself regularly informed and take the important decisions. It was not a question of energy or will . . . . It was the result of the sheer volume of business and the extreme variety of the matters concerned. In consequence while the Minister was responsible for all that was done, most things were done without his knowledge." It followed from this that a change of Minister had a profound effect on a department. "Precisely because the Minister knew of and decided relatively few of the matters for which he was responsible, it was important that officials who made the decisions on his behalf should know his mind and conduct their business in that knowledge." They must decide in accordance with the policy the minister would defend if it were challenged.

This account refers to the conditions of war when the nation was able to call on abilities of every kind and when it was informed by a passionate though quiet determination which is unthinkable in peace. But it does give point to a very different aspect of the problem of administration stated by another academic critic.[65] " A good administrative machine is made only as to 5 per cent. on a drawing board but as to 95 per cent. in the adjustment of human motives." Professor Jewkes would agree with Francis Bacon that " the life of the execution of affairs, resteth in the good choice of persons." It is not he wrote " the lines of responsibility running smoothly but the curves of temperament cunningly adjusted which count." For this reason the larger the organization the more difficult for it to move with pace and ease, for the head comes to know less and less about more and more, while the units in the hierarchy " steadily fanning out beneath him come to know more and more about less and less." This is sometimes hidden because "moribund administration has been galvanized into life by a good administrator." But the supply of good administrators is not unlimited. With the work of government ever increasing the supply may well fall seriously below the need. In a simple community the talents which nature casts up must suffice : Horatius had probably received no special training in the art of bridge defence and when Homer sang there were no simple guides to the telling of tales. The exigencies of the machine age will call for a dilution of the labour, a job analysis, even in the field of counsel. Some study of the mind and temper employed must do in the administrative art what motion study has done at the bench. It is perhaps true that administrative skill is not unlimited. But it is also true that the development of what there is has not gone very far. Already the Civil Service has begun a system of training which involves the simple principles of : estimating the varieties of skills which may be required; estimating the qualities which can be obtained ; explaining to the recruit what it is that he has joined. Not every private can have the field marshal's strategic eye but it is fairly certain that the military competence of a platoon can be increased ten-fold if it knows something of the plan in which it is to play a part. Any increase in efficiency which such a job analysis can give will not prevent the play of genius whenever it appears. If the general structure is as good as common skills can make it the opportunity for shaping genius is improved. A sound tradition can support and need not crush the innovator. The civil servant at his best requires " the force, the steadiness, the comprehensiveness, and the versatility of intellect, the command over our own powers, the instinctive just estimate of things as they pass before us, which sometimes is a natural gift but commonly is not gained without much effort and the exercise of years."[66] The administrator has in the world of actions to find those ordered lines which correspond to the ordered worlds which the creative artist makes with the materials of his art. The great administrator can inform the wills and deeds of men.

It was a great achievement before 1914 that a collection of relatively separated and unrelated staffs had been made into a unified service based on common methods of recruitment and that departmental allegiance had been deepened and not divided by a tradition of allegiance to the service as a whole. The Treasury had been responsible for finding the practical measure through which this unity could be expressed. The work of the Treasury after 1918 was not as successful as had been hoped. It has been criticized for failing to foster systematic studies of departmental organization and administrative techniques. The general lay-out of departments and the distribution of responsibility was not periodically overhauled or systematically reviewed. In the rearmament period of 1936-9 it had not been eager to give expert study to the administrative art. And at the outbreak of the war in 1939 it had no equipment to cope with the problems of reorganization and expansion which emerged. There was no body of expert knowledge to guide the staffing of new and expanding departments.

Between 1918 and 1939 as we have seen there had been developed a technique of consultation between the Treasury and those responsible in every department for problems of staffing and finance. But the response of the Treasury to the suggestion that expert knowledge and study might be brought to bear on the fundamental principles of departmental organization had been very thin. Establishment questions had remained in the hand of civil servants whose experience was usually limited to the departments in which they served. A mighty maze was empirically served but there lacked a theoretic plan.

The collective responsibility of the Cabinet for the political decisions was not paralleled by a collective expert machine. And of course it is not really practical to cut and fashion on utility lines the service which is the expert lining of the political cloak. An expert in organization and method has suggested that the British departmental pattern might be taken to pieces and put together in an efficient form. Such a thorough going survey is not really possible in a civil service which serves a responsible government because the Cabinet has to allocate functions for reasons which are never merely administrative.

In 1919 a few (never more than 4) Treasury Investigation Officers were introduced. But they did not cut very deep or range very wide. Between 1939 and 1942 they were increased from 4 to 46 and were named the Organization and Methods Division. Departments were invited but not compelled to use their skill. There was no tampering with the principle that the head of a department must be responsible for the management of his own organization. But five of the larger departments set up Organization and Methods branches of their own. In January, 1945, the Treasury Organization and Methods division issued a memorandum on the status and the functions of Organization and Methods branches in the departments and their relation to the Organization and Methods Division in the Treasury itself. The Treasury would do work for departments with no Organization and Methods branch of their own and undertake general investigations of matters covering several departments at once.[67]

One aspect of the subtle interplay between the different levels of knowledge and opinion on which the health of a political system depends is the information which a government can give the people and the information which it can have about them. Before the thronging troubles of our times, J. H. Newman stated the dilemma they would bring. " In this day the subject-matter of thought and belief has so increased upon us, that a far higher mental formation is required than was necessary in times past, and higher than we have actually reached. The whole world is brought to our doors every morning, and our judgment is required upon social concerns, books, persons, parties creeds, national acts, political principles and measures. We have to form our opinion, make our profession, take our side on a hundred matters on which we have but little right to speak at all. But we do speak upon them, though neither we nor those who hear us are well able to determine what is the real position of our intellect relatively to those many questions, one by one, on which we commit ourselves." It was necessary, he wrote, " if it is possible, to analyse the process of reasoning, and to invent a method which may act as a common measure between mind and mind, as a means of joint investigation, and as a recognized intellectual standard—a standard such as to secure us against hopeless mistakes, and to emancipate us from the capricious *ipse dixit* of authority."[68] Dimly aware of the strain that accelerating change imposes upon the life of reason in the individual, and the institutions which might support his freedom and his ease, it has been the wicked and the foolish aim of totalitarian powers to exploit it for their own ends. The life of reason is a fine and private growth upon the depths of passions we have barely glimpsed. The propagandist wishes to control the life of mind by operating on the emotional depths in which it grows.

He would :

> " . . . . tempt the frailty of our powers
> Presuming on their changeful potency "

315

" Propaganda " said Goebbels " has no fundamental method. It has only one purpose—the conquest of the masses." Using a technique of repetition in subtly varied contexts—the basis of the advertiser's art— the propagandist believes that individuals may be so bewildered, terrorized or tempted that they can be moved to mass action which would lead to their defeat, or in peace lured from the life of reason into the service of a new race of experimenting despots. During the 1939-45 war the method of the German propaganda machine was to adapt the technique of the advertiser, who creates a silly friendly world of perfect smiles and ardent bridegrooms won, of potions giving dreamless sleep and perfect nerves, for the creation of a nightmare world in which the reason would be numbed and the power to resist destroyed.

Such propaganda attacks are not successful in any country which has a vigorous and healthy party system. For such a system will be supported by a network of institutions in which the relation between ideas and action is ever tried and tested. A party system involves a continuous practice in the art of the possible, as a soccer league involves continuous practice in the control of a ball. Where it exists the world of difference which lies between an idea and its embodiment in a rule of law, or administrative device, will never be ignored. Where politics, which is the art of the possible, is understood at all, there men know the difference between voicing, in the lobby or the club, a fear, uncertainty, or hope and putting forward at a conference a proposal for action. Democratic political institutions allow for emotion to be earthed in orderly debate before action is determined by discussion in committee. The passions which may move men as individuals to their fall— fear, pride and anger—are in a healthy party system harnessed to the task of finding ways and means in the dreary details of the ordinary world for its preservation and slight amelioration. In the literature of a party system there will be found a continuous gradation from the loud vulgarities of a gutter press to the subtlest periods of the great pamphleteers. On the existence of this ladder from the gutter to the stars does the stability of the political order depend. It may be raised but it should not be broken.

While the propaganda of the Goebbels machine was wasting its sweetness on the desert air and finding a united people like the air invulnerable, some advances were being made in the useful and practical art of necessary government publicity. To meet the complaints of the Press about the lack of information a few government departments appointed officers to deal with press enquiries before and during the 1914-18 war. After 1918 the Foreign Office News division took over these duties from the wartime Ministry of Information, and the Service departments, the Ministry of Heath and the Ministry of Agriculture appointed press officers. The arrangements made were very small. But in 1931 a full time publicity officer was appointed to the Dominion and Colonial Offices and in 1932 the G.P.O. set up a publicity section. In 1934 the Treasury was given a full time publicity officer, and the ministries of Transport, Health, Education and Labour followed suit. In 1937 there were high ranking Public Relations Officers at the War Office and the Admiralty and at the Home Office for civil defence. By January, 1944, the total public relations staff of the civil ministries was 661, excluding the 2,700 employed by the Ministry of Information in Britain and the 530 employed by the War Office and the 370 by the Air Ministry and the 115 of the Admiralty.[69] These men were really necessary. It was not possible for thirty or forty newspapers and unnumbered journals and magazines to get the news and facts they needed from a large department by casual and unofficial contacts. In war time too it was essential that the people should know what it was that they had to do and receive every help in doing it. The people had given to the government the power to make whatever regulations might be necessary for the safety of the state. The regulations were inevitably complicated, touching as they did detailed problems of distribution (rationing and price controls) and production (dig for victory, industrial mobilization) and safety (air-raid shelters, evacuation) and the timing and the phrasing of their issue could not be left to chance.

This system of Public Relations Officers has been retained as an obvious necessity since the war. Some criticism has been made that they have not always limited themselves to the communication of administrative facts. The line between an explanation and a defence of governmental policy is difficult to draw. It has been said that some Ministers might use their Public Relations Officers as personal publicity officers—that the man who could create a Mr. Therm might give a radiance to the Minister of Home Security and give a touch of warmth to the icy clutch of Sir Stafford Cripps.[70] Some Ministers and their Public Relation Officers were as inseparable as Dick Whittington and his cat.

In the problem of information as in others one must not confuse the conditions of war and peace. In war it was essential that the government should get to know some things and give explanations about others with the speed which war requires. It was known that the enemy was all around and it was obvious that a fact or word out of place might be deadly to our cause. It was also desirable that the public should feel

317

that the government was so watching the problem of information that no spy mania could develop. After an initial period in which the headlines of newspapers and the chalked headlines of street corner newsvendors were of some concern to the new and donnish staff of the Ministry of Information a most practical arrangement of voluntary censorship was devised under a Director General, Sir Walter Moncton and Sir Cyril Radcliffe as Controller of News. Newspapers could submit to the Press Censorship Division any report which might contain information of value to the enemy and though they were not bound to take the advice which was given if they did so they were safe from prosecution. This system was successful because the men who ran it were practical journalists ; because it was known, to be temporary and those who ran it had every wish that it should be so ; because no control was exercised over the opinions which a newspaper might express but only over such facts as might be of importance for security reasons ; and also because in the background the government had powers under the Defence Regulations to suppress at once any newspaper which was a danger to the war effort.[71]

To help it obtain information needed in its work the government had through the Ministry of Information two widely different means. First a weekly report provided by Home Intelligence which was an odd amalgam of things heard and seen by voluntary observers who undertook to give their estimate of public feeling and morals.[72] These reports will perhaps one day give many a chuckle to scholars yet unborn. In the strange conditions of the time these records of little Caliphs who so loyally recorded the chatter heard in markets, queues and bars had their use. Secondly there was a War Time Social Survey which was a machine for obtaining factual information needed in the work of the administrative departments. It was run by the Ministry of Information but it worked mainly for other departments and got for them more or less accurate indications of the public needs, or wishes, or expectations in many practical affairs. When the government was responsible for the clothes, the food and the housing of the people it was useful to know what articles of clothing, what kinds of food and what shape of house were really in demand.[73] After the war, on 1st April, 1946, the Central Office of Information was set up and took over some of the duties of the Ministry of Information which had died the day before. It was to give professional and common services in the art of publicity to some departments.[74] It was not a policy department. The department responsible for a particular service had to decide whether or not the means of publicity or enquiry which it might suggest should be used. The Ministry of Health must decide whether the Central Office of

318

Information should use its skill to secure an increase in diphtheria immunization or a reduction in venereal disease. The Ministry of Agriculture must decide whether the instructional films it can make shall be used to help to increase the output of food. The Ministry of Labour must decide if it is to be asked to get more men down the mines. The Central Office of Information itself was to advise about the media to be used and the scale of activity which might be necessary to get a desired result. It has so far helped the departments : (1) by disseminating general information about public affairs. The cold if sometimes foggy statement of policy found in the white papers which comes direct from the government's planning brain may be given a dewy sparkle and rainbow glow in the lighter pamphlets which the C.O.I. can create. The heavy foot of policy is lent the lightness of the common touch ; (2) it has undertaken campaigns to secure a particular result, such as an increase in recruitment for an industry or service, sufficient blood donors, or more men and women to be trained as teachers ; (3) it has provided technical and specialized information for the use of people in their work. It has supplied films, booklets and even small exhibitions for the use of such bodies as the Agricultural Advisory Service, the Department of Scientific and Industrial Research, the Industrial Fuel Efficiency Service of the Ministry of Fuel and Power and the Food Advisory Service of the Ministry of Food. And (4) it has helped to diffuse information about the life of the people and their progress in certain fields. Matthew Arnold's sweetness and light are partly in its care.

Information about the work of particular departments is the responsibility of the Information Division of the department concerned. It is headed by a Chief Information Officer who is responsible to the Minister concerned. He must decide when the services of the Central Office of Information should be used, over and above the press and broadcasting, and he is responsible for telling the C.O.I. what is to be done and for passing its work. Although the individual departments are responsible for the issue of news and information and for all the field of press relations the existence of the Central Office of Information has made possible since 1946 the use of a central delivery service and a team of despatch riders. In 1939 news was sent out for the most part on foot by messengers from the originating departments whereas now complete delivery can be made within about 45 minutes to over a 100 separate places from the Central Office of Information.

In the conditions of the modern state the climate of opinion will be one of the things which no government can ignore. We have seen that very great care was taken to unravel the administrative pattern of the war. There was no disorder because the initial problems of peace had been foreseen as had the initial problems of the war itself. But the success in the technical matter of disarmament, while it is a witness to the competence of the Civil Service in its proper field, must not tempt us to underestimate the seriousness of the real adjustments which have yet to be made. In the grey horror of the war the springs of action, so long as the will to win is not broken, are always very simple. In 1939-45 they were for us particularly so. No compromise was possible. We could not win alone. We could make it possible for others to win and no sacrifice was worth avoiding until that common victory had occurred. We avoided the immeasurable disaster of a German victory but we did not avoid the sacrifice of our own economic and political life. For this we were prepared, but that it had occurred we could not really feel. Those who have staked their all when they do not lose their life may not notice for some time how much in fact has been lost. References have been made to the spiritual exhaustion of the British people after the long strain. The real problem has not always been understood. When an individual has escaped from death he feels that it is good to be alive and in most cases he will enjoy the convalescence after sickness, injury or shock which the community prescribes. But a nation is not an individual. The longer the struggle the more the world in which it must struggle to survive will have changed. To use a homely image a nation may find, like a man who feels some natural pride when he has rescued a drowning fellow creature, that he has ruined his only suit and lost his job while he has been away. The material losses of the war are not all. The dislocation of industry, the loss of markets, the sale of overseas investments may be serious enough. There is an intellectual price to pay as well. In the political field this can be serious indeed. During the war the functions of the Opposition have been undertaken by the enemy himself and when he goes a serious weakness in political life may be revealed. It is not I think cynical to suggest that the peculiar unity of war is not a good preparation for the future rivalries of peace. Of course where there has been defeat the disruption of political life is even more serious—the political climates of France and Germany are witnesses to that. But the more subtle disruption which may occur in an undefeated country may be serious too. The explanation is simple enough. During the war the normal exercise of political skills has been suspended. In peacetime the continuous adjustments of political life in a democracy are determined by a complex interplay of persuasion, interest and coercion, an election here, a strike there, and many conferences here and there : the subtle party structure is in continuous adjustment. But in war we have been so absorbed in adjusting ourselves to the malice of the enemy that we have had little time to adjust ourselves and our ideas to the life which peace will bring. The differences which on the world stage cause former allies to fall apart have their place too in the domestic sphere.

The case of foreign relations had a stark simplicity. In 1945 " the shape of things to come, and the policy which it required on the part of the British government . . . . seemed plain enough." The grand alliance of the United Nations would be transformed into a " peacetime organization." The partnership of the Great Powers was to provide the framework of a new world order. But all this was based on " the false axiom there was any real unity of purpose between the Soviet Union and the Western Powers." In fact " the post-war aims of the Soviet Union and of the Western Powers were as opposed as their wartime aims had been identical." So the story of British post-war policy was one of " the reluctant abandoning of false assumptions, and the gradual acceptance of unpleasant realities."[75] We now know that the Soviet system is a threat to every tradition of western civilization and that the latter can only be saved by finding in alliance with the New World a basis of resistance which Western Europe cannot provide alone. This revelation of the new shape of power politics has been concurrent with a deepening understanding of the shifts in the economic structure of the world. The world does not owe us a living and the political arts are no substitute for the ability to earn our daily bread.

In domestic policies the adjustments to the facts of peace have been more subtle. The first post-war election was a most gentlemanly affair and it has had an almost Victorian biography.[76] The Labour Party was better prepared for the contest than were the Conservatives. It had held a party conference every year and though it supported the Government in Parliament it had freely engaged in party propaganda about post-war problems. It did not see why it should not exercise the freedoms we were in arms to defend. The Conservatives had held no party conference during the war until 1943 and they and the Liberals had allowed their organizations in the constituencies to run down further than had the Labour Party.

The Labour Party went to the country with a compact and fully developed programme. It offered a tempting combination of pre-war aims and wartime means. *Let us Face the Future* " embodied the idea of planning and using all the resources of the country in the interests of the British people as a whole." " It made " writes the same party authority " a very definite appeal to all those sections of the thinking public who were beginning to believe in the need for a planned economy on democratic lines."[77] The spirit of the war was to be used for the aims of peace. The inevitability of gradualness was to give place to a Mulberry speed. Both sides in fact paid more attention to benefits than they did to burdens. 97 per cent. of the Labour candidates and 94 per cent. of the Conservatives dealt with the question of Housing in their election addresses and next in importance were Social Security and Full Employment. Nearly 12,000,000 votes were given for Labour, nearly 10,000,000 for the Conservatives and their allies, and more than 2,200,000 for the Liberals. The authors of *The British General Election of* 1945 estimate that there was a Socialist majority of 66,000 (12,008,000 against 11,942,000). With 48 per cent. of the votes Labour obtained 393 seats in a House of 640 members or 61 per cent. of the total giving them a clear majority of 146 over all the rest. The Conservative alliance was reduced from 397 to 213, a swing over in votes of 12 per cent. and the loss by the Conservatives " of a quarter of their supporters—more than doubled the Labour representation in Parliament and almost halved the Conservative strength." The two party system had revived with a bang and not with a whimper. It is perhaps remarkable that the Labour party should have obtained less than half the votes cast when one considers the inevitable attraction of the idea that planning for war should set the standard of planning for peace. If we could conquer Hitler why should we not conquer unemployment ? Let there be a D-day for disease and as many letters of the alphabet as might be required for the days which would bring fresh instalments of the elements of social justice. It is a very real tribute to the political sense of the country that the Conservatives held what they did. By far the most vital factor in the election was the use of party broadcasts. The B.B.C. estimated that 44.9 per cent. of the adult population listened in ; and " where the greater part of the electors are . . . in their own homes beside the wireless . . . the element of mass emotion is entirely absent." The historians of the election added that " it may well be that this method of radio campaigning has revolutionized the nature of British elections."[78] The still small voice of the spoken radio word is a new weapon in the armoury of sense and freedom in a dangerous world. In the election of 1931 it was one of the major factors to secure the heavy defeat of a divided party ; in 1940 with its magic power Mr. Churchill could address a world, as Prologue could address his " wooden O," as darkness fell upon the vasty fields of France and all the youth of England was on fire. With it Mr. Attlee has ended a strike, speaking to every docker as he might have spoken in any room to anyone. In a serious crisis it is a most potent tool and it is desirable that it should not be used to secure a decision on matters which have not been fully discussed before. The health of our political system requires that when a critical decision has to be taken, the facts which are relevant to it shall have been diffused far and wide by party, press and pamphlet.

During the first two years of its office, the Government was writing the Beveridge Report into the Statute book. It is a record in the speed of legislation that this should have been so quickly done. The aim of a national minimum in health, education and economic security was pursued with maximum speed. The poor law was abolished and the National Insurance, National Assistance, Industrial Insurance, and National Health Service Acts passed. The trade cycle and chronic unemployment were both to disappear and to that end the Bank of England, the coal mining industry, civil aviation, Cables and Wireless were nationalized in the first year, transport and the supply of electricity in the second, while Gas and Iron and Steel were to follow the latter over the hamstrung body of the Lords.[79]

APPENDIX I

THE PARLIAMENT ACT

1 and 2 Geo. V, Cap. 13, 1911

An Act to make provision with respect to the powers of the House of Lords in relation to those of the House of Commons, and to limit the duration of Parliament (18th August, 1911).

Whereas it is expedient that provision should be made for regulating the relations between the two Houses of Parliament :

And whereas it is intended to substitute for the House of Lords as it at present exists a Second Chamber constituted on a popular instead of hereditary basis, but such substitution cannot be immediately brought into operation :

And whereas provision will require hereafter to be made by Parliament in a measure effecting such substitution for limiting and defining the powers of the new Second Chamber, but it is expedient to make such provision as in this Act appears for restricting the existing powers of the House of Lords :

Be it therefore enacted by the King's Most Excellent Majesty, by and with the advice and consent of the Lords Spiritual and Temporal, and, Commons, in this present Parliament assembled, and by the authority of the same, as follows :

1.—(1) If a Money Bill, having been passed by the House of Commons and sent up to the House of Lords at least one month before the end of the session, is not passed by the House of Lords without amendment within one month after it is so sent up to that House, the Bill shall, unless the House of Commons direct to the contrary, be presented to His Majesty and become an Act of Parliament on the Royal Assent being signified, notwithstanding that the House of Lords have not consented to the Bill.

(2) A Money Bill means a Public Bill which in the opinion of the Speaker of the House of Commons contains only provisions dealing with all or any of the following subjects, namely, the imposition, repeal, remission, alteration, or regulation of taxation ; the imposition for the payment of debt or other financial purposes of charges on the Consolidated Fund, or on money provided by Parliament, or the variation or repeal of any such charges ; supply ; the appropriation, receipt, custody, issue or audit of accounts of public money ; the raising or guarantee of any loan or the repayment thereof ; or subordinate matters incidental to those subjects or any of them. In this subsection the expressions " taxation," " public money," and " loan " respectively do not include any taxation, money, or loan raised by local authorities or bodies for local purposes.

(3) There shall be endorsed on every Money Bill when it is sent up to the House of Lords and when it is presented to His Majesty for assent the certificate of the Speaker of the House of Commons signed by him that it is a Money Bill. Before giving his certificate, the Speaker shall consult, if practicable, two members to be appointed from the Chairmen's Panel at the beginning of each Session by the Committee of Selection.

2.—(1) If any Public Bill (other than a Money Bill or a Bill containing any provision to extend the maximum duration of Parliament beyond five years) is passed by the House of Commons in three successive sessions (whether of the same Parliament or not), and, having been sent up to the House of Lords at least one month before the end of the session, is rejected by the House of Lords in each of those sessions, that Bill shall, on its rejection for the third time by the House of Lords, unless the House of Commons direct to the contrary, be presented to His Majesty and become an Act of Parliament on the Royal Assent being signified thereto, notwithstanding that the House of Lords have not consented to the Bill : Provided that this provision shall not take effect unless two years have elapsed between the date of the second reading in the first of those sessions of the Bill in the House of Commons and the date on which it passes the House of Commons in the third of those sessions.

(2) When a Bill is presented to His Majesty for assent in pursuance of the provisions of this section, there shall be endorsed on the Bill the certificate of the Speaker of the House of Commons signed by him that the provisions of this section have been duly complied with.

(3) A Bill shall be deemed to be rejected by the House of Lords if it is not passed by the House of Lords either without amendment or with such amendments only as may be agreed to by both Houses.

(4) A Bill shall be deemed to be the same Bill as a former Bill sent up to the House of Lords in the preceding session if, when it is sent up to the House of Lords, it is identical with the former Bill or contains only such alterations as are certified by the Speaker of the House of Commons to be necessary owing to the time which has elapsed since the date of the former Bill, or to represent any amendments which have been made by the House of Lords in the former Bill in the preceding session, and any amendments which are certified by the Speaker to have been made by the House of Lords in the third session and agreed to by the House of Commons shall be inserted in the Bill as presented for Royal Assent in pursuance of this section :

Provided that the House of Commons may, if they think fit, on the passage of such a Bill through the House in the second or third session, suggest any further amendments without inserting the amendments in the Bill, and any such suggested amendments shall be considered by the House of Lords, and, if agreed to by that House, shall be treated as amendments made by the House of Lords and agreed to by the House of Commons ; but the exercise of this power by the House of Commons shall not affect the operation of this section in the event of the Bill being rejected by the House of Lords.

3. Any certificate of the Speaker of the House of Commons given under this Act shall be conclusive for all purposes, and shall not be questioned in any court of law.

4.—(1) In every Bill presented to His Majesty under the preceding provisions of this Act, the words of enactment shall be as follows, that is to say :—

" Be it enacted by the King's most Excellent Majesty, by and with the advice and consent of the Commons in this present Parliament assembled, in accordance with the provisions of the Parliament Act, 1911, and by authority of the same, as follows."

(2) Any alteration of a Bill necessary to give effect to this section shall not be deemed to be an amendment of the Bill.

5. In this Act the expression " Public Bill " does not include any Bill for confirming a Provisional Order.

6. Nothing in this Act shall diminish or qualify the existing rights and privileges of the House of Commons.

7. Five years shall be substituted for seven years as the time fixed for the maximum duration of Parliament under the Septennial Act, 1715.

8. This Act may be cited as the Parliament Act, 1911.

APPENDIX II

MINISTRIES

1835-41. Second Melbourne.
1841-6. Second Peel.
1846-52. First Russell.
1852. First Derby.
1852-5. Aberdeen.
1855-8. First Palmerston.
1858-9. Second Derby.
1859-66. Second Palmerston.
1866-8. . Third Derby and First Disraeli.
1868-74. First Gladstone.
1874-80. Second Disraeli.
1880-5. Second Gladstone.
1885-6. First Salisbury.
1886. Third Gladstone.
1886-92. Second Salisbury.
1892-5. Fourth Gladstone and Rosebery.

1895-1905. Third Salisbury and Balfour.
1905-15. Campbell-Bannerman and Asquith.
1915-16. Asquith Coalition.
1916-22. Lloyd George Coalition.
1922-4. Bonar Law and First Baldwin.
1924. First MacDonald.
1924-29. Second Baldwin.
1929-31. Second MacDonald.
1931. MacDonald-Baldwin Coalition or National.
1932-35. National Coalition— MacDonald.
1935-45. National Coalition—Baldwin.
1937—Chamberlain.
1940—Churchill.
1945. Labour Government—Attlee.

APPENDIX III

THE ELECTORATE AND THE HOUSE OF COMMONS

ELECTORATE

1831	...	...	435,391 ⎱ ...	... increase	217,386	...	... 49%
1833	...	...	652,777 ⎰				
1866	...	...	1,056,659 ⎱ ...	... increase	938,427	...	... 88%
1869	...	...	1,995,086 ⎰				
1883	...	...	2,618,453 ⎱ ...	... increase	1,762,087	...	... 67%
1885	...	...	4,380,540 ⎰				

1918 added 13,000,000 new voters making total of 21,000,000.
1928 added 5,000,000 new voters making total of 28,500,000.
1945 the number of voters was 32,836,419.

HOUSE OF COMMONS

	Before 1832	1832	1867-8	1885	1918
England and Wales	513	... 500	... 495	... 495	... 528
Scotland	45	... 53	... 60	... 72	... 74
Ireland	100	... 105	... 103	... 103	... 105
Totals	658	658	658	670	707

After creation of Irish Free State, Northern Ireland 13 and Total, 615.
1945 : England 505, Wales 36, Scotland 74, N. Ireland 13, Universities 12.
Total 640.

APPROXIMATE STRENGTH OF PARTIES IN THE HOUSE OF COMMONS

Elections.

Dec., 1832. Reformers 487, Tories 171.
Jan., 1835. ,, 365, ,, 293.
July, 1837. ,, 339, ,, 319.
July, 1841. ,, 289, ,, 369.
July, 1847. Liberals 337, Peelites 116, Protectionists 202.
1852. Liberals 323, Conservatives 331.
1857. ,, 373, ,, 281.
1859. ,, 347, ,, 307.
1865. ,, 360, ,, 298.
1868. ,, 382, ,, 278.
1874. ,, 249, ,, 352, Home Rulers 51.
1880. ,, 350, ,, 238, ,, 64.
1885. ,, 335, ,, 249, Nationalists 86.
1886. Conservatives 316, Liberal Unionists 78, Gladstone 191, Parnell 85.
1892. ,, 268, ,, 47, ,, 274, Irish 81.
1895. ,, 340, ,, 71, Rosebery 177, ,, 82.
1900. ,, 334, ,, 68, Liberals 186, Nationalist 82.
1906. Unionists 167, Liberals 377, Labour 43, Irish 83.
Jan., 1910. Unionists 273, Liberals 275, Labour 40, Nationalist 82.
Dec., 1910. ,, 272, ,, 272, ,, 42, ,, 84.
1918 Coupon election. Coalitionist 526, Labour 63, Independent Liberals 33, Irish 80, and Independents 5.
1922. Conservatives 347, Labour 142, Liberal 114.
1923. ,, 258, ,, 191, ,, 159.
1924. ,, 420, ,, 151, ,, 40.
1929. ,, 260, ,, 287, ,, 59.
1931. ,, 471, ,, 52, ,, 33.
1935. ,, 387, ,, 154, ,, 17.
1945. ,, 189, ,, 393, ,, 12.

APPENDIX IV

GROWTH OF THE CIVIL SERVICE

1832. 21,305.

1841. 16,750, exclusive of many clerks, messengers, and many engaged also in trade.

1851. 39,147.

1861. 31,943.

1871. 53,874, including some workmen.

1881. 50,859. Telephone and telegraph not included.

1891. 79,241.

1901. 116,413. G.P.O. included.

1914. 280,000. Scotland and Ireland included.[1]

1929. 434,000, including 122,000 Industrial workers ; 178,500 Manipulative staff employed mainly in the Post Office ; 16,500 messengers and porters, etc. ; *all other grades,* 117,000.[2]

1939. 408,000 ... ... + 211,000 (industrial staffs of government
(non-industrial). departments not classified to a particular industry, together with N.F.S., police and civil defence.

1946. 722,000 ... ... + 384,000.

1948. 715,000 ... ... + 389,000.

The Chancellor of the Exchequer on December 17th, 1946, gave the following figures of non-industrial civil servants :

	April, 1939.		October, 1946.	
	Men.	Women.	Men.	Women.
Administrative	2,068	52	3,442	556
Executive	18,276	1,031	34,324	9,550
Clerical and sub-clerical ...	77,540	35,313	127,921	137,073
Typing	64	15,273	70	30,209
Professional, scientific and technical	10,906	135	38,253	2,819
Minor and manipulative ...	127,420	35,192	124,998	65,886
Technical ancillary staff ...	24,151	1,717	43,035	7,285
Inspectorate	5,259	528	5,155	731
Messengers, porters, etc. ...	13,669	5,707	30,850	13,021

1 From Dr. Finer : *The Theory and Practice of Modern Government,* pp. 1294-5.
2 Treasury Memoranda for Royal Commission on Civil Service 1929-31, pp. 3-8.

APPENDIX V

TAXATION DIRECT AND INDIRECT

Indirect Taxation.			Direct Taxation.		
1874-5	£42.5 millions, 67.2%	... ...	£20.7 millions, 32.8%		
1894-5	£46.8 ,, 54.6%	... ...	£38.9 ,, 45.4%		
1914-15	£75.8 ,, 39.9%	... ...	£114.2 ,, 60.1%		
1919-20	£280.3 ,, 28.0%	... ...	£720.6 ,, 72.0%		
1938-39	£397.1 ,, 44.4%	... ...	£499.3 ,, 55.6%		
1941-2	£756.5 ,, 38.6%	... ...	£1,205.5 ,, 61.4%		
1945-6	£1,178.9 ,, 36.9%	... ...	£2,017.8 ,, 63.1%		

STANDARD RATE OF TAX IN THE POUND

	s.	d.		s.	d.
1913-14	1	2	1936-7	4	9
1927-28	4	0	1937-8	5	0
1928-29	4	0	1938-9	5	6
1929-30	4	0	1939*	5	0
1932-33	5	0	1940*	7	0
1934-35	4	6	1941*	8	6
1935-36	4	6	1942-5	10	0
	1946-49	9s.	0d.		

* in these years there was a change in the rate in the course of the financial year.

PERCENTAGE OF INCOME PAID IN DIRECT TAXATION

Year	Earned Income		
	£100	£500	£10,000
1903	—	3.5	4.7
1913-14	—	2.6	7.7
1923-24	—	3.2	35.9
1938-39	—	8.8†	56.6
1946-47	—	20.1†	79.4

†on income of £500–£1,000.

SELECT BIBLIOGRAPHY

The purpose of the following selection is twofold. First : to indicate the sources from which the facts and ideas of the preceding essay have been derived. Only a small part of so wide a field can have been covered by research in original authorities. Second : An exhaustive bibliography might run to over fifty pages and even then mislead because it was comprehensive but uncritical, while a select bibliography may put the general reader and the student in the way of finding what he wants to know. I have therefore included two kinds of works : (1) standard authorities which will usually contain exhaustive and critical bibliographies in their own field ; and (2) essays and books on special themes which have come my way and which may serve to supplement the former and to direct attention to underlying problems.

GENERAL SOCIAL CONDITIONS RELEVANT TO THE DEVELOPMENT

OF GOVERNMENT

The general history of the nineteenth century and the twentieth century to the war of 1914-18 is being gradually covered by a series of comprehensive studies. I have used Halévy : *History of the English People*, Vols. 1, 2, 3, from 1815 to 1841 ; Vol. 4, 1894-1905 ; Vol. 5, 1905-1915. J. H. Clapham : *An Economic History of Modern Britain.* G. M. Young : *Early Victorian England ;* 2 vols. 1934, provides a diversity of essays on many topics and includes a brilliant survey of the character of the period by G. M. Young. R. C. K. Ensor : *England, 1870-1914*, in the Oxford History of England, is the latest and best general book on the period.

The 1914-18 war is dealt with in the many monographs published by the Carnegie Endowment, e.g. :—E. M. H. Lloyd : *Experiments in State Control ;* Sir William Beveridge : *British Food Control ;* Humbert Wolfe : *Labour Supply and Regulation ;* T. H. M. Middleton : *Food Production in War ;* Francis Hirst : *The Consequences of the War to Great Britain ;* and many others.

The period between the wars is covered in various ways by D. C. Somervell : *The Reign of George V ;* J. A. Spender : *Great Britain, 1886-1935.* Economic conditions are best summarized in Bowley : *Economic Consequences of the War* (Home University Library) ; Sir W. T. Layton : *The Economic Situation of Great Britain ;* Pigou : *Economic Position of Great Britain*, 1927 ; and Pigou and Colin Clarke : *The Economic Position of Great Britain*, 1936 (the two latter both published by the London and Cambridge Economic Service). G. C. Allen : *British Industries* (1935) ; *Britain's Industrial Future*, the Liberal Industrial Report of 1928 ; the report and minutes of evidence of the *Macmillan Report on Finance and Industry*, Cmd. 3897, 1931 ; and J. H. Richardson : *British Economic Foreign Policy*, provide an introduction to contemporary economic history. For the period since 1939, W. K. Hancock and M. M. Gowing : *British War Economy* (1949); and Churchill : *Second World War* (in progress) are essential.

For the general reader of politics who requires the essential economic and social background : T. S. Ashton : *The Industrial Revolution* 1760-1830 (H.U.L. 1948) ; J. F. Rees : *A Survey of Industrial Development* (valuable because it links the pre- and the post-war world) ; Bowley's *England's Foreign Trade* (1922 edition) ; Layton's *Introduction to the Study of Prices ;* Loveday : *Britain and World Trade* would give the essentials.

BIBLIOGRAPHY

Political and Social Theory Relevant to the Development
of Government

Dicey's *Law and Opinion in England* is the best introduction to the interplay
between thought and political action in this period, but Halévy : *Philosophical
Radicalism ;* Leslie Stephen : *The English Utilitarians ;* Beer : *History of British
Socialism ;* Brinton : *English Political Thought in the Nineteenth Century ;* J. Bonar :
Philosophy and Political Economy ; and A. N. Whitehead : *Science and the Modern
World* are all vital. In the inter-war period the essential conflicts of theory will be
found in H. J. Laski : *The State in Theory and Practice ;* L. Robbins : *The Nature
and Significance of Economic Science ;* A. Salter : *Recovery ; Tariffs :* ' *The Case
Examined* by Sir William Beveridge and others ; The Liberal Industrial Report
on *Britain's Industrial Future in* 1928. For the period since 1939 F. G. Hayek :
Road to Serfdom (1944) ; J. E. Meade : *Planning and the Price Mechanism* (1948) ;
W. A. Lewis : *The Principles of Economic Planning* (1949).

Special studies.—The student or general reader who wishes to come most
swiftly to the underlying ideas should read :—Jacob Viner : *Adam Smith and
Laissez-Faire* (Chapter 5 of *Adam Smith,* 1776-1926, University of Chicago
Press, 1926) ; J. M. Keynes : *The End of Laissez-Faire ;* B. and S. Webb : *The
Decay of Capitalist Civilization ;* Bagehot's *Economic Studies ;* W. S. Jevons :
The State in Relation to Labour ; W. Y. Edgeworth's *Mathematical Psychics,* 1881 ;
J. A. Hobson : *Imperialism.* He may then embark with some security on the
contemporary flood of pro- and anti-communist literature.

The Nature of the Constitution

Four key books are Bagehot : *The English Constitution ;* Dicey : *The Law of
the Constitution ;* W. I. Jennings : *The Law and the Constitution ;* H. R. G. Greaves :
The British Constitution (1938). These are the best introductions to the constitution
before 1867, the constitution before the Parliament Act, 1911, and the constitution
before 1939. W. I. Jennings : *Cabinet Government* (1936) and *Parliament* (1939)
are complete and masterly for their period. For reference on legal minutiæ
Halsbury's *Laws of England* (the Volumes on Constitution Law) and the many
editions of Anson's *Law and Custom of the Constitution* are indispensable. A. L.
Lowell : *The Government of England,* 2 vols., provides an excellent survey of the
constitution before 1914.

Special studies.—Cabinet Government to the Accession of Queen Victoria, by
W. I. Jennings, *Economica,* November, 1931, and February, 1932 ; H. J. Laski : *The
British Cabinet : A Study of its Personnel,* 1801-1924 (Fabian Tract 223) ; *The
Constitution Under Strain,* by W. I. Jennings, *Political Quarterly,* 1932, p. 194 ;
Sidney Webb : *What Happened in* 1931 (Fabian Tract 237). R. L. Schulyer :
Parliament and the British Empire (New York, 1929), Chapter 5, is the best introduction to the constitutional development of the Empire. A. B. Keith's collection
of *Speeches and Documents on the British Dominions,* 1918-1931 (World's Classics) is
useful. For the period since 1939 L. S. Amery : *Thoughts in the Constitution*
(1947) ; W. Harrison : *Government of Britain.* Churchill's *Second World War* is
full of information about Cabinet organization and administrative machinery.

Parties and Politics

The essential documents are scattered among innumerable biographies and
autobiographies. No one of the political parties has yet inspired a good and
comprehensive history of itself. A few of the more important biographies, autobiographies and letters are :—*The Letters of Queen Victoria,* edited by A. C.
Benson, Viscount Esher and G. E. Buckle, in 9 vols. ; Sir Sidney Lee : *Edward
VII ;* C. S. Parker : *Sir Robert Peel* from his private papers, 3 vols., and *Life and
Letters of Sir James Graham ;* Morley's *Lives* of Gladstone and Cobden ; the *Life*

of Disraeli, by Moneypenny and Buckle ; Gwynn and Tuckwell : *Life of Sir C. W. Dilke;* G. M. Trevelyan : *Life of John Bright ;* Bernard Holland : *Life of the Duke of Devonshire;* Lady Victoria Hicks-Beach : *Life of Michael Hicks-Beach ;* Lady Gwendolen Cecil : *Life of Robert, Marquis of Salisbury* (in progress) ; The Marquis of Crewe : *Lord Rosebery ;* A. G. Gardiner : *Life of Sir William Harcourt ;* Lord Edmond Fitzmaurice : *Life of Lord Granville ;* J. A. Spender's *Life* of Campbell-Bannerman ; J. L. Garvin : *Life of Joseph Chamberlain* (in progress) ; The Earl of Ronaldshay : *Life of Lord Curzon ;* J. A. Spender and Cyril Asquith : *Life of Lord Oxford and Asquith ;* Lord Balfour's *Chapters of Autobiography* and Blanche E. C. Dugdale : *Arthur James Balfour, First Earl of Balfour ;* Sir Austen Chamberlain : *Down the Years* and *Politics from the Inside ;* D. Lloyd George : *War Memoirs ;* Lord Snowden's *Autobiography.*

For the early nineteenth century the *Greville Journal* and for the later the *Journals and Letters of Reginald Viscount Esher* have a special value.

Special studies.—J. R. M. Butler : *The Passing of the Great Reform Bill ;* H. W. C. Davis : *The Age of Grey and Peel* (1929) ; S. Maccoby : *English Radicalism ;* Charles Seymour : *Electoral Reform in England and Wales,* 1832-1885 ; C. S. Emden : *The People and the Constitution* (Oxford, 1933) ; W. E. Williams : *The Rise of Gladstone to the Leadership of the Liberal Party* (1934) ; Frank Hardie : *The Political Influence of Queen Victoria ;* Graham Wallas : *Human Nature in Politics* (1908) ; E. Wertheimer : *Portrait of the Labour Party ;* G. T. Garratt : *Mugwumps and the Labour Party* (1932). G. D. H. Cole : *British Working Class Politics* 1832-1914 (1941) ; Francis Williams : *The Triple Challenge* (1948).

PARLIAMENT

G. F. M. Campion : *Introduction to the Procedure of the House of Commons* (1929) provides a useful introduction to the standard and voluminous works of Anson : *Law and Custom of the Constitution ;* May : *Parliamentary Practice ;* and Redlich : *Procedure of the House of Commons* (3 vols., tr. by A. E. Steinthal, 1908). Jennings : *Parliament* (1938).

For the House of Lords, Lees-Smith : *Second Chambers in Theory and Practice ;* J. A. R. Marriott : *Second Chambers ;* G. B. Roberts : *Functions of an English Second Chamber* (1926) ; two Fabian Pamphlets : 183, *The Reform of the House of Lords ;* and 213, *The Problem of a Second Chamber* should also be consulted. Martin Lindsay : *Shall we Reform the Lords?* (1948) is wise and succinct.

Special studies.—J. A. Thomas : *The House of Commons,* 1832-67 ; *A Functional Analysis* in *Economica,* March, 1925 ; and a longer work by the same author on the same subject in MSS. at the University of London Library ; H. R. G. Greaves : *Personal Origins and Inter-relations of the Houses of Parliament* (since 1832), *Economica,* June, 1929 ; W. I. Jennings : *Parliamentary Reform,* 1934, the best critical survey of the problem of parliamentary procedure at the time. *The Third Report from the Select Committee on Procedure* (189 of 1946) has an excellent Appendix by the Clerk of the House giving a critical analysis of modern procedure.

ADMINISTRATION

There is no good general history of the development of government departments since 1832 though there are excellent studies of some departments. A. R. Lowell : *The Government of England* provides a good general survey. The *Whitehall* series, edited by Sir James Marchant, is a series of studies of individual departments. Among them are Sir Thomas L. Heath : *The Treasury ;* Sir Edward Troup : *The Home Office ;* Sir Evelyn Murray : *The Post Office ;* Sir H. Llewellyn Smith : *The Board of Trade.* H. Finer : *Theory and Practice of Modern Government* contains a study of the nature and necessity of administrative machinery.

Special studies of departments.—A. J. V. Durell : *Parliamentary Grants* (Gieves, 1917) is the best authority on all aspects of Treasury control. It contains an exhaustive bibliography of the relevant parliamentary reports. It should be supplemented by the *Minutes of Evidence to the Royal Commission on the Civil Service,* 1929-31, particularly the evidence of Sir Warren Fisher. The *Report on Machinery of Government,* Cmd. 9230, of 1918, is the key to many post-war developments. There is a collection of MSS. material in the library of the London School of Economics on which the report of this commission was based. The problem of a Ministry of Justice is discussed in R. C. K. Ensor : *Courts and Judges.*

The organization of the Civil Service.—The best introduction to the modern Civil Service is to be found in three government publications : *Report of the Royal Commission on the Civil Service,* 1929-31, Cmd. 3909, 1931 ; Introductory Memoranda relating to the Civil Service submitted by the Treasury, 1930 ; Appendix VIII to the *Minutes of Evidence of the Royal Commission on the Civil Service.* H. R. G. Greaves : *The Civil Service in the Changing State* (1947) is the best recent short study. W. K. Hancock and M. M. Gowing : *British War Economy* (1949) is an unsurpassed tribute to the Civil Service.

Special studies.—Sir William Beveridge : *The Public Service in Peace and War ;* Prof. H. J. Laski's Introduction to Sir Henry Taylor's *The Statesman* (reprint by Heffer) ; Flynn : *Problems of the Civil Service,* 1928. Also *The Development of the Civil Service* (P. S. King, 1922) ; Leonard D. White : *Whitley Councils in the British Civil Service.* There are many important articles in the *Journal of Public Administration* and in *The Political Quarterly* on general and technical problems of Civil Service organization. The 1939-45 war produced many special studies : Sir Oliver Franks : *Central Planning and Control in Peace and War* (1947) : *The Experience of a University Teacher in the Civil Service* (1947) ; Sir John Henderson : *The Organisation of Economic studies in Relation to the Problems of Government* (1947) : *The Machinery of Government* (Romanes Lecture 1946) ; H. V. Rhodes : *Setting up a New Government Department* (1949).

Delegated Legislation and Administrative Law.—On Delegated Legislation, Carr : *Delegated Legislation,* 1921 ; Willis : *Parliamentary Powers of English Government Departments* (Harvard) should be consulted. On Administrative Law, W. A. Robson : *Justice and Administrative Law* (1928 and later editions) ; F. J. Port : *Administrative Law,* 1929 : and the *Report on Ministers' Powers,* Cmd. 4060.

Local Government.—W. I. Jennings : *Principles of Local Government Law,* 1931 ; W. A. Robson : *The Development of Local Government ;* S. and B. Webb : *English Local Government.* There is a short *History of Local Government* by K. B. Smellie (1950). V. D. Lipman : *Local Government Areas* 1834-95 (1949) and Peter Self : *Regionalism* (1949) explain the problem of areas.

REFERENCES

CHAPTER I

[1] Jacob Viner : Adam Smith & Laissez-Faire. Chapter V of *Adam Smith* 1776-1926 (Lectures to commemorate the sesquicentennial of the publication of the *Wealth of Nations*), University of Chicago Press, p. 126.

[2] Jacob Viner, op. cit., p. 128.

[3] ibid., p. 144.

[4] ibid., pp. 144-145.

[5] Leslie Stephen : *English Utilitarians*, Vol. II., p. 218.

[6] ibid., p. 219.

[7] Dicey : *Law and Opinion in England*, 2nd edition, p. 306.

[8] Halevy : *Histoire du Peuple Anglais*, Vol. III., p. 79.

[9] Paine : *Rights of Man*, Part 2, Chap. 1.

[10] J. H. Clapham : *Economic History of Modern Britain*, Vol. I., p. 378.

[11] Dicey : *Law and Opinion in England*, 2nd edition, p. 306.

[12] Leslie Stephen : *English Utilitarians*, Vol. 2, p. 53.

[13] Hyde F. E. : *Gladstone at the Board of Trade*, pp. 54-8.

[14] Leslie Stephen : *English Utilitarians*, Vol. 3, p. 164.

[15] J. H. Clapham : *Economic History of Modern Britain*, Vol. I., p. 378.

[16] ibid., Vol. II., p. 389.

[17] F. E. Hyde : *Gladstone at the Board of Trade*, p. 35.

[18] Bowley : *England's Foreign Trade*, 2nd edition, p. 48.

[19] J. H. Clapham : *Economic History of Modern Britain*, Vol. 2, p. 398.

[20] F. E. Hyde : *Gladstone at the Board of Trade*, p. 51.

[21] Bowley : *England's Foreign Trade*, p. 55.

[22] F. E. Hyde : *Gladstone at the Board of Trade*, p. 186.

[23] ibid., p. 190.

[24] J. H. Clapham : *Economic History of Modern Britain*, Vol. II., p. 178.

[25] H. A. Shannon : The Coming of General Limited Liability. *Economic History* (Supp. to *Economic Journal*), January, 1931, p. 278.

[26] ibid., p. 286.

[27] ibid., p. 287.

[28] Milne-Bailey : *Trade Unions and the State* (1934), p. 175.

[29] ibid., p. 176.

[30] Dicey : *Law and Opinions in England*, p. 199.

[31] Milne-Bailey, *Trade Unions and the State*, 181-2.

[32] ibid., p. 183.

[33] McCulloch : Historical Sketch of the Bank of England, 1831, cited Vera C. Smith : *The Rationale of Central Banking* (1936), pp. 63-5.

[34] S. J. Loyd : Further Reflections on the State of the Currency, 1837, cited Vera C. Smith, p. 69.

[35] Tooke : *History of Prices*, Vol. III., p. 206, cited Vera C. Smith, p. 69.

[36] Vera C. Smith, op. cit., p. 125.

[37] Hyde F. E. *Gladstone at the Board of Trade*, p. 139.

[38] ibid., p. 136-7.

[39] Cleveland Stevens : *English Railways and their Relation to the State*, p. 60.

[40] J. H. Clapham : *Economic History of Modern Britain*, Vol. 2, p. 410.

[41] Farrer : *The State in its Relation to Trade*, pp. 130-131, quoting Giffen in the series *The English Citizen*, 1883.

REFERENCES

⁴² Knowles : *Industrial and Commercial Revolutions*, p. 116.
⁴³ W. Stanley Jevons : *The State in Relation to Labour*, p. 87.
⁴⁴ Macaulay : *Gladstone on Church and State*, p. 3.
⁴⁵ *Table Talk*, Feb. 22, 1832.
⁴⁶ Coleridge.
⁴⁷ Leslie Stephen : *English Utilitarians*, Vol. 2, p. 58.
⁴⁸ ibid., p. 60.
⁴⁹ J. A. Thomas : *The House of Commons*, 1832-1901.
⁵⁰ Halevy : *Histoire du Peuple Anglais*, Vol. 3, p. 228.
⁵¹ Peel : *Memoirs*, 1857 edition, Vol. II., pp. 72, 76, 78.
⁵² G. M. Young : *Early Victorian England*, Vol. II., p. 465.
⁵³ Frank Smith : *History of Education*, p. 258.
⁵⁴ Parker's *Life and Letters of Sir James Graham*, 1792-1861, Vol. I., p. 346.
⁵⁵ G. M. Young : *Early Victorian England*, Vol. 2, p. 465.
⁵⁶ For details of land tenure and land acts see M. Bonn : *Modern Ireland and her Agrarian Problem ;* and W. F. Bailey : *Irish Land Acts.*
⁵⁷ Sidney and Beatrice Webb :*Decay of Capitalist Civilization*, p. 155-6.
⁵⁸ J. H. Clapham : *Economic History of Modern Britain*, Vol. 2, p. 482.

CHAPTER II

¹ C. S. Parker : *Life and Letters of Sir James Graham*, 1792-1861, Vol. 2, pp. 367-8.
² Table Talk, Nov. 1, 1830.
³ J. R. M. Butler : *Passing of the Great Reform Bill*, p. 236.
⁴ G. T. Garratt : *Lord Brougham* (1935), p. 254.
⁵ S. Maccoby : *English Radicalism*, 1832-52 (1935), p. 60.
⁶ J. R. M. Butler, op. cit., 227.
⁷ Charles Seymour : *Electoral Reform in England and Wales* (1832-1885), 1915, p. 88.
⁸ ibid., p. 97.
⁹ Morley : *Life of Cobden* (1883 edition), p. 84.
¹⁰ M. Ostragorski : *Democracy and the Organisation of Political Parties* (1902 edition), Vol. 1, p. 142.
¹¹ J. K. Buckley : *Joseph Parkes of Birmingham* (1926), p. 138.
¹² C. S. Parker's *Sir Robert Peel*, Vol. 2, p. 368 (1899 edition), Nov. 8, 1838. Peel to Mr. Arbuthnot.
¹³ Palmerston to Gladstone.
¹⁴ Lord George Hamilton : *Parliamentary Reminiscences*, 1868-85, p. 3.
¹⁵ Parker's *Peel*, Vol. 2, p. 487. Mrs. Disraeli to Sir Robert Peel. Sept. 5, 1841 (confidential).
¹⁶ C. S. Parker's *Graham*, Vol. 1, p. 256.
¹⁷ T. H. Ward, *Reign of Queen Victoria*, Vol. 1, p. 33.
¹⁸ Buckley : *Joseph Parkes*, p. 154.
¹⁹ H. W. Carless Davis : *Age of Grey and Peel* (1929), p. 268.
²⁰ ibid., passim., Chap. XI.
²¹ Parker's *Peel*, Vol. 3, p. 617-618 (quotation from the summary of Peel's life by his grandson, the Hon. George Peel, pp. 561-622).
²² H. W. C. Davis : *Age of Grey and Peel*, p. 299.
²³ Halevy : *Histoire du Peuple Anglais*, Vol. 3, p. 179.
²⁴ T. E. Kebbel : *History of Toryism* (1886), p. 299.
²⁵ H. R. G. Greaves : *Personal Origins and Inter-relations of the Houses of Parliament* (since 1832), *Economica*, June, 1929.
²⁶ S. Maccoby : *English Radicalism*, p. 68.
²⁷ J. K. Buckley : *Joseph Parkes*, pp. 157-8.
²⁸ H. W. C. Davis : *Age of Grey and Peel*, p. 239.

[29] Halevy : *Histoire du Peuple Anglais*, Vol. 3, p. 183.
[30] Maccoby : *English Radicalism*, p. 65.
[31] ibid., pp. 130-131.
[32] ibid., pp. 143-144.
[33] Greville : *Journal*, Feb. 5, 1842.
[34] Scrope : *Life of Lord Sydenham*, p. 89.
[35] Trevelyan : *John Bright*, p. 184.
[36] ibid., p. 177.
[37] ibid., p. 177.
[38] Sir J. Graham to Mr. Lewis, April 22, 1848 : Parker's *Graham*, Vol. 2. p. 69.
[39] ibid., Vol. 2, p. 90.
[40] *Later Correspondence of Lord John Russell*, 1840-78, Vol. 2, p. 102.
[40A] ibid., Vol. 2, p. 222.
[40B] Parker's *Graham*, Vol. 2, p. 178.
[41] ibid., Vol. 2, pp. 295-6.
[42] W. E. Williams : *Rise of Gladstone to Leadership of the Liberal Party*, pp. 47-8.
[43] G. C. Brodrick : *English Land and English Landlords* (1881), p. 166. Cf.
Clapham : *Economic History of Modern Britain*, Vol. 2, p. 253.
[44] Walpole's *Russell*, p. 63.
[45] Holland's *Devonshire*. Palmerston to Devonshire, Feb. 7, 1863, Vol. 1, p. 55.
[46] H. W. C. Davis : *Age of Grey and Peel*, pp. 269-70.
[47] C. S. Emden : *The People and the Constitution*, p. 147.
[48] Hansard : 59, 3rd series, p. 71.
[49] C. S. Emden : *The People and the Constitution*, p. 148.
[50] *Letters of Queen Victoria*, 1837-43, Vol. 1, pp. 167-8, May 10, 1839.
[51] ibid., Vol. 2, p. 91. July 16, Queen to Russell.
[52] ibid., Vol. 2, pp. 62-3. Dec. 21, 1845, Peel to the Queen.
[53] Parker's *Graham*, Vol. 2, p. 42.
[54] Disraeli to Derby, Dec. 19, 1853. Buckle's *Disraeli*, Vol. III p. 529.
[55] Parker's *Graham*, Vol. 2, pp. 198-9.
[56] Morley's *Gladstone*, Vol. 1, p. 527.
[57] Fitzmaurice's *Granville*, Vol. 1, p. 293.
[58] Parker's *Graham*, Vol. 2, p. 376.
[59] Fitzmaurice's *Granville*, Vol. 1, pp. 340-41.
[60] Greville : *Journal*, Aug. 15, 1835.
[61] Morley's *Gladstone*, Vol. II., p. 208.
[62] *Later Correspondence of Lord John Russell*, Vol. 2, p. 351.
[63] A. D. Elliott's *Goschen*, Vol. 1, p. 84.
[64] Parker's *Graham*, Vol. 2, p. 316.
[65] Buckle's *Disraeli*, Vol. 4, p. 405.
[66] J. Redlich : *The Procedure of the House of Commons* (1908 edition), Vol. 1, Book 1, Part 2, for material here used.
[67] Parker's *Graham*, Vol. 1, pp. 288-9.
[68] ibid., Vol. 1, p. 239.
[69] W. H. Dawson : *Cobden and Foreign Policy*, p. 40.
[70] Buckle's *Disraeli*, Vol. 4, p. 156.
[71] Parker's *Graham*, Vol. 1, Chap. XV.
[72] Greville : *Journal*, Sept. 17, 1841.

CHAPTER III

[1] MSS. evidence before Haldane *Committee on Machinery of Government*, 1918. From material in the library of the London School of Economics. The phrase quoted is G. B. Shaw's.
[2] Miss Nightingale to Mr. Herbert, Nov. 18th, 1859, quoted Lord Stanmore : *Memoir of Sidney Herbert*, Vol. II., p. 369. For Army administration 1854-68 and subsequent reform see Sir Robert Biddulph : *Lord Cardwell at the War Office* (1904).

REFERENCES

3 J. W. Fortescue : *History of the British Army*, Vol. XI., p. 24.
4 Lord Edmond Fitzmaurice's *Life of Granville* : Vol. I, p. 140, Jan. 10, 1856.
5 *Life of Lord Ripon*, Vol. I., p. 171.
6 J. S. Omond : *Parliament and the Army*, 1642-1904 (Cambridge, 1933), p. 93.
7 Stanmore's *Sidney Herbert*, Vol. I. p. 292.
8 Omond : *Parliament and the Army*, p. 94.
9 ibid., p. 99.
10 ibid., pp. 111-112.
11 ibid., p. 108.
12 ibid., pp. 114.
13 ibid., p. 113.
14 ibid., p. 114.
15 H. W. Richmond : *National Policy and Naval Strength* (1928), p. 241.
16 ibid., p. 244.
17 ibid., p. 244.
18 Evidence of Sir James Graham, Parliamentary Papers, 1861, Vol. V., Q., 804-6.
19 H. W. Richmond : *International Policy and Naval Strategy*, p. 249.
20 Harold Nicolson : *Political Quarterly*, 1936, p. 209.
21 C. K. Webster : *Study of Nineteenth-Century Diplomacy*, p. 17.
22 Cambridge *History of British Foreign Policy*, Vol. II., p. 106.
23 Webster : *Study of Nineteenth-Century Diplomacy*, p. 15.
24 Cambridge *History of British Foreign Policy*, Vol. III., p. 588.
25 ibid., p. 577.
26 ibid., p. 589.
27 Maxwell's *Life of Clarendon*, Vol. II., p. 281.
28 Parliamentary Papers, 1864, Vol. VII., Q. 2450.
29 ibid., Q. 2581.
30 ibid., Q. 2563.
31 ibid., Q. 2581.
32 From unpublished study of Dr. H. L. Hall on *Colonial Office*.
33 Sir William Molesworth.
34 H. L. Hall, op. cit.
35 For Treasury control see A. J. V. Durell : *Principles and Practice of the System of Control over Parliamentary Grants* (1917) for full details and references to official papers.
36 Andrew Lang : *Sir Stafford Northcote* (1891 ed.), pp. 73 and 111.
37 These criticisms are to be found in the published memoranda on the Northcote and Trevelyan Report, 1853.
38 25 Feb., 1838. *Queen Victoria Letters*, 1837-61, Vol. I., p. 106.
39 Lady G. Cecil's *Life of Salisbury*, Vol. III., p. 205.
40 Algernon West : *Contemporary Portraits*.
41 Greville : *Journal*, Sept. 29, 1841.
42 Fitzmaurice's *Life of Granville* : p. 177 and cf. p. 29.
43 *Gladstone Papers* : Autobiography, 1897.
44 Seton Watson : *Gladstone, Disraeli, and the Eastern Question*, pp. 44-45.
45 *Quarterly Review*, Vol. 261, pp. 41-4.
46 ibid., pp. 42-43.
47 F. W. Maitland : *Justice and Police*, p. 21.
48 ibid., p. 21-22.
49 Justice Bowen in T. H. Ward's : *Reign of Queen Victoria*, Vol. I., pp. 282-3.
50 ibid., p. 285.
51 Viscount Birkenhead : *Points of View*, Vol. I., pp. 97-8. The Essay on the Ministry of Justice, pp. 92-129 would seem to be the official case against that institution.
52 Selborne *Memorials*, Part II., 1865-1895, Vol. I., p. 298.
53 ibid., p. 304.
54 ibid., p. 305.

[55] ibid., pp. 314-315.
[56] Maitland : *Justice and Police*, p. 23.
[57] *Quarterly Review*, Vol. 262, p. 196.
[58] Justice Bowen in T. H. Ward's *Reign of Queen Victoria*, Vol. I, p. 323.
[59] ibid., pp. 324-5.

CHAPTER IV

[1] A. L. Bowley's *England's Foreign Trade*, 1922 edition, pp. 112-113.
[2] For the most systematic eulogy see Leone Levi : *History of British Commerce* 1872.
[3] L. C. A. Knowles : *The Industrial and Commercial Revolutions in Great Britain during the Nineteenth Century*. Part IV.
[4] Morley's *Cobden* (1883 edition), p. 205.
[5] G. C. Allen : *British Industries*, p. 92 (1935 edition).
[6] R. C. K. Ensor : *England*, 1870-1914, p. 151.
[7] ibid., p. 110.
[8] ibid., p. 110.
[9] *Britain's Industrial Future*. (The report of the Liberal Industrial Inquiry 1928), p. 9.
[10] A. L. Bowley's *England's Foreign Trade*, pp. 15-16.
[11] ibid., p. 146.
[12] G. C. Allen : *British Industries*, p. 13.
[13] W. S. Jevons : *Methods of Social Reform* (edition 1883) Essay on Amusements of the People, published 1878, pp. 20-21.
[14] ibid., p. 5.
[15] ibid., p. 6.
[16] ibid., p. 3.
[17] *Representative Government*, 1861, *passim*.
[18] Sir Henry Maine : *Village Communities* (1871 edition), p. 60.
[19] ibid., p. 59.
[20] Report of *Cranworth Commission*, 1867.
[21] Holdsworth : *Introduction to the Land Law*, p. 320.
[22] A. V. Dicey, L.Q.R. XXI., p. 222.
[23] Frederick Pollock : *The Land Laws*, p. 185.
[24] Maitland : *Collected Papers*, Vol. I, p. 191.
[25] Holdsworth : *Introduction to the Land Law*, p. 319.
[26] cited J. P. Thomas : *Study of House of Commons*, 1832-1901.
[27] Bonn : *Modern Ireland and her Agrarian problem*, p. 60.
[28] Dicey : *Law and Opinion in England*, pp. 265-6.
[29] Bailey : *Irish Land Acts*, p. 18.
[30] Thomas : op. cit., p. 137.
[31] Bailey : *Irish Land Acts, passim*.
[32] Dec. 24, 1885, Harcourt to Hartington. A. G. Gardiner : *Life of Sir William Harcourt*, Vol. I, p. 553.
[33] Bailey : *Irish Land Acts, passim*.
[34] Ensor : *England 1870-1914*, p. 113.
[35] Cmd. 3897 of 1931. *Committee on Finance and Industry*, pp. 162-3.
[36] ibid., pp. 162-163.
[37] H. Feis : *Europe, the World's Banker* (Yale 1930), p. 83.
[38] Allen : *British Industries*, p. 11.
[39] H. Feis, op. cit. p. 83.
[40] ibid., p. 85.
[41] ibid., p. 87.
[42] ibid., p. 96.
[43] ibid., p. 87.
[44] ibid., p. 117.
[45] Cmd. 3897, pp. 14-15.

[46] ibid., *passim*.
[47] W. S. Jevons : *Methods of Social Reform*, p. 120.
[48] ibid., p. 108.
[49] J. R. Hicks : *Theory of Wages*, p. 165.
[50] W. S. Jevons : *Methods of Social Reform*, p. 108.
[51] F. Y. Y. Edgeworth : *Mathematical Psychics*, 1881, pp. 44-5.
[52] ibid., pp. 44-5.
[53] Sir Wm. Beveridge : *Unemployment* (1930 edition), p. 256.
[54] ibid., p. 216.
[55] Sir Wm. Beveridge : *Unemployment* (1930 edition), pp. 216 and 198.
[56] ibid., p. 197.
[57] ibid., p. 209.
[58] ibid., p. 200.
[59] ibid., p. 209.
[60] ibid., p. 211.
[61] ibid., p. 202.
[62] ibid., p. 199.
[63] ibid., p. 212.
[64] Cmd. 363 : *An Outline of the Practice of Preventive Medicine*, by Sir George Newman, 1919, p. 13.
[65] p. 18.
[66] ibid., p. 10.
[67] ibid., p. 60.
[68] Article, *Times*, 15-7-35.
[69] Mess H. A. : *Factory Legislation and its Administration*, 1891-1924 *passim* and cf. Times 20-7-33.
[70] Sympathetically described by Max Beerbohm in *Christmas Garland*.
[71] *Newcastle Report*, 1858-61, Vol. I, p. 93., pp. 1861, Vol. XXI.
[72] Morley's *Cobden* (1906 edition), p. 548.
[73] Thomas : *Study of House of Commons*, p. 173.
[74] Helen Wodehouse : *The History of Education*, p. 202.
[75] Thomas : *Study of House of Commons*, p. 119.
[76] R. C. K. Ensor, op. cit., p. 501, citing Marshall in Cmd. 321 of 1908.
[77] Lady G. Cecil's *Life of Lord Salisbury*. Reference mislaid. Might one not say *passim* ?
[78] See H. F. Egerton : *History of British Colonial Policy*, *passim*.
[79] cf. Sir James Stephen : *Letters with Biographical Notes*, (1906), pp. 49-52.
[80] Buckle's *Disraeli*, Vol. V. p. 195.
[81] and [82] For the development of Colonial Self Government, see Chap. 5 of R. L. Schuyler : *Parliament and the British Empire*, p. 207.
[83] *Report of the Inter Imperial Relations Committee Imperial Conference*, 1926. Cmd. 2768, p. 14.
[84] See *Colonial Military Defence Committee* 1861, XIII. (No. 423).
[85] ibid., Q. 2093.
[86] Morrell W. P. : *British Colonial Policy in the Age of Peel and Russell*.
[87] ibid.
[88] ibid.
[89] Lady G. Cecil : *Life of Lord Salisbury*, Vol. 3, Chapters 8-11 on the Partition of Africa.
[90] ibid., Vol. 4, pp. 225-6.
[91] L. C. A. Knowles : *Industrial and Commercial Revolutions*, pp. 332-59.
[92] ibid., page 328 footnote.
[93] ibid., p. 341-59.
[94] Lady G. Cecil : *Life of Salisbury*, Vol. 2, p. 80, Salisbury to Sir Louis Mallet, Jan. 14, 1876.
[95] ibid., Sept. 23, 1876, Salisbury to Beaconsfield, pp. 85-6.
[96] Buckle's *Disraeli*, Vol. 6, p. 367. Beaconsfield to Drummond Wolff.
[97] A. F. Pribram : *England and Europe*, 1871-1914, p. 14.

[98] ibid., p. 18.
[99] ibid., p. 28.
[100] Lady V. Hicks-Beach : *Life of Sir Michael Hicks-Beach*, Vol. 1, p. 162. Jan. 15, 1880, Hicks-Beach to Sir Bartle Frere.
[101] Bernard Holland : *Life of the Duke of Devonshire*, Vol. 1, p. 368.
[102] Granville to the Great Powers 1883, cited *Cambridge History of Foreign Policy*, Vol. 3, p. 174.
[103] A. F. Pribram : *England and Europe*, 1871-1914, p. 31.
[104] Gooch : *Before the War*, Vol. 1, p. 5.
[105] A. F. Pribram, op. cit., pp. 87-8.
[106] ibid., pp. 55-6.
[107] Gooch : *Before the War*, Vol. 1, p. 22.
[108] Pribram, op. cit., p. 83.
[109] Gooch, op. cit., Vol. 1, p. 70.
[110] ibid., p. 54.
[111] Pribram, op. cit., p. 94.
[112] ibid., p. 118.
[113] Esher : *Journal*, Vol. 2, p. 267.
[114] Balfour to Lord Lansdowne, Nov. 6, 1908.
[115] A. E. Gathorne Hardy : *Gathorne Hardy : A Memoir*, Vol. II., p. 193.
[116] Elliot : *Life of Goschen*, Vol. 1, p. 294 (1911, 2nd edition).
[117] 17 June, 1886, to Sir Arthur Gordon. Selborne : *Memorials*, Part II., Vol. II., p. 227.
[118] Garvin : *Chamberlain*, p. 512, Vol. 2.
[119] Holland. *Life of Devonshire*, Vol. 2, p. 71.
[120] *Gathorne Hardy*, Vol. 2, p. 345.
[121] Crewe : *Lord Rosebery*, Vol. 2, p. 623.
[122] Edgeworth : *Mathematical Psychics*.
[123] Buckle's *Disraeli*, Vol. V., p. 88.
[124] Esher : *Journal*, Vol. 1, p. 76, Sept. 30, 1880.
[125] Selborne *Memorials*, Part II, Vol. 2, p. 182, Nov. 5, 1885.
[126] Godfrey Elton : *England Arise*, p. 94, quoting Shaw.
[127] ibid., p. 113.

CHAPTER V

[1] Hansard, Vol. 186, 3rd series, pp. 1568-73.
[2] cf. Gathorne Hardy, August 9, 1867, in A. E. Hardy's *Gathorne Hardy*, Vol. I., p. 212.
[3] A. Elliot : *Life of Goschen*, Vol. I., p. 161.
[4] Seymour : *Electoral Reform in England and Wales*, Chap. X., p. 283.
[5] ibid., p. 346.
[6] Buckle's : *Disraeli*, Vol. V., p. 141 and see A. G. Gardiner's *Life of Harcourt*, Vol. I., p. 239.
[7] W. E. Williams : *Rise of Gladstone to leadership of Liberal Party*, p. 173.
[8] Selborne : *Memorials*, Part II., Vol. 2, p. 99.
[9] ibid., p. 122.
[10] Lady G. Cecil's *Salisbury*, Vol. III., pp. 122-4.
[11] A. E. Hardy's *Gathorne Hardy*, Dec. 3, 1884, Vol. II., p. 204.
[12] In *Representative Government*.
[13] Derby to Disraeli, Nov. 22, 1868. Buckle's *Disraeli*, Vol. V., p. 92.
[14] Selborne : *Memorials*, Vol. I., p. 330.
[15] ibid., p. 470.
[16] Cd. 5163, pr. 126, pp. 1910, XXVI.
[17] Holland's *Devonshire*, Vol. II., p. 142.
[18] Disraeli to Corry : Buckle's *Disraeli*, Vol. V., p. 89, Nov 3, 1868.
[19] Maxwell's *W. H. Smith*, Vol. II., p. 26.
[20] Buckle's *Disraeli*, Vol. V., p. 262.

[21] Gladstone.
[22] Buckle's *Disraeli*, Vol. VI., p. 518.
[23] Hill : *Toryism and the People*, p. 38.
[24] ibid., p. 81.
[25] Buckle's *Disraeli*, Vol. V., p. 185.
[26] ibid., p. 185.
[27] ibid., p. 520, Vol. VI.
[28] Lady Cecil's *Salisbury*, Vol. 3, p. 197.
[29] C. S. Emden : *The People and the Constitution*, p. 137.
[30] Holland's *Life of Devonshire*, Vol. I., p. 245.
[31] C. S. Emden, op. cit., p. 135.
[32] A. G. Gardiner : *Life of Harcourt*, Vol. II., p. 407.
[33] Crewe's *Rosebery*, Vol. II., p. 595.
[34] Selborne : *Memorials*, Part II., Vol. II., p. 189.
[35] ibid., p. 189.
[36] Crewe's *Rosebery*, Vol. I., p. 246.
[37] Buckle's *Disraeli*, Vol. V., p. 57.
[38] Esher : *Diary*, Dec. 4, 1879, Vol. I., p. 65.
[39] J. A. Spender : *Life of Campbell-Bannerman*, Vol. I., p. 206.
[40] ibid., p. 204.
[41] Article in *Round Table*, December, 1911, p. 75.
[42] Redlich : *Procedure of the House of Commons*, Vol. I., p. 140.
[43] ibid., p. 159.
[44] ibid., p. 170.
[45] *Round Table*, 1911, December, p. 83.
[46] ibid.
[47] ibid.
[48] ibid.
[49] Redlich, op. cit., pp. 198.
[50] *Round Table*, 1911, December, p. 92. Table F.
[51] To Hicks-Beach, Dec. 17, 1874. Lady Hicks-Beach's *Hicks-Beach, I.*, p. 46.
[52] Holland's *Devonshire*, Vol. I., pp. 121-2.
[53] F. Hardie : *Political Influence of Queen Victoria*, p. 55 (in 1878).
[54] Zetland : *Letters of Disraeli to Lady Bradford and Lady Chesterfield*, Vol. I., p. 92.
[55] Buckle's *Disraeli*, Vol. 4, p. 457.
[56] F. Hardie, op. cit., p. 245.
[57] ibid. (citing *Queen Victoria Letters*), p. 76.
[58] Buckle's *Disraeli*, Vol. VI., p. 528 (1880).
[59] H. H. Bolitho has, I think, pointed this out.
[60] Buckle's *Disraeli*, Vol. VI., 214.
[61] ibid., Vol. V., p. 337.
[62] Fitzmaurice : *Life of Granville*, Vol. II., p. 121.
[63] Buckle's *Disraeli*, Vol. V., p. 480.
[64] ibid., Vol. VI., p. 67.
[65] ibid., VI., p. 239.
[66] Acton's *Letters*, p. 78.
[67] Holland's *Devonshire*, Vol. I., pp. 260-2, Dec. 7, 1879.
[68] cf. *Queen Victoria Letters*, 2nd series, Vol. III., Chap. 2, *passim*.
[69] Buckle's *Disraeli*, Vol. V., p. 28.
[70] ibid., Vol. V., p. 33.
[71] ibid., Vol. V., p. 94.
[72] ibid., Vol. V., p. 95 (Disraeli to Queen, Nov. 28, 1868).
[73] Holland's *Devonshire*, Vol. I., pp. 117-9.
[74] Buckle's *Disraeli*, Vol. V., p. 206.
[75] His reason for resignation *Queen Victoria Letters*, 2nd series, Vol. II., p. 317 Mem. 17 Feb., 1874.

[76] Buckle's *Disraeli*, Vol. VI., p. 369.
[77] ibid., Vol. VI., p. 511.
[78] ibid., Vol. VI., p. 514.
[79] ibid., Vol. V., p. 114.
[80] ibid., Vol. IV., p. 586 (see *Queen Victoria Letters*, 2nd series, Vol. I., pp. 497).
[81] *Queen Victoria Letters*, 2nd series, Vol. I., pp. 492-509, for the actual change-over.
[82] *Queen Victoria Letters*, 2nd series, Vol. I., p. 564, Qu's Mem. 3 Dec., 1868.
[83] ibid.
[84] Morley's *Gladstone*, Vol. 2, p. 414.
[85] Parker's *Graham*, Vol. 2, p. 2 and Holland's *Devonshire*, Vol. 2, p. 77.
[86] Hardy's *Diary*, Vol. 2, pp. 364-5.
[87] Fitzmaurice's *Granville*, Vol. 2, p. 2.
[88] Selborne : *Memorials*, Part II., Vol. 2, p. 348.
[89] Knaplund : *Gladstone and Britain's Imperial Policy*, pp. 167-70.
[90] Fitzmaurice's *Granville*, Vol. II., p. 175.
[91] ibid., Vol. II., pp. 1 and 150.
[92] A. G. Gardiner : *Life of Harcourt* (App. II., being Harcourt's Mem. on Morley's chapter on the Cabinet in his *Walpole*).
[93] *Queen Victoria Letters*, 2nd series, Vol. II., p. 323, 23 Feb., 1874.
[94] Buckle's *Disraeli*, Vol. V., p. 295.
[95] *Queen Victoria Letters*, 2nd series, Vol. II., pp. 321-2. Mem. of 20 Feb., 1874.
[96] Buckle's *Disraeli*, Vol. VI., p. 272.
[97] ibid., p. 280.
[98] ibid., p. 280.
[99] Buckle's *Disraeli*, Vol. VI., pp. 194-5.
[100] Balfour : *Autobiography*, p. 113.
[101] Ensor : *England 1870-1914*, p. 30.
[102] Buckle's *Disraeli*, Vol. V., p. 370.
[103] Balfour - *Autobiography*, p. 114.
[104] Buckle's *Disraeli*, Vol. VI., p. 163.
[105] Ensor : *England 1870-1914*, p. 39.
[106] ibid., p. 60.
[107] ibid., p. 47.
[108] Lady Cecil's *Salisbury*.
[109] Introduction to *Radical Programme*.
[110] *Quarterly Review*, Oct., 1883. Article *Disintegration*, by W. E. Forster, p. 538.
[111] Elliot's *Goschen*, Vol. I., pp. 252-3.
[112] *Queen Victoria Letters*, 2nd series, Vol. 3, pp. 75-6, 8 April, 1880.
[113] Holland's *Devonshire*, Vol. I., 260-2 and 274.
[114] ibid., Vol. I., p. 276.
[115] Buckle's *Disraeli*, Vol. VI., p. 538.
[116] Fitzmaurice : *Granville*, Vol. II., pp. 421-2.
[117] Holland's *Devonshire*, Vol I., pp. 397-8.
[118] Lady Hicks-Beach : *Hicks-Beach*, Vol. I., p. 258.
[119] Ensor : *England 1870-1914*, p. 95.
[120] Holland's *Devonshire*, Vol. II., p. 173.
[121] Lady Cecil's *Salisbury*, Vol. III., p. 137.
[122] Garvin's *Chamberlain*, Vol. II., p. 538.
[123] Crewe's *Rosebery*, Vol. II., p. 507.
[124] Garvin's *Chamberlain*, Vol. III., p. 585.
[125] ibid., Vol. III., p. 593.
[126] ibid., Vol. III., p. 599.
[127] Holland's *Devonshire*, Vol. I., p. 397, Dec. 1883.
[128] Lady Cecil's *Salisbury*.
[129] ibid.
[130] Elliot's *Goschen*, Vol. II., pp. 50 and 87.

[131] Lady Cecil's *Salisbury*, Vol. III., p. 310.
[132] ibid., Vol. III., p. 167.
[133] ibid., Vol. III., p. 111.
[134] Lady Hicks-Beach : *Hicks-Beach*, Vol. I., p. 302.
[135] Garvin's *Chamberlain*, Vol. II., p. 423.
[136] *Queen Victoria Letters*, Vol. 2, 3rd series, pp. 172-5, Oct. 28, 1892.
[137] Crewe's *Rosebery*, Vol. II., p. 456.
[138] Gardiner's *Harcourt*, Vol. II., p. 337.
[139] ibid., Vol. II., pp. 338-9.
[140] ibid., Vol. II., p. 271.
[141] Crewe's *Rosebery*, Vol. II., p. 441.
[142] ibid., Vol. II., p. 462.
[143] Garvin's *Chamberlain*, Vol. III., p. 6.
[144] ibid., Vol. III., p. 7.
[145] *Hicks-Beach*, Vol. II., App. A., pp. 359-63.
[146] Garvin's *Chamberlain*, Vol. III., p. 295.
[147] Ensor : *England*, 1870-1914, p. 354.
[148] ibid., p. 372.
[149] J. A. Spender : *Campbell-Bannerman*, Vol. II., p. 101.
[150] ibid., Vol. II., p. 102.
[151] Holland's *Devonshire*, Vol. II., pp. 307-9.
[152] ibid., Vol. II., pp. 340 and 352.
[153] ibid., Vol. II., pp. 352-3.
[154] J. A. Spender : *Campbell-Bannerman*, Vol. II., p. 192.
[155] Ensor : *England* 1870-1914, p. 239.
[156] Esher : *Journals and Letters*, Vol. 2, p. 56.
[157] Spender : *Campbell-Bannerman*, Vol. II., p. 176.
[158] Halevy : *History of the English People*, Vol. 5, p. 6.
[159] Spender : *Campbell-Bannerman*, Vol. II., p. 197.
[160] ibid., Vol. II., p. 200.
[161] Halevy, op. cit., Vol. 5.
[162] Lee : *Edward VII.*, Vol. II., p. 449.
[163] Esher : *Journal and Letters*, Vol. II., p. 136.
[164] Spender : *Campbell-Bannerman*, Vol. II., p. 270.
[165] ibid., Vol. II., p. 281.
[166] Newton's *Lansdowne*, p. 352-3.
[167] Spender's *Campbell-Bannerman*, Vol. II., p. 356.
[168] ibid., p. 357.
[169] ibid., p. 275.
[170] *Life of Birkenhead*, Vol. I., p. 171.
[171] Spender's *Campbell-Bannerman*, Vol. 2, p. 305.
[172] Esher : *Diary*, Vol. II., p. 303.
[173] Ensor : *England* 1870-1914, pp. 413-14.
[174] ibid.
[175] Spender-Asquith : *Life of Asquith*, Vol. I., pp. 257-8.
[176] Esher : *Journal and Letters*, Vol. II., p. 424.
[177] Halevy, op. cit., p. 333, and Ensor, op. cit., p. 424.
[177A] Fitzmaurice's *Granville*, Vol. 2, p. 4.

CHAPTER VI

[1] Omond : *Parliament and the Army*, p. 119.
[2] Temperley : *Victorian Age in Politics*, p. 34.
[3] Ensor : *England* 1870-1914, pp. 10-11.
[4] Gladstone.
[5] Buckle's *Disraeli*, Vol. VI., p. 474, to Lady Bradford, Dec. 26, 1879.
[6] Omond : *Parliament and the Army*, pp. 129-30.

⁷ ibid., p. 132.
⁸ Hartington Commission, Cmd. 5979, pp. 1890, XIX, para. 73.
⁹ Omond, op. cit., pp. 136-7.
¹⁰ ibid., p. 135, citing *Wolseley's Life*, p. 241.
¹¹ ibid., pp. 145-8.
¹² Garvin : *Chamberlain*, Vol. 3, p. 452.
¹³ Lady Hicks-Beach's *Hicks-Beach*, Vol. 2, p. 148.
¹⁴ Omond : *Parliament and the Army*, p. 152.
¹⁵ ibid., p. 154.
¹⁶ *Report of the Committee*, pp. 1904, VIII., section II, para. 4.
¹⁷ Ensor : *England 1870-1914*, p. 287.
¹⁸ ibid., 121.
¹⁹ Lady Cecil's *Salisbury*, Vol. 3, p. 218, Feb 5, 1892.
²⁰ Lady Hicks-Beach : *Hicks-Beach*, Vol 2, p. 57.
²¹ Elliot's *Goschen*, Vol. 2, p. 180, Oct. 1888, W. H. Smith to Goschen.
²² Omond : *Parliament and the Army*, p. 110.
²³ Spender : *Campbell-Bannerman*, Vol. 1, p. 118.
²⁴ Crewe's *Rosebery*, Vol. 2, p. 497.
²⁵ *Royal Commission on War in South Africa*, pp. 1904, Vol. XI.
²⁶ Asquith, *Genesis of the War*, pp. 113-116.
²⁷ Ensor : *England 1870-1914*, p. 433.
²⁷ᴬ Material and quotations from Webb : *English Local Government*, Vol. 8. *English Poor Law History*, Part II., pp. 197-9.
²⁸ ibid., pp. 530-2.
²⁹ Haldane : *Report on Machinery of Government*, 1918, p. 59.
³⁰ See MSS. of Evidence for Haldane Report at London School of Economics.
³¹ John Willis : *Parliamentary Powers of English Government Departments* (Harvard Studies in Administrative Law, Vol. 4, 1933), p. 96.
³² Crewe's *Rosebery*, Vol. 1, p. 170.
³³ ibid., p. 212.
³⁴ Sir Lionel Earle : *Turn over the Page*, 230.
³⁵ Llewellyn Smith : *Board of Trade*, pp. 173 and 195.
³⁶ Lady Hicks-Beach : *Hicks Beach*, Vol. I., Chap. XII.
³⁷ Frank Smith : *Life of Sir James Kay-Shuttleworth*, p. 213.
³⁸ Buckle's *Disraeli*, Vol. 4, Chap. 2., p. 37.
³⁹ In Evidence before Commission.
⁴⁰ 1887 XIX, Q. 12.
⁴¹ ibid., Qu. 2.
⁴² 1865 X App. 1, 70.
⁴³ 1888 XXVII Qu. 10,623.
⁴⁴ ibid., 10,639.
⁴⁵ 1914, XVI., Qu 35,757.
⁴⁶ Lady Cecil's *Salisbury*, Vol. IV., pp. 176-7.
⁴⁷ Hamilton : *Parliamentary Reminiscences*, 1868-85, p. 304, Vol. I.
⁴⁸ In general on the Treasury, see Durell : *Parliamentary Grants*.
⁴⁹ 1870 XII.
⁵⁰ Haldane : *Report on Machinery of Government*, 1918, p. 19.
⁵¹ *Report on Ministers Powers*, Cmd. 4060, p. 5.
⁵² Willis : *Parliamentary Powers of English Government Departments*, p. 153.

CHAPTER VII

¹ Sir Frederick Maurice : *Governments and War*, p. 120.
² J. A. Spender and C. Asquith : *Life of Asquith*, Vol. 2, p. 123.
³ ibid., Vol. 2, p. 124.
⁴ ibid., Vol. 2, p. 127.
⁵ ibid., Vol. 2, p.95.

6 ibid., Vol. 2, p. 100.
7 A. Chamberlain : *Down the Years*, p. 116.
8 Ronaldshay : *Life of Lord Curzon*, Vol. 3, p. 124.
9 *Life of Asquith*, Vol. 2, p. 171.
10 Churchill : *World Crisis* 1915, p. 384.
11 *Life of Asquith*, Vol. 2, p. 130 and 180.
12 Asquith to Lloyd George, Dec. 1, 1916, *Life of Asquith*, Vol. 2, p. 253.
13 Chamberlain : *Down the Years*, p. 111.
14 *Life of Asquith*, Vol. 2, p. 273.
15 Chamberlain : *Down the Years*, p. 116.
16 *Life of Asquith*, Vol. 2, p. 248.
17 Chamberlain : *Down the Years*, p. 113 and 121.
18 ibid., p. 121.
19 It is possible that the King did not ask or that Asquith declined to tender advice as to who should be his successor. Chamberlain, op. cit., pp. 125-6.
20 *Life of Asquith*, Vol. 2, pp. 273-4.
21 Addison : *Politics from Within*, Vol. 1, pp. 267-272.
22 Lloyd George : *Memoirs*, p. 1039.
23 ibid., pp. 1077-9.
24 ibid., pp. 1067-1072.
25 Lloyd George : *Memoirs*, p. 1063.
26 ibid., p. 1051.
27 Chamberlain : *Down the Years*, p. 132.
28 *Empire Review*, Articles by C. Jones, Jan, 1924, p. 69.
29 ibid., Dec., 1923, p. 1412.
30 *Life of Asquith*, Vol. 2, p. 122.
31 ibid., Vol. 2, p. 121.
32 Lloyd George : *Memoirs*, p. 1151.
33 Joseph : *Logic*, pp. 184-5.
34 Lloyd George : *Memoirs*, p. 2341.
35 Sir Frederick Maurice : *Governments and War*, p. 124.
36 ibid., p. 127.
37 ibid., pp. 155-6.
38 ibid., p. 128.
39 ibid., p. 128.
40 ibid., p. 130.
41 ibid., p. 134.
42 *Life of Asquith*, Vol. 2, p. 132.
43 Sir F. Maurice : *Governments and War*, p. 132.
44 *Life of Asquith*, Vol. 2, p. 190.
44 Sir Fr. Maurice : *Governments and War*, p. 139.
46 Lloyd George : *Memoirs*, p. 2272.
47 ibid., pp. 2221, 1825.
48 ibid., p. 2192.
49 ibid., p. 2333.
50 ibid., p. 2333.
51 ibid., p. 2347.
52 ibid., p. 2344.
53 E. M. H. Lloyd : *Experiments in State Control*, p. 22.
54 Humbert Wolfe : *Labour Supply and Regulation*, p. 12.
55 ibid., p. 3.
56 ibid., pp. 1 and 2.
57 ibid., p. 3.
58 ibid., p. 3.
59 ibid., p. 297.
60 ibid., p. 217.
61 ibid., p. 120.
62 ibid., p. 99.

[42] ibid., pp. 101-2.
[43] ibid., p. 158.
[44] ibid., pp. 154-5.
[45] ibid., p. 136.
[46] ibid., p. 153.
[47] ibid., p. 50.
[48] ibid., p. 52.
[70] A. E. M. H. Lloyd : Experiments in State Control, p. 16.
[71] ibid., p. 21.
[72] ibid., p. 23.
[73] ibid., p. 25.
[74] Sir William Beveridge : British Food Control, p. 6.
[75] T. H. M. Middleton : Food Production in War, p. 35.
[76] Beveridge : British Food Control, p. 22.
[77] cited Beveridge, op. cit., p. 27.
[78] Beveridge, op. cit., p. 47.
[79] ibid., p. 52.
[80] ibid., p. 335.
[81] ibid., p. 336.
[82] T. H. Middleton : Food Production in War, p. 328.
[83] Beveridge : British Food Control, p. 73.
[84] C. Ernest Fayle : The War and the Shipping Industry, p. 404.
[85] ibid., p. 405.
[86] ibid., p. 404.
[87] ibid., p. 199.
[88] ibid., p. 402.
[89] ibid., p. 199.
[90] ibid., p. 205.
[91] ibid., p. 217.
[92] ibid., p. 239.
[93] ibid., p. 245.
[94] ibid., p. 248.
[95] ibid., p. 247.
[96] ibid., p. 247.
[97] ibid., p. 254.
[98] Official History of the War in the Air, Vol. 1, p. 211.
[99] Section 8.
[100] War in the Air, Vol. 3, p. 283.
[100] E. M. H. Lloyd : Experiments in State Control, pp. 352-3.
[101] Middleton : Food Production in War, p. 104.
[102] ibid., p. 168.
[103] Lloyd : Experiments in State Control, p. 272.
[104] Fayle : The War and the Shipping Industry, pp. 409 and 337.
[105] H. Wolfe : Labour Supply and Regulation, p. 151.
[106] ibid., pp. 120 and 141.
[107] E. M. H. Lloyd : Experiments in State Control, p. 50.
[108] ibid., p. 52.
[109] ibid., p. 64.
[110] Fayle : The War and the Shipping Industry, p. 221.
[111] China Mutual v. Maclay, 1918, 1.K.B. 33.
[112] Fayle, op. cit., p. 237.
[113] ibid., p. 216.
[114] E. M. H. Lloyd : Experiments in State Control, pp. 260-2.
[115] ibid., pp. 261-2.
[116] ibid., p. 264.
[117] Fayle : op. cit., p. 401.
[118] ibid., p. 337.
[119] E. M. H. Lloyd : op. cit., p. 390.

REFERENCES

¹¹⁰ ibid., p. 394.
¹¹¹ ibid., p. 390.

CHAPTER VIII

1 Minutes of Evidence to *Committee on Finance and Industry*, 1931, Cmd. 3897, Qu. 6673.
2 Fayle : *The War and the Shipping Industry*, p. 6.
3 Sir W. T. Layton : *Economic Situation of Great Britain*, 1931, p. 15.
Evidence Cmd. 3897, Niemeyer Qu. 6818.
5 Cmd. 3897, p. 4, para. 8.
6 A. C. Pigou and Colin Clark : *Economic Position of Great Britain*, p. 34.
7 D. H. Macgregor, p. 94.
8 League of Nations : *World Economic Survey*, 1934-5, p. 66.
9 Cmd. 3897, p. 116.
10 League of Nations, *World Economic Survey*, 1934-5, pp. 65-6.
11 Cmd. 3897, p. 92.
12 Cmd. 3897 Minutes of Evidence, Qu. 3.
13 ibid., Qu. 95.
14 ibid., Qu. 121.
15 J. H. Richardson : *British Economic Foreign Policy*, p. 33.
16 Sir B. Mallet : *British Budgets*, 3rd Series, p. 267, citing Horne's Budget, 1929.
17 J. H. Richardson, *op. cit.*, p. 36.
18 ibid., p. 40, citing Chamberlain, House of Commons, Dec. 21, 1934.
19 ibid., pp. 44-50.
20 Cmd. 3897, p. 7.
21 Cmd. 3897, p. 47.
22 Quoted J. H. Richardson, *op. cit.*, p. 20.
23 J. H. Richardson, *op. cit.*, p. 90.
24 ibid., p. 22.
25 ibid., pp. 94-5.
26 ibid., p. 94.
27 ibid., p. 100.
28 J. A. Spender : *Life of Campbell-Bannerman*, Vol. 2, p. 330.
29 Cd. 8462, pp. 1917 X, *Dominion Royal Commission*, Ch. XV, p. 163.
30 S. H. Bailey; article, *Economica* 1932. *Political Aspects of Discrimination in International Economic Relations*.
31 Churchill, House of Commons, 23 April, 1936, Hansard 1935/6, Vol. 311 p. 328.
32 Ward : *Reign of Queen Victoria*, Vol. 1, pp. 331-49.
33 Gertrude Williams : *The State and the Standard of Living*, p. 335.
34 Ensor : *England 1870-1914*, p. 217.
35 ibid., p. 396.
36 F. Hirst, *Consequences of the War*, p. 235.
37 Gertrude Williams, op. cit., p. 335.
38 Sir W. T. Layton : *Economic Situation of Great Britain*, p. 8.
39 Pigou and Clark, *op. cit.*, Tables, pp. 14-15.
40 League of Nations *Economic Survey* 1934-5, p. 192.
41 ibid., p. 192.
42 ibid., pp. 65-6.
43 G. C. Allen : *British Industries*, 2nd edition, pp. 283-5.
44 Pigou and Clark, *op. cit.*, p. 39.
45 ibid.
46 Ministry of Labour Report, 1936.
47 Committee of 1917.
48 D. H. Macgregor : *Enterprise, Purpose and Profit*, pp. 49-55 for analysis of causes of State control.
49 *Britain's Industrial Future* (report of the Liberal Industrial Enquiry), p. 75.

347

[50] p. 75.
[51] p. 85.
[52] ibid., p. 85.
[53] ibid., p. 85.
[54] Cmd. 3897, p. 166.
[55] *Britain's Industrial Future*, p. 91.
[56] Cannan : cited Geitrude Williams : *The State and the Standard of Living*, p. 321.
[57] D. H. Robertson in Minutes of Evidence to Cmd. 3897, Vol. I, p. 323.
[58] ibid.
[59] ibid., Vol I., Granet, Qu. 9029-36.
[60] ibid., Hopkins Qu. 5690.
[61] G. C. Allen : *British Industries*, p. 35.
[62] ibid., p. 45.
[63] Layton : *Economic Situation of Great Britain*, p. 21.
[64] H. S. Jevons : *British Steel Industry*, p. 29.
[65] ibid., 24-25 and cf. Allen, op. cit., p. 132.
[66] Astor and Murray : *The Planning of Agriculture*, p. 11.
[67] A. Salter, p. VIII of Introduction to Astor and Murray.
[68] *World Agricultural Report* of 1935.
[69] League of Nations *Survey of Economic Conditions* 1934-5, p. 86.
[70] Midland Bank Monthly Review, Aug.-Sept., 1934, p. 4.
[71] J. H. Richardson, op. cit., p. 188.
[72] ibid., p. 197.
[73] ibid., p. 197.
[74] Gertrude Williams : *State and the Standard of Living*, p. 47.
[75] ibid., p. 314.
[76] Pigou and Clark, op. cit., p. 39.
[77] Gertrude Williams, op. cit., p. 334.
[78] ibid., p. 317.
[79] ibid.
[80] ibid., pp. 319-20.
[81] ibid., pp. 319-20.
[82] ibid., p. 238.
[83] Robson : *Development of Local Government*, 1948 ed., pp. 116-117.
[84] Cmd. 4978, pp. 95-6.
[85] *Century of Municipal Progress*, Dr. Finer at p.284.
[86] ibid., p. 286.

CHAPTER IX

[1] P. Cambray : *The Great Game of Politics*.
[2] ibid.
[3] Asquith, cited Ronaldshay : *Curzon*, Vol. 3, p. 318.
[4] A. Chamberlain : *Down the Years*, pp. 139-43.
[5] Ronaldshay : *Curzon*, Vol. 3, p. 204.
[6] Spender and Asquith : *Life of Asquith*, Vol. 2, p. 337.
[7] Ronaldshay : *Curzon*, Vol. 3, p. 314.
[8] *Annual Register*, 1929, p. 58.
[9] ibid., 1930, p. 2.
[10] Mallet : *British Budgets*, p. 301, 3rd series.
[11] *Annual Register*, 1931, p. 64.
[12] *Political Quarterly*, 1932, p. 8-9.

CHAPTER X

[1] Cd. 9230, 1918.
[2] Aristotle : *Politics*, Book IV, p. 15.
[3] Cmd. 2649, VIII, 1926 Report of Committee on Amalgamation of Services Common to the Navy, Army, and Air Force, p. 49, para. 12.

REFERENCES

4 1926, VI, Qu. 297, Select Committee on Estimates.
5 For details see W. I. Jennings : *The Law Relating to Local Authorities.*
6 Sir John Anderson befoie the *Royal Commission on the Civil Service,* 1929-31, Qu. 2591.
7 Sir Warren Fisher before *Royal Commission on the Civil Service,* 1929-31 Qu. 18960.
8 ibid., 18, 840.
9 *Public Accounts Committee,* 1932, Sir R. Hopkins, Qu. 5377.
10 *Economy Committee* (Chairman, Sir George May), July, 1931, Cmd. 3920, para. 41.
11 Waldegrave : article in *Journal of Public Administration,* Vol. XIII, July, 1935.
12 Lord Eustace Percy : *J.P.A.,* XI, p. 6.
13 *Hansard,* 5th Series, Vol. 239, 1350, May 28, 1930.
14 Cmd. 3751, pr. 62, *Royal Commission on Transport Final Report.*
15 H. S. Morrison : *Socialization and Transport,* pp. 139-41.
16 ibid., p. 156.
17 *Hansard,* 5th Series, Vol. 193, 1698.
18 Cmd. 2599.
19 ibid., pr. 5.
20 ibid., pr. 8.
21 ibid., pr. 16.
22 Cmd. 4468, 1933 Report of Coal Mines Reorganization Commission.
23 *Agricultural Register,* 1933-4, p. 2.
24 Article in the *Economist,* March 25, 1933.
25 Lord Eustace Percy : *Democracy on Trial,* p. 30.
26 *Haldane Report,* Cd. 9230, p. 27.
27 Colin Clark : *J.P.A.,* 1932, X, p. 261.
28 and 29 ibid., p. 268.
30 Lloyd : *J.P.A.,* July 7, 1935.
31 Lord Eustace Percy : *Democracy on Trial,* p. 35.
32 Lloyd : *J.P.A.,* July 7, 1935, Vol XIII, p. 227.
33 ibid., p. 229.
34 Lord Eustace Percy, op. cit., pp. 37-8.
35 Colin Clark, J. P. A. Vol. X, 265-6.
36 and 37 Lord Eustace Percy : op. cit., 45-6.
38 Cmd. 320, 1919, pp. 12-14, Report of Committee of Privy Council in Scientific and Industrial Research, 1918-19.
39 Cmd. 2491, ibid. for 1924-5, p. 19.
40, 41 and 42 based on reports of *Department of Scientific and Industrial Research.*
43, 45 and 46 Reports of the *Development Commission.*
44 May : *Economy Committee,* 1931, pr. 280.
47 Cmd. 1937, Scientific and Industrial Research, 1922-3, p. 1-2.
48 Cmd. 1937, 1922-3.
49 Cmd. 4503, Repori of C. of P. C. for Medical Research, 1932-3.
50 Cmd. 4718, Report of Agricultural Research Committee for 1931-3, p. 5.
51 Morris R. Cohen : *Reason and Nature,* p. 85.
52 ibid., p. 87.
53 Julian Huxley : *Scientific Research and Social Needs,* Chapter XIII, for the general problems involved.
54 ibid., p. 253.
55 Cmd. 1938, XV, 1923, Recommendation of the National and Imperial Defence Committee, p. 14.
56 *Hansard,* Vol. 287, pr. 1325, March 21, 1934.
57 Trenchard : Letter to the *Times,* December 16, 1935.
58 May : *Economy Committee Report,* 1931, pr. 200-1.
59 ibid.
60 Cmd. 2029, X, 1924, pr. 33.

[61] ibid., pr. 28.
[62] Statement on Defence, March 3, 1936.
[63] Mr. Baldwin, February 22, 1936.
[64] Winston Churchill, House of Commons, July 20, 1936.
[65] R. T. Nightingale : *The Personnel of the British Foreign Office and Diplomatic Service, 1851-1929.* Greaves : *Reactionary Britain.* Tilley and Gaselee : *The Foreign Office.*
[66] Cd. 9230, p. 64.
[67] Fawcett : *Speeches,* 1872, p. 242.
[68] James Dickinson : Letter to *Times,* March 18, 1933, and cf. Article *Quarterly Review,* Vol. 262, p. 190.
[69] R. C. K. Ensor : *Courts and Judges,* p. 97.
[70] ibid., p. 97.
[71] Birkenhead : *Points of View,* Vol. I, p. 119.
[72] R. C. K. Ensor, op. cit., p. 100.
[73] Birkenhead : *Points of View,* Vol. I, pp. 112-3.
[74] ibid., p. 115.
[75] R. C. K. Ensor : *Courts and Judges,* p. 101.
[76] R. C. K. Ensor : *Courts and Judges,* p. I.
[77] ibid., p. 102.
[78] ibid., pp. 3-6.
[79] ibid., pp. 98-9.
[80] Anderson before *Royal Commission on Civil Service,* 1929-31, Qu. 2451.
[81] Henry Taylor : *The Statesman* (1836), pp. 206-7.
[82] Sir William Beveridge : *The Public Service in War and Peace* (1920).
[83] C. K. Webster : *Lord Palmerston at Work,* 1831-41 : *Politica,* 1934.
[84] Christopher Addison : *Four and a Half Years,* Vol. I, Chap. I ; a good account of departmental activity.
[85] and [86] Lloyd George, *Memoirs,* p. 1138.
[87] *Appendix VIII* to *Minutes of Evidence of Royal Commission on the Civil Service,* 1929-31, is a statement by the Association of First Division Civil Servants of their duties as they understand them, see para. 12.
[88] *Minutes of Evidence to Royal Commission on the Civil Service,* 1929-31, Qu. 22, 451.
[89] Appendix VIII, op. cit., para. 13.
[90] Sir Warren Fisher in evidence to *Royal Commission, op. cit.,* app. A. pt. 11, p. 1272, and Qu. 18,846 and 18,849.
[91] Morrison : *Socialization and Transport,* pp. 106-7.
[92] Gwyer evidence submitted to *Royal Commission on Civil Service, op. cit.*
[93] Lloyd George : *Memoirs,* pp. 1171-2.
[94] Addison : *Politics from Within,* Vol. I, p. 21.
[95] Cd. 8409.
[96] Minutes of Evidence *Royal Commission on the Civil Service,* 1929-31, see Index under *Registry,* p. 1011, pr. 16.
[97] *Journal of Public Administration,* Vol. VIII, p. 281, article by Sir Henry Bunbury.
[98] See *passim,* the *Whitehall Series,* edited by Sir James Marchant.
[99] Sir Edward Troup : *The Home Office,* pp. 255-6.
[100] 1871, VII, Select Committee on Diplomatic and Consular Services, Qu. 1146.
[101] 1888, XXVII, Qu. 10,994, Evidence to C. 5545, 2nd Report of Royal Commission on Civil Establishments.
[102] Dr. H. L. Hall : *The Colonial Office,* p. 19.
[103] *Royal Commission on the Civil Service,* 1929-31, Appendix VIII, pr. 27.
[104] ibid., Qu. 9396.
[105] ibid., Qu. 2185, and cf. *Statement of Case by Civil Service Clerical Association to Royal Commission on Civil Service,* 1929-31.

CHAPTER XI

[1] *The Times.*
[2] Wyndham : *Britain and the World*, p. 17 (Royal Institute of International Affairs Pamphlet, 1944).
[3] Whitehead : *Adventures of Ideas*, Chap. IV.
[4] *Times Literary Supplement*, March 8, 1947, p. 97.
[5] W. K. Hancock and M. M. Gowing : *British War Economy* (1949) pp. 32-35.
[6] ibid., p. 35.
[7] ibid., p. 37.
[8] ibid., pp. 41-2 and note 1 on page 42.
[9] ibid., 42-43.
[10] ibid., p. 45.
[11] Winston S. Churchill : *The Second World War*, Vol. 1, p. 117.
[12] ibid., p. 63.
[13] ibid., p. 177.
[14] Hancock and Gowing : *British War Economy*, p. 84.
[15] ibid., p. 4.
[16] ibid., p. 29.
[17] ibid., p. 26.
[18] ibid., p. 27.
[19] ibid., p. 10.
[20] ibid., pp. 47-49.
[21] ibid., p. 90.
[22] ibid., p. 91.
[23] ibid., p. 92.
[24] ibid., p. 93.
[25] ibid., p. 93.
[26] Churchill : *The Second World War*, Vol. 1, p. 439.
[27] Hancock and Gowing, op. cit., pp. 91-2.
[28] Churchill : *The Second World War*, Vol. 1, pp. 355-6 and p. 361.
[29] ibid., pp. 525-7.
[30] Churchill : *The Second World War*, Vol. 2, p. 8.
[31] ibid., pp. 9-12.
[32] Churchill : *The Second World War*, Vol. 1, p. 320.
[33] Vol. 2, p. 20.
[34] ibid., pp. 17-19.
[35] ibid., p. 439.
[36] Hancock and Gowing, op. cit., pp. 93-4.
[37] ibid., p. 541.
[38] ibid., 534-5.
[39] ibid., pp. 536-9.
[40] ibid., p. 542.
[41] ibid., p. 536.
[42] ibid., p. 519.
[43] Churchill : *The Second World War*, Vol. 2, pp. 308-9.
[44] Hancock and Gowing, op. cit., p. 522.
[45] ibid., p. 546.
[46] J. M. Keynes : *A Revision of the Treaty*, 1922, pp. 4-7.
[47] W. A. Robson : *The Machinery of Government*, 1939-47, in *Political Quarterly*, Jan.-March, 1948 and Francis Williams : *The Triple Challenge* (1948) chaps. 5, 6 and 7.
[48] Dr. Thomas Jones : *Prime Ministers and Cabinets*. The first Welsh National Lecture broadcast on Oct. 6 and published in *The Listener*, 13 Oct., 1938. Dr. Thomas Jones was once Deputy Secretary to the Cabinet.
[49] Churchill : *The Second World War*, Vol. 2, pp. 14-15.
[50] Keith Feiling : *Life of Neville Chamberlain*, p. 199.
[51] Churchill : *The Second World War*, Vol. 1, pp. 187 and 199.

[52] Cmd. 6923 of 1946, following Cmd. 6743.
[53] Churchill : *The Second World War*, Vol. 1, p. 368.
[54] *Hansard*, 27 Feb, 1946, Col. 1964.
[55] and [56] *Hansard*, 28 Feb., 1946, Cols. 2137-2140.
[57] W. H. Hancock and M. M. Gowing, *op. cit.*, p. 92.
[58] *Contribution of Scientists to Public Policy* (*The Times* 14/3/47).
[59] Sir John Anderson : *The Machinery of Government* (Romans Lecture 1949).
[60] Churchill : *The Second World War*, Vol. 2, p. 375.
[61] *The Economist*, Dec. 28, 1946, p. 1041, using *Hansard* Dec. 17.
[62] Cmd. 6525 of 1944 : the Assbeth Committee.
[63] F. Scott Fitzgerald : *The Last Tycoon*, p. 96 of English Edition, 1949.
[64] Sir Oliver Franks : *Central Planning and Control in War and Peace* (1947) ; *The Experience of a University Teacher in the Civil Service*. (Sidney Bace, Lecture 1947).
[65] Prof. Jewkes in *Time and Tide*.
[66] J. H. Newman : *A Grammar of Assent*.
[67] Fifth Report from the Select Committee in Estimates (143 of 1947). Organization and Methods and its effect in the staffing of Government Departments.
[68] J. H. Newman : *A Grammar of Assent*, p. 199.
[69] *P.R.O.s and Their Work* (*The Times* 11/4/44).
[70] *Who's Who* : Leslie S. C. 1946, Head of Economic Information Unit (Treasury) ; 1936-40 Publicity Manager to Gas, Light and Coke Company ; 1940-45, Public Relations Director Home Office and Ministry of Home Security, 1940-45.
[71] Francis Williams : *Press Parliament and People,* (1946) Chap. 2.
[72] ibid., pp. 6-7.
[73] ibid., p. 78.
[74] Cmd. 7567 of 1948. Report of Central Office of Information for 1947-8.
[75] W. N. Ewer : *The Labour Party's Record in Foreign Policy* in *The Political Quarterly*, Apl.-June, 1949.
[76] R. B. McCallum and Alison Readman : *The British General Election of* 1945 (pct. 1949).
[77] John Parker : *Labour Marches on* (1947) p. 27.
[78] R. B. McCallum and Alison Readman, *op. cit.*, p. 154.
[79] D. G. Macrae : *Domestic Record of the Labour Government* in the *Political Quarterly*, Jan.-March, 1949.

INDEX OF PERSONS

Chancellor of the Exchequer, 59, 68, 165, 166. *See* Treasury
Chapels, 125. *See* Liberal Party
Chartered Companies, 114
Chartists, 27, 38
Chiefs of Staff, reorganization of, 260-3; after 1918—285, 290, 291, 292-3
Church of England, 25, 26, 36, 118, 119, 123, 124, 125
Civil Aviation, Ministry of, 299
Civil Service, general character and conventions of, 266-79; Departmental organization 272-4; development and reform, 69-77, 170-1, 309-10; in war, 174; recruitment and grading problems, 167-71, 274-8; relation to Minister, 269-72, 312; training of, 311, 313; Treasury's relation to, 246-7, 314-5
Closure, 128-9, 233, 234
Colonial Defence Committee, 159
Colonial Office, 57, 58, 65, 76; Secretary of State for, 60, 65; traditions of, 110, 112; Chamberlain and, 147
Colonies. *See* Empire
Commander-in-Chief, 58-61, 131, 155-7. *See* War Office
Committees and Commissions:
Balfour Committee on Industry and Trade, 200; Haldane Committee on Machinery of Government, 167; Committee on Ministers' Power, 173; Macmillan Committee on Finance and Industry, 200; May Committee on Economy on Admiralty in 1861, 61; on Army, 58, 157 (Esher); on Civil Service, 68, 71-4, 163 (Northcote and Trevelyan); on Education, 164 (Bryce); on Poor Law, 1905-9, 102, 104, 160; on Sanitation, 1869, 67, 103, 159
Committee of Imperial Defence, 145, 146, 159, 175, 238, 260-3, 282-9, 302; secretariat, 284; and economic policy, 285
Committees of House of Commons. *See* House of Commons
Communism, 226, 280, 281
Company Law, 17-9, 98-9
Congress of Berlin, 115
Conservative Party, 37-8, 86, 119, 125, 130, 144, 221, 228, 232, 294, 321, 322
Constantinople, 115
Constituencies, equalization of, 220; and working of, 221
Constitution, 41-2, 123-4, 130, 132, 146, 148; Lords and, 148; testing of,

149-50; Crown and, 229; Parliament Act and, 151-2; effect of delegated legislation, 171; in war, 175; flexibility of, 179; after 1918, 218
Contract, freedom of and place in social order, 95-6
Control, Board of, 160
Conventions, 132. *See* Cabinet:
Bedchamber Question; Corn Laws; Dismissal of Melbourne. Constitution: Parliament Act, 1911
Corruption after 1832, 33-4
County Councils, 164
Course of Prices in a Great War, 288
Courts, Common Law, 79; Chancery, 79; County, 78; and Trade Unions, 102. *See* Justice
Crimean War, 59, 60, 70, 155, 159, 172, 203
Crown, Cabinet relation to, 42, 150; constitution and, 229; servants of, 172; (Queen Victoria, 123, 124, 130, 239; Disraeli misleads 130-1; Gladstone opposes, 132, 133, 138; intrigues of, 139, 141, 142, 143; plagues Rosebery, 144; relation with army, 156, 157); (Edward VII sends for Balfour, 144; for Campbell-Bannerman, 146; Liberals and, 1906, 147, 148; Peers and, 148; Parliament Act, 1911, 150-1); (George V sends for Bonar Law, 177; Lloyd George, 177; 1919 Cabinet and, 231; Bonar Law and, 231; Baldwin, Curzon and, 232; MacDonald and, 235)
Crown Colony, 113
Crown Lands, Office of, 162
Currency, State and, 20-21, 199-204

DEBATES, character of, 240
Defence, Departments, 151-9; amalgamation of Services common to, 245; Ministry of, 262-3, 292, 299-300, 302; Minister for Co-ordination of, 285, 290, 302; Committee (Supply) 293; Committee (Operations) 293; Requirements Committee, 285; Policy and Requirements Committee, 285; peacetime policy, 302
Delegated Legislation, 171-3
Demobilization, problems of, 296
Democracy, 1906 election and, 147; prospects of, 196-8; character of, in England, 218; two-party system and, 222, 240